Special Issue of Sustainable Asia Conference 2014

Special Issue of Sustainable Asia Conference 2014

Special Issue Editors

Yongrok Choi
Ning Zhang

MDPI • Basel • Beijing • Wuhan • Barcelona • Belgrade

MDPI

Special Issue Editors

Yongrok Choi
Inha University
Korea

Ning Zhang
Jinan University
China

Editorial Office
MDPI
St. Alban-Anlage 66
Basel, Switzerland

This is a reprint of articles from the Special Issue published online in the open access journal *Sustainability* (ISSN 2071-1050) from 2014 to 2015 (available at: http://www.mdpi.com/journal/sustainability/special_issues/asia-conference-2014)

For citation purposes, cite each article independently as indicated on the article page online and as indicated below:

LastName, A.A.; LastName, B.B.; LastName, C.C. Article Title. *Journal Name* **Year**, *Article Number*, Page Range.

ISBN 978-3-03897-109-2 (Pbk)
ISBN 978-3-03897-110-8 (PDF)

Contents

About the Special Issue Editors

Yongrok Choi is a distinguished research professor (Inha Fellow Professor) of the Inha University. He is the president of the Asia Business Forum and the organizer of the Sustainable Asia Conference (SAC). He has published more than 100 papers, including many SCI and SSCI level of journals such as *Energy Economics, Energy Policy, Tech. For. & Social Change*, etc. He also managed more than 10 special editions of the SCI level of journals such as *Energy Policy, Tech. For. & Social Change, Sustainability*, etc. His research focuses are on energy and environmental policy analyses, Green IT applications and sustainable management.

Ning Zhang is a Full Professor at the Department of Economics, Jinan University. He obtained his B.E. degree in international trade from Shandong University, and Ph.D. degree in environmental economics from Inha University. His current research interests include sustainability measurement and energy economics. His international reputation for sustainability measurement in developing countries has resulted in more than 60 publications, and he has participated in policy-making international conferences and committees including the UNFCCC COP conference. His publications have appeared in many highly ranked journals such as *Science, Nature Climate Change, Nature Geoscience, Resource and Energy Economics, Energy Economics, Ecological Economics, Energy Policy, Energy, Applied Energy*, etc. Among these, two of his papers were selected as the ESI top 0.1% hot papers and 14 were selected as the ESI top 1% highly-cited papers. Based on IDEAS/RePEc database, he ranked in the top 10 among all economists in the world (5 years or less). He received the outstanding scholar award from China Scholarship Council (CSC), best scholar award from Korea Energy Management Corporation (KEMCO), and best paper award from the Ministry of Knowledge Economy Korea (MKE). Regarding editorial work, he is serving as an editorial member of *Technological Forecasting and Social Change* and an associate editor of *Social Science Journal*. He has guest-edited many Special Issues in highly regarded journals; he is also the co-organizer of the Sustainable Asia Conference which is a collaborator of *Sustainability* (MDPI). He is also a referee for over 50 journals and national foundations related to sustainability.

Preface to "Special Issue of Sustainable Asia Conference 2014"

This special edition consists of 12 papers, including the Editorial. Most of the papers were presented at the Sustainable Asia Conference (SAC) 2014, in Nanchang, China. Since the most of sustainable issues are newly emerging challenges, international cooperation is crucial, and thus SAC has been promoting the research network since its inauguration in 2009, at Inha University, Korea. The SAC is a very important platform for researchers, not just to present papers, but to share all the possible future challenges such as co-research, project proposals, job-sharing information, and many more potential issues. For further information regarding the SAC conference, you are welcomed to visit our official website (http://abf.inha.ac.kr/).

Yongrok Choi, Ning Zhang
Special Issue Editors

![sustainability logo] *sustainability*

MDPI

Editorial

Introduction to the Special Issue on "the Sustainable Asia Conference 2014"

Yongrok Choi [1,*] and Ning Zhang [2,*]

[1] Department of International Trade and Regional Studies, Inha University, 100 Inha-ro, Nam-gu, Incheon 402-751, Korea
[2] Institute of Poyang Lake Eco-economics, Jiangxi University of Finance and Economics, Nanchang 330032, China
[*] Authors to whom correspondence should be addressed; yrchoi@inha.ac.kr (Y.C.); zn928@naver.com or zhangn@jxufe.edu.cn (N.Z.); Tel.: +82-032-860-7760 (Y.C.); Fax: +82-032-876-9328 (Y.C.).

Academic Editor: Marc A. Rosen
Received: 29 January 2015; Accepted: 29 January 2015; Published: 2 February 2015

Abstract: The continuous expansion and change in Asia is attracting increasing attention from the rest of the world. Thus, the papers from the Sustainable Asia Conference 2014 (SAC 2014) could provide a platform to examine outperforming governance factors and mechanisms in this dynamically growing region. This editorial for SAC 2014 will highlight the contents and methodologies of selected papers, presenting diverse issues in sustainable policies and strategies.

Keywords: Sustainable Asia Conference (SAC); governance; paradigm shift; network management

1. Background of the Special Issue

Although sustainability science shifts the academic paradigm from traditional one-way maximization to collaborative value creation, most of the existing theories are still missing the link of sustainability. When an author visited a university in the United States eight years ago, he was shocked to find new approaches around the campus such as sustainable development economics, a sustainable management seminar, sustainable literature reviews, a sustainable history special lecture, *etc.* The traditional paradigm of economics focuses on efficiency or economies, which means maximizing outputs while minimizing inputs. The traditional framework cannot accommodate external economic variables such as social responsibility and environmental pollution issues, and thus remains focused within the realm of market failure. Similarly, the paradigm of traditional business management is still based on maximizing profits on behalf of stockholders. Therefore, this traditional approach is unable to effectively handle the diverse requirements of interest groups such as consumers, society, and government. All these traditional paradigms are based solely on mechanical approaches to get one-way enhancement. Sustainability science is based on the harmonizing partnership around diverse entities, creating the opportunity for the field to be the platform field of study for human behavioral, social, and even environmental sciences. The cornerstone potential of sustainability science has become a strong motivation for international networking for the diverse studies.

The rapid growth of Asian countries is generating more attention worldwide [1]. Countries such as Korea and China are characterized as some of the fastest growing countries in the world due to their rates of economic growth. This growth presents challenges in the new frontier of sustainability academics; technological innovations are being outperformed over time, necessitating the recalibration of cultural or local governance mechanisms to better address these distinct phenomena. It is noteworthy that an eco-friendly economic system implies that harmonized mutual feedback is crucial for sustainable performance in Asia. Even if this kind of eco-systematic approach is liberally applied in worldwide practices and theories, the Asian approach is different from that in advanced western countries. Advanced countries such as the United States and European Union countries are emphasizing the role of markets too heavily and thus the harmonized outcome of the interoperational networking of sustainable activities takes too long to effectively diffuse this market-heavy mix. In contrast, Asian countries are keen to obtain an optimal path of control as a result of cultural adaptation or outperforming leadership by top decision makers such as presidents and executives of major corporations. For example, the Chinese government argued they were not ready to participate in official international talks on environmental issues, while in their national policies, they moved toward more emphasis on awareness of carbon dioxide (CO_2) emissions beginning in 2005, reflecting this policy change in the national five-year economic plan and soon enhancing eco-friendly efficiencies nationwide [2]. This Chinese policy of "sustainable growth" supports the environmental Kuznets curve (EKC) hypothesis, which posits that environmental improvements occur after a certain level of income is reached (*i.e.*, the turning point) and government leadership could tunnel through the EKC as a shortcut for improving performance [2]. The approach is quite different from those of western countries, where the role of the market is emphasized and thus government intervention may result in worsened economic performance.

Therefore, the Sustainable Asia Conference could be an important cornerstone for a new platform for academic networking to discover outperforming governance in the most rapidly growing region in the world. Since Korean president Lee announced the launching of "green growth" in Korea in 2008, the country has hosted the Green Climate Fund and has become one of the world's green growth hubs in a short period of time. The papers presented in this special issue will provide insight into the Asian model for sustainable governance.

2. Important Issues for a Sustainable Asia

Sustainability science is composed of the three pillars of environment, economics, and social studies. Therefore, most of the papers in this issue are based on the harmonization of these perspectives. Even so, individual sustainability issues range from the macro views of policy implications to the micro views of practical suggestions. Of course, most of the papers handle environmental issues in Asian countries, particularly in China. China is the largest greenhouse gas (GHG) emitter in the world, and recently the country's serious pollution problems have heightened the awareness of environmental issues by the Chinese government as well as the public. The Chinese government's response to this issue should be to assess the feasibility of economic growth against the constraints of resources and the environment. One study presented in this issue takes constraints on resources and the environment into account and uses frontier technology boundary analysis and directional distance function (DDF) to propose a decomposition of the sources of economic growth within the green growth accounting framework and then measures the sources of China's economic growth between 1998 and 2012 based on the new biennial Malmquist–Luenberger productivity index [MLPI] [3]. Using MLPI and based on the data envelopment analysis (DEA) and DDF, Chinese economic growth is decomposed with seven components: (1) technical efficiency change; (2) technological change; (3) labor effect; (4) capital effect; (5) energy effect; (6) output structure effect; and (7) environmental regulation effect. The empirical results show that, in general, physical capital accumulation is the most important driving force for economic takeoff, while CO_2 emissions with environmental regulation restrain economic growth in some provinces. It is argued that high growth by simply increasing factor inputs will not only result in a waste of resources, but also in environmental pollution [3]. The more serious task for the Chinese government comes from the fact that carbon emission reduction targets will not be met by controlling economic development [4]. Based on the extended Stochastic Impacts by Regression on Population, Affluence and Technology (STIRPAT) model (incorporating factors that drive carbon emissions), the determinant factors for the scale and intensity of carbon emissions could be much more important [4]. The study found the negative and significant impact of spatial-lagged variables, meaning that the carbon emissions among regions are highly correlated. Therefore, the role of provinces with low-carbon emissions could be crucial in developing a nationwide low-carbon economy. In recent years, the rural environmental pollution problem has intensified with the acceleration of urban–rural integration, especially in developed regions and countries in Asia. By utilizing the same STIRPAT model, Hongjun Dai *et al.* [5] conducted an empirical study of rural nonpoint source pollution problems in the process of urbanization and concluded that technical progress, transformation of the mode of production, and increasing the scale of financial support in rural areas are effective measures to solve the ever-increasing metropolitan pollution dilemma [5].

If we focus on the micro approach to CO_2 emission regulatory issues, the first and most important area should be the power generation industries. In China, biomass resources from agriculture and forestry are quite rich and thus a biomass power generation plant could be a good alternative compared with traditional coal-based power plants. However, carbon emissions should be considered carefully because they are influenced by the supply of straw fuel as well [6]. Without a sufficient straw supply, the plant's performance may be quite poor, resulting in lower economic benefit and higher carbon emissions. Thus, using a linear multi-objective integer program model, the research found that the straw acquisition range could be a determining factor for the straw-based power generation plant's performance [6]. New challenges from nuclear power plants present another issue on the power generation front. The Fukushima nuclear disaster in 2011 has created severe social, political, and economic impacts worldwide, causing the public to perceive nuclear power as a threat. Influenced by the worldwide spread of anti-nuclear attitudes, people who live near nuclear power plants have shown increasing concerns about nuclear risks, also known as the "not in my backyard" or NIMBY syndrome [7]. For the sustainable development of nuclear power in China despite the NIMBY syndrome, the feasibility study for the Chinese public willingness to pay (WTP) is analyzed. Using the contingent valuation method (CVM), the research found that there is an increase of 56.7% and 69.1% of respondents' WTP for a nuclear power plant located 80 km and 30 km, respectively, from their neighborhoods, resulting in stronger NIMBY attitudes toward nuclear power plants (especially for those who live in inland areas). Even if monetary compensation has its limitations, more trust should be given to the government and the public should approach nuclear power in a more rational manner [7].

Transportation presents another issue for CO_2 emissions. According to the investigation by the Intergovernmental Panel on Climate Change (IPCC), transportation accounts for approximately 13% of total greenhouse gas emissions worldwide [8]. The logistics field is especially important for sustainable development because it includes all product life cycle treatment by carbon footprint, with carbon footprint being defined as the CO_2 emission quantity produced either directly or indirectly throughout the entire life cycle of a service or a product [9]. To plan a vehicle route with the smallest carbon footprint, instead of the conventional approach of shortest route distance, the improved vehicle routing problem (VRP) equation combined with variables in the Lagrangian approach mathematical model is adopted. When there are many alternative paths between each pair of customers, and the vehicle speed differs at different times of the day, determining a balance among various objectives is critical to minimizing the carbon footprint on the route [9].

As sustainable development gets more and more attention from the public, NIMBY syndrome forces the government to treat environmental issues with a market-oriented approach, particularly given the pressure for eco-friendly development. From the ecological perspective of a market-oriented solution, the research examines the determinants of farmers' WTP and their payment levels for ecological compensation for the Poyang Lake Wetland, which is the largest lake in China. Using CVM and Heckman's two-step model, the survey shows that 46.58% of farmers are willing to pay ecological compensation, with an average price of $64.39 per household every year [10]. Based on the heterogeneity of the variables, it can be argued that the government should develop differentiated ecological compensation standards according to the diverse characteristics of NIMBY syndrome [10].

Among GHG emissions, CO_2 presents the most serious concern for sustainable development. Considering the aggravating effects on the ozone layer, sulfur dioxide (SO_2) could be even more harmful, and is a particularly important issue for manufacturing industries. Recognizing the need for action, the Chinese government introduced the SO_2 Emissions Trading Pilot Scheme (SETPS) in 2002 to reduce industrial SO_2 emissions. Four provinces (including Shandong), three municipalities (including Shanghai), and one business entity (the China Huaneng Group) were selected as pilot participants [11]. For the feasibility of this project, the empirical test evaluates the effects of SETPS on pollution abatement costs (PAC) from the past and future perspectives in a total of 29 Chinese provinces (including all of the pilot 'provinces') over the period 1998–2011. Results showed even if SETPS failed to reduce PAC as a whole, PAC reduction efforts had become increasingly important since 2009, implying that Chinese government involvement could improve the system to correct any design and operational deficiencies in the present emissions trading pilot policies [11]. As a global factory, China is considered to be a black hole for global resources as well. To stabilize China's strategic diversification of global outsourcing, especially in oil supply security (seriously restricted by the imbalance of oil reserves), the empirical research analyzes the feasibility of these diversification policies. Using the oil import source diversification index, the research concludes that China, compared with the United States, has more stable diversified import sources and the government's attention has resulted in more effective import sources than in the past. In the future, however, China should adjust the distributions of regional sources rather than focusing on the "number" of sources in its diversification strategy [12].

For sustainable governance, the role of information and communication technology (ICT) and its e-business utilization is crucial because ICT and its applications serve as another platform for all continuous performance policies and practices. There are two papers on the role of ICT in sustainability science. One paper explores the macro view of ICT application in sustainable development within the context of "smart e-government," which has been proposed as sustainable, cooperative government to strengthen the bilateral partnership between the public and private sectors [13]. The study empirically examines the correlation between the quality of e-government and trust in government in Korea. Using an index developed to measure the quality of e-government services (including factors such as openness, sharing, communication, and collaboration), the survey results show a partial correlation between the quality of e-government services and trust in government, suggesting that an open attitude toward information sharing could be more important regardless of the complexity or the technicality of the issues [13]. Likewise, from a microeconomic or business perspective, the research analyzes the success of e-businesses in China. It is well known that the global leaders in the field such as eBay, Amazon, and Facebook cannot compete effectively in the Chinese market against local companies such as Alibaba and its twin, Taobao. The reason may come from the cultural competitive advantage of Chinese trust (Guanxi) [1]. Based on the structural equation model (SEM), the paper analyzes the role of Guanxi in the success of outperforming web marketing mix strategies. In general, the empirical tests show the web marketing mix is important for creating value based on relationship management in China. Of note, the web marketing strategies of communication, content, and commerce are crucial for incorporation of Guanxi with full mediation effects [1].

3. Methodologies of Sustainability Science

The issues in Asia's sustainability model raise the common paradigm of value creation based on network management. Since sustainability science is based on the harmonized partnership among interrelated entities or the activities of those entities, network management is crucial to harmonizing the relationship and to creating value from the partnership network [1]. Of course, feasibility studies for the harmonization of conflicting interests are not easy to perform and thus the methodological approaches could be diverse, but with more emphasis on the importance of sustainable performance. Thus, the research methodologies used could give us greater insights, opening new frontiers to handle new challenges in sustainable governance.

Since most papers on sustainable governance handle conflicting interests as well as multi-inputs/outputs for their models, traditional regression analyses may not match these purposes. Therefore, most papers handle the multi-input/output models using DEA and SEM. DEA is especially important in the field of environmental economics since it handles desirable outputs as well as undesirable outputs such as CO_2 [2,3,10]. SEM is also another popular approach for handling diverse survey related issues because it clarifies the role of intermediation resulting from the complexity among the variables [1,13].

The linear regression or linear transformation of multivariant variables is introduced as well. Using the STIRPAT model variation, carbon emissions are modeled stochastically via regressing it on population, wealth, and technology in log function [4,5]. To compensate for NIMBY syndrome, two papers utilized survey data with CVM to calculate the invisible values for ecological development [10] and nuclear power plant site selection [7].

Linear programming is also used. A multi-objective mixed-integer programming model is introduced to solve the site selection problem for a straw-based power generation plant [6]. Using integer programming, the study optimizes two objectives of the economic and environmental outcomes of straw-based power generation, with the supply and demand of straw as constraints. The oil import diversification index is used to determine the Lorenz curve and the Gini coefficient for the unbalanced level of the market [12]. In diversification strategies, China showed higher balanced indexes than the United States. The stepwise optimal path control approach is introduced, a genetic algorithm is developed for solving the minimal-carbon-footprint time-dependent heterogeneous-fleet vehicle routing problem with alternative paths, and the optimal vehicle routing is obtained by the stepwise numerical experiment [9].

Due to the interdisciplinary character of sustainable science, diverse approaches could and should be imported and utilized for better understanding of multivariate complexity as well as for more systematic implications and suggestions.

4. Conclusions

While environmental strategies are becoming increasingly important over time, Asian countries such as China and Korea still need to give priority to economic growth from the perspective of overall economic performance. While Korea has announced its leading role in international cooperation for development of green growth policies, daily life in China has been getting worse due to increasing pollution and other environmental issues. These environment-related initiatives need to be harmoniously promoted among diverse, and often complicated, entities and associated activities. Fortunately, these Asian countries are quickly changing their paradigms toward eco-friendly development, and the role of political and business leadership in each country's policies and business practices could enhance the performance of sustainable strategies.

However, due to the complexity of a sustainable operation for cooperative networking, it is really difficult to visualize the performance of these sustainable policies and practices. That is the reason most papers in this special issue evoke the importance of creating a new paradigm of sustainable development as well as sustainable management geared toward value creation based on harmonized network management. Networking participants will need to adopt a more field- and performance-oriented approach to create these invisible, but precious, values—this is called sustainable governance [1] (p. 4115). In order to discover sustainable governance factors, sustainable issues as well as their methodologies should be highlighted in this rapidly changing Asian model.

Acknowledgments: The National Research Foundation of Korea Grant funded by the Korean Government (NRF-2014S1A5B1011422) and National Science Foundation of China (41461118) supported this work.

Author Contributions: All of the authors made equal contributions to the work in this editorial paper.

Conflicts of Interest: The authors declare no conflict of interest.

References

1. Choi, Y.; Gao, D. The Role of Intermediation in the Governance of Sustainable Chinese Web Marketing. *Sustainability* **2014**, *6*, 4102–4118. [CrossRef]

2. Yu, Y.; Choi, Y. Measuring Environmental Performance under Regional Heterogeneity in China: A Metafrontier Efficiency Analysis. *Comput. Econ.* **2014**. [CrossRef]

3. Du, M.; Wang, B.; Wu, Y. Sources of China's Economic Growth: An Empirical Analysis Based on the BML Index with Green Growth Accounting. *Sustainability* **2014**, *6*, 5983–6004. [CrossRef]

4. Liu, Y.; Xiao, H.; Zikhali, P.; Lv, Y. Carbon Emissions in China: A Spatial Econometric Analysis at the Regional Level. *Sustainability* **2014**, *6*, 6005–6023. [CrossRef]

5. Dai, H.; Sun, T.; Zhang, K.; Guo, W. Research on Rural Nonpoint Source Pollution in the Process of Urban-Rural Integration in the Economically-Developed Area in China Based on the Improved STIRPAT Model. *Sustainability* **2015**, *7*, 782–793. [CrossRef]

6. Lv, H.; Ding, H.; Zhou, D.; Zhou, P. A Site Selection Model for a Straw-Based Power Generation Plant with CO_2 Emissions. *Sustainability* **2014**, *6*, 7466–7481. [CrossRef]

7. Sun, C.; Lyu, N.; Ouyang, X. Chinese Public Willingness to Pay to Avoid Having Nuclear Power Plants in the Neighborhood. *Sustainability* **2014**, *6*, 7197–7223. [CrossRef]

8. IPCC. *Climate Change 2007: Synthesis Report*; Intergovernmental Panel on Climate Change: Geneva, Switzerland, 2007; pp. 45–54.

9. Liu, W.; Lin, C.; Chiu, C.; Tsao, Y.; Wang, Q. Minimizing the Carbon Footprint for the Time-Dependent Heterogeneous-Fleet Vehicle Routing Problem with Alternative Paths. *Sustainability* **2014**, *6*, 4658–4684. [CrossRef]

10. Kong, F.; Xiong, K.; Zhang, N. Determinants of Farmers' Willingness to Pay and Its Level for Ecological Compensation of Poyang Lake Wetland, China: A Household-Level Survey. *Sustainability* **2014**, *6*, 6714–6728. [CrossRef]

11. Tu, Z.; Shen, R. Can China's Industrial SO_2 Emissions Trading Pilot Scheme Reduce Pollution Abatement Costs? *Sustainability* **2014**, *6*, 7621–7645. [CrossRef]

12. Xu, J.; Zhang, J.; Yao, Q.; Zhang, W. Is It Feasible for China to Optimize Oil Import Source Diversification? *Sustainability* **2014**, *6*, 8329–8341. [CrossRef]

13. Myeong, S.; Kwon, Y.; Seo, H. Sustainable E-Governance: The Relationship among Trust, Digital Divide, and E-Government. *Sustainability* **2014**, *6*, 6049–6069. [CrossRef]

sustainability

MDPI

Article

Research on Rural Nonpoint Source Pollution in the Process of Urban-Rural Integration in the Economically-Developed Area in China Based on the Improved STIRPAT Model

Hongjun Dai [1,2,*], Tao Sun [1], Kun Zhang [1,3] and Wen Guo [1]

1 College of Economic and Management, Nanjing University of Aeronautics and Astronautics, Nanjing 211106, China; nuaastao@163.com (T.S.); zhkun_033@163.com (K.Z.); guowen_870608@163.com (W.G.)
2 College of Economic and Management, Huainan Normal University, Huainan 232000, China
3 College of Information Science and Technology, Shandong University of Political Science and Law, Jinan 250014, China
* Author to whom correspondence should be addressed; dhj@hnnu.edu.cn; Tel.: +86-554-686-2873.

Academic Editor: Yongrok Choi
Received: 26 June 2014; Accepted: 31 December 2014; Published: 12 January 2015

Abstract: The process of urban-rural integration has led to severe ecological environmental pollution in rural areas of China, particularly in the economically-developed areas. This is an urgent issue to be solved. We select Jiangsu Province as a case study. From the perspective of the population, economic scale, energy consumption and financial support, we perform an empirical study of rural non-point source pollution problems in the process of urbanization based on the improved STIRPAT model. We apply the ridge regression method to avoid the multicollinearity of the variables in the STIRPAT model. The results show that the technological level, the size of the population and financial support are important factors affecting rural non-point source pollution. Therefore, we believe that technical progress, transformation of the mode of production and increasing the scale of financial support in rural areas are effective measures to solve the current rural nonpoint source pollution.

Keywords: urban-rural integration; rural non-point source pollution; STIRPAT model; ridge regression method; measures

1. Introduction

With the development of the economy, environmental pollution has become more and more serious in China. Environmental protection has become a priority of government work. Additionally, more and more scholars have begun to study China's pollution control problems from different angles [1–3]. In recent years, the rural environmental pollution problem has increasingly intensified with the speeding up of the urban-rural integration, especially in developed regions.

Urban-rural integration is centered on cities, small towns serving as a link, based on the country, the rural areas driven by urban areas and township-promoted agriculture, which established a new urban-rural relationship of mutual benefit and reciprocity, as well as mutual promotion, coordinated development and promoted common prosperity. Urban-rural integration is not the basic driving force to ensure China's future economic growth, but a fundamental way to seek coordinated development between urban and rural areas, as well as to solve the "three agricultural problems" (referring in particular to agriculture, rural areas and farmer issues). From years of practice, urban-rural integration has greatly promoted the development of rural non-agricultural industries, achieving rural lifestyle urbanization and stimulating the free flow of the factors of production, narrowing the urban-rural gap. However, it has also exacerbated the extent of environmental pollution in rural areas of China, especially in developed regions. Rural pollution has a serious impact on regional economic development, endangers people's health and, in turn, hinders urban-rural integration. As one of the largest and fastest-growing economic regions in China, Jiangsu Province was the first region to promote urban-rural integration starting in 1983. Tremendous achievements have been accomplished, but rural environmental problems remain.

As can be seen in Table 1, the pollution problems of rural areas in Jiangsu Province gradually increased along with the development of the economy, which directly causes the deterioration of our natural environment. It was shown that the rural area's surface water was slightly polluted in nine monitoring stations in the 2011 Report on the State of the Environment in Jiangsu Province in China. Additionally, it shows that the water quality was exceeded in 2011 by 30%. It is necessary to analyze the rural non-point source pollution and put forward a targeted approach, for the purpose of facilitating the smooth implementation of the urban and rural integration process and of achieving sustainable development goals. Thus, many scholars have begun to focus on the rural environmental pollution in the process of urban-rural integration.

Non-point source pollution has four main features: private ownership, complex and diverse causes, great harm and a large influence scope. Therefore, it is difficult to clean up non-point source pollution in rural areas. The research on rural non-point source pollution control abroad began in the 1980s, mainly focused on technical measures, control theory, economic policy, *etc.* In 1991, two economists, Grossman and Krueger, proposed the famous EKC (Environmental Kuznets Curve) curve for describing the relationship between environmental population and per capita income [4]. Bell and Russell presented the view that the quantitative measurement of non-point source pollution is the foundation of the sewage charges and the issuance of sewage discharge permits [5]. Ribaudo *et al.*, Isik, Russel and Clark, Egli and Steger and Speir studied the feasibility of economic means and policy instruments to solve rural non-point source pollution [6–10]. They also discussed the implementation difficulties and corresponding countermeasures. Kaplowitz *et al.* studied non-point source pollution control using the selected experimental investigation methods and by understanding the public's preferences [11]. The results show that the involvement of stakeholders can increase the public recognition of the pollution control plan, thereby improving the effectiveness of pollution control. Camacho-Cuena *et al.* and Cason *et al.* also studied non-point source pollution from different aspects through experimentation [12,13].

Table 1. Economic and environmental data of Jiangsu Province in China (1990–2009).

Index	Units	1990	2009	Annual Average Growth %
Urbanization rate of population	%	21.56	55.60	3.71
Agriculture GDP [1]	Billion Yuan	355.17	798.74	6.24
The proportion of non-agriculture	%	72.0	94.6	1.57
The proportion of non-agriculture labor	%	38.48	67.15	3.73
Rural households per capita net income	Yuan	263.81	786.71	9.91
Rural Engel coefficient	%	52.30	39.20	−1.25
COD emissions [2,3]	Tons	64.20	96.88	2.55
TP emissions [2,4]	Tons	4.78	8.33	3.71
TN emissions [2,5]	Tons	54.29	72.87	1.71

[1] Constant prices in 1978; [2] research data from the College of Resources and Environment, Nanjing Agricultural University; [3] COD indicates chemical oxygen demand; [4] TP indicates total phosphorus; [5] TN indicates total nitrogen.

Non-point source pollution has also been studied from the technology and economic policy viewpoint in China. Li *et al.* thought that it showed an inverted U-shaped curve between fertilizer non-point source pollution and macroeconomic growth [14]. There are several key factors of the fertilizer non-point source pollution in rural areas, including the level of residents' wealth, the proportion of nonfarm employment of farmers, the urban-rural dualistic environmental management system, and so on. Guo and Sun have also researched the EKC curve between rural non-point source pollution and economic growth empirically in different ways [15]. Gao *et al.* calculated the equivalent pollution load and equivalent pollution index of Shandong Province in 2007, using the "Equivalent pollution load method" [16]. Yang *et al.* investigated the measures that could solve the problem of rural non-point source pollution and proposed an optimized management model about small watershed water quality [17]. Jin *et al.* investigated the acceptability of Macao residents to a solid waste management policy through the selection model [18]. Ge and Zhou proposed that China's policy of fertilizer price control and fiscal subsidies to farmers led to the distortion of the fertilizer market, which increased the emission of agricultural fertilizer non-point source pollutants [19].

Tremendous changes have occurred in the development scale, industrial structure, standards of living and lifestyle in rural areas due to urban-rural integration. These changes will have a great influence on rural non-point pollution. However, only a few studies have explored this area. Xiao thought that the environment should be protected through creating beautiful villages and ecological construction [20]. Luo took the rural areas of Chongqing as an example and proposed a measure of rural pollution control based on the perspective of urban and rural overall development [21]. Fei *et al.* discussed the ecological environmental issues in the process of urban-rural integration and presented the countermeasures correspondingly [22]. Fu took the rural areas of Changtu in Liaoning Province as an example, studied the status and issues of rural environmental governance and also put forward some measures on the issues [23]. As can be seen from the literature above, there has been a great deal of achievement in urban-rural integration. However, few of these works involve rural environmental pollution. If any, they put emphasis on the theoretical analysis and countermeasures instead of empirical analysis. This paper applies the improved STIRPAT model to research the rural non-point source pollution in the process of urban-rural integration. We use the ridge regression method to estimate the model parameters in order to avoid collinearity between the variables of the study based on theoretical analysis. Additionally, we use the ridge regression method to estimate model parameters in order to avoid collinearity between the variables of the study. In this paper, Jiangsu Province is selected as the study area, due to the fact that it is one of the most developed areas in China, the urban-rural integration in Jiangsu is representative of China and it has great influence. This paper empirically investigates the factors influencing rural non-point environmental pollution in the process of urban-rural integration and confirms the main factors that can influence rural non-point pollution. Finally, this paper provides the theoretical basis for rural environmental governance measures.

2. Analysis of Environmental Effects on the Construction of Urban and Rural Integration

2.1. Analysis of Population Factors

The rural population continues to decline, resulting in the decrement of the employment of the rural population with the urban and rural integration. Because of the lack of a rural labor force, the traditional mode of agricultural production is very hard to continue. Thus, farmers will increase their input of pesticides and fertilizers, machinery and other production factors as much as possible to replace the labor input for agricultural production. According to the statistics, the rural population has been reduced from 53,079,600 to 34,296,800 from 1990 to 2009, while the proportion of the employment of the rural population decreased from 74.69% to 58.81%. Fertilizer use increased from 2,217,900 tons to 3,440,000 tons, and = pesticide use increased from 79,800 tons to 92,300 tons. Plastic film use rose from 35,400 tons to 94, 300 tons at the same time. It is inevitable that non-point source pollution will continuously increase due to the wide use of chemicals.

2.2. Analysis of Economic Factors

Rural areas had experienced rapid economic development with urban and rural integration. Currently, chemicals, mainly fertilizers, pesticide, and plastic film significantly contribute to the development of agriculture in China. The increase of the agricultural economic scale means a large consumption of chemicals. At the same time, the income of the farmer's increases accordingly. Therefore, farmers will require better environmental quality. This will promote the improvement of environmental quality.

2.3. Analysis of Financial Factors

The government will pay more attention to the development of rural areas in the process of urban-rural integration. The government will provide funds and technology to rural areas. The technical level of agricultural production will be increased. The farmers will reduce the use of fertilizer, pesticide and other factors of production. By increasing the expenditure in rural areas, we can effectively support construction in rural areas, including environmental infrastructure. Once the environmental infrastructure increases, the processing capacity for environmental pollutants will be enhanced and non-point source pollutants will decrease. Consequently, the ecological environment can be improved at the same time. The increased expenditure is also able to increase funding for the publicity of environmental protection and to promote rural residents' environmental awareness, thereby reducing pollutant emissions.

3. Model, Variables and Method

3.1. Improved STIRPAT Model

Ehrlich and Holdren put forward the IPAT model ($I = PAT$) to research carbon emissions in 1971 [24]. I represents the amount of carbon emissions; P represents population size; A represents the degree of affluence; and T represents the technical level or energy efficiency. Dietz and Rose established the STIRPAT model ($I = aP^b A^c T^d e$) based on the IPAT model in 1994 [25]. The model allows for adjustment and improvement according to different research purposes. Therefore, the applicability of this model is stronger.

The model was applied extensively to research environmental issues. However, few researchers have applied it to rural non-point source pollution. We apply it to rural non-point source pollution in the process of urban-rural integration in this paper. We improved and decomposed the related variables of the STIRPAT model according to the analysis conclusions above. P represents the rural population size. A represents the size of the economy. T represents energy efficiency. Finally, we introduce a new index, F, to represent the financial support for rural areas. In order to verify the existence of the EKC curve in rural non-point source pollution, we establish a non-linear model with reference to the method of York (2003) [26]. We take the logarithm of the variables to eliminate the heteroscedasticity of the data and to explain the results better. The improved STIRPAT model is as follows:

$$\ln I = \ln a + b_1 (\ln P) + \left[c_1 (\ln A) + c_2 (\ln A)^2 \right] + d(\ln T) + e(\ln F) \tag{1}$$

3.2. Variables and Data

The research data on *COD* emissions per year, *TP* emissions per year and *TN* emissions per year is cited from the research data of the College of Resources and Environmental Science, Nanjing Agricultural University [27]. All other research data are taken from the "Jiangsu Statistical Yearbook" (from 1990 to 2009). We discount the data value indicators according to the 1978 value to eliminate the influence of price changes.

At first, we apply principal components analysis methods to analyze the three kinds of non-point pollutants. The results show that the coefficient of the KMO (Kaiser-Meyer-Olkin) test is 0.748, which indicates that the variables correlate closely with each other and are suitable to be analyzed with principal components. The first principal component takes into account 97.30% of the original data. Finally, we get a pollutant comprehensive value according to its proportion in the first principal component at last.

$$Pollutant\ comprehensive\ value = 0.3349 \times COD + 0.3295 \times TN + 0.3356 \times TP \tag{2}$$

Table 2. Research variables and research data.

	I	*P*	*A*	*T*	*F*
	Pollutant Comprehensive Value	Rural Population	Rural per GDP	Efficiency of the Use of Chemical Fertilizer	the Proportion of Fiscal Expenditure on Agriculture
1990	40.993303	5307.96	671.83	30.83	8.37
1991	41.641868	5255.96	685.40	28.63	8.17
1992	42.814612	5267.48	671.83	27.47	8.65
1993	44.77097	5293.69	742.48	25.77	10.96
1994	48.108065	5287.53	915.99	24.63	7.92
1995	51.597425	5136.93	1043.15	22.83	7.90
1996	54.239611	5167.66	1022.49	21.70	7.57
1997	51.841629	5014.22	972.63	20.61	7.47
1998	54.87332	4919.99	972.63	19.89	7.25
1999	55.840211	4693.04	962.95	22.47	7.20
2000	57.111186	4286.43	1043.15	22.44	5.87
2001	58.181257	4221.72	1085.72	22.15	5.93
2012	58.902019	4081.68	1130.03	21.95	5.94
2003	58.22738	3942.12	1261.43	21.88	6.29
2004	58.363574	3851.52	1540.71	21.36	5.77
2005	58.937756	3699.88	1652.43	21.07	5.83
2006	59.137562	3631.31	1719.86	20.89	6.08
2007	55.676315	3568.27	1978.31	20.77	7.58
2008	57.358569	3508.02	2230.54	20.77	8.50
2009	59.251325	3429.68	2321.57	20.44	10.04

3.3. Ridge Regression Method

The multiple regressions are sensitive to the collinearity. The coefficient standard deviation will falsely estimate at the higher degree of collinearity based on the least squares regression method (OLS). The ridge regression method is improved based on the least squares regression method and can avoid the collinearity of the model. Therefore, we apply it in this paper.

4. Empirical Results and Analysis

4.1. Unit Root Tests

In order to avoid the phenomenon of "spurious regression", we perform ADF (Augmented Dickey-Fuller test) unit root tests for all variables using EVIEW6.0 to examine their stationarity. We present test results as shown in Table 3.

Table 3. ADF unit root test results.

Variables	Test Type	Original Sequence	Test Type	First Difference	Conclusion
ln$I$	(C,T,0)	−1.232	(C,1,7)	−13.674 ***	First order stationary
ln$A$	(C,T,0)	−2.375	(C,T,1)	−3.670 **	First order stationary
ln$T$	(C,T,0)	−2.146	(C,T,7)	−20.269 ***	First order stationary
ln$P$	(C,T,0)	−2.280	(C,0,7)	−4.400 ***	First order stationary
F	(0,0,0)	0.198	(0,0,1)	−2.428 **	First order stationary

*, **, *** indicate the levels of significance at 10%, 5%, 1%, respectively; (C,T,K) denote the intercept, time trend and lag order, respectively.

As can be seen from the test results, not all of the original sequences of variables are stable. After the first difference, the time sequence data of total variables reject the original hypothesis at the level of significance of 5% and consider that they are first-order difference stationary sequences.

4.2. Co-Integration Tests

Since total variables are I (one) sequences, the co-integration test can be carried out to determine whether there are long-run equilibrium relationships between them. The Johansen co-integration test method is used in this article, because it is more suitable for a multivariate co-integration test, and the test potential is higher than the EG (Engle-Granger) two-step method. The optimal lag order of VAR (Vector Auto-regression Model) (P) is two, determined by using the AIC (Akaike Information Criterion) and the SC (Schwarz information criterion) information criterion. Therefore, the optimal lag order of the Johansen co-integration test is one. Accordingly, the results of the Johansen co-integration test are obtained in Table 4.

Table 4. Test results of the Johansen co-integration approach.

Original Hypothesis	Eigenvalues	Trace Statistic	Critical Value (5%)
None **	0.9986	271.6813	83.9371
At most 1 **	0.9888	153.9545	60.0614
At most 2 **	0.9097	73.0420	40.1749
At most 3 **	0.5534	29.7621	24.2760
At most 4 **	0.4856	15.2536	12.3209
At most 5 **	0.1670	3.2894	3.1299

** indicates that original hypothesis is rejected at the 5% level.

From the results of Johansen co-integration, we can see that both the trace test and max-eigenvalues test reject the original hypothesis at the 5% confidence level, suggesting that there are co-integration relationships between total variables.

4.3. Estimation Results of the Model

Due to the existence of a co-integration relationship between total variables, we estimate the parameters of Model (1). We apply a ridge regression method with Maekmay software 5.0 to avoid the multicollinearity of the model variables. We get the ridge regression coefficient and the ridge trace plot after setting up the ridge parameter K from zero to 0.50, and a step of 0.05. We present test results as shown in Table 5 and Figure 1.

Total regression coefficients of independent variables have a large variation range when the ridge parameter goes from zero to 0.05. These are the abnormal changes caused by multicollinearity. The regression coefficients of independent variables tends to be stable when the ridge parameter is larger than 0.05. The bigger the ridge parameter, the greater the standard error of the model. Therefore, we set the ridge parameter to 0.05. At last, we get the parameters' estimated values. We present test results as shown in Table 6.

As can be seen from the estimation results, the model works well. The adjusted R^2 of the model is greater than 0.900, which means that the explanation capacity of all of the variables reaches above 90%. The empirical results are consistent with what we expect. The technological factor is the highest. The second is the size of the population. The third is the prosperity and financial support. Lastly is the size of economy. The EKC curve in rural non-point source pollution does not exist currently.

Table 5. Estimated results of the ridge regression.

K	SD	C	ln*I*	ln*A*	$(\ln A)^2$	ln*T*	F
0.00	0.0301	−2.9573	−0.5073	3.6578	−0.2611	−0.5218	0.0055
0.05	0.0384	7.5076	−0.1983	0.0181	0.0002	−0.5926	−0.0209
0.10	0.0398	6.8697	−0.1582	0.0284	0.0013	−0.5355	−0.0219
0.15	0.0411	6.5396	−0.1415	0.0342	0.0019	−0.4962	−0.0221
0.20	0.0423	6.3314	−0.1330	0.0377	0.0022	−0.4659	−0.0219
0.25	0.0435	6.1843	−0.1282	0.0401	0.0024	−0.4412	−0.0216
0.30	0.0446	6.0723	−0.1253	0.0418	0.0026	−0.4204	−0.0213
0.35	0.0457	5.9825	−0.1233	0.0430	0.0027	−0.4025	−0.0209
0.40	0.0469	5.9078	−0.1219	0.0439	0.0028	−0.3868	−0.0205
0.45	0.0479	5.8439	−0.1207	0.0446	0.0028	−0.3728	−0.0201
0.50	0.0490	5.7880	−0.1198	0.0450	0.0029	−0.3603	−0.0197

Table 6. Estimation results of the model.

	Coefficients	Standardized Coefficient
C	7.5076	
ln*P*	−0.1983	−0.2585
ln*A*	0.0181	0.0553
$(\ln A)^2$	0.0002	0.0071
ln*T*	−0.5926	−0.5732
ln*F*	−0.0209	−0.2386
Adjusted R^2	0.907	
F	38.100 ***	

*** indicates that original hypothesis is rejected at the 1% level.

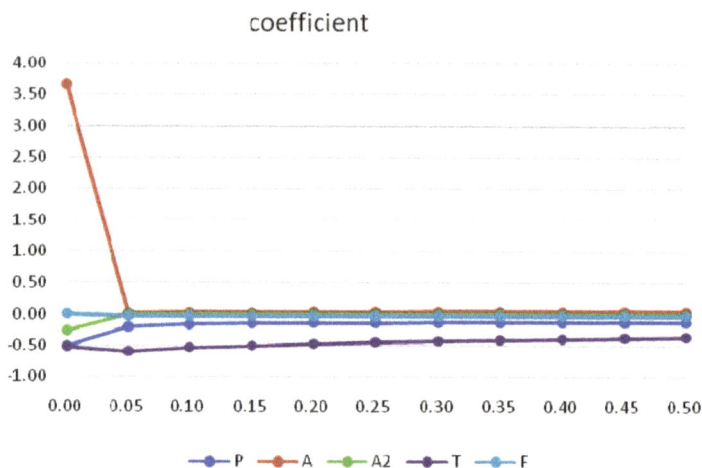

Figure 1. Ridge trace plot.

5. Conclusions and Policy Suggestions

According to the data about economic development and environmental pollution from 1990 to 2009 in Jiangsu Province, we apply the improved STIRPAT model and the ridge regression method to study the rural pollution problem in a developed area in the process of urban-rural integration. The results show that technological level and the size of the population are important factors to reduce rural non-point source pollution. Financial support can reduce rural non-point source pollution, too. Accordingly, we put forward the following policy suggestions:

(1) Balance urban and rural development, speed up industrial adjustment and speed up scientific and technological progress. Currently, an extensive and predatory development model has inspired the increase in agricultural nonpoint source pollution. Hence, balancing urban and rural development, taking economic and policy measures to guide rural industrial structure adjustment, introducing green industry and eco-industries instead of polluting non-agricultural industries and speeding up scientific and technological progress will reduce rural non-point source pollution effectively.

(2) Increase financial support and improve rural environmental infrastructure. The dual urban-rural environmental protection system is an important factor for ineffective rural non-point source management. For a long time, the focus of China's environmental protection work has been in big cities, large industries and large projects, while rural environmental protection basically has remained in a marginalized status. In recent years, though the situation has improved, it still cannot meet the needs of the current pollution situation. Therefore, the government should take on policies of various forms: on the one hand, increasing financial input to environmental infrastructure in rural areas and improving the capacity to control pollution; and on the other, setting up a special fund for rural governance. In this way, the trend of the deterioration of the rural ecological environment can be reversed.

Of course, there are some limitations in this paper that need to be improved in future research. Due to variability of the data, such as population urbanization and the proportion of non-farm labor, being unstable, they are not included in the model for the empirical analysis; therefore, the study of the influencing factors is not comprehensive.

Acknowledgments: This study was supported in part by: the Ministry of Education Foundation for Humanities and Social Science (No. 11YJA790133), the Jiangsu Province Foundation for Philosophy and Social Sciences

(No. 12EYA001), the Bidding Project of the Research Center for Resource-based Cities' Development of Huainan Normal University (No. SK2014A099), the Program for Innovative Research Team in Huainan Normal University, the CNAC Foundation for Generalized Virtual Economics (No. GX2012-1023(Y)).

Author Contributions: All of the authors made contributions to the work in this paper. Tao Sun and Hongjun Dai designed the research. Hongjun Dai contributed to model development, data collection. Kun Zhang and Wen Guo analyzed the data. Tao Sun provided guidance for writing this paper. Hongjun Dai wrote the paper. All authors have read and approved the final manuscript. We would like to acknowledge the reviewers for the comments that enhanced the quality of the manuscript.

Conflicts of Interest: The authors declare no conflict of interest.

References

1. Zhang, N.; Kong, F.; Choi, Y.; Zhou, P. The effect of size-control policy on unified energy and carbon efficiency for Chinese fossil fuel power plants. *Energy Policy* **2014**, *70*, 193–200. [CrossRef]

2. Zhang, N.; Choi, Y. Total-factor carbon emission performance of fossil fuel power plants in China: A metafrontier non-radial Malmquist index analysis. *Energy Econ.* **2013**, *40*, 549–559. [CrossRef]

3. Choi, Y.; Zhang, N.; Zhou, P. Efficiency and abatement costs of energy-related CO_2 emissions in China: A slacks-based efficiency measure. *Appl. Energy* **2012**, *98*, 198–208. [CrossRef]

4. Grossman, G.M.; Krueger, A.B. Environment Impacts of a North American Free Trade Agreement. Available online: http://www.nber.org/papers/w3914 (accessed on 30 December 2014).

5. Bell, R.G.; Russell, C. Environmental Policy for Developing Countries. *Issues Sci. Technol.* **2002**, *69*, 63–70.

6. Ribaudo, M.; Horan, R.D.; Smith, M.E. *Economics of Water Quality Protection from Nonpoint Sources: Theory and practice*; Economic Research Service: Washington, DC, USA, 1999.

7. Isik, H.B.; Sohngen, B. *Performance-Based Voluntary Group Contracts for Nonpoint-Source Water Pollution*; Ohio State University: Columbus, OH, USA, 2003.

8. Russell, C.S.; Clark, C.D. *Economic Instruments and Nonpoint Source Water Pollution*; Biswas, A.K., Tortajada, C., Braga, B., Eds.; Springer: Berlin, Germany, 2006.

9. Egli, H.; Steger, T.M. A Dynamic Model of the Environmental Kuznets Curve: Turning Point and Public Policy. *Environ. Resour. Econ.* **2007**, *36*, 15–34. [CrossRef]

10. Khanna, M.; Speir, C. Motivations for Proactive Environmental Management. *Sustainability* **2013**, *5*, 2664–2692. [CrossRef]

11. Kaplowitz, M.D.; Lupi, F. Stakeholder preferences for best management practices for non-point source pollution and stormwater control. *Landsc. Urban Plan.* **2012**, *3*, 364–372. [CrossRef]

12. Camacho-Cuena, E.; Requate, T. The regulation of non-point source pollution and risk preferences: An experimental approach. *Ecol. Econ.* **2012**, *1*, 179–187. [CrossRef]

13. Cason, T.N.; Gangadharan, L. Empowering neighbors *versus* imposing regulations: An experimental analysis of pollution reduction schemes. *J. Environ. Econ. Manag.* **2012**, *9*, 87–96.

14. Li, T.; Zhang, F.; Hu, H. Authentication of the Kuznets Curve in Agriculture Non-point Source Pollution and Its Drivers Analysis. *China Popul. Resour. Environ.* **2011**, *21*, 118–123.

15. Guo, W.; Sun, T. Empirical Research of Rural Non-point Source Pollution Based on the Theory of "EKC". *Hunan Agric. Sci.* **2012**, *23*, 117–120.

16. Gao, X.; Jiang, L.; Li, X.; Liu, Z.; Xu, Y.; Wei, J. Using Equivalent Standard Pollution method to evaluate impacts of agricultural non-point pollution resources on water environment in Shandong Province. *Chin. J. Ecol. Agric.* **2010**, *18*, 1066–1071. [CrossRef]

17. Yang, Y.; Yan, B. Optimal Non-point Source Pollution Control Practices for a Small Watershed. *J. Ecol. Rural. Environ.* **2011**, *27*, 11–15.

18. Jin, J.; Wang, Z. Choice Experiment Method and Its Application to Solid Waste Management in Macao. *Environ. Sci.* **2006**, *27*, 821–826.

19. Ge, J.; Zhou, S. Does Factor Market Distortions Stimulate the Agricultural Non-oint Source Pollution? A Case Study of Fertilizer. *Issues Agric. Econ.* **2012**, *3*, 92–100.

20. Xiao, J. To promote integral construction of cities and villages to accordinate the development of economy, society and environment. *Environ. Pollut. Control* **2004**, *26*, 198–202.

21. Luo, D.; Bai, J.; Zhu, L. Study on the Cause and Strategy of Country Pollution in Chongqing by the Angle of Viewing Urban and Country Plan as a Whole. *Ecol. Econ.* **2009**, *4*, 166–169.

22. Fei, Y.; Zhang, J.; Cheng, Q. Strengthening Eco-Environmental Protection during the Process of Urban-rural Integration Construction. *Pollut. Control Technol.* **2010**, *23*, 89–93.

23. Fu, S. How to improve rural living environment and accelerate the integration of urban and rural. *Agric. Econ.* **2012**, *4*, 41–42.

24. Ehrlich, P.R.; Holdrens, J.P. Impact of population growth. *Science* **1971**, *171*, 1212–1217. [CrossRef] [PubMed]

25. Dietz, T.; Rosa, E.A. Rethinking the environmental impacts of population, affluence and technology. *Hum. Ecol. Rev.* **1994**, *1*, 277–300.

26. York, R.; Rosa, E.A.; Dietz, T. STIRPAT, IPAT and ImPACT: Analytic Tools for Unpacking the Driving Forces of Environmental Impacts. *Ecol. Econ.* **2003**, *46*, 351–365. [CrossRef]

27. Jiang, F.; Cui, C. Temporal and spatial characteristics and source apportionment of agricultural non-point source pollution in Jiangsu province based on inventory analysis. *J. Anhui Agric. Univ.* **2012**, *39*, 961–967.

sustainability

MDPI

Article

Is It Feasible for China to Optimize Oil Import Source Diversification?

Jian Xu [1,2], Jin-Suo Zhang [2,*], Qin Yao [1] and Wei Zhang [1,2]

[1]   School of Management, Xi'an University of Science and Technology, Xi'an 710054, China;
      jxu@xust.edu.cn (J.X.); yaoqin@xust.edu.cn (Q.Y.); zhangwei@xust.edu.cn (W.Z.)
[2]   Research Center for Energy and Economics, Xi'an University of Science and Technology, Xi'an 710054, China
*   Author to whom correspondence should be addressed; zhangjinsuo@xust.edu.cn; Tel.: +86-29-8558-3906.

External Editor: Marc A. Rosen

Received: 29 June 2014; in revised form: 27 October 2014; Accepted: 13 November 2014; Published: 21 November 2014

Abstract: In 2013, China imported 282 million tons of crude oil with an external dependence of 58.1%, surpassing the USA as the world's largest net oil importer. An import source diversification strategy has been adopted by China to ensure oil supply security and to prevent oil supply disruption. However, the strategy is restricted by the imbalance of oil reserves. What is the reasonable and clear objective of the diversification strategy under an imbalanced environment? How do we assess the natural imbalance? This paper analyzes the oil import diversification of China and the USA, as well as the oil production of oil export countries by the oil import source diversification index (OISDI). Our results are as follows: the distribution of oil import sources for China tends to coincide with the oil production distribution of oil exporters in the world. Compared with the USA, China has more diversified import sources. The Chinese government paid much attention to import sources in the past. In the future, China will adjust the distributions of regional sources rather than focus on the number of sources to further optimize the structure of imported regions in the course of implementing the import source diversification strategy.

Keywords: energy security; oil import source diversification index (OISDI); China; oil export countries

1. Introduction

In 2013, China imported 282 million tons of crude oil with an external dependence of 58.1%, surpassing the USA as the world's largest net oil importer. China's oil imports have increased over the years, as shown in Figure 1, and in response to the rapid growth in world oil demands, China has adopted a positive import source diversification strategy, which has been recognized by countries all over the world as preventing some individual countries from reducing or stopping their oil supply.

Since China became a net oil importer in 1996, the number of major oil importing countries has increased from 11 to 35. Nearly a decade later, the top five oil importing countries have remained stable, accounting for about 60% of the total oil imports, and some adjustments have been made in countries from the sixth to tenth place, whose import proportion remains at about 20%. At the same time, China has developed some overland oil import channels, building oil pipelines with Kazakhstan, Russia and Myanmar, which, to some extent, has reduced the risk from oil importing that China faces. However, there still exist some problems: (1) China's major import sources are focused in some politically unstable regions, such as the Middle East and Africa. China's top ten source countries are Saudi Arabia, Angola, Iran, Russia, Yemen, Oman, Sultan, Iraq and Venezuela, which have high risks. The oil supply is susceptible to emergencies and political sanctions; (2) The production of major import source countries illustrates a downward trend, which can be in Figure 2. Except for Saudi Arabia and

Russia, who maintain higher yields, many other countries, such as Iraq, Angola and Oman, show a downward trend; (3) Because the geographical location of the source countries is concentrated in the Middle East and Africa, the mode of transportation is too singular. Although there are overland pipeline transportation routes, China depends on marine channels to import two thirds of the oil, most of which relies on foreign shipping corporations. Additionally, the Malacca strait, Somalian waters and the Gulf of Aden are vital shipping routes, which have suffered many pirate attacks [1]. Thus, the import source diversification strategy of China does not fundamentally reduce the risk of importing oil, and it is difficult to guarantee China's oil import demands in the future.

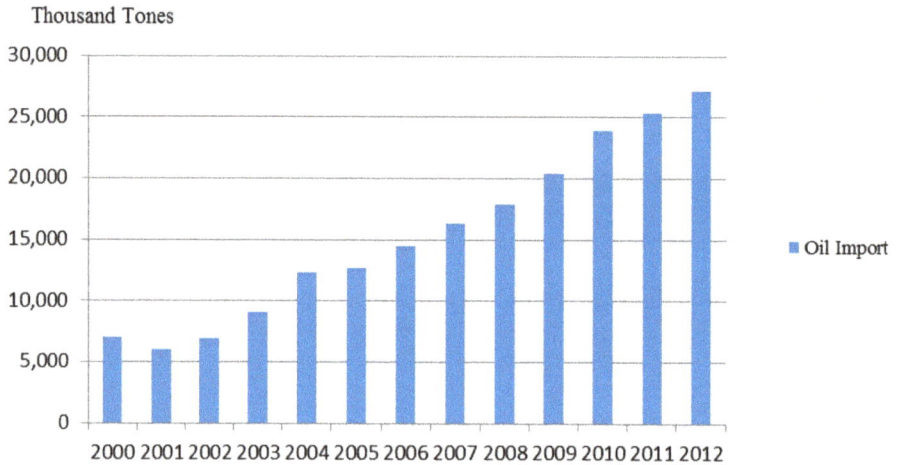

Figure 1. 2000–2012 China oil import volume.

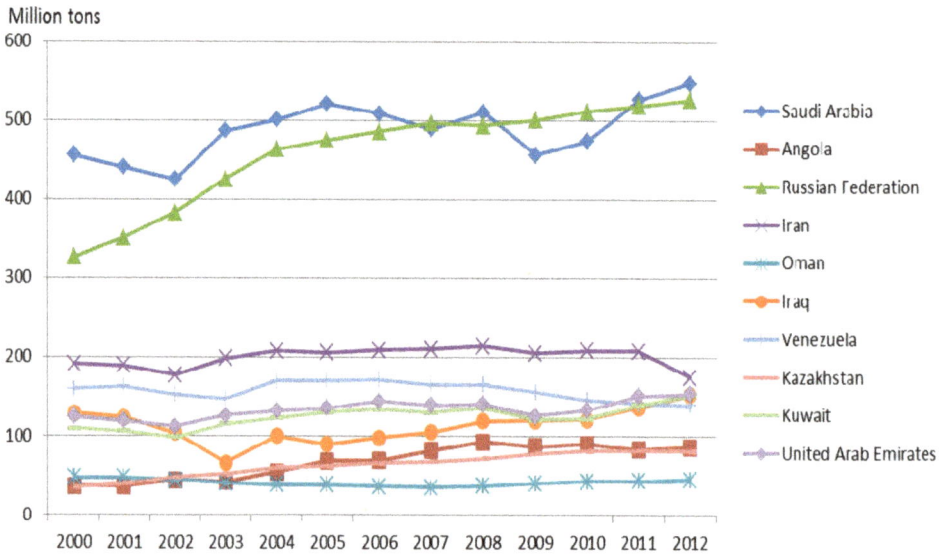

Figure 2. 2000–2012 oil production of China's oil import sources.

The International Energy Agency (IEA) predicts that the oil gap for China will increase to 400 million tons by 2020. China will face cut-throat competition with both traditional oil importers and emerging oil importers, dealing with complex geopolitical relationship and all kinds of emergencies and problems of oil export regions. Meanwhile, there is a huge imbalance in the oil reserves in the whole world. In detail, the proven oil reserves of North America account for 13.6%, South and Central America 19.5%, Europe and Eurasia 8.8%, the Middle East 47.9%, Africa 7.7%, Asia Pacific 2.5% of oil reserves worldwide. The oil reserves of Africa, the former Soviet Union, the Middle East and South America account for 83.6% of the whole world, while their consumption is only 24.8% [2]. Oil reserves are unbalanced across all countries; there is a huge imbalance between oil producing and consuming countries. However, because of the political nature of oil, there is fierce competition among countries. If the importers want to have access to a safe and stable supply, they should resort to political, economic and even military force. This implies that the number of import source countries will not be increased unlimitedly. If the traditional import source diversification strategy is still adopted, could China's oil supply be sustainable under the imbalanced conditions of oil reserves? Is it feasible for China to optimize oil import source diversification?

The paper is organized as follows: after the Introduction, the Section 2 gives a brief overview of the import source diversification strategy that is necessary to ensure oil supply security. Section 3 addresses the model built by the oil import source diversification index. In Section 4, we describe the oil import source diversification index of China (2012) and the USA (2012), as well as the oil production distribution index of oil exporters in the world. In the final section, policy implications are derived.

2. Literature Review

Energy security is very important for any country, but its concept is very confusing and has been broadened over time. Many authors give different definitions [3–9]. Christian Winzer [10] "suggests narrowing down the concept of energy security to the concept of energy supply continuity". An importer takes insurance measures against the disruptions of energy importing at reasonable prices to support its economic growth and social welfare [11–13].

Despite the fact that there are different risk sources [14,15], import source diversification strategies has been recognized by countries all over the world [16] and studied in various countries and regions [17–20]. Oil import source diversification refers to the mix of state providers of oil [19]. Diversification was quantified by using one or more of the scientific measures of diversification. Neff [19] utilized the Herfindahl–Hirschman index (HHI) for market concentration to value energy supply dependence across the fuels of Asia Pacific. Most of the literature [18–21] uses HHI to measure diversification.

From the review of the literature, it is clear that an importer should enhance the diversification degree against the disruption of the oil supply. However, the exact objective is not given. Many scholars chose to use the HHI method to build a diversified index. The HHI method can give a company with a bigger market share more weight, amplify the company's influence and reflect the impact of large-scale companies on the changes of market concentration sensitively and in an exaggerated way. However, the method cannot react to the unbalanced market truthfully and accurately; hence, it is not intuitive. Therefore, we will use the oil import diversification index based on the Gini coefficient method to analyze oil import diversification situations, the imbalanced oil production characteristics of export countries and oil reserve distribution of exporters. Finally, we put forward the goal of China's oil import diversification strategy.

3. Data and Method

3.1. Data Sources

The data for China's oil importing (2012) are taken from China's Customs Statistics Yearbook (2012). The data for the USA's oil importing (2012) and the oil production of oil export countries are taken from the Energy Information Administration (EIA), U.S. Department of Energy.

3.2. Model of Oil Import Source Diversification Index

Lorenz proposed using the cumulative percentage curve as a method to test the degree of social income imbalance in 1905, namely the Lorenz curve. By mapping the Lorenz curve of a country, one can observe and analyze the degree of balance and concentration of its income distribution. In order to accurately reflect the changing degree of income distribution, C. Gini proposed a measure to indicate the balance level of income distribution, namely the Gini coefficient. The index values are between 0 and 1. A value of zero means that the income is absolutely balanced. A value of one means that the income is absolutely unbalanced. A larger index value means a less balanced income distribution.

According to the principles of the Lorenz curve and the Gini coefficient, we build a function of the oil import diversification curve and calculate the oil import diversification index. The import diversification curve (Figure 3) is a function that describes the relation between the proportion of import sources and the percentage of imported oil.

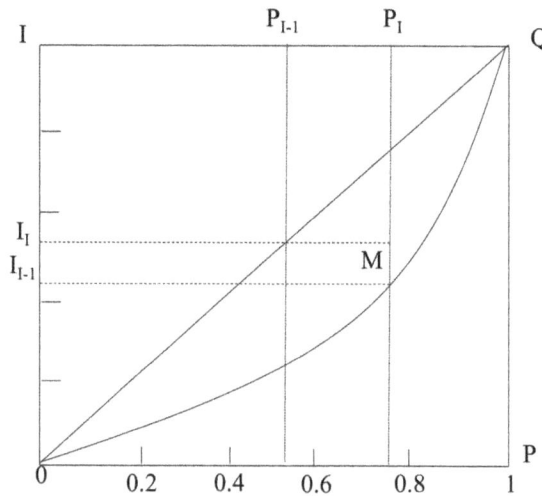

Figure 3. Import diversification curve.

The import diversification function is $I = I(P)$. I is the cumulative percentage of import volume, and P is the cumulative percentage of the oil import source.

The oil import diversification index is defined as:

$$
\begin{aligned}
Diversification\ \ index \\
= \frac{Area\ of\ the\ dagram\ formed\ by\ 45°\ OQ\ and\ actual\ diversification\ curve\ OMQ}{Area\ of\ the\ right\ below\ the\ 45°\ line} \\
= \frac{\int_0^1 [P - I(P)]dP}{\int_0^1 PdP}
\end{aligned}
\tag{1}
$$

3.3. Method

The most important step is to calculate the area of the diagram formed by 45° OQ and actual diversification curve OMQ. Firstly, draw the oil import diversification scatter plot based on the oil import data. Then, preliminarily judge the shape of the curve and carry out the curve regression and statistical tests to get the acceptable function expressions. Finally, calculate the oil import index using the diversification index model.

4. The Empirical Analysis

4.1. Analysis of China's Oil Imports in 2012

Using SPSS (16.0 Version, IBM, USA), we draw the scatter plot on the basis of China's oil import data and select linear, exponential and logistic models to estimate the curve. We find that the logistic function is the best by comparison. Its goodness of fittest (R^2) is 0.924. The greater the R^2 value, the better the fitting result. Because we only use the logistic function to calculate the area and select all of the data, this paper does not analyze the coefficients.

Drawing the oil import diversification curve (Figure 4) and carrying out the coefficients (Table 1), we obtain China's oil import diversification curve function: $I = 1/[1/1000 + (5.427 \times 0.938^P)]$. The import diversification index is 0.67.

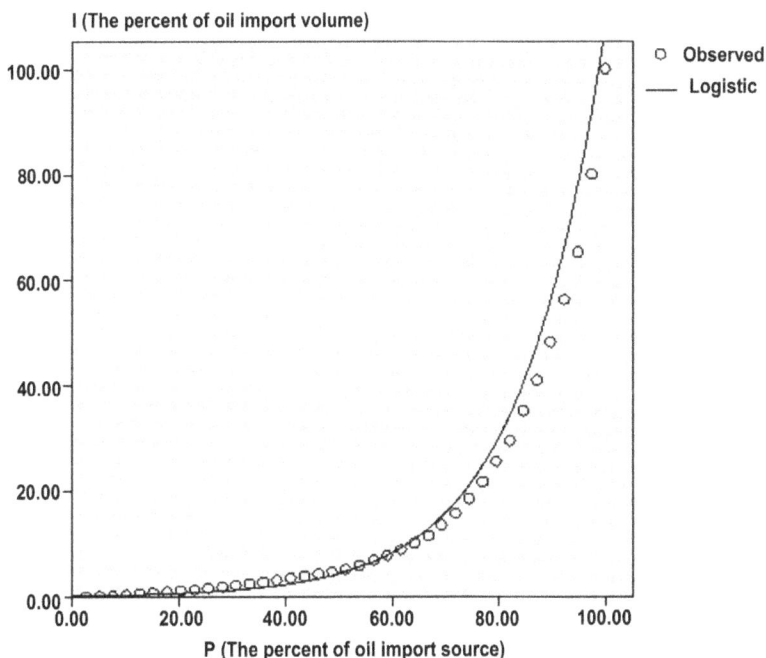

Figure 4. China's oil import diversification curve.

Table 1. Coefficients.

	Unstandardized Coefficients		Standardized Coefficients	t	Significance
	B	Standard Error	Beta		
P	0.938	0.003	0.382	332.703	0.000
Constant	5.427	0.960	-	5.654	0.000

4.2. Analysis of the USA's Oil Imports in 2012

Drawing the oil import diversification curve (Figure 5) and carrying out the coefficients (Table 2) using SPSS (16.0 Version, IBM, USA) on the basis of USA oil import data (2012), we obtain the USA's oil import diversification function: $I = 1/[1/1000 + (28.087 \times 0.924^P)]$. The import diversification index is 0.77.

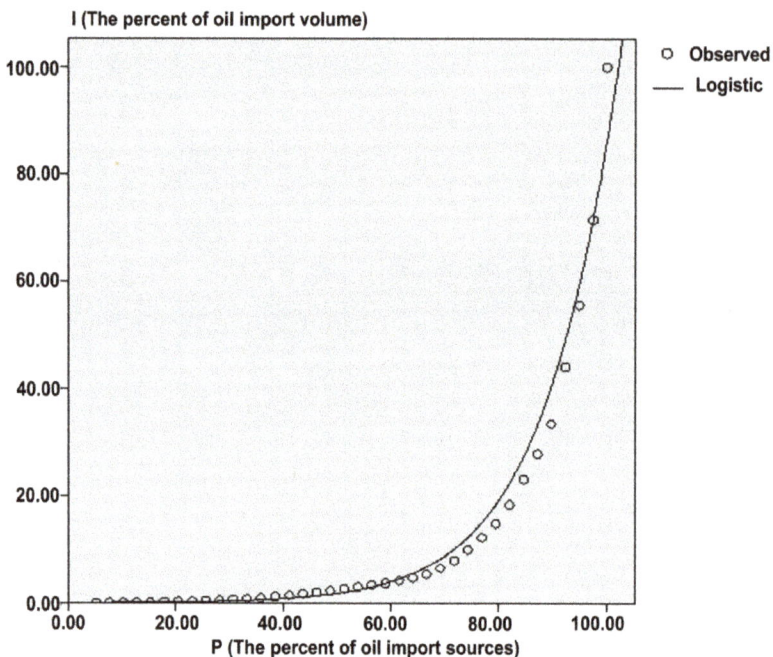

Figure 5. The USA's oil import diversification curve (2012).

Table 2. Coefficients.

	Unstandardized Coefficients		Standardized Coefficients	t	Significance
	B	Standard Error	Beta		
P	0.924	0.002	0.374	413.066	0.000
Constant	28.087	4.053	-	6.929	0.000

4.3. Analysis of the Oil Production of Oil Exporting Countries

Drawing the oil production distribution curve (Figure 6) and carrying out the coefficients (Table 3) using SPSS (16.0 Version, IBM, USA) on the basis of the oil production of oil exporting countries, we obtain the oil production diversification function of oil exporting countries: $I = 1/(1/1000 + 70.09 \times 0.91^P)$. The production diversification index is 0.62. The production diversification index of oil exporting countries shows the degree of the concentration of oil markets in the short term.

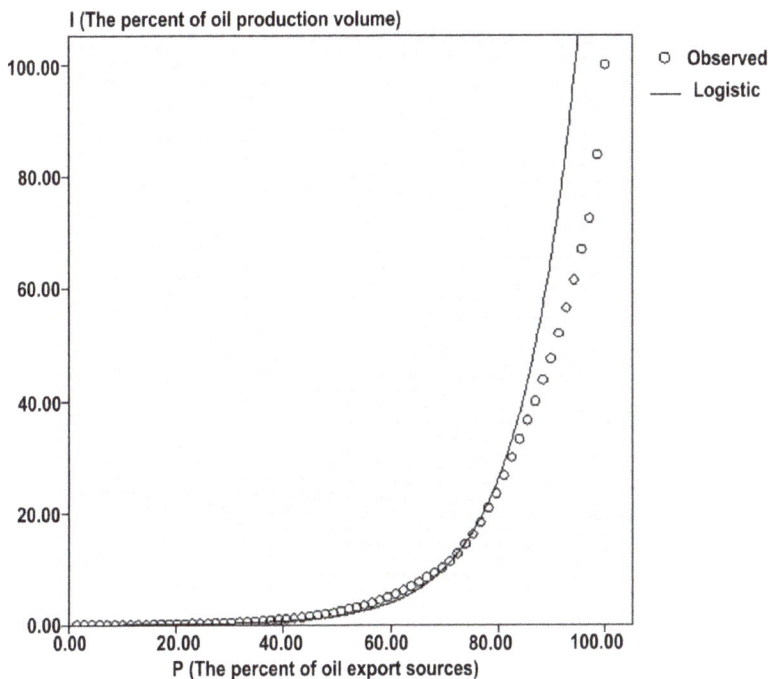

Figure 6. The oil production distribution curve.

Table 3. Coefficients.

	Unstandardized Coefficients		Standardized Coefficients	t	Significance
	B	Standard Error	Beta		
P	0.910	0.002	0.373	535	0.000
Constant	70.086	7.635	9.180	0.753	0.000

4.4. Analysis of the Oil Reserves of Oil Exporting Countries

Drawing the oil exporting countries' reserve distribution curve (Figure 7) and carrying out a coefficient statistical test (Table 4) using SPSS (16.0 Version, IBM, USA), on the basis of the oil reserves of the oil exporting countries, we obtain the oil reserve diversification function of oil exporting countries: $I = 1/(0.001 + 11.65 \times 0.935^P)$. The reserve diversification index is 0.79. Because a country's oil production is mainly constrained by its oil reserves, the oil reserve diversification index of oil exporting countries illustrates the concentration degree of the long-term oil supply in the future.

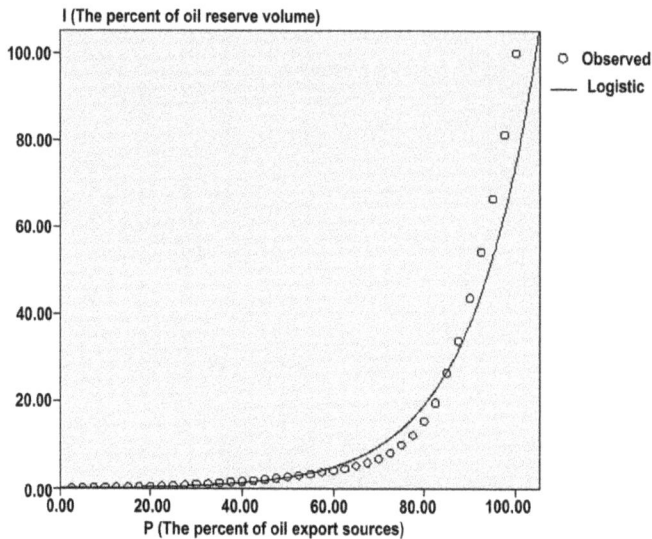

Figure 7. The oil reserve distribution curve.

Table 4. Coefficients.

	Unstandardized Coefficients		Standardized Coefficients	t	Significance
	B	Standard Error	Beta		
P	0.935	0.001	0.373	654.272	0.000
Constant	11.656	1.048	-	11.124	0.000

5. Results and Discussions

5.1. Market-Oriented Diversification Strategy

China's oil import diversification strategy is market-oriented, which focuses on a short-term market and can meet the demands of the domestic markets in the short term; thus, it is also more susceptible to short-term fluctuations of the oil market.

As the world's second largest oil importing country, China's oil import diversification index is 0.669, which is close to the oil production diversification index of oil exporters, 0.622, and lower than the oil exporters' reserve diversification index, 0.79. This shows that, currently, China's oil import diversification strategy is a market-oriented diversification strategy rather than a long-term market strategy. This phenomenon has a close relationship with the rapid growth of domestic demand for oil. In the past 10 years, the average growth rate of China's oil consumption was 7.1%, and its foreign-trade dependence rose from 36% in 2003 to 56.4% in 2012. To meet the rapid economic development of China, China always purchases oil by short-term contract trading in spot markets, so China's oil import diversification index is similar to the oil production diversification index of oil exporters. What is more, China is a developing country, which has little advantage in competing with the developed countries to gain a long-term contract with exporters with political stability and with rich oil reserves in the world oil markets. According to the information provided by the general administration of customs, in 2012, about 49.8% of China's oil imports were from the Middle East, 23.9% from Africa, 13.1% from the former Soviet Union and Europe and 10.4% from America. As we can see, more than 70% of China's oil imports are imported from the Middle East and Africa, and the political situation of these two regions has been unstable for a long time. Influenced by the political situation, in 2012, Iran's oil exports to China fell by 20.7% compared to the previous year, and Sudan experienced a four-month supply interruption. Thus, the import source diversification strategy cannot reasonably avoid political risks of source imports; instead, it pays more attention to the current short-term oil production distribution in order to solve the pressing domestic oil consumption demands. Therefore, under the condition of oil reserve disequilibrium, excessive dependence on short-term trade and politically unstable regions is not sustainable.

As the world's largest oil importer, America's diversification index is 0.767, which is higher than the oil exporter production diversification index, 0.622, and close to the oil exporters' reserve diversification index, 0.79. This shows that America's diversification strategy not only focuses on short-term market supply, but also is concerned with the long-term market supply. According to the information from EIA, we know that 2% of oil imports come from five oil exporters: Canada, Saudi Arabia, Iraq, Mexico and Venezuela. These countries are America's allies or neighbors and have huge storage capacities. Canada's oil reserves are 173 billion barrels, ranking third. Saudi reserves are 267.02 billion barrels, ranking first. Iraqi reserves are 143.1 billion barrels, ranking fifth. Mexican reserves are 10.36 barrels, ranking 13th. Venezuelan reserves are 211.17 billion barrels, ranking second.

5.2. The Future Diversification Strategy of China

We propose that China's oil import diversification strategy be reserve-oriented. This fact, coupled with the future development of import source economies, means that some export countries will transform into importers, which will not provide a large quantity of oil to guarantee the oil imports of China, increasing the risk to China's oil imports in the future. To provide a sustainable and stable oil import guarantee for future oil consumption, the oil import diversification strategy should be directed toward optimizing the structure of import sources, focusing on long-term, stable import sources. China's objective should aim at the oil reserve diversification index of export countries, which reflects the long-term market supply guarantee, instead of the market-oriented diversification strategy.

According to IEA [22], in 2020, China's net oil import will be 400 million tons (mt), which is a 68% increase over 2011; the EU's net oil import will 450 mt, which is down by nearly 9% compared to 2011; India's net oil import will be 190 mt, which is a 72% increase over 2011; the United States' net oil import will be 290 mt, which is down by nearly 39% compared to 2011; Japan's net oil import will be 190 mt, which has a nearly 2% decline over 2011. From that, we can see that the United States will significantly reduce oil imports in the future, and the European Union and Japan will have a small cut, as well. India has relatively rapid growth, but its amount is not very great. With an energy independence strategy implemented, the United States will significantly reduce its imports, until North America becomes a net oil exporter in about 2030. This trend will shift the international oil trade direction to Asia much faster. Canada, Mexico and Venezuela are eager to seek new trading partners, which provides strategic space for China to adjust its oil import strategy. At the same time, the European Union is actively exploring new oil suppliers to reduce its dependence on Russia; Russia is also trying to break the situation of relying too much on the EU. Therefore, China has an opportunity to expand its oil imports from Russia. In 2013, China put forward the idea of the "Silk-Road Economic Belt", and China has strengthened energy cooperation with central Asian countries, including: Kazakhstan, which has 30 billion barrels of oil reserves; Turkmenistan, which has 600 million barrels of oil reserves; Uzbekistan, which has 600 million barrels; and Azerbaijan, which has seven billion barrels. They have in total 125.2 billion barrels of oil reserves. This situation will increase China's imports from the land, reducing the transportation risk of oil imports. Based on the above analysis, we suggest that in the future, China's oil import diversification strategy should be guided by oil reserves and diversified transport channels. The oil import source distribution in 2020 is shown in Table 5, and we find that our import diversity index is 0.81, which is close to the oil reserve diversification index.

Table 5. China oil import sources distribution (2020).

Import Sources	2012	2020	Import Sources	2012	2020
Indonesia	54.85	55	Sudan	250.59	1500
Vietnam	74.46	74	Equatorial Guinea	200.13	200
Malaysia	111.47	111	Cameroon	57.63	58
Australia	371.56	372	South Africa	44.33	44
Brunei	40.5	41	Congo-Kinshasa	85.5	86
Thailand	72.29	72	Others	120.87	121
Mongolia	45.79	46	Total Africa	6469.91	8073
Other Asia Pacific	4.14	4	Russian Federation	2432.97	4000
Total Asia Pacific	775.06	775	Kazakhstan	1070.37	2300
Oman	1957.38	1957	Azerbaijan	-	600
Yemen	358.45	358	Turkmenistan	-	500
Iran	2,200.96	1000	Uzbekistan	-	500
United Arab Emirates	874.37	874	Others	45.19	-
Saudi Arabia	5390.06	6000		3548.53	7900
Iraq	1568.47	3000	Venezuela	1529.03	4000
Kuwait	1049.19	1000	Ecuador	89.37	89
Qatar	99.55	-	Argentina	120.69	121
Total Middle East	13,498.43	14,190	Brazil	607.05	607
Angola	4015.63	4,000	Colombia	290.86	291
Nigeria	93.65	-	Canada	66.37	3000
Libya	730.7	731	Mexico	101.55	1000
Algeria	257.19	257	Others	12.3	12
Congo	536.55	1000	Total America	2817.22	9120
Egypt	77.14	77	Total Import Sources	27,109.12	40,059

6. Conclusions

Since China became a net oil importer in 1996, China has adopted a positive import source diversification strategy. However, the strategy is restricted by the imbalance of oil reserves. Analyzing the oil import diversification of China and the USA, as well as the oil reserve and production distribution of oil exporting countries by the oil import source diversification index (OISDI), we arrive at the following conclusions:

(1) The oil import diversification index based on the principles of the Lorenz curve and the Gini coefficient can react to the unbalanced market truthfully and accurately, and it is intuitive. China's oil import diversification index is 0.67. The USA's oil import diversification index is 0.77. The production diversification index of oil exporting countries is 0.62. The reserve diversification index of oil exporting countries is 0.79.

(2) China's oil import diversification strategy is market-oriented, which focuses on a short-term market and can meet the demands of the domestic markets in the short term, but it does not fundamentally reduce the risk of oil importing; it is difficult to guarantee China's oil import demands in the future.

(3) China's oil import diversification strategy should be reserve-oriented. China's objective should aim at the oil reserve diversification index of export countries, which reflects the long-term market supply guarantee, instead of the market-oriented diversification strategy. In the future, China should increase the oil imports from Eurasia and America.

Acknowledgments: This work was financially supported by the Natural Science Foundation (71273206) and Shaanxi provincial department of education (Higher) social science research base construction projects (No. 12JZ018) and Shaanxi province characteristic disciplines construction project. We would like to acknowledge the reviewers for the comments that enhanced the quality of the manuscript.

Author Contributions: Jian Xu and Jin-suo Zhang designed the research. Jian Xu built the model. Qin Yao and Wei Zhang analyzed the data. Jian Xu wrote the paper. All authors have read and approved the final manuscript.

Sustainability **2014**, *6*, 8329–8341

Conflicts of Interest: The authors declare no conflict of interest.

References

1. Wu, G.; Wei, Y. Analysis of marine transportation risks of China's oil imports. *China Energy* **2009**, *31*, 9–13. (In Chinese)
2. Statistical Review of World Energy 2014. Available online: http://www.bp.com/statisticalreview (accessed on 18 November 2014).
3. Chevalier, J.M. Security of Energy Supply in Europ: Continuous Adaptation. Available online: http://ec.europa.eu/energy/publications/doc/20110601_the_european_files_en.pdf (accessed on 18 November 2014).
4. Checchi, A.; Egenhofer, C.; Behrens, A. Long-Term Energy Security Risks for Europe: A Sector-Specific Approach. Available online: http://www.ceps.eu/book/long-term-energy-security-risks-europe-sector-specific-approach (accessed on 14 November 2014).
5. Chester, L. Conceptualising energy security and making explicit its polysemic nature. *Energy Policy* **2010**, *38*, 887–895. [CrossRef]
6. International Energy Agency. World Energy Outlook 2007—Special Report—China and India insights. Available online: http://www.iea.org/publications/freepublications/publication/weo-2007---special-report---focus-on-china-and-india.html (accessed on 14 November 2014).
7. Kruyt, B.; van Vuuren, D.P.; de Vries, H.J.M.; Groenenberg, H. Indicators for energy security. *Energy Policy* **2009**, *37*, 2166–2181. [CrossRef]
8. Löschel, A.; Moslener, U.; Rübbelke, D.T.G. Indicators of energy security in industrialised countries. *Energy Policy* **2010**, *38*, 1665–1671. [CrossRef]
9. Asia Pacific Energy Reseach Centre (APERC). *Emergency Oil Stocks and Energy Security in the APEC Region*; Asia Pacific Energy Research Centre: Tokyo, Japan, 2000.
10. Winzer, C. Conceptualizing energy security. *Energy Policy* **2012**, *46*, 36–48. [CrossRef]
11. Bauen, A. Future energy sources and systems—Acting on climate change and energy security. *J. Power Sources* **2006**, *157*, 893–901. [CrossRef]
12. Lesbirel, S.H. Diversification and Energy Security Risks: The Japanese Case. *Jpn. J. Politi. Sci.* **2004**, *5*, 1–22. [CrossRef]
13. Dorian, J.P.; Franssen, H.T.; Simbeck, D.R. Global challenges in energy. *Energy Policy* **2006**, *34*, 1984–1991. [CrossRef]
14. Van Kooten, G.C. Wind power: The economic impact of intermittency. *Lett. Spat. Resour. Sci.* **2010**, *3*, 1–17. [CrossRef]
15. Mabro, R. On the security of oil supplies, oil weapons, oil nationalism and all that. *OPEC Energy Rev.* **2008**, *32*, 1–12. [CrossRef]
16. Vivoda, V. Diversification of oil import sources and energy security: A key strategy or an elusive objective? *Energy Policy* **2009**, *37*, 4615–4623. [CrossRef]
17. Wu, G.; Liu, L.-C.; Wei, Y.-M. Comparison of China's oil import risk: Results based on portfolio theory and a diversification index approach. *Energy Policy* **2009**, *37*, 3557–3565. [CrossRef]
18. Gupta, E. Oil vulnerability index of oil-importing countries. *Energy Policy* **2008**, *36*, 1195–1211. [CrossRef]
19. Neff, T.L. Improving energy security in Pacific Asia: Diversification and risk reduction for fossil and nuclear fuels. Available online: http://oldsite.nautilus.org/archives/papers/energy/NeffPARES.pdf (accessed on 14 November 2014).
20. Wu, G.; Wei, Y.-M.; Fan, Y.; Liu, L.-C. An empirical analysis of the risk of crude oil imports in China using improved portfolio approach. *Energy Policy* **2007**, *35*, 4190–4199. [CrossRef]

21. Le Coq, C.; Paltseva, E. Measuring the security of external energy supply in the European Union. *Energy Policy* **2009**, *37*, 4474–4481. [CrossRef]
22. World energy outlook 2012—Oil market outlook. Available online: http://www.worldenergyoutlook.org/publications/weo-2012/ (accessed on 18 November 2014).

MDPI

Article

Can China's Industrial SO$_2$ Emissions Trading Pilot Scheme Reduce Pollution Abatement Costs?

Zhengge Tu [†] and Renjun Shen [†,*]

School of Economics and Business Management, Central China Normal University, 152 Luoyu Road, Wuhan 430079, China; tuzhengge@163.com

* Author to whom correspondence should be addressed; shenrenjun@mails.ccnu.edu.cn; Tel.: +86-131-6321-9835.

† These authors contributed equally to this work.

External Editor: Ning Zhang

Received: 28 July 2014; in revised form: 17 October 2014; Accepted: 27 October 2014; Published: 31 October 2014

Abstract: This paper evaluates the effects of China's industrial SO$_2$ emissions trading pilot scheme (SETPS) on the pollution abatement costs (PAC) from the past and future perspective. We apply the kernel-based propensity score difference-in-difference method to examine the effects of SETPS on the average pollution abatement costs (APAC) and the marginal pollution abatement costs (MPAC) based on the environment data from the industrial sector of 29 provinces in China over the period of 1998 to 2011. Our findings are that SETPS failed to reduce PAC as a whole. During 2002 to 2011, SETPS increased APAC by 1310 RMB per ton on average and had an insignificant negative effect on MPAC. Nevertheless, the conclusions would be markedly different if we separately investigated the effects of SETPS each year of the pilot period. The positive effects of SETPS on PAC started to appear since 2009, and SETPS significantly reduced both APAC and MPAC, especially in 2009 and 2011.

Keywords: SO$_2$ emissions trading pilot scheme (SETPS); pollution abatement costs (PAC); difference-in-difference method; network DEA

---

1. Introduction

China's economy has maintained a high-rate of growth since the reform and opening up in 1978. Meanwhile, the environment has been deteriorating. In order to restore the environment, Chinese governments have adopted both traditional administrative measures (e.g., command-and-control regulations) and market-oriented policy instruments (e.g., tradable permit scheme) to ease the environmental pollution. China used to solely rely on a charging scheme by imposing mandatory pollution taxes on business firms. However, the charging scheme failed to curb the environmental pollution. Chinese governments thus attempted to take some more market-oriented measures to reduce industrial emissions of SO$_2$ and other pollutants. As a result, the SO$_2$ emissions trading pilot scheme (SETPS) was initiated in 2002. Four provinces (*i.e.*, Shandong, Shanxi, Jiangsu and Henan), three municipalities (*i.e.*, Shanghai, Tianjin and Liuzhou) and one business entity (*i.e.*, China Huaneng Group) were selected as the emissions trading scheme pilot regions or entity, which were known as the "4 + 3 + 1" project. These pilot regions and entity were responsible for 18.5% of SO$_2$ emissions in the acid rain and SO$_2$ control zones and included 131 cities and 727 firms, including Shanghai and Jiangsu, which were among the most developed areas of China, Shandong, which suffered the most serious SO$_2$ pollution, Henan, which was the biggest industrial province in central China and had the largest population in China, Shanxi, which was one of the heavy industry and energy bases of China, Tianjin, which was also a typical industrial city, Liuzhou, which was a typical acid district, and China Huaneng Group, which possessed one tenth of the thermal power generation capacity in China.

Sustainability **2014**, *6*, 7621–7645

SETPS has been in effect in China for nearly twelve years since 2002. Can it really reduce the pollution abatement costs (PAC)? How does one measure the PAC? In this paper, we choose the average pollution abatement costs (APAC) and the marginal pollution abatement costs (MPAC) of SO_2 to evaluate the effects of SETPS on the economic growth and environment improvement in China. APAC, a historical cost concept in a static or past perspective, reflects the economic costs per unit of emissions reduction under the current environmental technical level. While MPAC, a future cost concept in a dynamic or future perspective, reflects the abandoned economic output per unit of additional emission abatement under the Pareto optimal level, which is gained through improving the environmental technical efficiency of each province. SETPS would be proven effective in the past if it could reduce APAC in a real sense. Furthermore, SETPS would be effective in the future if it could reduce MPAC, and thus, the environmental technology efficiency of each province could achieve the Pareto optimal level.

In order to examine whether SETPS is effective in China, we apply the kernel-based propensity score difference-in-difference method to analyze the effects of SETPS on APAC and MPAC. The empirical evidence indicates that SETPS had failed to reduce PAC if the pilot period as a whole sample were taken into account. SETPS increased APAC by 1,310 RMB per ton on average from 2002 to 2011 and reduced MPAC by 72,400 RMB per ton on average, which was not significant. Nevertheless, the conclusion would be soundly different if we separately investigated the effects of SETPS each year of the pilot period. SETPS began to show positive effects on PAC since 2009 and significantly reduced both APAC and MPAC, especially in 2009 and 2011. Therefore, the effects of SETPS on reducing PAC are expected to be stable if the emissions permits trading market could be improved reasonably in the future.

The paper is unfolded as follows: Section 2 provides a literature review; Section 3 develops several theoretical models to measure MPAC and to evaluate the effects of SETPS; Section 4 introduces how the data were used in the research; Section 5 shows the empirical evidence; Section 6 serves as the conclusion of this research; the last section discusses the limitations of the paper and provides an outlook for further research on this subject.

2. Literature Review

Economists generally believe that the emissions permit trading scheme is a more effective measure than environmental taxes. Coase (1960) suggested that emission permits allocated through a market mechanism are the most efficient mechanism to solve pollution problems [1]. Crocker [2] (1966), Dales [3] (1968) and other researchers further pointed out that the emissions permit trading scheme is effective at dealing with external environmental resources. Montgomery [4] (1972) proved that market-oriented emissions trading schemes are superior to traditional environmental governance measures. Compared with traditional environmental governance measures, the emissions trading policy has an advantage in reducing PAC. Tietenberg [5] (1985) demonstrated it and argued that the emissions trading scheme reduces PAC by allowing these firms with high abatement costs to purchase emissions permits until the emissions trading market reaches equilibrium. This indicates that each firm's marginal abatement costs are equal and that the social abatement costs will be reduced entirely through this process. Some scholars also found relevant evidence in empirical studies. Grubb [6] (2003) proposed that Annex I countries in the Kyoto Protocol can reduce emissions costs largely through the carbon emissions trading market. In addition, Rose *et al.* [7] (2006) examined the U.S. data and concluded that the more participants in the carbon emissions trading markets there are, the more cost-saving effects there will be.

China is a large country with huge emissions. Therefore, an increasing number of researchers have engaged themselves in studying the effects and rationality of China's emissions trading. Among them are Li and Shen [8] (2008), Wang and Tu [9] (2009), He and Xiao [10] (2010), Zheng [11] (2010), Tan and Chen [12] (2012), Yan and Guo [13] (2012), *etc.* They demonstrated two unique opinions. One is An and Tang [14] (2012), who diverted the analysis on quota-based trading market in most literatures to the analysis on the project-based trading market [14]. The other one is Fan [15,16] (2012), who mainly focused on the consumption aspect of the emissions trading market, adhering to Ferng's [17] (2003) idea that it is consumers, not producers, who should be blamed for driving up pollution in manufacturing sectors.

Cui *et al.* [18] (2013) proposed a provincial emissions trading model and concluded that in the effort to achieve the emission reduction targets of every province, a unified national carbon emissions trading market can save 23.44% in abatement costs, while a carbon emissions trading pilot market, which involves only six pilots, can save 4.42% when both are compared with the scenario of no carbon emissions trading. From a regional perspective, the cost-saving effects are much more significant in eastern and western China.

Nevertheless, the existing literature aiming at evaluating SETPS focuses primarily on the environmental impacts, such as emissions mitigation (e.g., total emissions reduction and/or emissions intensity mitigation), and rarely considers environmental and economic factors. Therefore, they are not in compliance with the core ideology of sustainable development. This paper argues that PAC is one of the best evaluation indexes when examining the effectiveness of emissions trading schemes. Cui *et al.* [18] (2013) applied this evaluation method. However, their research was based on simulation instead of the data from the emissions trading pilots in practice [18]. As a result, an evaluation approach with a "natural experiment" character was initiated in six pilot provinces in 2002, with Liuzhou and China Huaneng Group as an exception. This paper adopts thekernel-based propensity score difference-in-difference method to evaluate whether SETPS can reduce PAC or not. Differing from the other research up to now, this paper defines PAC in a much more comprehensive way by admitting that APAC reflects historical costs, while MPAC reflects future costs. In this case, we can evaluate the effects of SETPS on PAC in the past and future.

3. The Theoretical Underpinnings

3.1. How to Measure PAC

Following Li *et al.* [19] (2010), who divided the total environmental costs of industrial production into paid environmental costs and unpaid environmental costs [19], the paper divides SO_2 abatement costs into the following two categories. One is paid abatement costs, which refers to the abatement expenditure that industrial enterprises pay for desulfurization and other environmental treatments of SO_2 generated in the process of production. The other is unpaid abatement costs, which are the additional abatement costs or opportunity costs generated by reducing SO_2 emissions to the required levels by current environmental regulations. Therefore, this paper defines unpaid abatement costs to a small extent. This is slightly different from Li *et al.* [19] (2010), who define unpaid abatement costs as whole governance expenses needed under the current governance and technology level. These abatement costs are determined by the desulfurization rate and technology. Because the desulfurization rate is determined by the intensity of environmental regulations, the implementation of an environmental policy will indirectly affect PAC by changing the desulfurization rate. However, the economic development level and the size of the population are different across provinces in China. A difference within a certain spectrum in SO_2 emissions across provinces is considered reasonable. Therefore, it is reasonable to use unit or marginal costs rather than total costs when making a comparative analysis across provinces or cities in cross-sectional dimensions. Based on the above economic logic, this paper extends two categories of SO_2 abatement costs to average or marginal concepts, namely APAC and MPAC, in order to test the effectiveness of environmental policies. APAC is the paid abatement costs that take into account the investment in the treatment of industrial pollution in terms of per unit desulfurization. MPAC is the unpaid abatement costs, which are measured by network DEA in this paper. The following paragraph will focus on the measurement of MPAC.

Boyd *et al.* [20] (2002) and Chen [21] (2011) employed the directional distance function (DDF) to construct the formulas of MPAC by comparing command-and-control regulations with standard energy saving and emissions reduction regulations in terms of potential outputs and potential emissions However, according to Färe *et al.* [22] (2011) and Tu and Shen [23] (2013), this may cause a serious deviation, because the traditional measuring method of environmental technology efficiency underestimates environment governance efficiency. Therefore, there must be bias in the potential output and the potential emissions measured with the traditional method. In addition, an accurate MPAC could not be calculated. In accordance with the calculation methodology of Boyd *et al.* [20] (2002) and Chen [21] (2011), this paper builds a formula for MPAC by using the environmental directional distance function, which is based on network DEA proposed by Färe *et al.* [22] (2011) and Tu and Shen [23] (2013).

In accordance with the study of Färe *et al.* [22] (2011) and Tu and Shen [23] (2013), this paper divides the production process into two main phases: production and abatement, which are denoted as P_1 and P_2, respectively. When inserting input x_1 into the production process, we can get output y and pollution b_1. While, when inserting input x_2 into the abatement process, we can reduce pollution b_1 to pollution b_2. We illustrate this setup in Figure 1.

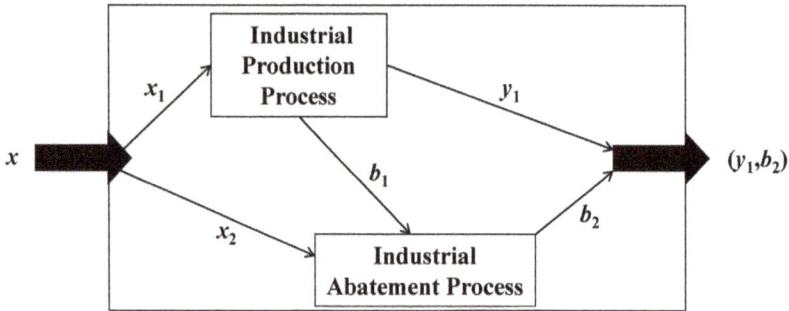

Figure 1. Industrial environmental technology based on network DEA.

Define the environmental technology based on network DEA as:

$$P(x) = \{(y, b_2) : (y, b_1) \in P_1(x_1), b_2 \in P_2(x_2, b_1)\} \tag{1}$$

Thus, the directional environmental distance function based on network DEA can be expressed as:

$$\overrightarrow{ND}_o^t(y^t, x_1^t, x_2^t, b_2^t; g_y^t, -g_b^t) = \sup[\beta : (y^t + \beta g_y^t, b_2^t - \beta g_b^t) \in P^t(x^t)] \tag{2}$$

When implementing command-and-control regulations, we can choose directional vector $g^t = (y_1^t, 0)$, so that the directional environmental distance function based on network DEA can be calculated by solving the following mathematical programming if producer $k'(y_{1,k'}^t, x_{1,k'}^t, x_{2,k'}^t, b_{2,k'}^t)$ takes reference technology $P^t(x^t)$ into consideration:

$$\overrightarrow{ND_o^t}(y_{1,k'}^t, x_{1,k'}^t, x_{2,k'}^t, b_{2,k'}^t; y_{1,k'}^t, 0) = \max\beta_c \qquad s.t.$$

$$industrial \quad production \quad processs:$$

$$\sum_{k=1}^{K} z_{k_1} y_{1,k,m_1}^t \ge (1+\beta_c) y_{1,k',m_1}^t, m_1 = 1, \cdots, M_1,$$

$$\sum_{k=1}^{K} z_{k_1} b_{1,k,j_1}^t = b_{1,k',j_1}^t, j_1 = 1, \cdots, J_1,$$

$$\sum_{k=1}^{K} z_{k_1} x_{1,k,n_1}^t \le x_{1,k',n_1}^t, n_1 = 1, \cdots, N_1,$$

$$z_{k_1} \ge 0, k_1 = 1, \cdots K \qquad (3)$$

$$industrial \quad abatement \quad process:$$

$$\sum_{k=1}^{K} z_{k_2} b_{2,k,j_2}^t = b_{2,k',j_2}^t, j_2 = 1, \cdots, J_2,$$

$$\sum_{k=1}^{K} z_{k_2} b_{1,k,j_1}^t \le b_{1,k',j_1}^t, j_1 = 1, \cdots, J_1$$

$$\sum_{k=1}^{K} z_{k_2} x_{2,k,n_1}^t \le x_{2,k',n_2}^t, n_2 = 1, \cdots, N_2,$$

$$z_{k_2} \ge 0, k_2 = 1, \cdots K$$

Now, we can get the potential output y_c:

$$y_c = (1+\beta_c)y \qquad (4)$$

When enforcing standard energy saving and emissions reduction regulations, we can choose directional vector $g^t = (y_1^t, -b_2^t)$, so that the directional environment distance function based on network DEA can be calculated by solving the following mathematical programming if producer $k'(y_{1,k'}^t, x_{1,k'}^t, x_{2,k'}^t, b_{2,k'}^t)$ takes reference technology $P^t(x^t)$ into consideration:

$$\overrightarrow{ND_o^t}(y_{1,k'}^t, x_{1,k'}^t, x_{2,k'}^t, b_{2,k'}^t; y_{1,k'}^t, -b_{2,k'}^t) = \max\beta_r \qquad s.t.$$

$$industrial \quad production \quad processs:$$

$$\sum_{k=1}^{K} z_{k_1} y_{1,k,m_1}^t \ge (1+\beta_r) y_{1,k',m_1}^t, m_1 = 1, \cdots, M_1,$$

$$\sum_{k=1}^{K} z_{k_1} b_{1,k,j_1}^t = b_{1,k',j_1}^t, j_1 = 1, \cdots, J_1,$$

$$\sum_{k=1}^{K} z_{k_1} x_{1,k,n_1}^t \le x_{1,k',n_1}^t, n_1 = 1, \cdots, N_1,$$

$$z_{k_1} \ge 0, k_1 = 1, \cdots K \qquad (5)$$

$$industrial \quad abatement \quad process:$$

$$\sum_{k=1}^{K} z_{k_2} b_{2,k,j_2}^t = (1-\beta_r) b_{2,k',j_2}^t, j_2 = 1, \cdots, J_2,$$

$$\sum_{k=1}^{K} z_{k_2} b_{1,k,j_1}^t \le b_{1,k',j_1}^t, j_1 = 1, \cdots, J_1$$

$$\sum_{k=1}^{K} z_{k_2} x_{2,k,n_1}^t \le x_{2,k',n_2}^t, n_2 = 1, \cdots, N_2,$$

$$z_{k_2} \ge 0, k_2 = 1, \cdots K$$

Now, we can get the potential output y_r and the potential pollution b_r:

$$y_r = (1+\beta_r)y \qquad (6)$$

$$b_r = (1-\beta_r)b_2 \qquad (7)$$

The potential output and the potential pollution under different environmental policies are indicated in Figure 2. Point A represents the producer's initial output and emissions. Producers can reach the frontier Point B by improving their technical efficiency under no environmental regulations. Producers can reach the frontier Point C by improving their technical efficiency and expanding production under command-and-control regulations with a given emissions level. Producers can reach the frontier Point D by improving their technical efficiency in the case of production expansion and emissions reduction under the standard energy saving and emissions reduction regulations in place. Comparing Point C with D, it is shown that producers may lose the potential output $(y_c - y_r)$ for reducing the emissions $(b - b_r)$ with standard energy saving and emissions reduction regulations rather than the command-and-control regulations in place. Therefore, in accordance with the methodology of Boyd *et al.* [20] (2002) and Chen [21] (2011), MPAC is calculated as follows:

$$MPAC = (y_c - y_r)/(b - b_r) = (\beta_c - \beta_r)y/(\beta_r b_2) \qquad (8)$$

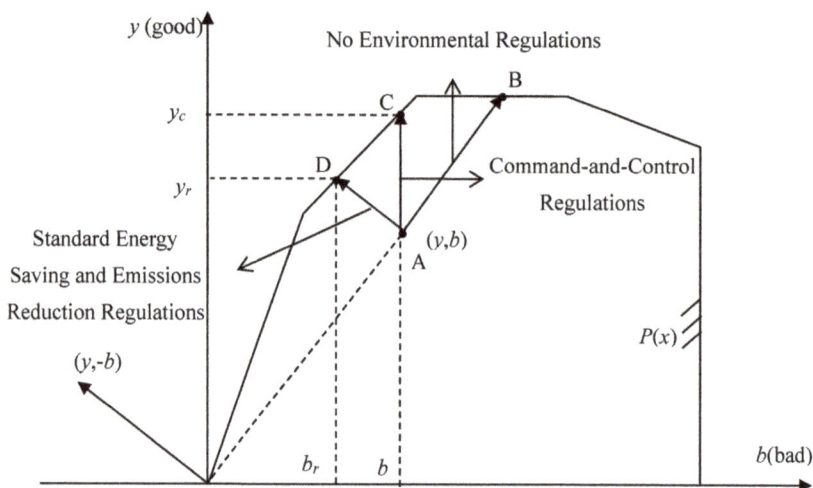

Figure 2. The potential output and potential emissions under different environmental schemes.

3.2. Kernel-Based Propensity Score Difference-in-Difference Method

In order to examine the effects of SETPS, we adopt the difference-in-difference method, which is normally used to assess the effectiveness of public policies. We regard SETPS as a policy experiment or natural experiment, the pilot provinces (*i.e.*, Tianjin, Shanxi, Shanghai, Jiangsu, Shandong, Henan) as the treated group or experimental group, non-pilot provinces as the control group, the non-pilot period from 1998 to 2001 as the before treatment period and the pilot period from 2002 to 2011 as the after treatment period. As seen from the model, Y represents APAC and MPAC, and dummy variables *period* and *treated* denote period and province, respectively, whether SETPS is implemented or not. Therefore, we can formulate the regression model as follows:

$$Y_{it} = \beta_0 + \beta_1 period_t + \beta_2 treated_i + \beta_3 period_t \cdot treated_i + \mu_{it} \qquad (9)$$

In Model (9), β_3 examines the effects of SETPS on PAC (including APAC and MPAC) in the past and future. However, the pilot provinces are not randomly chosen, but determined by Chinese governments. It does not meet the requirements of random sampling of the treatment group (or experimental group) in the policy experiment (or natural experiment). Pilot provinces probably obtain this pilot opportunity because of some factors. Therefore, it is difficult to ensure that the PAC changes in both pilot provinces and non-pilot provinces from the non-pilot period to pilot period are due to the same reasons. On the contrary, it is possible that some specific factors cause different changes in PAC between the pilot provinces and non-pilot provinces. In this case, this will lead to a serious estimation bias if using the difference-in-difference method to directly estimate Model (9). The kernel-based propensity score difference-in-difference method is employed to solve this estimation problem in this paper. This estimation method consists of three steps. Firstly, the probit model (or logit model) is used to estimate the propensity score of the samples. Then, the principle of similar propensity score is obeyed to match one or more control groups with treatment groups (or experimental groups). Through this process, we can eliminate the self-selection problem of the treated group (or experimental group) to achieve random selection. Finally, with the matching results, the propensity score is used to formulate a weighting function based on the kernel density function. After that, we can calculate the effect of policy experiments (or natural experiments), namely β_3 estimated in Model (9).

The key issue to apply the kernel-based propensity score difference-in-difference method is to make a reasonable choice on the explanatory variables that determine the pilot provinces in SETPS. This paper considers the fact that Chinese governments may weigh over these six determinants (*i.e.*, emissions intensity, energy intensity, GDP per capita, the proportion of industry sector in GDP, the proportion of urban population and the proportion of state-owned and state-holding industrial enterprises) to make the choice. These six determinants can be classified into three categories as follows:

- Environmental and energy factors: SO_2 emissions intensity (*SI*) and energy intensity (*EIP*). In general, the intensity of environmental regulations is determined by the basic conditions of the environment and energy of each province. Emission intensity refers to the SO_2 emissions per unit of energy consumption, which reflects the energy consumption structure. A low emission intensity indicates a large proportion of clean energy (e.g., hydropower, nuclear power and solar energy) or low-carbon energy in the total energy consumption. Energy intensity refers to the energy consumption per unit of the industrial gross output and reflects in the level of energy efficiency or energy-saving technology. A low energy intensity indicates a high energy efficiency or energy-saving technology.

- Macro-economic factors: GDP per capita (*GDPP*), the proportion of the industrial sector in GDP (industrialization) and the proportion of urban population (urbanization). These indicators reflect the economic development level, the industrialization level and the urbanization level, respectively. Generally speaking, the relatively developed regions are more inclined to implement SETPS.

- Micro-enterprise factor: the proportion of state-owned and state-holding industrial enterprises (state_rate). In terms of the cost-benefit function, the national protection level and the environmental constraints vary across state-owned enterprises and private enterprises (Yan and Guo, 2012) [13]; the efficacy of environmental policies will be significantly different across enterprises of different ownership. Meanwhile, a lower proportion of state-owned and state-holding industrial enterprises implies a higher degree of marketization and is also conducive to the implementation of market-oriented policies. Thus, the proportion of state-owned and state-holding industrial enterprises reflects the ownership structure, as well as the degree of marketization.

In summary, the probit model can be formulated as follows:

$$P(treated = 1|x) = \Phi(\alpha_1 SI_i + \alpha_2 EIP_i + \alpha_3 GDPP_i + \alpha_4 industrialization_i + \alpha_5 urbanization_i + \alpha_6 state\_rate_i + v_i) \tag{10}$$

4. Data

This study employs balanced panel data covering 29 provinces in China over the period from 1998 to 2011. The industrial enterprises of above designated size are examined as representative of China's industrial sector in the empirical analysis. The Industrial enterprises of the above designated size are all state-owned enterprises and non-state owned enterprises with annual revenue from principal business over 5 million RMB from 1998 to 2006, and they are industrial enterprises with annual revenue from principal business over 5 million RMB from 2007 to 2010 and are industrial enterprises with annual revenue from principal business over 20 million RMB after 2011. Considering that Qinghai's volume of SO_2 removed in the period of 2001–2006 was very small (close to 0 if we use units of tons) and that Tibet had lots of missing data, which would affect the relevant calculations in this paper, these two provinces are therefore excluded here. All kinds of data in this paper are obtained mainly from "China Statistical Yearbook from 1999 to 2012" [24], "China Energy Statistical Yearbook from 1997 to 2012 [25]", "China Compendium of Statistics from 1949 to 2008" [26], "China Statistical Yearbook on Environment 2012" [27] and "China Industry Economy Statistical Yearbook from 2001 to 2012" [28].

The variables in this study are constructed in accordance with Tu and Shen [23] (2013). As for the industrial production process, we choose annual average of employees in the industrial sector (l), net value of the fixed assets in the industrial sector (k) and industrial end-use energy consumption (e) as input variables, while we use industrial gross output (y) as the output variable and the volume of SO_2 emissions by industrial production (s_1) as the emission variable. With regard to the industrial abatement process, we choose the volume of SO_2 emissions by industry production (s_1) and the number of facilities for the treatment of industrial waste gas (GMS) as input variables, while we use the volume of terminal SO_2 emissions by industry (s_2) as the output variable. Paid abatement costs are measured by the investment in the treatment of industrial pollution. Each province's net value of the fixed assets in the industrial sector and investment in the treatment of industrial pollution are converted into the comparable value, with 1998 as the base year, by using the price index of investment in fixed assets. The industrial gross output and the output of state-owned and state-holding industrial enterprises of each province are also converted into the comparable value, with 1998 as the base year, by using the producer price index for industrial products. Four indicators of industrial enterprises of the above designated size, which are volume of terminal SO_2 emissions, volume of SO_2 removed, end-use energy consumption and number of facilities for treatment of wastes gas, have not been released. Considering that the industrial enterprises of the above designated size account for a large proportion of the industrial sector, we use industrial-level data instead.

The economic data in this study are collected mainly from "China Statistical Yearbook" [24] and partly from "China Compendium of Statistics from 1949 to 2008" [26] and "China Industry Economy Statistical Yearbook from 2001 to 2012" [28]. Meanwhile, missing data are filled by using the linear interpolation method. As for the specific process of industrial end-use energy consumption (please see Tu and Shen [29] (2013)), this paper uses the sum of 20 kinds of end-use energy consumption. In addition, the data on GDP per capita, the proportion of the industrial sector in GDP and the proportion of urban population are sourced from Tu and Shen [29] (2013).

Table 1 gives a brief statistical description of the final sample in terms of output, input and price variables.

Table 1. Statistical description of outputs, inputs and prices variables.

Variable	Observations	Mean	SD	Min	Max
Investment in the Treatment of Industrial Pollution (100 million RMB)	406	4.44	4.70	0.01	33.71
Industrial Gross Output (100 million RMB)	406	9644.52	14,826.62	183.20	93,960.53
Producer Price Indices for Industrial Products (1998 = 1)	406	1.11	0.25	0.85	2.56
Net Value of the Fixed Assets in Industrial Sector (100 million RMB)	406	3032.35	2833.34	181.37	16,896.21
Price Indices for Investment in Fixed Assets (1998 = 1)	406	1.15	0.15	0.96	1.56
Annual Average of Employees in Industrial Sector (10,000 persons)	406	244.20	255.58	11.60	1,568.00
Industrial End-use Energy Consumption (10,000 tons of standard coal equivalent (SCE)	406	3335.09	2773.92	67.46	16,285.17
Number of Facilities for Treatment of Industrial Wastes Gas (set)	406	5348.20	3449.14	292.00	21,702.00
Volume of SO_2 Emissions by Industry Production (10,000 tons)	406	115.12	84.93	2.11	592.88
Volume of Terminal SO_2 Emissions by Industry (10,000 tons)	406	62.54	38.72	1.93	176.01
Emissions Intensity (ton/ton of SCE)	406	0.02	0.01	0.00	0.08
Energy Intensity (ton of SCE/10,000 RMB)	406	0.76	0.68	0.06	8.47
GDP per Capita (10,000 RMB/person)	406	1.43	1.07	0.22	6.13
The Proportion of Industry Sector (%)	406	42.75	9.34	12.68	63.29
The Proportion of Urban Population (%)	406	45.02	16.21	19.93	89.30
The Proportion of State-owned and State-holding Industrial Enterprises (%)	406	50.16	20.70	10.73	89.88

5. Main Empirical Results

5.1. APAC and MPAC

Since the paid abatement costs are measured in terms of the investment in the treatment of industrial pollution, APAC is calculated in terms of the paid abatement costs per unit of desulfurization. Based on the network DEA to measure the MPAC proposed above, we make an estimation on the MPAC for each province in China from 1998 to 2011. By contrast, we also use the traditional method, namely DDF, to measure MAC, and we find that there is a significant difference between the two results. Please see the Appendix, Table A1, for details. As shown in Table 2, we calculate the national APAC and MPAC from 1998 to 2011 by taking the simple arithmetic average of the 29 provinces.

Table 2. The average pollution abatement costs (APAC) and the marginal pollution abatement costs (MPAC) in China.

Year	APAC (10,000 RMB/ton)			MPAC (10,000 RMB/ton)		
	Non-pilot provinces	Pilot provinces	All provinces	Non-pilot provinces	Pilot provinces	All provinces
1998	0.27	0.35	0.28	0.32	0.16	0.29
1999	0.54	0.27	0.49	0.28	0.24	0.27
2000	0.46	0.32	0.43	0.77	0.46	0.71
2001	0.29	0.24	0.28	0.91	0.65	0.86
Subtotal	*0.39*	*0.29*	*0.37*	*0.57*	*0.38*	*0.53*
2002	0.29	0.23	0.28	1.40	1.03	1.33
2003	0.30	0.35	0.31	2.94	1.11	2.56
2004	0.28	0.36	0.30	3.83	1.47	3.35
2005	0.29	0.42	0.32	2.10	2.26	2.13
2006	0.23	0.21	0.23	4.06	4.53	4.16
2007	0.15	0.43	0.21	5.36	4.10	5.10
2008	0.15	0.19	0.16	6.13	6.28	6.16
2009	0.21	0.10	0.19	7.40	7.18	7.35
2010	0.06	0.05	0.06	8.89	2.81	7.63
2011	0.06	0.07	0.06	10.44	3.97	9.10
Subtotal	*0.20*	*0.24*	*0.21*	*5.25*	*3.47*	*4.89*
Total	*0.26*	*0.26*	*0.26*	*3.92*	*2.59*	*3.64*

As we can see from Table 2, China's APAC remained relatively stable with fluctuations around the mean value of 0.26 (10,000 RMB/ton) during 1998 to 2009, but sharply declined to 0.06 (10,000 RMB/ton) in 2010 and 2011. The mean value of non-pilot provinces and that of the pilot provinces was alternately greater than the other. During the pilot period starting from 2002, the APAC of the pilot provinces was larger than that of non-pilot provinces in the majority of the years. The difference of APAC between the pilot and non-pilot province even reached 0.28 (10,000 RMB/ton) in 2007. However, the APAC in the pilot provinces was less than or equal to non-pilot provinces since 2009.

By contrast, China's MPAC kept rising in general from 0.26 (10,000 RMB/ton) in 1998 to 9.10 (10,000 RMB/ton) in 2011 and reached 3.64 (10,000 RMB/ton) on average during 1998 to 2011. Comparing the mean value of MPAC between non-pilot provinces and pilot provinces, the MPAC of the pilot provinces was less than that of non-pilot provinces during the non-pilot period, but alternately greater than the other during the pilot period. Nevertheless, the MPAC in the pilot provinces has been lower than non-pilot provinces since 2009.

Additionally, as is shown in Table 3, we calculate the APAC and MPAC of China's 29 provinces by taking the simple arithmetic annual average of each province.

Table 3. APAC and MPAC of China's 29 provinces.

Province/City	APAC (10,000 RMB/ton)	MPAC (10,000 RMB/ton)	Province/City	APAC (10,000 RMB/ton)	MPAC (10,000 RMB/ton)
Beijing	2.03	0.00	Chongqing	0.04	0.00
Hebei	0.14	0.00	Sichuan	0.15	0.00
Inner Mongolia	0.11	0.34	Guizhou	0.09	0.06
Liaoning	0.07	0.00	Yunnan	0.05	0.00
Jilin	0.29	0.50	Shaanxi	0.17	0.22
Heilongjiang	0.66	79.57	Gansu	0.04	0.00
Zhejiang	0.16	0.00	Ningxia	0.23	0.00
Anhui	0.03	0.00	Xinjiang	0.50	8.71
Fujian	0.50	0.00	**Tianjin**	**0.44**	**0.00**
Jiangxi	0.02	0.00	**Shanxi**	**0.20**	**15.54**
Hubei	0.08	0.67	**Shanghai**	**0.44**	**0.00**
Hunan	0.07	0.00	**Jiangsu**	**0.16**	**0.00**
Guangdong	0.26	0.00	**Shandong**	**0.16**	**0.00**
Guangxi	0.05	0.00	**Henan**	**0.14**	**0.00**
Hainan	0.19	0.00			
Eastern	*0.38*	*0.00*	*Western*	*0.16*	*1.12*
Central	*0.18*	*10.74*	*Nationwide*	*0.26*	*3.64*

Note: Pilot provinces in bold type. *"Eastern"*, *"Central"* and *"Western"* represent eastern areas, central areas and western areas in China, respectively. Eastern areas include twelve provinces (*i.e.*, Beijing, Tianjin, Hebei, Liaoning, Shanghai, Jiangsu, Zhejiang, Fujian, Shandong, Guangdong, Guangxi and Hainan); central areas include nine provinces (*i.e.*, Shanxi, Inner Mongolia, Jilin, Heilongjiang, Anhui, Jiangxi, Henan, Hubei and Hunan); and western areas include eight provinces (*i.e.*, Chongqing, Sichuan, Guizhou, Yunnan, Shaanxi, Gansu, Ningxia and Xinjiang).

As Table 3 shows, Jiangxi exhibits the lowest APAC among all of the 29 provinces with only 0.02 (10,000 RMB/ton), while Qinghai has the highest APAC, and Beijing follows. In terms of regional APAC, eastern areas rank the first, central areas follow and western areas take the last seat.

The "three stages" concept proposed by Tu [30] (2009) is employed to evaluate the change of MPAC for each province during the 1998 to 2011. At the first stage (called the steep stage), MPAC is relatively higher, which means that a huge reduction in output only results in a small reduction in emissions. Therefore, provinces at this stage should put economic development in the first place. At the second stage (called the flat stage), MPAC tends to decline, which means that a slight reduction or even no change in output will lead to a huge reduction in emissions. Provinces at this stage should enhance environmental governance, because a substantial reduction in emissions can be achieved at a low price. Otherwise, they might endure high environmental costs for output growth. At the third stage (called the plateau stage), MPAC is negative, which means that the output will increase instead of decrease, even though the emissions are largely reduced. This is similar to the two-factor model of labor and capital, which indicates that the marginal output declines or even becomes negative when one of two factors grows to a certain level. It is the best opportunity for the provinces at this stage to carry out industrial structure adjustment.

As Table 3 exhibits, 21 of the 29 provinces' MPAC (include Beijing's, Tianjin's, and so on) is zero, which implies that standard energy saving and emissions reduction regulations, compared to command-and-control regulations, are able to meet emission reduction targets without sacrificing economic growth. This conclusion seems inconsistent with common sense, owing to the fact that the calculation of MPAC in this paper is based on network DEA, which takes full account of environmental governance efficiency. To some extent, this proves that it is an effective way to reduce MPAC by improving environmental governance efficiency. These provinces' MPAC, together with Guizhou's, Shaanxi's, Inner Mongolia's, Jilin's and Hubei's, are approximately zero. They are at the flat stage defined by Tu [30] (2009). They should strengthen environmental governance, but pay only a small price for a substantial emissions reduction. Helongjiang exhibits the highest MPAC of 79.57 (10,000 RMB/ton). Shanxi and Xinjiang also exhibit a higher MPAC. These three provinces are at the steep stage and should focus on economic development. In terms of the regional MPAC, central areas rank the first and eastern areas lie at the bottom. In this case, eastern areas are at the flat stage and should enhance environmental governance. Central and western areas are at the steep stage and should encourage economic development. These results are slightly different from Tu [30] (2009), who demonstrated that central areas exhibit the highest MPAC, but western areas exhibit the lowest. This difference is probably due to different calculation ideology. Tu [30] (2009) constructed the calculation formula with the marginal effect of pollution's inter-period changes on output, while this paper calculates it by comparing different environmental policies under the current reference technology.

5.2. The Effect of SETPS on PAC

As for the dataset of China's 29 provinces over the 1998–2011 period, the period of 1998–2001 is regarded as a non-pilot period and the period of 2002–2011 as the pilot period. Tianjin, Shanxi, Shanghai, Jiangsu, Shandong and Henan are the six pilot provinces, while the other 23 provinces are non-pilot provinces. Based on the kernel-based propensity score difference-in-difference method, this paper estimates Model (9). At first, this paper calculates the mean of the key variables in pilot and non-pilot provinces over the two periods and then makes a comparison between these two groups of provinces, as shown in Table 4.

Table 4. Comparison on the mean of key variables in pilot and non-pilot provinces (1998–2011).

Variables	Non-pilot period (1998–2001)				Pilot period (2002–2011)			
	Non-pilot provinces		Pilot provinces		Non-pilot provinces		Pilot provinces	
	Obs.	Mean	Obs.	Mean	Obs.	Mean	Obs.	Mean
APAC (10,000 RMB/ton)	92	0.39	24	0.29	230	0.20	60	0.24
MPAC (10,000 RMB/ton)	92	0.57	24	0.38	230	5.25	60	3.47
Emissions Intensity (ton/ton of SCE)	92	0.03	24	0.03	230	0.02	60	0.02
Energy Intensity (ton of SCE/10,000 RMB)	92	1.17	24	0.79	230	0.67	60	0.43
GDP per Capita (10,000 RMB/person)	92	0.67	24	1.22	230	1.45	60	2.61
The Proportion of Industry Sector (%)	92	36.45	24	45.90	230	42.46	60	52.27
The Proportion of Urban Population (%)	92	37.65	24	46.88	230	45.17	60	54.98
The Proportion of State-owned and State-holding Industrial Enterprises (%)	92	66.59	24	46.12	230	48.20	60	34.13

Note: Dependent variables in bold type. Obs.: Observation.

As Table 4 shows, the APAC of the pilot provinces is lower than that of non-pilot provinces in the non-pilot period, but higher than that of non-pilot provinces in the pilot period. This can be explained by the law of diminishing marginal utility. Specifically, when the intensity of environmental governance reaches a certain extent, its effect on emissions reduction tends to diminish. The intensity of environmental regulations in the pilot provinces is higher than that in non-pilot provinces. Therefore, the pilot provinces will incur higher costs in order to achieve the same amount of emissions reduction. The MPAC of the pilot provinces is lower than that of non-pilot provinces in both the non-pilot period and pilot period. This means that the pilot provinces, compared to non-pilot provinces, are in a better place to strengthen environmental governance. In other words, this is the reason, to certain extent, why these provinces are chosen to be the pilots of SO_2 emissions trading. Comparing the environmental and energy factors, no significant difference in the energy structure can be observed between the pilot provinces and non-pilot provinces in both the non-pilot period and pilot period. The energy intensity of the pilot provinces is lower than that of non-pilot provinces in both the non-pilot period and the pilot period. This implies that the level of energy efficiency or energy-saving technology is higher in the pilot provinces, compared to non-pilot provinces. With regard to the macro-economic factors, the pilot provinces outperform non-pilot provinces in both the non-pilot period and pilot period. This result is also in line with the previous judgment that relatively developed regions are more inclined to impose SETPS. As far as the micro-enterprise factors are concerned, the proportion of state-owned and state-holding industrial enterprises in the pilot provinces is smaller than that in non-pilot provinces in both the non-pilot period and pilot period. This is also in line with another previous judgment that a higher marketization level is conducive to the implementation of a market-oriented policy.

Based on Model (10), this paper makes an estimate of propensity score based on the probit model. With regard to the scarcity of non-pilot samples, poor results for propensity scores and matching may occur if merely using one year of data of the 29 provinces in 2001. As is shown in Table 5, this paper regards the dataset of four non-pilot years from 1998 to 2001 as a whole sample to estimate the probit model of the propensity score in order to prevent the sample estimating problem. The environmental and energy factors have a significant positive effect on determining whether a province is qualified as the pilot province for SETPS. It is shown that a province, which has a problematic heavy energy structure and a lower level of energy efficiency (or energy-saving technology), is more likely to be a part of SETPS with other conditions remaining constant. However, the above result is different from the initial understanding of the environmental and energy factors, due to the given simple arithmetic average of provinces when comparing the pilot provinces with non-pilot provinces in Table 4. Table 4 shows that the energy intensity is lower in the majority of the pilot provinces, with Shanxi as an exception, whose energy intensity is 2.20 (ton of SCE/10,000 RMB) on average over the period of 1998 to 2001 and is much higher than the nationwide mean of 1.09 (ton of SCE/10,000 RMB). In addition to the variable of the proportion of urban population, other macro-economic factors show a significant positive effect, as well. In the period from 1998 to 2001, the GDP per capita of the pilot provinces is higher than the nationwide mean of 0.79 (10,000 RMB/person), with Shanxi and Henan as an exception. The proportion of the industrial sector of the six pilot provinces is larger than the nationwide mean of 38.40 (%), among which Tianjin ranks the first with 50.48 (%). The proportions of urban population of Shanxi, Jiangsu, Shandong and Henan are much smaller than the nationwide mean of 39.56 (%), among which Henan only exceeds Hainan with 22.60 (%) over 22.26 (%). As shown in Table 5, the estimated sign of the proportion of urban population is negative, which deviates from the preliminary results in Table 4. This is determined by the higher proportion of urban population in some pilot provinces, such as Tianjin and Shanghai, whose proportion is 76.80 (%) and 84.24 (%), respectively. The micro-enterprise factor of the proportion of state-owned and state-holding industrial enterprises is in line with the expectation. It has a negative, but not significant, impact. In the period from 1998 to 2001, the proportion of state-owned and state-holding industrial enterprises of the pilot provinces was smaller than the nationwide mean of 63.36 (%), with Shanxi as an exception. Among them, Jiangsu has 30.10 (%), which is only larger than Zhejiang's 21.01 (%) and Guangdong's 25.96 (%). By the way, Guangdong was approved to be a carbon emissions trading pilot in 2011.

Table 5. Estimated results of the probit model. *SI*, SO_2 emissions intensity; *EIP*, energy intensity.

Environmental and energy factors		Macro-economic factors			Micro-enterprise factor	
SI	*EIP*	*GDPP*	*industrialization*	*urbanization*	*state_rate*	*Constant*
28.734	0.621	2.305	0.187	−0.047	−0.002	−10.124
17.177 *	0.324 *	0.913 **	0.066 ***	0.022 **	0.014	3.502 ***
Observations	116	*log likelihood*		−33.076	*pseudo-R-squared*	0.441

Note: Standard errors in parentheses; *** $p < 0.01$; ** $p < 0.05$; * $p < 0.1$.

Upon the estimations of the probit model, we can get propensity scores and then match one or more non-pilot provinces with the pilot provinces according to the principle of similar propensity score. The matching results show that 83.33% of the pilot provinces and 34.78% of non-pilot provinces are matched in the non-pilot period (1998–2001), while 91.67% of the pilot provinces and 44.78% of non-pilot provinces are matched in the pilot period (2002–2011). As seen from Figure 3, this paper chooses the result in 2001 as an example to illustrate the geographic distribution of matching pilot provinces and non-pilot provinces, due to there being little change in matching results over time. In the pilot provinces, Tianjin, Shanxi, Shandong and Henan are matching provinces, but Shanghai and Jiangsu are exceptions. As to the geographic distribution of matching non-pilot provinces, they lie mainly nearby the matching pilot provinces or surround coastal areas.

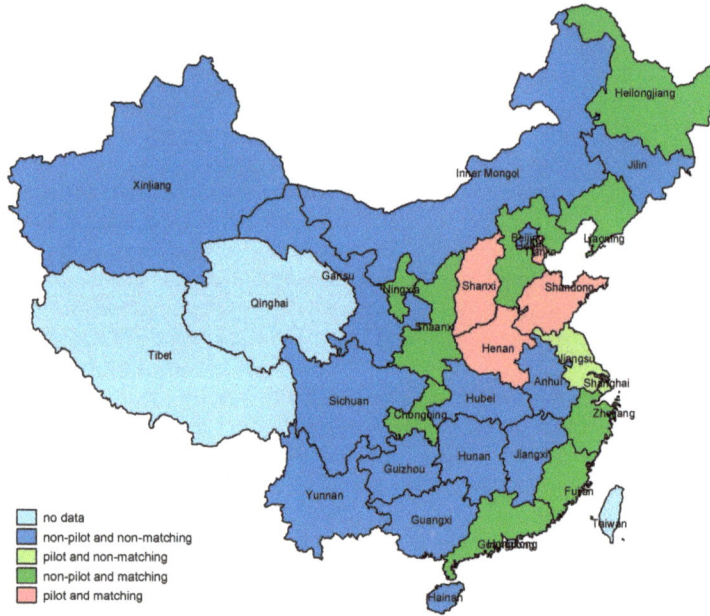

Figure 3. Geographic distribution of matching pilot provinces and non-pilot provinces in 2001.

As is shown in Table 6, we perform a *t*-test, which is called the balancing test in this case, on the matching variables between the pilot provinces and non-pilot provinces. It is not difficult to find that each absolute value of difference among matching variables is less than 20, and all of the results of the *t*-test do not reject the null hypothesis that there is no significant difference among the matching variables between the pilot provinces and non-pilot provinces. In short, the matching results by using the kernel-based propensity score method are proven to be reliable in this paper.

Table 6. Matching balancing test.

Variables	Mean of non-pilot provinces	Mean of pilot provinces	Difference	*t*-value	Probability
APAC	0.288	0.284	−0.004	0.050	0.959
MPAC	0.935	0.484	−0.451	0.530	0.599
SI	0.027	0.027	0.000	0.100	0.920
EIP	0.943	0.887	−0.055	0.250	0.803
GDPP	0.936	0.983	0.047	0.380	0.703
industrialization	46.019	45.543	−0.476	0.440	0.664
urbanization	42.835	41.823	−1.012	0.210	0.835
state_rate	46.548	46.720	0.172	0.030	0.975

Based on the results of propensity score and matching in the probit model, as shown in Tables 7 and 8, we can formulate the weighting function by applying the kernel density function and then calculating the effects of SETPS on PAC. This paper regards the dataset of ten pilot years from 2002 to

2011 as a whole sample to obtain the estimates in Table 7, regardless of chronological order. In Table 8, this paper takes chronological order into account and examines the dynamic effects of SETPS on PAC.

Table 7. The effects of SETPS on PAC.

Variables	Non-pilot period (1998–2001)			Pilot period (2002–2011)			Difference-in-difference
	Non-pilot provinces	Pilot provinces	Difference	Non-pilot provinces	Pilot provinces	Difference	
APAC	0.288	0.284	−0.004	0.118	0.246	0.127	0.131
	(0.064)	(0.058)	(0.087)	(0.038)	(0.066)	(0.076)	(0.067) *
MPAC	0.935	0.484	−0.451	10.699	3.008	−7.691	−7.240
	(1.001)	(0.435)	(1.092)	(10.581)	(2.838)	(10.955)	(9.932)

Note: Clustered standard errors in parentheses; *** $p < 0.01$; ** $p < 0.05$; * $p < 0.1$.

As indicated in Table 7, SETPS has a significant positive effect on APAC, but a negative effect on MPAC, which is not significant. Compared with the mean value in the pilot provinces during the non-pilot period, the APAC in the pilot provinces increased by 45.17% on average, while the MPAC decreased by 2585.7% on average. This shows that SETPS failed to reduce PAC from the past and future perspective. However, this conclusion is based on the dataset of ten pilot years from 2002 to 2011 as a whole sample. Would it be quite different if we investigate the SETPS of each year during the pilot period?

Table 8. The dynamic effects of SETPS on PAC.

Year	APAC		MPAC	
	Quantity changes	Percentage changes	Quantity changes	Percentage changes
2002	0.077 (0.178)	26.55	−7.497 (6.371)	−2677.50
2003	0.161 (0.267)	55.52	−6.051 (6.709)	−2161.07
2004	0.098 (0.120)	33.79	3.769 (2.623)	1346.07
2005	0.096 (0.109)	33.10	7.589 (4.995)	2710.36
2006	0.002 (0.093)	0.69	0.058 (0.712)	20.71
2007	0.082 (0.091)	28.28	0.435 (1.113)	155.36
2008	−0.203 (0.191)	−70.00	−42.220 (48.084)	−15,078.57
2009	−0.486 (0.084) ***	−167.59	−143.008 (4.507) ***	−51,074.29
2010	−0.031 (0.083)	−10.69	−81.807 (50.890)	−29,216.79
2011	−0.159 (0.068) ***	−54.83	−106.000 (53.962) *	−37,857.14

Note: Clustered standard errors in parentheses; *** $p < 0.01$; ** $p < 0.05$; * $p < 0.1$. "Percentage changes" are compared with the mean value in pilot provinces during the non-pilot period.

As shown in Table 8, the effect of SETPS on APAC showed a general downward trend from 2002 to 2011. SETPS has had a negative effect on APAC since 2008, which reached a peak in 2009 with an APAC reduction of 0.486 (10,000 RMB/ton) and 167.59% in percentage changes. SETPS hardly had a positive effect on APAC before 2008. Such a trend indicates that SETPS has played a certain, but not very outstanding, role in reducing PAC. Meanwhile, the effect of SETPS on MPAC also followed a general downward trend from 2002 to 2011. In the years of 2002 and 2003, SETPS reduced MPAC by 7.497 (10,000 RMB/ton) and 6.051 (10,000 RMB/ton), respectively, up to 2677.50% and 2161.07% in percentage changes. SETPS has been making a positive effect on MPAC since 2004, which once increased by 7.589 (10,000 RMB/ton) and 2710.36% in percentage changes in 2005. After 2008, the effect of SETPS reversed to negative, which reached a bottom in 2009 with −143.008 (10,000 RMB/ton) and −51,074.29% in percentage changes. Such trends are consistent with the conclusion on the mean value comparison between non-pilot and pilot provinces, as shown in Table 2. The APAC and MPAC in the pilot provinces have been constantly lower than non-pilot provinces since 2009. In summary, the year 2009 is a cut-off point for which SETPS began to cause a reduction in PAC.

The previous analyses can lead to the conclusion that the effect of SETPS on MPAC is not significantly negative if we investigate the dataset of ten pilot years from 2002 to 2011 as a whole sample, but the effect is significantly negative in 2009 and 2011 if we investigate each year separately during the pilot period. Meanwhile, the effect of SETPS on APAC was not significantly positive initially, but turned out to be significantly negative in 2009 and 2011. In other words, SETPS began to play a certain role in reducing PAC since 2009. This is in line with the practical experience in other countries that the practical effects of environmental policies needs some time to appear.

6. Conclusions

This paper examines the effects of SETPS on PAC in China during 1998 to 2011. First, this paper calculates MPAC based on the estimated potential output and potential emissions by using network DEA under two different policy scenarios, *i.e.*, command-and-control regulations and standard energy saving and emissions reduction regulations. Then, we analyze the effects of SETPS on APAC and MPAC in the past and future by using the kernel-based propensity score difference-in-difference method. This paper reaches the following conclusions through empirical analysis:

First, SETPS started to show positive effects on reducing PAC since 2009. During 2001 to 2011, SETPS raised APAC by 1,310 RMB per ton on average and reduced MPAC by 72,400 RMB per ton on average, which was not significant. In other words, SETPS failed to reduce PAC as a whole. However, the conclusion would be markedly different if we investigated the effects of SETPS each year of the pilot period separately. SETPS began to show positive effects since 2009 and significantly reduced both APAC and MPAC, especially in 2009 and 2011. Therefore, SETPS began to play an important role in reducing PAC only since 2009.

Second, China, especially non-pilot provinces, should keep putting economic growth in first place because of high PAC. China's APAC has been fluctuating steadily around the mean value, meanwhile showing a downward trend in recent years. For example, there was a decrease from 0.19 (10,000 RMB/ton) in 2009 to 0.06 (10,000 RMB/ton) in 2010 and 2011. At the same time, China's MPAC showed an upward trend from 0.29 (10,000 RMB/ton) in 1998 to 9.10 (10,000 RMB/ton) in 2011. This indicates that China is at the stage that it should focus on economic development. Combining the findings on APAC's and MPAC's trends, PAC in China, especially in non-pilot provinces, is at the high level. Therefore, China should keep putting economic growth in first place.

Third, the eastern areas should enhance environmental governance, while the central and western areas should encourage economic development. Since these regions are at different stages of environmental governance, the eastern areas rank first in APAC, the central areas follow and western areas lag behind them. However, the conclusion on MPAC is converse. The eastern areas exhibit the lowest MPAC, which indicates that they are at the flat stage. Therefore, the eastern areas should enhance environmental governance; while the central and western areas should encourage economic development, because of their higher MPAC, which indicates that they are at the steep stage.

Based on the above findings, this paper argues that the following counter-measures should be carried out to adjust China's emissions trading scheme. First of all, China should identify the deficiency of the present emissions trading pilot policies and improve them with respect to their design, as well as their operation. Secondly, China still needs to give priority to economic growth from the perspective of overall economic and environmental development, due to the effects of decreasing APAC and increasing MPAC. Furthermore, China's PAC has a significant difference among regions. Accordingly, the coordination between economic growth and environment and resources in central and western areas needs to be improved through economic support policies and energy saving technology transfer policies.

7. Limitations and Avenues for Further Investigation

This paper examines the effects of SETPS on PAC by using the kernel-based propensity score difference-in-difference method. Owing to the difficulty in obtaining the official micro-level data in China, we used provincial-level dataset instead in this paper. However, this study paves the way for further research that will be able to obtain a much more reliable estimation with micro-level data. In order to reduce the possibility of unreliable estimation due to the limitation of data, this paper selects a more appropriate estimation method. On the one hand, this paper uses the kernel-based propensity score difference-in-difference method to solve the self-selection problem of the pilot provinces. On the other hand, this paper does a remedial job, such as using four non-pilot years' data from 1998 to 2001 as a whole sample to estimate the probit model of the propensity score in order to prevent the likely poor results of propensity scores and matching due to the small sample size. In addition, this paper directly uses the difference-in-difference method to estimate Model (9). The results are shown in Appendix Table 2 and demonstrate that the kernel-based propensity score difference-in-difference method is reliable in this paper, according to the results of the difference-in-difference method with the same estimated symbol. Nevertheless, the kernel-based propensity score difference-in-difference method is also proven to be a more appropriate estimation method in this paper, because all of the results of the difference-in-difference method are insignificant, due to the self-selection problem.

Acknowledgments: This work is supported by the New Century Talent Support Program funded by China's Ministry of Education (NCET-10-0409) and the Excellent Doctoral Dissertation Cultivation granted by Central China Normal University (2013YBYB02).

Author Contributions: This research was designed and written by the first author. The data were performed and analyzed by the coauthor, as well as the corresponding author.

Conflicts of Interest: The authors declare no conflict of interest.

Appendix A

Table A1. Comparison of MPAC estimated by network DEA and the directional distance function (DDF) (units: 10,000 RMB/ton).

Province/City	MPAC	1998	1999	2000	2001	2002	2003	2004	2005	2006	2007	2008	2009	2010	2011	Mean
Beijing	1	0.00	0.00	0.00	0.00	0.00	0.00	0.00	0.00	0.00	0.00	0.00	0.00	0.00	0.00	0.00
	2	-12.66	108.37	2.39	253.40	0.00	363.96	0.00	0.00	0.00	0.00	0.00	0.00	0.00	0.00	51.10
Tianjin	1	0.00	0.00	0.00	0.00	0.00	0.00	0.00	0.00	0.00	0.00	0.00	0.00	0.00	0.00	0.00
	2	-9.45	122.60	-29.60	39.60	49.67	-20.13	-20.68	0.00	0.00	0.00	0.00	0.00	0.00	0.00	9.43
Hebei	1	0.00	0.00	0.00	0.00	0.00	0.00	0.00	0.00	0.00	0.00	0.00	0.00	0.00	0.00	0.00
	2	-6.31	-11.51	-14.25	-13.72	-15.49	-10.57	-20.68	-30.14	-28.43	-36.99	-58.05	-62.37	-86.03	-75.20	-33.55
Shanxi	1	0.94	1.46	2.74	3.92	6.21	6.68	8.84	13.53	27.19	24.61	37.70	43.06	16.84	23.82	15.54
	2	1.06	3.09	2.47	2.21	7.26	10.66	10.37	10.80	29.90	30.32	34.30	37.54	5.94	14.39	14.31
Inner Mongolia	1	0.78	1.90	2.14	0.00	0.00	0.00	0.00	0.00	0.00	0.00	0.00	0.00	0.00	0.00	0.34
	2	1.29	4.13	0.63	-0.30	-6.95	-11.52	-18.66	-20.24	-25.43	0.00	-97.94	0.00	0.00	0.00	-12.50
Liao	1	0.00	0.00	0.00	0.00	0.00	0.00	0.00	0.00	0.00	0.00	0.00	0.00	0.00	0.00	0.00
	2	1.09	21.51	0.54	39.83	59.71	47.06	41.13	-0.97	17.23	-9.21	-0.25	-53.05	-74.03	-61.19	2.10
Jilin	1	5.66	1.40	0.00	0.00	0.00	0.00	0.00	0.00	0.00	0.00	0.00	0.00	0.00	0.00	0.50
	2	11.62	75.02	6.16	85.54	92.58	84.90	69.87	14.02	44.36	-0.05	26.89	-59.15	-84.42	-75.12	20.87
Heilongjiang	1	0.00	0.00	15.63	20.91	31.20	59.91	88.17	47.47	91.65	112.61	123.79	147.75	172.26	202.68	79.57
	2	9.83	81.44	31.58	171.39	214.03	143.14	164.49	64.83	105.74	119.96	116.90	134.61	144.82	189.20	120.85
Shanghai	1	0.00	0.00	0.00	0.00	0.00	0.00	0.00	0.00	0.00	0.00	0.00	0.00	0.00	0.00	0.00
	2	0.00	0.00	0.00	0.00	0.00	0.00	0.00	0.00	0.00	0.00	0.00	0.00	0.00	0.00	0.00
Jiangsu	1	0.00	0.00	0.00	0.00	0.00	0.00	0.00	0.00	0.00	0.00	0.00	0.00	0.00	0.00	0.00
	2	0.00	0.00	0.00	0.00	0.00	0.00	-20.68	0.00	-28.42	0.00	118.27	0.00	0.00	-42.88	1.88
Zhejiang	1	0.00	0.00	0.00	0.00	0.00	0.00	0.00	0.00	0.00	0.00	0.00	0.00	0.00	0.00	0.00
	2	0.00	0.00	0.00	0.00	0.00	11.22	-20.68	91.71	163.07	176.60	226.52	169.30	38.91	-52.30	57.45
Anhui	1	0.00	0.00	0.00	0.00	0.00	0.00	0.00	0.00	0.00	0.00	0.00	0.00	0.00	0.00	0.00
	2	6.64	4.59	6.62	24.26	28.35	16.66	-18.91	-17.11	-24.63	-36.99	-25.06	-59.15	-64.10	-42.88	-14.41
Fujian	1	0.00	0.00	0.00	0.00	0.00	0.00	0.00	0.00	0.00	0.00	0.00	0.00	0.00	0.00	0.00
	2	5.16	89.16	-17.46	79.40	100.97	84.40	137.10	31.99	-18.15	-36.89	-51.43	-54.67	0.00	0.00	24.97
Jiangxi	1	0.00	0.00	0.00	0.00	0.00	0.00	0.00	0.00	0.00	0.00	0.00	0.00	0.00	0.00	0.00
	2	9.83	19.36	0.20	18.98	27.65	-0.10	-20.56	-21.35	-28.43	-36.89	-32.82	-98.99	-72.32	-82.23	-22.69
Shandong	1	0.00	0.00	0.00	0.00	0.00	0.00	0.00	0.00	0.00	0.00	0.00	0.00	0.00	0.00	0.00
	2	-18.78	-30.18	-43.97	-26.66	-33.11	-27.28	-20.68	-28.47	-28.43	-36.89	-51.43	-59.15	-64.10	-42.88	-36.57

Table A1. Cont.

Province/City	MPAC	1998	1999	2000	2001	2002	2003	2004	2005	2006	2007	2008	2009	2010	2011	Mean
Henan	1	0.00	0.00	0.00	0.00	0.00	0.00	0.00	0.00	0.00	0.00	0.00	0.00	0.00	0.00	0.00
	2	4.06	4.23	-3.63	6.22	5.42	1.91	-11.72	-28.47	-28.43	-36.89	-51.43	-59.15	-64.10	-42.88	-21.78
Hubei	1	0.00	0.00	0.00	0.00	0.00	7.69	0.00	0.00	1.72	0.00	0.00	0.00	0.00	0.00	0.67
	2	9.83	9.28	6.81	25.50	24.48	65.69	18.51	22.23	41.89	50.48	86.20	77.27	-32.79	-54.79	25.04
Hunan	1	0.00	0.00	0.00	0.00	0.00	0.00	0.00	0.00	0.00	0.00	0.00	0.00	0.00	0.00	0.00
	2	1.05	-0.24	-6.87	-6.30	-0.72	-3.53	-15.04	-23.50	-27.24	-36.89	-51.43	-55.72	-64.10	-42.88	-23.81
Guangdong	1	0.00	0.00	0.00	0.00	0.00	0.00	0.00	0.00	0.00	0.00	0.00	0.00	0.00	0.00	0.00
	2	0.00	0.00	0.00	0.00	0.00	0.00	0.00	0.00	0.00	0.00	0.00	0.00	0.00	0.00	0.00
Guangxi	1	0.00	0.00	0.00	0.00	0.00	0.00	0.00	0.00	0.00	0.00	0.00	0.00	0.00	0.00	0.00
	2	-6.08	-7.58	-13.71	-16.45	-19.67	-18.12	-21.56	-23.78	-24.38	-32.96	-45.14	-64.25	-79.23	-13.19	-27.58
Hainan	1	0.00	0.00	0.00	0.00	0.00	0.00	0.00	0.00	0.00	0.00	0.00	0.00	0.00	0.00	0.00
	2	0.00	-40.50	-36.16	63.09	120.68	70.48	67.54	18.65	-67.67	-33.12	11.49	-35.85	-55.49	-57.78	1.81
Chongqing	1	0.00	0.00	0.00	0.00	0.00	0.00	0.00	0.00	0.00	0.00	0.00	0.00	0.00	0.00	0.00
	2	0.81	-7.42	-14.89	-20.12	-24.36	0.00	0.00	0.00	0.00	0.00	0.00	0.00	0.00	0.00	-4.71
Sichuan	1	0.00	0.00	0.00	0.00	0.00	0.00	0.00	0.00	0.00	0.00	0.00	0.00	0.00	0.00	0.00
	2	3.16	21.25	-14.04	-14.85	-10.87	-2.21	-13.29	-25.42	-40.49	-36.99	-51.43	-59.15	-64.10	-51.39	-25.70
Guizhou	1	0.00	0.00	0.00	0.00	0.00	0.00	0.00	0.85	0.00	0.00	0.00	0.00	0.00	0.00	0.06
	2	-5.96	-8.16	-9.89	-12.00	-13.76	-4.95	-8.44	-6.58	-15.84	-20.78	-28.35	-39.02	-44.76	-39.35	-18.42
Yunnan	1	0.00	0.00	0.00	0.00	0.00	0.00	0.00	0.00	0.00	0.00	0.00	0.00	0.00	0.00	0.00
	2	-7.33	-5.33	-10.89	-11.80	-13.24	-5.11	-31.57	-24.08	-19.33	-21.32	-21.29	-33.09	31.79	-44.42	-20.04
Shaanxi	1	0.00	0.00	0.00	0.00	1.04	0.00	0.00	0.00	0.00	0.00	0.00	0.00	0.00	1.98	0.22
	2	-0.90	-18.48	-22.32	-25.65	-5.47	-28.18	-33.71	-35.00	-39.49	-49.20	-62.53	-80.08	-88.28	-26.98	-36.88
Gansu	1	0.00	0.00	0.00	0.00	0.00	0.00	0.00	0.00	0.00	0.00	0.00	0.00	0.00	0.00	0.00
	2	3.43	16.40	3.37	4.49	-1.41	5.35	7.48	-7.39	9.52	-0.34	-0.81	-5.07	-1.33	-21.93	0.84
Ningxia	1	0.00	0.00	0.00	0.00	0.00	0.00	0.00	0.00	0.00	0.00	0.00	0.00	0.00	0.00	0.00
	2	-9.02	-9.57	-10.88	-14.60	-14.82	-4.89	-10.61	-18.92	-16.19	-23.18	-29.30	-38.26	-45.82	-39.16	-20.37
Xinjiang	1	0.90	3.17	0.00	0.00	0.00	0.00	0.00	0.00	0.00	10.73	17.13	22.39	32.25	35.35	8.71
	2	3.01	18.60	-19.68	-34.59	-33.10	-8.64	-17.65	-11.73	-6.88	0.16	-9.44	4.47	1.61	-3.52	-8.39

Note: "1" is MPAC estimated by network DEA, which was used in this paper; "2" is MPAC estimated by DDF.

Table 2. The effects of SETPS on PAC based on the difference-in-difference method.

Year	APAC	MPAC
2002–2011	0.246 (0.243)	−5.147 (8.725)
2002	−0.068 (0.088)	−0.214 (1.301)
2003	0.030 (0.135)	−2.061 (2.890)
2004	0.111 (0.215)	−2.852 (4.592)
2005	0.120 (0.215)	0.271 (3.152)
2006	0.029 (0.225)	0.054 (7.110)
2007	0.256 (0.353)	−2.119 (8.018)
2008	0.137 (0.287)	0.035 (10.102)
2009	−0.001 (0.338)	−0.264 (12.107)
2010	0.103 (0.312)	−8.709 (11.790)
2011	0.100 (0.273)	−9.103 (13.969)

Note: Clustered standard errors in parentheses; *** $p < 0.01$; ** $p < 0.05$; * $p < 0.1$.

References

1. Coase, R.H. The Problem of Social Cost. *J. Law Econ.* **1960**, 3, 1–44. [CrossRef]
2. Crocker, T.D. The Structuring of Atmospheric Pollution Control Systems. In *The Economics of Air Pollution*; Harold, W., Ed.; W.W. Norton: New York, NY, USA, 1966.
3. Dales, J.H. *Pollution, Property and Prices*; University Press: Toronto, ON, Canada, 1968.
4. Montgomery, W.D. Markets in Licenses and Efficient Pollution Control Programs. *J. Econ. Theory* **1972**, 5, 395–418. [CrossRef]
5. Tietenberg, T.H. Emissions Trading: An Exercise in Reforming Pollution Policy. *J. Polit.* **1986**, 48, 220–222. [CrossRef]
6. Grubb, M. The Economics of the Kyoto Protocol. *World Econ.* **2003**, 4, 143–189.
7. Rose, A. Equity Considerations of Trading Carbon Emission Entitlements. In *Combating Global Warming: Study on a Global System of Tradable Carbon Emission Entitlements*; Barrett, S., Ed.; United Nations: New York, NY, USA, 1992.
8. Li, Y.; Shen, K. Emission Reduction of China's Pollution Control Policy—An Empirical Study Based on Provincial Industrial Pollution Data. *Manag. World* **2008**, 7, 8–17. (In Chinese)
9. Wang, J.; Tu, Z. Emissions Trading: Theory and Practice. *Hubei Soc. Sci.* **2009**, 3, 103–106. (In Chinese)
10. He, J.; Xiao, B. The Pilot Start-up of the Emissions Trading and the Definition of Market Player. *Reform* **2010**, 1, 155–159. (In Chinese)
11. Zheng, W. Assessment of Development Trend of Emission Right Trade System under the Background of Low-Carbon Economy. *Reform* **2010**, 4, 104–110. (In Chinese)
12. Tan, Z.; Chen, D. Regional Carbon Trading Mode and Its Implementation Path. *China Soft Sci. Mag.* **2012**, 4, 76–84. (In Chinese)

13. Yan, W.; Guo, S. Can Sulfur Dioxide Emissions Trading Policy Reduce Pollution Intensity?—An Empirical Study Based on the Difference in Difference Model. *Shanghai J. Econ.* **2012**, *6*, 76–83. (In Chinese)

14. An, C.; Tang, Y. Research on Decision Model of Enterprises' Carbon Emission Reduction under Emission Trading System. *Econ. Res. J.* **2012**, *8*, 45–58. (In Chinese)

15. Fan, J.; Zhao, D.; Guo, T. Research on Carbon Emission Trading Mechanism from Consumer Perspective. *China Soft Sci. Mag.* **2012**, *6*, 24–32. (In Chinese)

16. Fan, J.; Zhao, D.; Jin, H. The Effects of Consumption Emissions Trading on Consumer's Choice—Evidence from Experimental Economics. *China Ind. Econ.* **2012**, *3*, 30–42. (In Chinese)

17. Ferng, J. Allocating the Responsibility of CO_2 Over-emissions from the Perspectives of Benefit Principle and Ecological Deficit. *Ecol. Econ.* **2003**, *46*, 121–141. [CrossRef]

18. Cui, L.; Ying, F.; Zhu, L.; Bi, Q.; Zhang, Y. The Cost Saving Effect of Carbon Markets in China for Achieving the Reduction Targets in the "12th Five−Year Plan". *Chin. J. Manag. Sci.* **2013**, *21*, 37–46. (In Chinese)

19. Li, G.; Ma, Y.; Yao, L. The Intensity and Upgrade Path for China's Industrial Environmental Regulation—An Empirical Study of the Costs and Benefits of China's Industrial Environmental Protection. *China Ind. Econ.* **2010**, *3*, 31–41. (In Chinese)

20. Boyd, G.A.; George, T.; Pang, J. Plant Level Productivity, Efficiency, and Environmental Performance of the Container Glass Industry. *Environ. Resour. Econ.* **2002**, *23*, 29–43. [CrossRef]

21. Chen, S. Marginal Abatement Cost and Environmental Tax Reform in China. *Soc. Sci. China* **2011**, *3*, 85–100. 222. (In Chinese)

22. Färe, R.; Grosskopf, S.; Carl, A.P., Jr. Joint Production of Good and Bad Outputs with a Network Application. In *Encyclopedia of Energy, Natural Resources and Environmental Economics*; Elsevier: San Diego, CA, USA, 2011.

23. Tu, Z.; Shen, R. Dose Environment Technology Efficiency Measured by Traditional Method Underestimate Environment Governance Efficiency? From the Evidence of China's Industrial Provincial Panel Data Using Environmental Directional Distance Function Based on the Network DEA Model. *Econ. Rev.* **2013**, *5*, 89–99. (In Chinese)

24. National Bureau of Statistics of China. *China Statistical Yearbook 1999–2012*; China Statistics Press: Beijing, China, 2013.

25. National Bureau of Statistics of China. *China Energy Statistical Yearbook 1997–2012*; China Statistics Press: Beijing, China, 2013.

26. National Bureau of Statistics of China. *China Compendium of Statistics 1949–2008*; China Statistics Press: Beijing, China, 2010.

27. National Bureau of Statistics of China. *China Statistical Yearbook on Environment 2012*; China Statistics Press: Beijing, China, 2013.

28. National Bureau of Statistics of China. *China Industry Economy Statistical Yearbook 2001–2012*; China Statistics Press: Beijing, China, 2013.

29. Tu, Z.; Shen, R. Industrialization's, Urbanization's Dynamic Marginal Carbon Emissions—The Analytical Framework Based on LMDI "Two−Level Perfect Decomposition" Method. *China Ind. Econ.* **2013**, *9*, 31–43. (In Chinese)

30. Tu, Z. The Shadow Price of Industrial SO_2 Emission: A New Analytic Framework. *China Econ. Q.* **2009**, *91*, 259–282. (In Chinese)

sustainability

MDPI

Article

A Site Selection Model for a Straw-Based Power Generation Plant with CO_2 Emissions

Hao Lv [1,2], Hao Ding [1,2,*], Dequn Zhou [1,2] and Peng Zhou [1,2]

[1] College of Economics and Management, Nanjing University of Aeronautics and Astronautics, 29 Jiangjun Avenue, Nanjing 210016, China; lvhao@nuaa.edu.cn (H.L.); dqzhou88@163.com (D.Z.); rocy_zhou@hotmail.com (P.Z.)

[2] Research Centre for Soft Energy Science, Nanjing University of Aeronautics and Astronautics, 29 Jiangjun Avenue, Nanjing 210016, China

[*] Author to whom correspondence should be addressed; dding2009@nuaa.edu.cn; Tel.:+86-156-5175-6806.

External Editor: Yongrok Choi

Received: 28 August 2014; in revised form: 24 September 2014; Accepted: 15 October 2014; Published: 23 October 2014

Abstract: The decision on the location of a straw-based power generation plant has a great influence on the plant's operation and performance. This study explores traditional theories for site selection. Using integer programming, the study optimizes the economic and carbon emission outcomes of straw-based power generation as two objectives, with the supply and demand of straw as constraints. It provides a multi-objective mixed-integer programming model to solve the site selection problem for a straw-based power generation plant. It then provides a case study to demonstrate the application of the model in the decision on the site selection for a straw-based power generation plant with a Chinese region. Finally, the paper discusses the result of the model in the context of the wider aspect of straw-based power generation.

Keywords: straw-based power generation; carbon emissions; project location; mixed-integer programming

---

1. Introduction

Straw-based power generation is a kind of stable and reliable method to utilize co-product energy sources. Bioenergy now makes up most part of the total renewable energy consumption in the world [1]. The total electricity generated from renewable energy in 2012 was 992 TWh (except hydro-power); the electricity generated from biomass was 424 TWh, and it accounts for nearly 9.5% of the whole electricity generated [2].

In China, biomass resources from agriculture and the forestry are quite rich. The total production of straw crop in 2010 was about 720 million tons. It is expected to reach 800 million tons by 2020. The research and appliance of technologies related to biomass utilization are listed as the key scientific research projects continuously in the recent four Five-year Plans of China. By the end of 2013, the cumulative capacity of biomass power generation checked and approved by the Chinese government (checked and approved capacity) was 12,226.21 MW, and the capacity of straw-based power generation connected to the grid (on-grid capacity) reached 7790.01 MW, which accounts for about 63.72% of the total checked and approved capacity. Among the on-grid capacity, agricultural and forestry biomass-based power generation accounted for 53.85%, whose installed capacity was 4195.3 MW [3].

Straw-based power generation is a kind of resource-oriented power generation form, which means that the resource has a great influence on the operation and performance. In richer areas for agriculture and forestry biomass resources, the electricity generation cost could be less, because of economies of scale. Operation is also affected by factors related to the resource endowment and production characteristics of different areas. At present, the total installed capacity in Eastern China is 3514.84 MW, accounting for 45.12% of the whole country. The installed capacities in Central China and the southern area of China are 1438 MW and 1096 MW, respectively [3].

In the operation process of straw-based power generation, the fuel cost takes up more than 60% of the total electricity cost [4]. Compared with traditional energy, the fuel purchasing cost, warehousing cost and transportation expense, which dominate straw-based power generation plants' fuel cost, are all influenced by the location of the plant. However, currently, most of the studies on straw-based power generation have been concentrated on assessing the technologies and related public policies, and research studies on the location problems are lacking, especially in China. Liuqin Chen discussed the current problems for biomass power generation in China, including the technology problems, the policy problems, and so on [5]. Tianyu Qi *et al.* adopted the optimized cost calculating methods to analyze the electricity costs of biomass power generation in different provinces and areas in China. They identified the provinces and areas whose electricity costs are less than others [6]. Lin Zhao applied fuzzy synthetic evaluation techniques in her analysis of planning and site selection for straw-based power generation plants to compare the characteristics of different regions and introduced the concept of regional suitability [7].

The site selection of the project has two phases: region and site selection. The first phase usually considers the straw resources and different policies on straw-based power generation plants in different regions, the economic levels and social environments of the regions. In the second phase, the problem is which site in the chosen region is the best choice for the plant. It usually concentrates on the total cost of the plant and its environmental performance. The straw-based power generation's regional choice has effects on its investment, fuel purchasing cost, incentives, and so on. Site selection affects the fuel's transporting cost greatly. Zhimei Guo *et al.* used a conditional logit model (CLM) to make a straw-based power generation plant's location decision. They assumed that each firm screens locations based on a latent profit function that is dependent on a variety of state attributes where it plans to locate. They use the function $\pi_{ij} = \beta'X_j + \mu_{ij}$ as the latent profit function, where π_{ij} are the expected profits of firm i if locating the new plant in state j, X_j is a vector of the observable characteristics of state j, β' is a vector of estimated coefficients and μ_{ij} is the random disturbance term. According to the model, the economic benefit of biomass power generation is determined by the decision of the location problem [8].

Traditional solutions of site selection problems include the iterative gravity method and the linear programming method [7–13]. Matt Kocoloski *et al.* used a mixed-integer program (MIP) to locate ethanol refineries and connected these refineries to biomass supplies and ethanol demands in a way that minimizes the total cost [11]. Cong Dong *et al.* and Cong Chen *et al.* introduced the concept of uncertainty into the program method and use a mixed-integer interval program model to solve the location decision for biomass power generation. They replaced the imprecise integer number with the interval to deal with the uncertainties [12,13]. Lin Zhao analyzed the cost of the electricity generated from biomass resources [7]. She used an iterative gravity method for biomass power generation that has no candidate sites to obtain the optimal location with the least total cost for a straw-based power generation plant to generate electricity over the whole life cycle.

All of the studies discussed above take the economic benefit optimization as the objective. Based on the traditional theory of project site selection, most of them are conducted by dealing with the optimization of the total electricity cost. Some of them considered the uncertainties of the system and combined methods to deal with these uncertainties with the traditional linear program method to obtain a location model that accords with reality. On the basis of current research, this paper further talks about the objectives of the model. It introduces the objective of the minimization of carbon emissions during the whole life of the project, which is of equal importance to the economic benefit. It gives a multi-objective mixed-integer linear programming model to solve the site selection problem for a straw-based power generation plant and considers the model's application.

2. The Regional Distribution of Biomass Power Generation in China

The first straw-based power generation plant in China was built in 2006. Since then, straw-based power generation has been growing at a rapid speed. From the end of 2013, the regional distribution of agricultural and forestry biomass power generation is shown in Table 1.

From the perspective of the resource distribution among the regions, the cumulative straw resources of the nine province areas in Table 1 account for nearly 56.49% of China's total straw resources. Meanwhile, the straw-based power generation in the nine provinces takes up nearly 75.99% of the whole country. It can be observed that the distribution of the straw-based power generation does not accord with the distribution of straw resources. Take Henan Province as an example, the installed capacity of straw-based power generation in Shandong Province is 45.97%, more than that of Henan Province, but its straw resources are almost the same as that of Henan Province; the straw resources of Heilongjiang Province are much less than those of Henan Province, but it has a larger installed capacity than Henan Province. We can conclude that the distribution of straw-based power generation is not in accordance with the resource supply.

From the perspective of the regional electricity demand distribution, the cumulative annual electricity consumption of the nine provinces takes up about 45.3% of China's annual electricity consumption. However, the percentage of the nine provinces' accumulative installed capacity with respect to the whole country is far more than that. Then, it will also cost money to transport electricity from the plant to the whole country. Therefore, we can observe that the biomass power generation's regional distribution is not in accordance with the regional demand distribution of the electricity.

In Table 1, the regional straw-based power generation's annual equivalent full load operation hours reflect the utilization efficiency of a straw-based power generation plant's production ability: the more hours the straw-based power generation can operate annually, the more efficiently the generation's capacity is used. On the perspective of site selection, the project's annual equivalent full load operation hours are mostly influenced by the straw fuel's supply and collection. If the supply of straw is sufficient, the straw-based power generation is expected to operate for many hours, and the utilization of equipment is great. As a result, we can take straw-based power generation's annual equivalent full load operation hours as an indicator to assess the regional biomass resource supply ability.

Table 1. The agricultural and forestry biomass resource distribution in some regions of China.

Province	Electricity consumption (100 million kWh)	Annual equivalent full load operation hours (h)	Total installed capacity (MW)	Percentage that this province's straw resource makes up in China (%)
Henan	2988	4940	422	10.24%
Shandong	4083	6018	616	9.98%
Heilongjiang	845	4987	465	8.44%
Hebei	3251	5436	218	7.53%
Jiangsu	4956	-	380	5%
Anhui	1528	6166	406	4.76%
Hunan	1423	5396	242	4.63%
Hubei	1629	5157	374	4.27%
Zhejiang	3453	5897	65	1.46%
Others	29,067	-	1007.3	43.51%
Cumulative	53,223	-	4195.3	1

Data resources: National Bureau of Statistics of China, renewable energy database [14], Science and technology education department of Ministry of Agriculture of the People's Republic of China, 2010. The report on national straw crop resource survey and assessment.

3. Methodology

3.1. Candidate Sites Selection for Straw-Based Power Generation

During the candidate site selection for straw-based power generation, some important factors need to be considered. They are general site requirements, community impacts, environmental impacts, economic impacts and land use impacts.

Firstly, the location of straw-based power generation should comply with the overall urban planning and the national government's regulations. Secondly, the straw-based power generation plant should be located near rivers, as it will consume large amounts of water in its operation. The selected site for straw-based power generation should have access to municipal service facilities, such as fire-fighting service and road service, because of the storage and transportation of straw. These are all the general site requirements.

During the site selection, the straw-based power generation plant's community impacts have to be taken into consideration. Located in areas where people's attitudes toward straw-based power generation are friendly, the plant's construction and operation will be smooth. Otherwise, it would come up against many impediments from local residents [7].

The environmental impacts of straw-based power generation plants include the carbon emissions, water pollution and ash [7]. The water pollution and ash can be controlled by specific methods and technologies; while carbon emissions can be minimized during the site selection period of the plant. The straw-based power generation plant should be located in places where the price of straw and the labor costs are both low, to reduce the construction and operation costs. The transportation cost for straw can also be minimized with a reasonable location decision. These economic factors are the most frequently used ones in recent research studies [6–13].

Land occupation is a specific characteristic of straw-based power generation, for it needs large amounts of land to store straw resources. In the location decision of straw-based power generation plants, the land cost would be an important factor. The plants should be located in places with low land costs. Meanwhile, the selected sites need to be open spaces without construction or residences, so that the construction and operation of the plants will not cause the removal and relocation of residents. Another requirement is that straw-based power generation plants should try not to occupy farmland or to take up as little as possible; because the occupation of farmland may influence the farmers' production, which could causes community impacts.

3.2. Mathematical Model

To take both optimizations of the economic benefit and environmental influences of straw-based power generation into consideration simultaneously, this paper uses a two-objective integer linear programming model to get the optimal location for the straw-based power generation plant from a set of candidate sites. The two objectives here are minimizing the total cost and total carbon emissions of the biomass power generation plant, respectively. The model presented in this paper is based on the mixed-integer programming model of Matt Kocoloski *et al.*, which only has one objective: the economic benefit [11]. The model here recognizes the carbon emissions to be one of the key factors that will have an impact on the real performance of straw-based power generation. During the whole life cycle of the power generation system, the total carbon emissions may be more than expected without reasonable planning and scheduling of the system. By including the carbon emissions as one of the model's objectives, this paper tries to obtain the optimal operation performance with respect to carbon emissions. In the original model, the project's operation cost is the main optimization objective of the MIP model. According to the authors, the plant's operation cost consists of the biomass resources' and the ethanol's transportation fees, the investment of purchasing the equipment and the operation and maintenance costs of the equipment. The constraints of the original model are the size of the facilities and the supply of the resources. In this paper, it is assumed that the straw-based power generation's location will be selected from the candidate sites in a chosen region. The given region is divided into some sub-regions (see Figure 1). Every sub-region is a straw supplier for straw-based power generation. It then translates the location decision problem of the biomass power generation into a transportation planning problem.

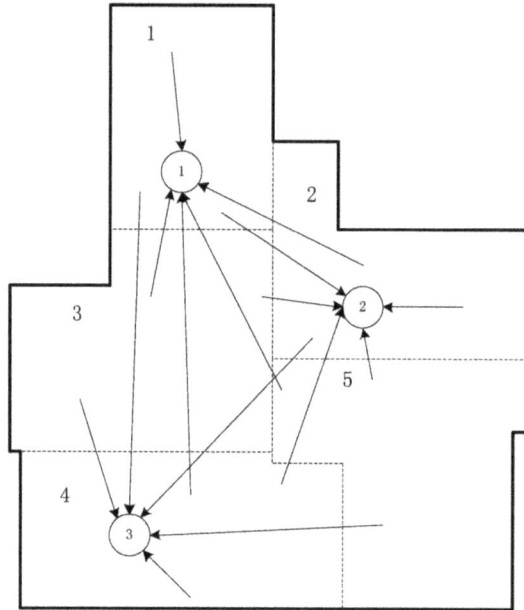

Note: the number 1 to 5 represents the five sub-regions.

Figure 1. The candidate sites of the biomass power generation and the division of the region.

As show in Figure 1, there are three candidate sites for the biomass power generation from which to select. The region can be divided into five sub-regions, and the straw crop collection is in the five sub-regions independently. However, the straw resources can be translated across different sub-regions to a large degree. During the collection process of straw resource in sub-regions, the acquisition range is limited to less than 10 kilometers for the economic benefits. The transportation machines include small-sized agricultural trucks and electro-tricycles. When the straw is transported across the sub-regions, the machines used are usually trucks, whose full load is between 20 tons and 25 tons to minimize the transportation cost.

Here, it is defined that xij ($i = 1,2,3 \ldots, j = 1,2,3 \ldots$) is the number of straw resources transported from sub-region i to site j. $y_j = \begin{cases} 0 \\ 1 \end{cases} . j = 1,2,3 \ldots$ When $y_i = 0$, this means that straw-based power generation will not be located in site j. In this scenario, other sub-regions seem not to transport their straw resources to this site and this sub-region ($x_{.j} = 0$). When $y_i = 1$, this means that in site j, there will be straw-based power generation, so that other sub-regions can transport the straw resources to this site.

The objectives of this model are the optimization of the economic benefit of the straw-based power generation and the carbon emissions of the whole system.

Objective 1: optimizing the economic benefit of straw-based power generation. The scale of the plant is given. Here, we assume that in the selected region, the on-grid price of the electricity is determined. Therefore, the optimization of the economic benefit is the same as the minimization of the total cost of the generation.

Sustainability **2014**, *6*, 7466–7481

Mohammad Asadullah assessed the economic benefit of biomass gasification power generation. In the assessment, he pointed out that the cost of biomass gasification power generation contains the initial investment of the plant and the operation and maintenance costs [15]. The operation and maintenance costs of the plant are calculated by summing up the biomass fuel cost, the labor cost and the fossil fuel cost. Daniel G. Wright *et al.* said that the total cost of biomass power generation is calculated by using the sum of the initial investment, the operation and maintenance cost and the fuel cost minus the sum of the economic incentives and the benefits from supplying heat [16]. Then, they made a mathematical model to calculate the levelized cost of electricity generated from biomass resource. Almost 60% of the unit cost of the electricity generated in the biomass power generation is the biomass fuel cost, including the purchasing price of the straw in the field, the transportation cost, the pre-processing cost and the storage cost [17–21]. Lihuan Chen *et al.* adopted the activity-based cost method to calculate the straw resources' transportation cost. They took the straw purchase center belonging to the biomass power generation as the activity center in the study and analyzed the transportation cost of different straw crops in Jiangsu, Henan, Hebei, *etc.* According to the research, the total transportation cost for the rice straw is 226 RMB yuan/ton, and the total transportation costs for the wheat straw, the corn straw and the cotton straw are 228 RMB yuan/ton, 217 RMB yuan/ton and 192 RMB yuan/ton, respectively [22].

Rogers, J.G. and Brammer, J.G. claimed to set pre-disposing points in the collection field of the biomass resource when analyzing the electricity cost of the biomass gasification power generation [23]. They made a model to estimate the average logistic cost per GJ for a given plant to calculate the total transportation cost of the biomass resources.

As described by Ruiz, J.A. *et al.*, 75% of the transportation cost of the biomass from the temporary acquisition points to the plant is the cost of the trucks, including their purchasing cost, their operation and maintenance costs, the fossil fuel cost, the drivers' salary, and so on [24]. At the same time, the two key factors that influence the straw's total transportation cost are the travel distances and the travel durations for the trucks. The travel distance mainly affects the fossil fuel consumption of the truck. Therefore, this has effects on the total transportation cost. Meanwhile, travel duration has a greater influence on the total transportation cost, as it determines the salary paid to the drivers. It seems to be true that the labor cost is the most important factor of the biomass resource's total transportation cost [25].

We give the empirical function of the total cost of the biomass power generation as Equation (1).

$$TC = C_{investment} + C_{O\&M} + C_F - R_{incentive} \tag{1}$$

where TC is the total cost of the biomass power generation, $C_{investment}$ is the initial investment of the project, $C_{O\&M}$ is the operation and maintenance costs of the plant, C_F is the total cost of the biomass resource and $R_{incentive}$ is the economic incentives from the government. As we have discussed in Section 1, in a certain region, the initial investment, the operation and maintenance costs and the economic incentives are almost the same in different sub-regions and different candidate sites for the plant. The cost of the biomass resource consists of the purchase price of the straw, the disposal cost of the straw and the transportation cost. Among these three parts, the purchase cost of the straw is determined by the economic level of the selected region and the technology level of the agricultural crops' harvest. The differences in purchase costs among different sub-regions are so small, that they can be ignored. Therefore, we can reduce the objective of minimizing the total cost of the biomass power generation into the minimization of the total transportation cost of the straw.

The total transportation cost of the biomass power generation contains the cost to transport the straw in the sub-region and the cost to transport the straw from the supplying sub-region to the selected site. The first part of the total transportation cost can be calculated by Equation (2).

$$C_{transporting,i} = \lambda \sum_j x_{ij} \tag{2}$$

where λ is the collection cost ratio on the supply side (RMB yuan/ton).

The cost to transport the straw from the supply side to the selected site can be calculated by Equation (3).

$$C_{transport,ij} = \alpha_{ij} \times x_{ij} \qquad (3)$$

where α_{ij} is the cost to transport per ton of straw from sub-region i to selected site j (RMB yuan/ton).

Objective 1 is then described by Equation (4).

Objective 1:

$$\min z_1 = \sum_i \sum_j \lambda x_{ij} + \sum_i \sum_j \alpha_{ij} x_{ij} \qquad (4)$$

Objective 2: minimizing the total carbon emission during the whole life cycle of straw-based power generation. Biomass power generation is famous for its characteristic of having "few carbon emissions or zero carbon emission". In fact, however, during the operation of the straw-based power generation plant, there will be some carbon emissions produced. Most of the carbon emission produced is in the collection and transportation processes of the straw. All of the pre-processing, collecting and transporting of straw consume fossil fuels and then emit carbon into the atmosphere. Those carbon emissions will influence the performance of biomass power generation. Guoliang Cao *et al.* estimated by experiment that the carbon emission ratio of the straw crop's burning in the field is between 1400 g/kg and 1800 g/kg. It is discovered that the amount of straw burned in the field in China has a great and obvious effect on the whole carbon emissions of the country [26]. Zhen He *et al.* utilized a simplified full life cycle model (FLCM) to estimate the total carbon emissions of the biomass power generation. They divided the whole life cycle of biomass power generation into three parts, which are the growing process of biomass crops, the collecting, storage and transporting process of straw and the straw utilization and electricity production process. They then calculated the carbon emissions during these three parts independently by their activities and their links to the environment of the system. It is pointed out in the study that the carbon emissions of the straw-based direct burning power generation is associated with the straw fuel it burns. During the burning process in a straw-based direct burning power generation with a capacity of 25 MW, the carbon emission coefficients for different kinds of straw are: 377.1 kgC/ton for rice straw, 395.8 kgC/ton for corn straw and 389.9 kgC/ton for wheat straw; the carbon emission coefficients for different kinds of straw during the transporting process are, respectively: 0.1435 kgC/(ton·km) for rice straw, 0.1270 kgC/(ton·km) for corn straw and 0.3403 kgC/(ton·km) for wheat straw [27].

According to Chao Feng and Xiaoxi Ma, burning 100 kg of rice straw directly to generate electricity will emit 164.24 kg CO_2, during the transportation of the straw, consume about 0.07 L diesel and emit nearly 1.7 g CO and 0.03 kg CO_2 during the burning process of the straw; it will emit almost 136.77 kg CO_2 [28]. Yin Li and Jing Li analyzed the appliance of the CDM (Clean Development Mechanism) method's ACM0006 technique, which is designed to calculate the projects' real carbon emissions [29]. Amit Thakur *et al.* listed the energy consumption of related machines when analyzing the total carbon emissions during the full life cycle of forestry biomass power generation. In that study, a truck with a load capacity of 25 tons is the main transportation machine for the biomass resource [30].

The total carbon emissions during the whole life cycle of the biomass power generation mostly comes from the consumption of fossil fuels. Fossil fuels' consumption usually happens in the straw resource transportation process. Most of the fossil fuels are consumed by the transportation machines and some of the pre-processing machines. The total fossil energy consumption during the whole life cycle of the biomass power generation can be calculated by Equation (5).

$$Total\_Energy = Energy_{processing} + Energy_{transporting} \qquad (5)$$

where $Energy_{processing}$ is the fossil energy consumed to pre-process the straw, which is mainly determined by the amount of biomass resources demanded by the plant and the biomass resources' characteristics. $Energy_{transporting}$ is the fossil energy consumed during the transportation of the biomass resources, and it is mainly related to the straw fuel's travel distance. We can calculate the total carbon emissions by multiplying the total energy consumption with the corresponding emission coefficients of the fossil fuels. Therefore, Objective 2 can be described as Equation (6).

Objective 2:

$$\min z_1 = \sum_i \sum_j \eta x_{ij} + \sum_i \sum_j \beta_{ij} x_{ij} \tag{6}$$

where η is the carbon emission coefficient during the collecting process of the biomass in the sub-regions. β_{ij} is the carbon emission coefficient for transporting the biomass resources between different sub-regions; it can be described as the carbon emissions from transportation per ton of biomass per kilometer from sub-region i to selected site j.

The constraints of the model include:

(1) Straw fuels collected from the whole region and transported to the selected site of the biomass power generation are sufficient to meet the demand of the straw-based power generation plant to generate the electricity planned. It can be described as Equation (7).

$$\sum_i x_{ij} = D \times y_j \tag{7}$$

where D is the annual demand of the straw-based power generation plant, which is only related to the capacity of the plant.

(2) The total amount of the crop straw collected in the sub-region cannot be more than what the sub-region itself can really supply as a kind of energy resources. This means that only part of the total straw in the sub-region can be collected and utilized as the energy resource. It can be described as Equation (8).

$$\sum_j x_{ij} \leq R_i \tag{8}$$

where R_i is the amount of biomass resources that can be utilized as the energy resource and that can be collected in sub-region i. It can be calculated by multiplying the total production of straw crop with the use ratio of biomass as energy.

(3) The plant can only choose one site from the candidate sites as its location, and there must be one site to be selected as the result. This can be described as Equation (9).

$$\sum_j y_j = 1 \tag{9}$$

In conclusion, we present Equation (10) as the whole model.

$$
\begin{aligned}
\min \quad & w = \varphi z_1 + (1 - \varphi) z_2 \\
& z_1 = \sum_i \sum_j \lambda x_{ij} + \sum_i \sum_j \alpha_{ij} x_{ij} \\
& z2 = \sum_i \sum_j \eta x_{ij} + \sum_i \sum_j \beta_{ij} x_{ij} \\
& \sum_i x_{ij} = D \times y_i \\
& \sum_j x_{ij} \leq R_i \\
& \sum_j y_j = 1 \\
& 0 < \varphi < 1
\end{aligned} \tag{10}
$$

where φ is the weight of Objective 1. When φ is larger than 0.5, the weight of Objective 1 is larger than Objective 2, *vice versa*. Through solving this model, we can get the optimal location of the straw-based power generation plant.

4. Case Study and Discussion

An electric power group has decided to develop a 25-MW straw-based power generation plant in Nantong, Jiangsu Province, China. The total demand of the straw is estimated to be about 270 thousand tons. Nantong consists of Chongchuan District, Gangzha District, Tongzhou District, Hai'an County, Rudong County, Rugao County and Haimen County. The first three districts together form the municipal district. The whole area of Nantong is nearly 8544 square kilometers. Its total straw production is almost 4.7 million tons [31]. The production of crop straw in the sub-regions in Nantong is shown in Table 2. We find that Rudong County has the most biomass straw production in Nantong. Rugao County has the second largest amount of straw production, and Hai'an has the third largest amount of straw production in Nantong. To efficiently reduce the amount of straw transported between different sub-regions, three candidate sites were chosen in Rudong, Rugao and Hai'an, respectively. The three candidate sites are labeled 1, 2 and 3. The cumulative straw production of these three sub-regions is equal to 3.224 million tons. According to Zhang *et al.*, by the end of 2012, the utilization of straw as energy is expected to reach 26% [4]. Take the completion of other straw-based power generation plants and other uses for straw, where it is hypothesized that the real utilization of straw as energy is about 10%. Therefore, the total supply ability of these three sub-regions is about 320 thousand tons. Rudong County can supply nearly 129 thousand tons every year. Rugao County can supply about 102 thousand tons every year, and Hai'an County can supply about 90 thousand tons of straw every year. Meanwhile, because there are two counties that are next to these three sub-regions, but outside Nantong (these two counties are Dongtai and Taixing), the total straw production for them is 1.33 million tons and 0.98 million tons, respectively. Their straw supply ability is, respectively, 133 thousand tons and 98 thousand tons. The distances between the sub-regions and the other coefficients related to the system can be found in Table 3.

Assume that crop straw is collected and transported in the sub-region mainly by small agricultural machines whose load abilities are less than 10 tons; the machines used to transport the straw from the sub-regions to the biomass power generation plant are trucks with load abilities between 20 tons and 25 tons. During the collecting process of the straw in the sub-regions, the cost coefficient for the transportation is about 1.5 RMB yuan/(ton·km), and the energy consumption coefficient and carbon emission coefficient for the transportation are almost 0.15 L/(ton km) and 0.24 kgC/(ton km), respectively. When the straw is transported from the sub-regions to the plant side, the cost coefficient for the transportation is nearly 1 RMB yuan/(ton km); the fossil energy consumption coefficient and carbon emission coefficient for the transportation are nearly 0.02 L/(ton km) and 0.03 kgC/(ton km), respectively [4,27,32].

Table 2. The cultivated area and crop production in the sub-regions of Nantong.

Sub-region	The grain plantation area (1000 ha)	The production of the crops (10,000 tons)	The cotton plantation area (1000 ha)	The production of cotton (tons)	The total production of biomass straw (10,000 tons)
Municipal area	92.2	59.53	6.78	7535	84.6
Hai'an County	79.19	64.43	0.14	171	90.4
Rugao County	110.53	72.81	0.21	200	102.2
Rudong County	131.87	90.8	12.55	17,281	129.8
Haimen County	40.97	17.83	11.43	12,859	26.8
Qidong County	70.85	24.09	14.73	16,349	36.2
Cumulative	525.61	329.49	45.84	54,395	470

Table 3. The parameters related to this case.

	Candidate Site 1 (y₁)			Candidate Site 2 (y₂)			Candidate Site 3 (y₃)		
	Travel distance of straw (km)	Cost coefficient for transportation (RMB yuan/ton)	Carbon emission coefficient for transportation (kgC/ton)	Travel distance of straw (km)	Carbon emission coefficient for transportation (kgC/ton)	Travel distance for straw (km)	Travel distance for straw (km)	Carbon emit coefficient for transportation (kgC/ton)
Dongtai	35	50	5.05	80	95	6.4	100	115	7
Hai'an	0	15	2.16	45	60	3.51	75	90	4.41
Rugao	45	60	4.46	0	15	3.11	55	70	4.76
Rudong	75	90	6.01	55	70	5.41	0	15	3.76
Taixing	55	70	3.84	40	55	3.39	90	105	4.89
Municipal district	85	100	5.11	50	65	4.06	20	35	3.16
Haimen	111	126	4.33	75	90	3.25	50	65	2.5

Note: both the cost coefficient for transportation and the carbon emission coefficient for transportation contain the collection of straw in the sub-region and transporting the straw from the sub-regions to the plant site.

According to the assumptions presented above and the model given in this paper, we present results as shown in Table 3, making the number of φ 0.5. The minimum transportation cost of the plant is estimated to be about 8735 thousand RMB yuan. The price of straw at the plant is nearly 200 RMB yuan/ton. The total carbon emission during the transportation is about 963.04 ton C (carbon). Candidate Site 3 is the best choice for the straw-based power generation plant to be built. Therefore, the electric power group should build the straw-based power generation plant at the candidate site in Rudong County to get the best economic benefits and the least carbon emissions.

Table 4. The result of the model for the case study (units: 10,000 tons).

	Candidate Site 1 (y1 = 0)	Candidate Site 2 (y2 = 0)	Candidate Site 3 (y3 = 1)
Dongtai	x11 = 0	x12 = 0	x13 = 0
Hai'an	x21 = 0	x22 = 0	x23 = 0
Rugao	x31 = 0	x32 = 0	x33 = 3.1
Rudong	x41 = 0	x42 = 0	x43 = 12.9
Taixing	x51 = 0	x52 = 0	x53 = 0
Municipal District	x61 = 0	x62 = 0	x63 = 8.4
Haimen	x71 = 0	x72 = 0	x73 = 2.6
The demand of the site	D1 = 0	D2 = 0	D3 = 27

Compared with the model given by Matt Kocoloski *et al.*, in which the optimal site for the straw-based power generation plant in this case is also Site 3, the model presented in this paper considers the impacts of carbon emissions. In these two models' results, Site 1 is preferable to Site 2. However, if taking Objective 2 as the only objective of the model, we would choose Site 2 as the optimal selection for the plant. When the weight of Objective 1 (φ) is less than 0.4 in this case, Site 2 would be preferable to Site 1 by the results of our model.

One of the key parameters having an influence on the total cost of the straw-based power generation plant is the price of straw. Take the municipal district as an example. The price of straw could be higher than other sub-regions. When the price of straw in the municipal district is 25 RMB yuan/ton higher than those in other sub-regions, the optimal site will remain as Site 3. When the price of straw in the municipal district is 26 RMB yuan/ton higher than in other sub-regions, the optimal site will be Site 1.

It can be recognized from the results of the case study that Rudong County has the most biomass straw production in Nantong. It is also the best choice of the three candidate sites for the straw-based power generation to be located. Taking both the economic benefit and carbon emissions of the plant into consideration, we can infer that the total transportation cost and carbon emissions of the straw's transportation and collection are usually determined by the transportation process of straw between sub-regions. It also proves that the acquisition range of straw has a great influence on both the straw-based power generation's economic benefit and total carbon emission. The straw-based power generation technology is a kind of resource-oriented technology. In the location decision for the biomass power generation, the supply abilities of the sub-regions should be adequately considered.

5. Conclusions

Biomass power generation is currently a mature and reliable technology for utilizing this renewable energy source. A biomass power generation plant's economic benefit and carbon emission are both influenced by the supply of straw fuel. Without sufficient straw supply, the plant's performance may be quite poor, the economic benefit may be negative and the carbon emissions may be larger than expected. This problem can be avoided by the location decision of the plant. This paper studied a solution to site selection for a biomass power generation plant. It introduces the objective of minimizing the total carbon emissions into the traditional site selection model. A linear multi-objective integer program model was then developed to get the best location for the plant.

Sustainability **2014**, *6*, 7466–7481

Through the case study, an example shows how to apply the model to make the location decision. We find that when the weight of the carbon emission optimization objective is large enough, the results of our model will be different from those of models considering only economic benefits. This further demonstrates that carbon emissions really have a great influence on the site selection of the straw-based power generation plant. We also find from the results that the transportation of straw between sub-regions has more influence on the straw-based power generation total cost and total carbon emissions than the straw's collection and transportation in sub-regions. This conclusion also demonstrates that the straw acquisition range is a determining factor for the straw-based power generation plant's performance. During the location decision, we need to take full consideration of the straw fuel supply abilities of the sub-regions.

Acknowledgments: The authors gratefully acknowledge the financial support provided by the Natural Science Foundation of China (No. 71203151 and 71373122), the Jiangsu Natural Science Foundation for Distinguished Young Scholar (No. BK20140038), the Ph.D. Programs Foundation of the Ministry of Education of China (No. 20123218110028), the NUAA fundamental research fund (No. NE2013104), and the major project in college's key research base for Philosophy and Social Science in Jiangsu Province (No. 2010JDXM012).

Author Contributions: All of the authors made contributions to the work in this paper. Hao Lv proposed the idea and partly contributed to the model development. Hao Ding contributed to model development, data collection and analysis. Dequn Zhou contributed to policy analysis and formulation. Peng Zhou provided guidance for writing this paper. Hao Lv and Hao Ding were the main authors for the writing of this paper.

Conflicts of Interest: The authors declare no conflict of interest.

References

1. World Energy Council (WEC). World Energy Resources (2013 survey). Available online: http://www.worldenergy.org/publications/2013/world-energy-resources-2013-survey/ (accessed on 24 September 2014).
2. International Energy Agency (IEA). World Energy Outlook 2013-Chapter 6: Renewable Energy Outlook. Available online: http://www.worldenergyoutlook.org/publications/weo-2013/ (accessed on 24 September 2014).
3. China Renewable Energy Engineering Institute, China National Renewable Energy Center. *Statistic Report on China's Biomass Power Generation Development in 2013*; China Renewable Energy Engineering Institute & China National Renewable Energy Center: Beijing, China, 2014.
4. Zhang, Q.; Zhou, D.Q.; Zhou, P.; Ding, H. Cost Analysis of Straw-based Power Generation in Jiangsu Province, China. *Appl. Energy* **2013**, *102*, 785–793. [CrossRef]
5. Chen, L. Analysis on the problems of biomass power generation power generation in China. *Decision-Making Consult.* **2012**, *1*, 18–24. (In Chinese)
6. Qi, T.; Zhang, X.; Ou, X.; Liu, Z.; Chang, S. The regional cost of biomass direct combustion power generation in China and development potential analysis. *Renew. Energy Resour.* **2011**, *29*, 115–124. (In Chinese)
7. Zhao, L. Research of Planning and Site Selection Method of Straw Burning Power Plant. Master's Thesis, North China Electric Power University, Beijing, China, 2012.
8. Guo, Z.; Hodges, D.G.; Young, T.M. Woody biomass policies and location decisions of the woody bioenergy industry in the southern United States. *Biomass Bioenergy* **2013**, *56*, 268–273. [CrossRef]
9. Leduc, S.; Schwab, D.; Dotzauer, E.; Schmid, E.; Obersteiner, M. Optimal location of wood gasification plants for methanol production with heat recovery. *Int. J. Energy Res.* **2008**, *32*, 1080–1091. [CrossRef]
10. Shabani, N.; Sowlati, T. A mixed integer non-linear programming model for tactical value chain optimization of a wood biomass power plant. *Appl. Energy* **2013**, *104*, 353–361. [CrossRef]
11. Kocoloski, W.M.; Griffin, H.M.; Matthews, S. Impacts of facility size and location decisions on ethanol production cost. *Energy Policy* **2011**, *39*, 45–76. [CrossRef]
12. Dong, C.; Li, W.; Li, Y.; Xie, Y.; Cui, L. Establishment of optimization model for location of biomass power plants and its application. *Acta Energy Sol. Sin.* **2012**, *33*, 1732–1737. (In Chinese)
13. Chen, C.; Li, W.; Li, Y.; Zhu, Y. Biomass power plant site selection modeling and decision optimization. *Trans. CSAE* **2011**, *27*, 255–230. (In Chinese)

14. Renewable Energy Database. National Bureau of Statistics of China. Available online: http://red.renewable. org.cn:9080/RED/index.action (accessed on 28 August 2014).

15. Asadullah, M. Biomass gasification gas cleaning for downstream applications: A comparative critical review. *Renew. Sustain. Energy Rev.* **2014**, *40*, 118–132. [CrossRef]

16. Wright, D.G.; Dey, P.K.; Brammer, J. A barrier and techno-economic analysis of small-scale Bchp (biomass combined heat and power) schemes in the UK. *Energy* **2014**, *71*, 332–345. [CrossRef]

17. Song, Y. Technical and economic analyse of biomass power generation. Master's Thesis, Henan Agriculture University, Zhengzhou, China, 2010.

18. Wang, X.; Cai, Y.; Dai, C. Evaluating China's biomass power production investment based on a policy benefit real options model. *Energy* **2014**, *73*, 751–761. [CrossRef]

19. Algieri, A.; Morrone, P. Techno-economic analysis of biomass-fired ORC systems for single-family combined heat and power (CHP) applications. *Energy Procedia* **2014**, *45*, 1285–1294. [CrossRef]

20. Bouchard, S.; Landry, M.; Gagnon, Y. Methodology for the large scale assessment of the technical power potential of forest biomass: Application to the province of New Brunswick, Canada. *Biomass Bioenergy* **2013**, *54*, 1–17. [CrossRef]

21. Nikolaos, G.T.; Petros, A.P.; Apostolos, L.P. An economic comparison assessment of lignite and biomass IGCC power plants. *Appl. Therm. Eng.* **2012**, *38*, 26–30. [CrossRef]

22. Chen, L.; Li, Y.; Ding, W.; Liu, J.; Shen, B. Analysis on straw logistics cost of direct-fired power generation using activity-based costing. *Trans. CSAE* **2012**, *28*, 199–203. (In Chinese)

23. Rogers, J.G.; Brammer, J.G. Analysis of transport costs for energy crops for use in biomass pyrolysis plant networks. *Biomass Bioenergy* **2009**, *33*, 1367–1375. [CrossRef]

24. Ruiz, J.A.; Juárez, M.C.; Morales, M.P.; Muñoz, P.; Mendívil, M.A. Biomass logistics: Financial & environmental costs. Case study: 2 MW electrical power plants. *Biomass Bioenergy* **2013**, *56*, 260–267. [CrossRef]

25. Delivand, M.K.; Barz, M.; Gheewala, S.H. Logistics cost analysis of rice straw for biomass power generation in Thailand. *Energy* **2011**, *36*, 1435–1441. [CrossRef]

26. Cao, G.; Zhang, X.; Wang, Y.; Zheng, F. Estimation of regional carbon emissions from the crop straw's open firing in agriculture field in China. *Chin. Sci. Bull.* **2007**, *52*, 1826–1831.

27. He, Z.; Wu, C.; Yin, X. Carbon cycle analysis of biomass power generation system. *Acta Energiae Sol. Sin.* **2008**, *29*, 705–710. (In Chinese)

28. Feng, C.; Ma, X. Life cycle assessment of the straw generation by direct combustion. *Acta Energ. Sol. Sin.* **2008**, *29*, 711–715. (In Chinese)

29. Li, Y.; Li, J. A study on calculation method of carbon emission in power generation with biomass. *Energy Environ. Prot.* **2012**, *26*, 5–8. (In Chinese)

30. Amit, T.A.; Canter, C.E.; Kumar, A. Life-cycle energy and emission analysis of power generation from forest biomass. *Appl. Energy* **2014**, *128*, 246–253. [CrossRef]

31. Zhang, Q.; Zhou, D. Analysis on Present Situation of Generating Electricity by Burning Straw in Jiangsu Province. *China Soft Sci.* **2010**, *10*, 104–111. (In Chinese)

32. Rentizelas, A.A.; Tolis, A.J.; Tatsiopoulos, I.P. Logistics issues of biomass: The storage problem and the multi-biomass supply chain. *Renew. Sustain. Energy Rev.* **2009**, *13*, 887–894. [CrossRef]

sustainability

MDPI

Article

Chinese Public Willingness to Pay to Avoid Having Nuclear Power Plants in the Neighborhood

Chuanwang Sun [1], Nan Lyu [1] and Xiaoling Ouyang [2,*]

[1] Collaborative Innovation Center for Energy Economics and Energy Policy, School of Economics, Xiamen University, Xiamen 361005, China; scw@xmu.edu.cn (C.S.); barcelonana@126.com (N.L.)
[2] Department of Economics, Business School, East China Normal University, 500 Dongchuan Road, Shanghai 200241, China
* Author to whom correspondence should be addressed; xlouyang@jjx.ecnu.edu.cn; Tel./Fax: +86-21-5434-4958.

External Editor: Ning Zhang

Received: 30 July 2014; Accepted: 23 September 2014; Published: 18 October 2014

Abstract: In spite of the decreasing share of nuclear power all over the world, China resumed the approval of large-scale construction of nuclear power plants in 2012. However, influenced by the worldwide spreading anti-nuclear attitudes, people who live near nuclear power plants showed increasing concerns about nuclear risks. Consequently, the Not In My Backyard (NIMBY) syndrome of nuclear power plants should be evaluated prudently to support the healthy development of nuclear power in China. Based on the face-to-face survey data, this study estimates Chinese public willingness to pay (WTP) to avoid having nuclear power plants in the neighborhood. The respondents include both residents who currently live near and those who would live near nuclear power plants in the future. Considering the possible presence of the sample selection bias caused by protest responses, this paper constructs a two-step sample selection model with the protest responses and the double bounded dichotomous choice (DBDC) questions. Using the Contingent Valuation Method (CVM), we measure the effects of influencing factors of public WTP and study the decay of WTP with longer distances from nuclear power plants. The results suggest that most people are willing to pay higher electricity prices to avoid having nuclear power plants in the neighborhood. Comparing the WTP to avoid having nuclear power plants nearby with the current electricity price, we find that there is an increase of 56.7% and 69.1% of respondents' WTP for a nuclear power plant located 80 km and 30 km, respectively.

Keywords: Not In My Backyard (NIMBY); nuclear power; Contingent Valuation Method (CVM); sustainability

1. Introduction

The Fukushima nuclear disaster in 2011 has made severe social, political and economic impacts worldwide, making nuclear power come to the fore as threats to global society [1,2]. Opinion polls show that public support for nuclear power has declined dramatically since the Fukushima nuclear disaster [3]. Public attitude towards nuclear power has played an important role in energy policy-making since the accident, and has made public rejection towards nuclear power a critical problem for nuclear policy all over the world [4], especially for countries with a high density of nuclear power reactors and extensive operational experience of nuclear power plants [5]. Most public protests can be attributed to the Not In My Backyard (NIMBY) attitude regarding nuclear power facilities. This phenomenon, which has been widely reported [6–9], is the case that the construction of new nuclear facilities is often strongly opposed by residents who live in the neighborhood [10]. Due to the sharp decline of public acceptance, the share of nuclear power in electricity generation decreased from

16.8% in 2011 to 13.5% in 2012 [11]. For example, Japan has shut all 50 nuclear power plants down. Countries such as Germany, Switzerland and Belgium have confirmed the closing-down policies under the public pressure [12].

By contrast, China has the most ambitious nuclear expansion plan after the Fukushima nuclear disaster [13]. The government has showed determinations to accelerate the development of nuclear power. Specifically, by the end of 2014, China would increase 8.64 gigawatt-electric (GWe) of nuclear power installed capacity, three times the increment in 2013 [14]. According to the National Nuclear Long-and-medium Term Development Planning (2011–2020) [15], China plans to realize 88 GWe of nuclear power installed capacity by 2020. This goal implies that nuclear power in China will exceed the total electricity consumption in Canada in 2012 [16]. More long-term plans for future capacity are 200 GWe by 2030 and 400 GWe by 2050 [17]. Most of China's nuclear power reactors are located in the coastal regions, which involves only 5.8% of the whole population [18] and small towns and cities. In addition, nuclear power generation only accounts for 2.1% of total power generation in China [19], far below the world average level (11%) [20]. According to the research by Nature News in cooperation with Columbia University [21], 75 million people live near 49 nuclear power reactors in China, which includes nuclear power plants under construction and in operation, and the distances are in the range of 75 kilometers (km). Different from the anti-nuclear activities in other countries, in the past, nuclear power plants did not have a wide impact in China in view of the large population base and vast land. However, we should note that China is currently facing a rapid nuclear power expansion (13 times the current installed nuclear power capacity by 2050) [22]. Considering that the nuclear power installed capacity will be twice as great as before, and China will expand nuclear power from coastal to inland regions in the near future, the number of residents who live near nuclear power plants will have a rapid growth. After the Fukushima nuclear disaster, the voice of anti-nuclear seems to be louder, especially from those who live in the neighborhood. People living nearby have, apparently, shown their anxiety [23]. There have been several anti-nuclear activities in local areas in recent years, which have affected the attitude of people who live in other places of China. Hence, a concern is provoked that China's nuclear expansion could possibly lead to a more severe NIMBY attitude among the public, as more residents and regions will be affected. This attitude in turn may have a negative impact on nuclear power expansion in the future. To summarize, studies of Chinese public willingness to pay to avoid having nuclear power stations in the neighborhood are believed to be mandatory.

The NIMBY phenomena are highly complex, representing a wide range of facilities and participants [24]. There are definite regulations about the location and safe distance of NIMBY facilities in many countries [25], but evaluation of safety distance by residents in terms of the vicinity of the facilities is always greater than that identified by the government. Similar to nuclear power plants, paraxylene (PX, a chemical essential) plants are also NIMBY facilities, which have been strongly opposed by the general public in China in recent years. PX plants are common in many countries [26], which are usually kept 4 km away from the city center in Korea [27], and 5 km from the city center in Singapore [28]. However, a planned PX project with a distance of 7 km from the city center in Xiamen was stopped because of the public protest. This phenomenon shows that the distance by regulation doesn't fall in line with the accepted distance by the public. In this context, this study tries to find out how the public reacts to the location of a new nuclear power plant in the distance of 30 km and 80 km separately, based on data from the survey of China's Public Perception of Nuclear Power (CPPNP). The survey of CPPNP, launched by China Center for Energy Economics Research at Xiamen University once or twice a year from 2013, is a nationwide face-to-face survey focuses on the public perception of nuclear power.

This paper attempts to answer three questions as follows:

First, is there a NIMBY attitude towards nuclear power plants among residents in China, including both the residents who currently live near and those who will live near the plants in the future? How do socio-economic characteristics, such as income, age and gender, affect Chinese public willingness to pay to avoid having nuclear power stations in the neighborhood?

Second, will residents show different WTP at different construction phases of the NIMBY facilities? In our study, we explore this by evaluating and comparing the WTP of residents who live in coastal areas where nuclear power plants have already constructed, and those who live in inland areas where nuclear power plants would be built in the future.

Third, how does the public WTP change with the dwelling distance from nuclear power plants? What's the residents' estimated safety distance from nuclear power plants? Does the safety distance accepted by the public fall in line with that regulated by the government?

The remainder of this paper is organized as follows. Section 2 reviews the main research on NIMBY of nuclear power plants and the evaluation methods of WTP. Section 3 describes the data from CPPNP and the methodological approach used in this study, which corrects the possible selection bias due to protest responses. Section 4 presents the empirical results, in which we analyze public WTP by answering the three questions above. Finally, Section 5 provides conclusions and gives policy suggestions.

2. Literature Review

2.1. Research of Public Attitude towards Nuclear Power

Considering the global environmental and economic development [29,30], nuclear energy has been attached worldwide attention to its impacts on greenhouse gases emissions reduction [13,31,32]. However, the Fukushima nuclear disaster reminds the public to refocus on the risks of nuclear power [33], and pay more attention to nuclear policies [34]. Plenty of research has investigated risk perceptions associated with nuclear power [1,25,35–37]. For example, Kim *et al.* [35] examined the effects of knowledge, trust, risk and benefit-related factors on the public acceptance of nuclear power across 19 countries, and found that trust in inspection authorities was crucial for the decision between opposition and reluctant acceptance. Some researchers analyzed the nuclear energy policies and strategies in the future [12,38–43]. Aoki and Rothwell [39] analyzed the causes, responses and consequences of the Fukushima nuclear disaster by comparing them with those of the Three Mile Island and the Chernobyl, and suggested the introduction of an independent Nuclear Safety Commission. Other scholars explored the public acceptance and change of attitudes toward nuclear power and other renewable energy [44–46]. For instance, using a longitudinal study design, Siegrist and Visschers [44] found that the Fukushima nuclear disaster had a negative impact on the acceptance of nuclear power.

NIMBY is an important public attitude, which has attracted increasing attentions from scholars. The NIMBY syndrome is an evidence for the opposition to the local siting of nearly all-environmental and technological hazards [47]. The public attitude of NIMBY indicates that certain services are in principle beneficial to the majority of the population, but are in practice often strongly opposed by local residents who live near the proposed facilities [48]. Since China has resumed the approval of new nuclear power plants, the NIMBY attitude about nuclear power would be an urgent problem for China. Research about public attitudes toward nuclear power after the Fukushima nuclear disaster is relatively scarce in China. He *et al.* [10] analyzed public participation and trust in nuclear power development by investigating residents who live near the Haiyang nuclear power plant in China. Results indicated that the Chinese respondents had a high level of trust in governmental authorities rather than in nuclear power companies and the media. Results also demonstrated that respondents with lower levels of education were more convinced by government information and had more confidence in government response capacities. Zhang and Tong [49] comprehensively analyzed factors that affect NIMBY attitude towards nuclear power plants, and showed that residents who lived near nuclear power plants had strong NIMBY attitudes after the Fukushima nuclear disaster, and the main concerns included health risk, long-term risks and economic benefits. Studies of both He *et al.* [10] and Zhang and Tong [49] only focused on residents who live near the existing nuclear power plants and excluded residents who lived far away from the plants. With the rapid development of nuclear power, some residents who currently live far away from the plants may be adjacent to the plants in the future; hence, it is inaccurate to measure public perceptions with only residents who live near the nuclear power plants. Our study tries to contribute to literatures by including both residents in the evaluation of public WTP to avoid having nuclear power stations in the neighborhood. Although Zhang and Tong [49] explored the respondents' perception on the distances of nuclear power plants, they paid more attention to affecting factors of the living distance. Our study also tries to figure out the change of WTP with longer living distances to analyze the relationship between the living distance and NIMBY attitude more precisely.

2.2. Methods of Testing the NIMBY Syndrome

Few studies covered the issue of NIMBY syndrome after the Fukushima nuclear disaster [50]. Before that, plenty of studies had investigated the WTP to avoid having NIMBY facilities constructed in the neighborhood [51]. The analysis methods can be divided into two categories: the qualitative attitude analysis and the quantitative numerical estimate.

Many scholars analyzed the NIMBY syndrome by attitude analysis [25,48,52], of which, the investigations covered many aspects including the public risk perception, the cognition degree, distance, and individual characteristics such as age, gender, income, education, and so on. Qualitative attitude analysis is a basic analysis in the research of NIMBY syndrome, which directly collects and truly presents respondents' attitudes with little bias. Conclusions of the above studies showed how distance affects residents' attitude towards the NIMBY facilities. Several studies showed that people who lived near the nuclear power plant of Three Mile Island had stronger stress reactions than people who lived far away [53,54]. Huppe and Weber [52] found an inverted U-shaped relationship between the strength of opposition towards nuclear power plants and the distance of dwelling place to the plant. The above studies focused on residents who lived near the nuclear power plants for many years, but overlooked the time factor (which is a key element that differentiates public attitudes [55]). More research showed that opposition would be the strongest at the planning phase, and would be weaker before a project was proposed or after the facility was in operation [56]. The apparent "gap" in attitudes between "before" and "during" the planning of a local project is a key problem [57]. Hence, our study selects samples including both the areas with nuclear power plants and those nuclear power plants will be built in the future.

Researchers also tried to quantify the NIMBY syndrome and evaluate the scale and intensity of protests provoked by facilities that perceived to be risky [58]. They made use of property values or willingness to pay (WTP)/willingness to accept (WTA) of the public [59–61]. For example, Ansolabehere and Konisky [51] measured the public attitude towards nuclear power construction, and found that most Americans oppose having nuclear power plants in their neighborhood. Gawande and Jenkins-Smith [62] found that being five miles away from a nuclear waste shipment route means a 3% increase of average house value compared to properties right on the route. However, Zweifel *et al.* [63] questioned the approach of testing the NIMBY syndrome based on real estate property values. They pointed out that the estimates of individual WTP based on the analysis of the compensating differentials found in market data would be distorted and incomplete, because market prices depend on demand and supply, which in turn made the results affected by zoning laws and building regulations. Therefore, the Contingent Valuation Method (CVM) had been used by researchers to estimate public willingness to pay (WTP) or willingness to accept (WTA) [63–65]. CVM is a method designed to elicit preference [66]. It is a stated-preference valuation method that directly surveys individuals or households to estimate the values of non-market goods or services [64]. Respondents are asked to state their WTP for an improvement of a public good (*i.e.*, environmental quality) or the avoidance of a public "bad" (*i.e.*, risks or pollution) in a hypothetical market. In this way, researches can evaluate some non-market goods such as public defense, environmental amenities, death risks reduction and so on [67]. Zweifel *et al.* [63] investigated residents' WTP for risk reduction of nuclear power plants nearby, and found a linear relation between the WTP and the distance. Studies about waste disposal facilities mainly focused on the WTP analysis to quantify NIMBY. For instance, Ferreira and Gallagher [64] chose the WTP and the WTA to analyze using host community compensation to solve the NIMBY issue, and found that the WTP was lower than the WTA. Pelekasi *et al.* [68] presented a contingent valuation survey aimed at investigating a local community's willingness to accept (WTA) compensation for allowing the establishment and operation of a marble quarry nearby and exploring the determinants of NIMBY reactions against the marble quarrying activity. Zhou *et al.* [65] focused on residents' WTA of the compensation in waste incineration facilities in China. They emphasized that standardized management, publicity mechanism, and whole-process supervision should be built. In this way, the ecological compensation can turn the NIMBY attitude into acceptance. According to the previous studies on the WTP, factors, such as gender, age, income, education, distance, risk perception, trust, *etc.*, have effects on the public WTP. Therefore, our study chooses some of these factors to investigate how they affect Chinese WTP to avoid having nuclear power plants in the neighborhood. Table 1 shows results of relative research publications briefly.

Table 1. Main previous research publications of the NIMBY syndrome.

Author	Country	Method	Factor	Result
Huppe and Weber [32]	Germany	Attitude analysis	Distance, Age, Gender	An inverted U-shaped relationship between firmness of negative attitudes toward nuclear power plants and the distance of dwelling to the plant.
Gawande and Jenkins-Smith [62]	US	Hedonic model	Distance, Age of residence, Race, Education, Income, *etc.*	Being five miles away from a nuclear waste shipment route was associated with a 3% increase of average house value compared to the property on the route.
Zweifel *et al.* [63]	Switzerland	WTP	Distance, Attitude, Gender, Income, *etc.*	For residents who live at the power plant, the maximum of lifetime WTP is $2280. It decreases by $24 per km, or $15 per mile.
Van der Horst [48]	UK	Attitude analysis	Distance, Time, *etc.*	Proximity does have a strong influence on public attitudes toward the proposed NIMBY projects. However, the nature, strength and spatial scale of this effect may vary according to the local context and value of the land.
Greenberg [25]	US	Attitude analysis	Distance, Age, Race, Worry, Trust, Income, *etc.*	More than half of the respondents who live near the nuclear power plants oppose constructing more nuclear power plants nearby.
Ferreira and Gallagher [64]	Ireland	WTP/WTA	Gender, Occupation, Dwelling breakdown, Education, *etc.*	The rejection rates for WTA CV study with between 78% and 91.5% of respondents rejecting the offer of compensation. Most rejections are protest responses (which range between 65% and 90.3% of the zero responses).
Zhang and Tong [49]	China	Regression analysis	Distance, Age, Gender, Education, Risk, Benefit, *etc.*	80.2% of respondents were against nuclear power construction in their neighborhood; 78.7% of respondents proposed that nuclear power plants should be constructed in other provinces which are far away from the places they live; 33.1% of respondents planed to relocate if there were nuclear power plants in their neighborhood. Health risks, long-term hazards and benefits are three critical factors of their concerns.

Quantitative numerical estimates of the Chinese public WTP to avoid having nuclear power plants in the neighborhood are still scarce. We intend to make contributions to literature in this filed. In this paper, we analyze residents' WTP for other high-cost clean energies [69] to replace nuclear power. Since respondents have to be definite about their WTP, they are required to be more rational in measuring both the risks and benefits of nuclear power plants. Unlike the previous efforts to quantify the NIMBY syndrome, our study explores the decay of NIMBY associated with distance to analyze the difference between public acceptable living distance and the distance proposed by safety regulations of nuclear power. Considering that the inevitable NIMBY attitudes at the planning phase, we collect samples in the areas where nuclear power plants will be built in the future to compare their NIMBY attitudes with those of the respondents who currently live near nuclear power plants. Our study can also be an important reference for further studies about the time factor of NIMBY, as well as a part of the temporal extent of studies with regard to nuclear power plants (before people are informed about the plan, during the planning process, or after the plant has in operation) [48].

It should be noted that Contingent Valuation Method (CVM) typically uses survey techniques to elicit individuals' willingness to pay (WTP) for the hypothetical provision of a public good (or environmental good) or willingness to accept (WTA) compensation for the hypothetical loss of this good. Both of the estimation methods are common. Literature, such as Saz-Salazar *et al.* [60] and Carson [61], has compared WTA and WTP in detail. The data used in this paper are from the CPPNP, which gathers information by asking questions of WTP.

3. Methods and Data

3.1. Two-Step Sample Selection Model

CPPNP is a systematic survey of public attitudes about nuclear power in China (The specific introduction of CPPNP can be found in Appendix A). The survey of CPPNP uses dichotomous choice (DC) format questions to obtain the WTP for replacing nuclear power nearby, because the DC format has been frequently used in the literature [70]. Respondents may refuse to accept bids for elicitation questions for reasons that differ from the genuine zeros [71,72]. Considering the possible presence of the sample selection bias caused by protest responses, this paper constructs a two-step sample selection model with the protest responses and the double bounded dichotomous choice (DBDC) questions.

Protest responses can be reflected by a system of two-step sequential questions in the survey of CPPNP. The first-step is that, before asking the DBDC question, we ask each respondent an initial question (sample selection question, SSQ), which is, if he or she were willing to use other clean energies to replace nuclear power stations in his or her neighborhood by paying higher electricity tariffs (The specific structure of the questionnaire can be found in Appendix A). After obtaining answers of the first question from the respondents, we set two situations in the second-step. One situation is that if the respondents replied "Yes" to the first question, a follow up DBDC question would be posed to elicit the WTP. That is, the respondents should reply that whether their WTP equals or exceeds a sequence of two bids. If respondents' WTP is lower than the first bid, investigators will ask the question again with a smaller bid. On the contrary, if the WTP were equal to or higher than the first bid, the second bid would be higher. The other situation is that if the respondents replied "No" to the first question, investigators would further inquire the motives behind their answers. The above treatment can be used to determine whether the respondents are with genuine zeros or with protest responses (The specific questions can be found in Appendix A). Finally, we discuss the difference between the WTP of nuclear power plants located 80 km and the WTP of nuclear power plants located 30 km in the neighborhood. Figure 1 illustrates the process of the two-step sample selection.

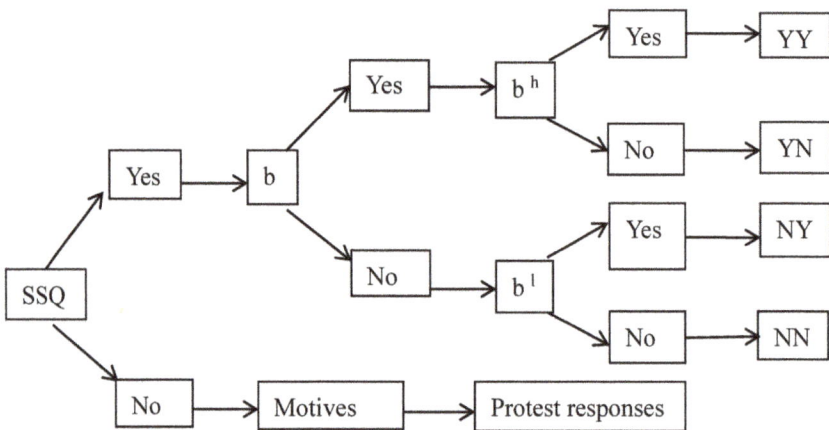

Figure 1. The schematic diagram of sample selection and DBDC questions.

According to studies of Heckman [73], Calia and Strazzera [74], and Ramajo-Hernández and Saz-Salazar [72], two-step sequential questions can be modeled by the following two equations: the first one is the selection equation, and the second one is the elicitation equation.

For each respondent, the binary variable Y_i can be defined by the selection equation, which represents whether or not the respondent i has protest responses. In turn, the latent variable Y_1^* can be represented:

$$Y_i = \begin{cases} 1, & \text{if } Y_i^* \geq 0, \ i \text{ without protest responses} \\ 0, & \text{if } Y_i^* < 0, \ i \text{ with protest responses} \end{cases} \tag{1}$$

$$Y_i^* = \alpha_1 + w_i'\gamma + v_i \tag{2}$$

where α_1 is the constant item in the selection equation, vector w_i represents factors that influence the probability of giving protest responses from respondents, and γ is the vector of estimated parameter in the selection equation. According the pilot study for the pre-test survey, we commonly assume that the error term v_i has a normal distribution with mean zero [73], thus, the selection equation of Y_i is the probit model, and $P(Y_i = 1|\alpha_1, w_i) = \Phi(\alpha_1 + w_i'\gamma)$.

We define that the WTP_i represents the willingness to pay of each respondent, and whether the WTP_i can be observed depends on whether Y_1 equals 1.

$$WTP_i = \begin{cases} \text{Observable}, & \text{if } Y_i = 1 \\ \text{Unobservable}, & \text{if } Y_i = 0 \end{cases} \tag{3}$$

The zero choice of Y_i is a threshold for the available data of WTP_i.

The WTP function (elicitation equation) are represented below:

$$WTP_i = \alpha_2 + z_i'\beta + u_i \tag{4}$$

In that case, the respondent will say "Yes" only when his true WTP_i is higher than the given bid. α_2 is the constant item in the elicitation equation, z_i is a vector of explanatory variables affecting the value of WTP_i, β is a vector of parameters, the error term u_i has a normal distribution with mean zero.

Considering the sample selection bias caused by protest responses, the conditional expectation can be expressed as:

$$\begin{aligned} E(WTP_i|\text{Observable}) &= E(WTP_i|Y_i^* \geq 0) \\ &= E(\alpha_2 + z_i'\beta + u_i|\alpha_1 + w_i'\gamma + v_i > 0) \\ &= E(\alpha_2 + z_i'\beta + u_i|v_i > -\alpha_1 - w_i'\gamma) \\ &= \alpha_2 + z_i'\beta + E(u_i|v_i > -\alpha_1 - w_i'\gamma) \end{aligned} \tag{5}$$

Under the assumption that the error terms are jointly normal, and according to the expectation formula of incidental truncation [74], we have:

$$E(WTP_i|Y_i^* \geq 0) = \alpha_2 + z_i'\beta + \rho\sigma_u\lambda(-\alpha_1 - w_i'\gamma) \tag{6}$$

where ρ is the correlation between u_i and v_i, σ_u is the standard deviation of u, and $\lambda(-\alpha_1 - w_i'\gamma)$ is the Inverse Mill's Ratio (IMR).

Obviously, under the condition of taking the sample selection bias into consideration, if we use $E(WTP_i) = \alpha_2 + z_i'\beta$ directly to estimate the sample data, the omitted item $\rho\sigma_u\lambda(-\alpha_1 - w_i'\gamma)$ will be resulted. Generally, w_i and z_i will include the same variables, therefore, they may probably correlated. Only under the condition of $\rho = 0$, estimates can be consistent by directly estimating the elicitation equation of the omitted item IMR. Therefore, it is necessary to use the two-step sample selection model and address the possible presence of self-selection caused by protest responses [72].

The specific estimation method for the two-step sample selection model is as follows: the first step is obtaining α_1 and γ by estimating the selection equation $P(Y_i = 1|\alpha_1, w_i) = \Phi(\alpha_1 + w_i'\gamma)$, and

$\lambda(\cdot)$ (IMR); the second step is estimating the elicitation equation and including $\lambda(\cdot)$ as an additional explanatory variable. Therefore, the elicitation equation can be rewritten as the following format. And testing the null that the coefficient θ on $\lambda(\cdot)$ is zero is equivalent to testing for sample selection bias.

$$WTP_i = \alpha_2 + z_i'\beta + \theta\lambda(\cdot) + u_i \qquad (7)$$

The elicitation question in this paper adopts the DBDC format. According to Liao *et al.* [75] and Jun *et al.* [76], the bid price is offered twice in the DBDC question model, and the second bid price is determined by the answer of the first bid b. If the answer is "Yes" for the first question, a higher bid b^h will be given; otherwise, a lower bid b^l will be given.

In this way, there are four categories of WTP:

(1) The answers are both "No" for two bids: $WTP < b^l$, P_{NN} is the corresponding probability.
(2) The answer is "No" for the first bid, and "Yes" for the second bid: $b^l \leq WTP < b$, P_{NY} is the corresponding probability.
(3) The answer is "Yes" for the first bid, and "No" for the second bid: $b \leq WTP < b^h$, P_{YN} is the corresponding probability.
(4) The answers are both "Yes" for both the first and the second bids: $b^h \leq WTP < \infty$, P_{YY} is the corresponding probability.

Since u_i with a normal distribution, the DBDC elicitation equation can be estimated by the Probit model which includes the additional explanatory variables b, b^h and b^l. The probability functions are denoted as:

$$
\begin{aligned}
P_{NN} &= 1 - \Phi\left(\frac{\alpha_2 + z_i'\beta + \theta\lambda(\cdot)}{\sigma_u} - \frac{b^l}{\sigma_u}\right) \\
P_{NY} &= \Phi\left(\frac{\alpha_2 + z_i'\beta + \theta\lambda(\cdot)}{\sigma_u} - \frac{b^l}{\sigma_u}\right) - \Phi\left(\frac{\alpha_2 + z_i'\beta + \theta\lambda(\cdot)}{\sigma_u} - \frac{b}{\sigma_u}\right) \\
P_{YN} &= \Phi\left(\frac{\alpha_2 + z_i'\beta + \theta\lambda(\cdot)}{\sigma_u} - \frac{b}{\sigma_u}\right) - \Phi\left(\frac{\alpha_2 + z_i'\beta + \theta\lambda(\cdot)}{\sigma_u} - \frac{b^h}{\sigma_u}\right) \\
P_{YY} &= \Phi\left(\frac{\alpha_2 + z_i'\beta + \theta\lambda(\cdot)}{\sigma_u} - \frac{b^h}{\sigma_u}\right)
\end{aligned}
\qquad (8)
$$

Here, we obtain the estimated parameters using the maximum likelihood estimation (MLE). The log-likelihood function that needs to be maximized is:

$$\ln L = \sum_{i=1}^{N} \left(I_i^{YY} \ln P_{YY} + I_i^{YN} \ln P_{YN} + I_i^{NY} \ln P_{NY} + I_i^{NN} \ln P_{NN} \right) \qquad (9)$$

where $I_i^{YY}, I_i^{YN}, I_i^{NY}, I_i^{NN}$ are index variables, which will be 1 when the answer from respondent i is "Yes"-"Yes", "Yes"-"No", "No"-"Yes", "No"-"No" to each bid price, respectively; otherwise, will be zero. Once the estimated parameters are obtained, we can estimate the fitted value of WTP (for a detailed description of the DBDC model, please see Jun *et al.* [76]).

3.2. Variables and Data Source

Variables and data used in this paper are based on the survey of CPPNP, of which the main structure can be found in Appendix A. The explanatory variables in this study include the socio-economic characteristics of respondents such as gender, age, educational level (have a bachelor degree or not), income level, job (a civil servant or not), and whether the concerns of nuclear power come from the subjective pressures. The explanatory variables and their main descriptive statistics are listed in Table 2. These characteristics are considered being related with respondents' protest responses and the WTP. The gender ratio is kept close to balance with 52.19% of male and 47.81% of female. The size of the sample is 799.

Table 2. Explanatory variable descriptions and statistics.

Variable	Description	Mean	Standard deviation	Min	Max
Gender	Dummy variable (male = 1)	0.522	0.500	0	1
Age	Respondents' age	35.73	8.469	18	65
College	Dummy variable (have a bachelor degree = 1)	0.427	0.495	0	1
Income	Net annual personal income (10,000 USDs)	0.824	0.600	0.080	4.013
Job	Dummy variable (a civil servant = 1)	0.239	0.427	0	1
Risk	Dummy variable (from subjective pressures = 1)	0.063	0.242	0	1

The survey data indicate that a part of respondents were unwilling to pay higher electricity tariffs to replace nuclear power plants nearby by using other clean energies. Table 3 shows the questions concerning the sample selectivity, and data of the motives behind a "No" WTP response. Specifically, when the scenario assumption in the sample selection question (SSQ) of CVM is "replacing the nuclear power plant located 80 km in the neighborhood", 199 respondents are unwilling to pay. In which, responses of 91 respondents (45.7%) are genuine zeros, indicating that nuclear power and other clean energies are indifferent to them, and thus they accept the construction of nuclear power rather than paying higher electricity tariffs. However, responses of 108 respondents (54.3%) are protest responses in which, 72 respondents hold the views that the government should be responsible for the issue, and 36 respondents believe that they had already paid enough fees or taxes, and, therefore, are unwilling to pay more.

However, when the scenario assumption in the sample selection question (SSQ) of CVM is "replacing the nuclear power plant located 30 km in the neighborhood", only 97 respondents are unwilling to pay. The results are much smaller compared to the nuclear power plant that located 80 km in the neighborhood. In which, responses of 82 respondents are genuine zero responses, while only 15 responses are protest responses. Results indicate that, respondents are more willing to pay when the distance of nuclear power plants is shortened from 80 km to 30 km. Particularly, the number of protest responses reduced dramatically when the distance of nuclear power plants is shorter. The difference in acceptance level that reflected by different distance indicates the existence of the NIMBY syndrome. In other words, people have higher willingness to pay to replace nuclear power when the location of nuclear power plants is quite close.

On the basis of evaluating WTP using the two-step sample selection model, we set three models to analyze the NIMBY attitude towards nuclear power plants in China. Model 1 describes residents' WTP for avoiding a new nuclear power plant located 80 km in the neighborhood and the factors affecting their WTP. Model 2 describes residents' WTP for avoiding a new nuclear power plant located 30 km in the neighborhood and the factors affecting their WTP. In Model 3, we analyze the difference of NIMBY attitudes between inland areas and coastal areas.

Table 3. The motives for a "No" WTP response.

The condition of distance	Motives	Description	Number
Are you willing to pay higher electricity tariffs in order to substitute the nuclear power plant located 80 km in the neighborhood by using other clean energies?	Genuine zero responses	I am indifferent to nuclear power; therefore, I am unwilling to pay an extra amount of money.	91
	Protest responses	The government should be responsible for the issue.	72
		I have paid enough costs and taxes, and therefore I do not want to pay more.	36
	Total number		199
Are you willing to pay higher electricity tariffs in order to substitute the nuclear power plant located 30 km in the neighborhood by using other clean energies?	Genuine zero responses	I am indifferent to nuclear power; therefore, I am unwilling to pay an extra amount of money.	82
	Protest responses	The government should be responsible for the issue.	9
		I have paid enough costs and taxes, and therefore I do not want to pay more.	6
	Total number		97

The choices of 30 km and 80 km as signifying site regions in the survey of CPPNP were made on the basis of comprehensive discussions. According to United States Nuclear Regulatory Commission (U.S.NRC) [77], in order to facilitate a preplanned strategy for protective actions during an emergency, there are two emergency planning zones (EPZs) around each nuclear power plant, and the range of EPZ is 50 miles regulated by U.S.NRC. Table 4 shows the EPZs of three main nuclear power plants in China. The survey chooses 30 km and takes the EPZs of China's nuclear power plants as references. Moreover, Greenberg *et al.* [25] also choose 50 miles to signify a nuclear power site region when exploring the NIMBY syndrome in the USA. A distance of 80 km is suggested as the range of site evaluation of nuclear power plant by the International Atomic Energy Agency (IAEA) [78] after the Fukushima nuclear disaster. Beyond 80 km, there are no regulations for implementing emergency measures. Thus, 30 km and 80 km in the survey of CPPNP offer reasonable references in investigating the relationship between distance and residents' NIMBY attitudes. If respondents were willing to pay for other clean energies so as to avoid having a new nuclear power plant in the neighborhood, we can regard there exist the syndrome of NIMBY.

Table 4. The rules of EPZ of three nuclear power plants in China.

Zone		Da Yawan	Qinshan	Tianwan
Plume Exposure Pathway EPZ	I	0–5 km	0–3 km	0–4 km
	II	5–10 km	3–7 km	4–8 km
Ingestion Exposure Pathway EPZ		0–50 km	0–30 km	0–25 km

Note: Data in Table 4 are collected from the research of Zhao *et al.* (2003) [79].

4. Results and Discussion

4.1. NIMBY Attitude towards Nuclear Power Plants and Its Influencing Factors

Results of Model 1 and Model 2 are shown in Table 5. From the results of the first step (sample selection equation, SSQ), we can see that in Model 1, the probability of willingness to replace nuclear power by paying for higher electricity tariffs is higher for respondents with high-income and have college degrees. Moreover, respondents who are worried about the subjective risks of nuclear power are more likely to give protest responses. In addition, factors such as gender, age and job have no significant effects on the probability of giving protest responses. However, in Model 2, all results of the sample selection equation are insignificant.

The comparison of results of Model 1 and Model 2 indicate that some of these explanatory variables can significantly influence the probability of giving protest responses from respondents under the scenario of constructing a nuclear power plant that located 80 km in the neighborhood. However, when the scenario changes to be constructing a nuclear power plant that located 30 km nearby, the probability of giving protest responses from respondents would no longer be significantly influenced by these explanatory variables. The above results show that the probabilities of giving protest responses from respondents are different due to different distances of nuclear power plants. That is, if nuclear power plants were located closer to the places they live, respondents would have stronger willingness pay an extract amount of money to avoid having nuclear power plants in their neighborhood.

According to the econometric results in the sample selection equation, we calculate $\lambda(\cdot)$ (lambda), and add it as an explanatory variable in the elicitation equation. Results in the second step are shown in Table 5. As can be seen, the coefficients of the lambda terms are different in Model 1 and Model 2. In Model 1, the lambda term is significant and positive signed, which suggests that the error terms in the selection and elicitation equations are positive correlated. While in Model 2, the coefficient of lambda term is not statistically different from zero, so that the protest response does not lead to any significant sample selection bias. In other words, under the scenario of constructing a nuclear power plant that located 80 km in the neighborhood, the protest decision of respondents is interdependent with WTP to replace nuclear power by paying higher electricity tariffs. However, under the scenario of constructing a nuclear power that located 30 km nearby, the relationship between the protest responses of respondents and WTP is insignificant. That is, the public has stronger willingness pay an extract amount of money when nuclear power plants are located closer. In other words, respondents are quite sensitive to the distance of nuclear facilities

Results of elicitation equation indicate that factors of age, income, education, and job affect the outcome. Besides, these explanatory variables have similar effects in both Model 1 and Model 2. Some previous research showed that gender has an impact on WTP of nuclear facilities or the attitude towards the facilities [52,63]. However, the relationship between gender and the WTP is not remarkable in our study. The coefficients of the explanatory variables show that age has a negative impact on the WTP. For example, Kim *et al.* [5] declared in their study that younger people were less likely to strongly accept nuclear power than older people. Our result corresponds with negative correlations between age and risk rating claimed by Huppe and Janke [80].

Table 5. The econometric results of the two-step sample selection models.

	Model 1 (80 km)		Model 2 (30 km)	
Sample selection equation	Estimates	*p*	Estimates	*p*
Gender	0.1423	0.225	0.2054	0.350
Age	−0.0096	0.156	−0.0137	0.287
Income	0.1242	0.000	0.0471	0.282
College	0.3025	0.034	0.0685	0.801
Job	0.1888	0.211	−0.0016	0.995
Risk	−0.4746	0.026	−0.0550	0.898
Constant	0.6807	0.010	2.2379	0.000
Log likelihood	−297.1487		−72.8221	
% Correct predictions	86.5%		98.1%	
Pseudo R2	0.0611		0.0224	
Elicitation equation	Estimates	P	Estimates	P
Gender	0.0339	0.267	0.0881	0.096
Age	−0.0070	0.000	−0.0101	0.006
Income	0.0508	0.000	0.0364	0.000
College	0.1300	0.001	0.0888	0.003
Job	0.1151	0.003	0.0730	0.018
Risk	−0.1308	0.124	−0.0155	0.771
lambda	0.8756	0.008	3.9562	0.107
Constant	0.4765	0.000	0.7562	0.000
Log likelihood	−561.1972		−663.0475	
% Correct predictions	66.1%		63.9%	
Pseudo R2	0.0521		0.0371	

Table 6 shows the evaluation of respondents' WTP of Model 1 and Model 2. The mean WTP to avoid having a new nuclear power plant within 80 km is 0.1285 USD/kWh, and it increase to 0.1387 USD/kWh when the distance is shortened as 30 km. The empirical result shows a higher average WTP to avoid having nuclear power plants located 30 km nearby than for those located 80 km in the neighborhood. Assuming that residents are entitled to choose between nuclear power and other clean energies, and more risks would be suffered if respondents lived nearer to nuclear power plants, respondents who live closer to nuclear power plants might have stronger WTP to avoid having nuclear power plants in the neighborhood. The change of WTP for different distances indicates the change of their NIMBY attitudes.

Table 6. WTP evaluation of Model 1 and Model 2.

Model	Value of mean WTP (USD/kWh)	Standard Error	*p*	95% Confident Interval	
Model 1	0.1285	0.0023	0.000	0.1240	0.1330
Model 2	0.1387	0.0020	0.000	0.1347	0.1426

In order to verify the impact of distance on the WTP, or whether the public shows a greater WTP for the closer nuclear power plants, thereby reflects the syndrome of NIMBY, we conduct a robustness test on results in Model 1 and Model 2. We include both the scenario of nuclear power plants located 80 km and the scenario of nuclear power plants located 30 km into one model, and introduce a distance dummy variable (if the nuclear power located 30 km nearby, the value would be 1). Results of the robustness test are shown in Table 7. The coefficients of the distance variable are significantly positive in results of the selection equation and the elicitation equation, indicating the distance factor affects the public WTP for replacing nuclear power. Therefore, distance is a sensitive factor in the consideration of whether replacing nuclear power or not. Furthermore, under the condition of constructing a nuclear power plant located 30 km nearby, the probability of willing to pay an extract amount of money for higher electricity prices to replace nuclear power is much higher. The above conclusions are consistent with the results in Model 1 and Model 2.

Table 7. The robust test results.

Sample selection equation	Estimates	p	Elicitation equation	Estimates	p
Gender	0.1542	0.135	Gender	0.0149	0.440
Age	−0.0105	0.079	Age	−0.0053	0.000
Income	0.1084	0.000	Income	0.0300	0.000
College	0.2547	0.043	College	0.0866	0.000
Job	0.1478	0.265	Job	0.0774	0.001
Risk	−0.3830	0.038	Risk	−0.0092	0.831
Distance	1.0072	0.000	Distance	0.1273	0.003
Constant	0.7964	0.001	lambda	0.3180	0.125
Log likelihood	−371.6542		Constant	0.6928	0.000
% Correct predictions	92.3%		Log likelihood	−1228.4354	
Pseudo R2	0.1428		% Correct predictions	64.1%	
-	-	-	Pseudo R2	0.0447	

4.2. Regional Difference of NIMBY Attitude

Up to now, all nuclear power plants are operating or under construction in coastal areas in China [81]. Therefore, residents in coastal areas have more chances to obtain information about nuclear power than residents in inland areas. We explore whether regions play a role in the NIMBY attitude, and whether public opposition would be more serious for new nuclear power construction in inland areas. Answers to these questions can be found by dividing samples into different groups. Electricity prices are different in regions of China, and respondents would have different baselines of electricity prices in the estimation of WTP. Results in Table 8 show that the mean WTP would be higher in groups of which the local electricity prices are higher. Thus, in order to compare the NIMBY attitude among different regions, we need to investigate the variation between respondents' WTP and the present electricity prices.

In order to consider the regional factors, samples are divided into three groups: Group 1 consists of respondents from coastal areas, where the existing nuclear power plants are located; Group 2 consists of respondents from inland areas, where there are no nuclear power plants at present, but would be built in the future according to government planning; Group 1a consists of respondents who currently live near the existing nuclear power plants in coastal areas. The samples in inland and coastal areas in China are illustrated in Figure 2.

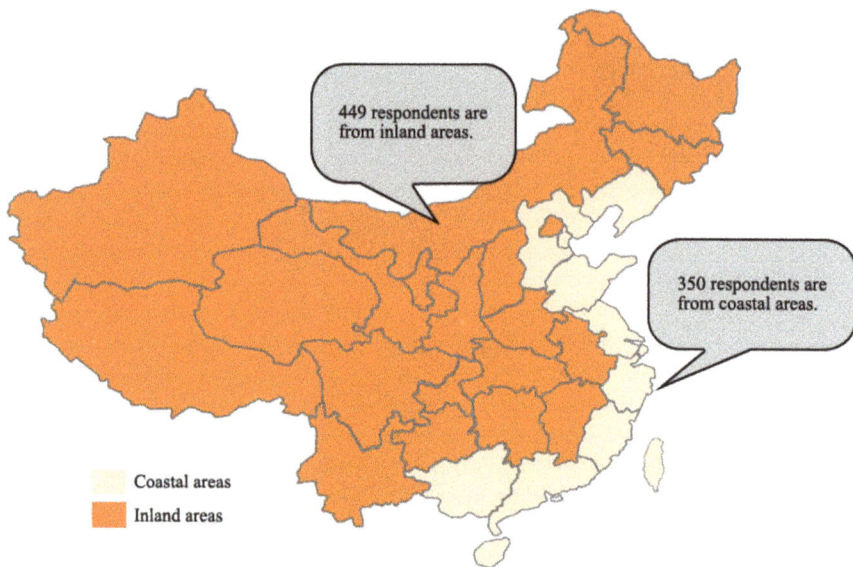

Figure 2. Illustration of the samples in inland and coastal areas in China.

Referring to Table 8, though Group 2 has the lowest mean WTP, it also pays the lowest price for electricity locally. Both Vari. 1 and Vari. 2 suggest that the mean WTP of Group 2 has the largest increase rate: the WTP for nuclear power plants located 80 km is 1.55 times the local electricity price, and the WTP for nuclear power plants located 30 km is 1.72 times the local electricity price. Variation of Group 1a is the smallest among the three groups: respondents who currently live near nuclear power plants have the highest WTP, but the local electricity prices are also the highest among the three groups. The mean WTP and the current electricity price of Group 1 are both found between Group 1a and Group 2. From Vari. 1 and Vari. 2, we come to the conclusion that people in inland areas have the strongest NIMBY attitude, and people who live in the vicinity of the existing nuclear power plants have the weakest NIMBY attitude. Results are in accordance with the findings of the previous studies, which indicate that opposition would be the strongest at the planning phase, and then would become weaker before the local projects were proposed or after the NIMBY facility had become operational [55–57]. This result demonstrates that residents have a strong NIMBY attitude towards nuclear power plants, especially those who live in inland areas.

Table 8. WTP evaluation of Model 3.

Group	Current price of electricity (USD/kWh)	WTP (USD/kWh) (80 km)	WTP (USD/kWh) (30 km)	Vari. 1	Vari. 2	Vari. 3
Group 1a	0.1033	0.1466	0.1496	41.9%	44.8%	2.0%
Group 1	0.0913	0.1376	0.1421	50.7%	55.6%	3.3%
Group 2	0.0780	0.1210	0.1345	55.1%	72.4%	11.2%
Total	0.0820	0.1285	0.1387	56.7%	69.1%	7.9%

Note: Vari. is the abbreviation of Variation. Variation 1 represents the increase between WTP for 80 km and the current electricity price; Variation 2 represents the increase between WTP for 30 km and the current electricity price; Variation 3 is the difference between Variation 1 and Variation 2, which is the variation between WTP for 80 km and WTP for 30 km.

4.3. Decay of NIMBY with Longer Distance

Table 8 shows that the NIMBY attitude decays as distance increases. In an ideal situation, the public tends to accept the safety distance regulated by laws or rules. The NIMBY attitude will apparently decay when the living distance increases to 80 km. Nevertheless, an empirical survey proposes that the NIMBY attitude does decay as distance increases both in coastal and inland areas, but the trend is not obvious. In total, the average of the present electricity price is 0.0820 USD/kWh; and there is a 56.7% increase of respondents' WTP for nuclear power plants located 80 km, and an additional 7.9% increase for nuclear power plants located 30 km. Respondents' WTP in inland areas has a larger percentage increase: the mean WTP for nuclear power plants located 80 km increases by 55.1% compared to the present electricity price, and the mean WTP for nuclear power plants located 30 km has an additional increase of 11.2%. As for respondents who live in the vicinity of nuclear power plants, the mean WTP only increases 2% when the distance is shortened from 80 km to 30 km.

Variation of WTP for nuclear power plants located 30 km and 80 km reflects respondents' sensitivity to distance. The Vari. 3 in Table 8 indicates that people are less sensitive to the distance change if they currently live close to the nuclear power plants. A 2% difference in Group 1a shows that respondents are indifferent to nuclear power plants located 30 km or 80 km. In their opinions, they face the same risks within the ranges of 80 km and 30 km, and the best way is having no nuclear power plants in the neighborhood. Nevertheless, the situation is different in inland areas. People in inland areas focus more on the specific location of the plant. An 11.2% difference apparently shows their sensitivity of distance. Therefore, the location of the new plant is more important in solving the problem of NIMBY in inland areas. Hence, in order to decrease the effect of NIMBY attitudes, strategies should be differentiated in different regions.

The gap between WTP for nuclear power plants located 80 km and the present electricity price in Vari. 1 shows that distance in regulation or in actual situation is inconsistent with the accepted distance in public. Zweifel *et al.* [63] showed that the safety distance is 95 km for public. They studied the public WTP for the insurance of living near nuclear power plants, and found that the pay fell to zero with the distance of 95 km. Assuming the decrease of WTP has a linear relationship with the increase in distance [63], we can figure out the distance where the WTP equals the present electricity price. Results show that the pay falls to the present electricity price when the distance is 354 km. Even though 80 km is the largest distance for nuclear monitor in regulations, the safety distance that the public can accept is far greater than this.

Previous studies suggested monetary compensations to reduce the NIMBY effect. In Taiwan, the aggregate WTP for a decrease in the nuclear energy ratio is $675 million New Taiwan Dollar (NTD) [75]. In the case of Korea, the yearly public WTP is 278 million USDS [76]. These WTP estimates provide preliminary information about compensation. We can estimate the compensation for residents who live near nuclear power plants by calculating the yearly public WTP. For more than 75 million people who are living near nuclear power plants in the distance of 80 km [21], the yearly WTP should be $1150.9 million. Result in our paper is much greater compared to the countries mentioned above. Since the CVM is based on an assumed situation, the real amount of compensation could be even larger than the assumed value considering the implementation process of nuclear power policy. Thus, the compensation estimated by the WTP only reflects the minimum quantity, and the amount of compensation would show an increasing trend in China with the growing number of nuclear power plants.

5. Conclusions and Policy Implications

Nuclear power has become an important energy source in the context of deteriorating energy and environmental security. It is particularly crucial for China to restructure its energy layout and solve the environmental problems. At the meeting of the State Energy Commission held on 18 April 2014, Premier Li announced that more nuclear power plants will be launched on the eastern coast. However, public acceptance is still a major barrier for further nuclear power development worldwide after the Fukushima nuclear disaster. The Chinese government is more than prudent in re-launching the nuclear power projects. The purpose of this paper is to provide references for future nuclear power policy in China.

Our study finds that the NIMBY attitude is an important potential impediment to nuclear power development, which could even impact the power structure in China. Most respondents prefer to pay more for other clean energies to replace nuclear power plants in the neighborhood. By comparing the WTP for avoiding nuclear power plants nearby with the current electricity price, we find that there is an increase of 56.7% of WTP for a nuclear power plant located 80 km, and an increase of 69.1% of WTP for a nuclear power plant located 30 km. Results indicate that there exists a strong NIMBY attitude among the public. Therefore, the public attitude cannot be ignored in choosing the new nuclear power locations. Social-economic characteristics have impacts on the public NIMBY attitude: age has a negative impact on the WTP, and income has a positive impact on the WTP. We also find that civil servants, who have a higher WTP than others, play an important role in determining the research outcome. Unlike previous studies, the effect by gender is not taken into consideration in view of the lack of knowledge of nuclear power in China.

Regional difference also has an effect on the NIMBY syndrome. People in inland regions have the strongest NIMBY attitude towards nuclear power plants, and people who live near nuclear power plants have the weakest NIMBY attitude. This implies that the problem of public opposition would be more serious when nuclear power expands to inland regions. Since the apparent "attitude gap" between "before" and "during" the planning of a local project was a key problem [57], the government should pay more attention to the public attitude at the planning phase of a new nuclear power project. Therefore, actions should be taken to enhance the information interchange among the public, government and nuclear enterprises.

The analysis about the decay of NIMBY suggests that the safety distance that public can accept is much farther than 80 km. People in inland areas are more concerned about the location of nuclear power plants and are more sensitive to the distance. Their WTP increases when the distance is shortened from 80 km to 30 km. The safety distance suggested by nuclear power regulations cannot be easily accepted. For monetary compensation, the yearly compensation would be no less than $1150.9 million in total for people who live near nuclear power plants that located 80 km nearby. Considering that people in inland regions are more sensitive to distance, monetary compensation based on distance could be considered in these regions.

However, monetary compensation has its limitations, and cannot fundamentally solve the issue. Individuals may ease their opposition to the proposed facilities, if they have been properly compensated for accepting the costs; however, the effects of compensation are not uniform across all types of facilities [82]. According to the previous studies, compensation for nuclear power plants cannot work in every case. Based on the survey of CPPNP, we find that the public in China lacks the cognition of nuclear power and relative regulations, which is easily influenced by the media. This indicates the importance of communication with honest information between the public and the stakeholders [76]. Thus, a transparent system for information exchanging about nuclear power development should be built, so that the local dwellers can participate in the decision-making about the location and provision of a nuclear power plant. Public participation does not mean being persuaded, but the right to deny or adjust the project. In this way, more trust can be given to the government, and the public can treat nuclear power with a more rational manner [83].

Results indicate that decision makers should pay more attention to the public attitude than ever before due to the existence of NIMBY attitude towards building a new nuclear power plant in the neighborhood. Although our study contributes to the literature on nuclear energy policy by exploring the public NIMBY attitude of nuclear power plants, and by providing policymakers with compensation suggestions, there are also limitations in the study. Due to the limitation of the CPPNP survey, it only estimates public WTP to avoid having nuclear power plants in the neighborhood by introducing two kinds of distance. Therefore, a series of additional surveys are required to explore the spatial factor and to find the relationship between the NIMBY syndrome and distance. In addition, further investigations on each region's characteristics that affect the public WTP are required. More data on acknowledge about nuclear power can help us obtain more results from a broader perspective. Periodical surveys about respondents' attitudes toward nuclear power plants in the neighborhood can show the time factor of WTP by further study on WTP in the same regions during the planning process or after the nuclear power plant has become operational. Therefore, deep and comprehensive research will give us more profound and valuable information as well as insights for nuclear energy policies. In addition, the data used in this paper are obtained by asking the questions of WTP. WTA could be estimated without the need to refer to an alternative "clean" power source, therefore, we will consider estimating the willingness to Accept (WTA) in the future research.

Acknowledgments: We would like to express our sincere gratitude to the three anonymous referees for their insightful and constructive comments. This article is supported by National Natural Science Foundation of China (Grant Nos. 71303199 and 71373218), Ministry of Education Foundation of China (Grant Nos. 13YJC790123 and 13JZD010), Soft Science Plan Funded Project of Fujian Province (Grant No. 2014R0088), Natural Science Foundation of Fujian Province (Grant No. 2014J01269), Social Science School of Fujian (Grant No. 2014B100), Social Science School of Xiamen (Grant No. [2014]15), Major Program of the National Social Science Foundation of China (Grant No. 13&ZD167), Youth Project of the National Social Science Foundation of China (Grant No. 12CTJ014), General Project of the Social Science Foundation of Fujian Province (Grant No. 2014B100) and the College Students Innovation and Entrepreneurial Training Plan of Xiamen University (Grant Nos. DC2013041 and DC2013135).

Author Contributions: Chuanwang Sun gave the framework of this research and made substantial contribution to the study design. Nan Lyu constructed the model and provided a wide range of support throughout the study. Xiaoling Ouyang gave some core advices, checked the whole paper, and revised the manuscript. All authors have read and approved the final manuscript.

Conflicts of Interest: The authors declare no conflict of interest.

Appendix A

The purpose of CPPNP is to explore public perceptions and attitudes toward nuclear power plant construction in the context of restarting the large-scale nuclear construction program in China. The topic has policy implications because the general public would be more sensitive to nuclear power after the Fukushima nuclear disaster in 2011. The survey of CPPNP, launched by China Center for Energy Economics Research at Xiamen University once to twice a year from 2013, is a nationwide face-to-face survey focuses on the public perception of nuclear power. The face-to-face interview is conducted because some questions are relatively professional and technical which require oral explanations. More importantly, the face-to-face interview is a good way to enhance communication with interviewees and convey information required by the Contingent Valuation Method (CVM). For instance, the interviewees could obtain information about substitutes and budget constraints reminders as suggested by the NOAA Panel [84]. Particularly, the pre-test survey is conducted in order to identify issues related to questionnaire design, statement expressions, payment vehicle, the transmission of energy policy and bid amount, and conduct the pre-pilot study and evaluation.

The questionnaire can be divided into four parts. *The first part* is the introduction, which includes information of the current price level of electricity, the average household budget for electricity expenditure, information channels of nuclear power development. Meanwhile, the first part also introduces the general background and characteristics of the different forms of power generation, in order to make interviewees clearly understand the situation of nuclear power development. *The second part* is the personal understanding or perception and concern of nuclear power. For example, the most worried risks of nuclear power, the most effective measures to reduce public concerns and attitudes about the development of nuclear power in China. *The third part* is the introduction of the contingent valuation scenario and dichotomous questions. According to the two-step sample selection method, we first explore whether the public is willing to pay and identify the protesters, then we investigate how much are they willing to pay for electricity tariffs [74]. *The fourth part* is composed of demographic and social-economic questions, including the respondents' gender (this question is not included in the questionnaire, because the answers can be obtained by visual observations and communications), age, education, income and job, *etc.* We can obtain explanatory variables of the WTP by asking the above questions.

Specifically, in the third part mentioned above, the sequential questions are as follows:

Question 1: In order to meet the rising demand for electricity and reduce emissions, we assume that the government plans to construct a nuclear power plant (located 80 km/30 km in the neighborhood). If you disagree with the nuclear power construction, you are entitled to convince the government to use other higher-cost clean energies to replace nuclear power. However, such substitution would inevitably increase electricity price. Are you willing to pay higher electricity tariffs in order to substitute nuclear power?

Yes, I am willing to pay. No, I am unwilling to pay.

Question 2: According to the results of Question 1, Question 2 is divided into two parts.

If the respondents are willing to replace nuclear power, we will ask the first bid amount (Chinese Yuan) for electricity tariffs. It should be noted that the unit of Chinese Yuan (CNY) for electricity tariffs is adopted as the payment vehicle, because the respondents are more familiar with and sensitive to electricity price. The above settlement is also determined by the results of the pre-survey. If the respondents were willing to make the first bid, we would continue to ask if they were willing to pay the second higher bid amount for electricity tariffs. If not, we would ask if they were willing to pay the second lower bid amount.

If the respondents were unwilling to replace nuclear power, we will ask them reasons. If the respondents display apathetic indifference towards the construction of nuclear power, we can regard their WTP as genuine zeros. If the respondents hold the views that the government should be responsible for the issue, or they think that they have already paid enough costs or taxes and therefore refuse to pay the proposed additional charges on electricity tariffs, we can regard their responses as protest responses. In this way, we can distinguish the protest responses from the genuine zero responses by their motives behind the answers, and then construct a sample selection model. According to Calia and Strazzera [74], a sample selection model with the protest responses should be preferred to the model without protest responses, since it takes into account the uncertainty about the estimates of the WTP for the public good.

Meanwhile, in order to enhance respondents' understanding of contingent valuation scenario, the following sentences are emphasized in both the questionnaire and the face-to-face survey when asking dichotomous questions: "Please answer questions according to your personal budget and the sensitivity to the risk of nuclear power. Your actual WTP will help to slow down or even stop the construction of nuclear power plants in your neighborhood". The settlement above makes the contingent valuation scenario more understandable. In other words, if the respondents were in a relatively more convinced scenario, their responses would be more accurate. For example, the government is considering implementing a policy, and public responses will be used to help inform that decision [85]. In this context, individuals would have incentives to truly respond as long as they believe that their responses can probabilistically influence government decisions [86]. Table A1. presents major questions about the NIMBY syndrome and the WTP.

Table A1. Major questions about the NIMBY syndrome and the WTP.

Category	Questions	Answers
Sample selection questions	In order to meet the rising demand for electricity and reduce emissions, we assume that the government plans to construct a nuclear power plant nearby (80 km/30 km). If you disagree with the nuclear power construction, you are entitled to convince the government to use other higher-cost clean energies to replace nuclear power. However, such substitution would inevitably increase electricity price. Are you willing to pay higher electricity tariffs in order to substitute nuclear power?	Yes, I am willing to pay. No, I am unwilling to pay.
The WTP elicitation questions	If the answer of the sample selection question is "Yes, I am willing to pay", we will continue to ask: how much are you willing to pay (first bid amount) for the electricity tariff (Chinese Yuan)?	If the respondents were willing to make the first bid, we would continue to ask if they were willing to pay the second higher bid amount for electricity tariffs. If not, we would ask if they were willing to pay the second lower bid amount.
Protest responses questions (distinguishing protest responses from genuine zero responses)	If the answer of the sample selection question is "No, I am unwilling to pay".	There is no need to replace nuclear power because it has no negative impact on me. The government should address the issue. I have paid enough costs and taxes, and do not want to increase electricity tariffs.
Demographic and social-economic questions	Age; Educational level; Annual personal income; Job.	Taking notes according to the specific circumstances.

Note: It should be noted that other questions are also included in the survey of CPPNP, which comprehensively investigates the public attitudes about nuclear power. We do not present all questions in the questionnaire due to the space limitation. Other questions, which are designed for exploring related nuclear policy, are used for our further studies.

References

1. Hartmann, P.; Apaolaza, V.; D'Souza, C.; Echebarria, C.; Barrutia, J.M. Nuclear power threats, public opposition and green electricity adoption: Effects of threat belief appraisal and fear arousal. *Energy Policy* **2013**, *62*, 1366–1376. [CrossRef]
2. Laes, E.; Meskens, G.; van der Sluijs, J.P. On the contribution of external cost calculations to energy system governance: The case of a potential large-scale nuclear accident. *Energy Policy* **2011**, *39*, 5664–5673. [CrossRef]
3. Ramana, M.V. Nuclear power and the public. *Bull. At. Sci.* **2011**, *67*, 43–51. [CrossRef]
4. Visschers, V.H.M.; Wallquist, L. Nuclear power before and after Fukushima: The relations between acceptance, ambivalence and knowledge. *J. Environ. Psychol.* **2013**, *36*, 77–86. [CrossRef]
5. Kim, Y.; Kim, M.; Kim, W. Effect of the Fukushima nuclear disaster on global public acceptance of nuclear energy. *Energy Policy* **2013**, *61*, 822–828. [CrossRef]
6. Gamson, W.A.; Modigliani, A. Media discourse and public opinion on nuclear power: A constructionist approach. *Am. J. Sociol.* **1989**, *95*, 1–37. [CrossRef]
7. Kemp, R. Why not in my backyard? A radical interpretation of public opposition to the deep disposal of radioactive waste in the United Kingdom. *Environ. Plan. A* **1990**, *22*, 1239–1258. [CrossRef]
8. Wolsink, M. Wind power and the NIMBY-myth: Institutional capacity and the limited significance of public support. *Renew. Energy* **2000**, *21*, 49–64.
9. Devine-Wright, P. Public engagement with large-scale renewable energy technologies: Breaking the cycle of NIMBYism. *Clim. Chang.* **2011**, *2*, 19–26. [CrossRef]
10. He, G.; Mol, A.P.J.; Zhang, L.; Lu, Y. Public participation and trust in nuclear power development in China. *Renew. Sustain. Energy Rev.* **2013**, *23*, 1–11.
11. International Energy Statistics. Available online: http://www.eia.gov/cfapps/ipdbproject/IEDIndex3.cfm (accessed on 4 September 2014).
12. Kunsch, P.L.; Friesewinkel, J. Nuclear energy policy in Belgium after Fukushima. *Energy Policy* **2014**, *66*, 462–474. [CrossRef]
13. Srinivasan, T.N.; Gopi Rethinaraj, T.S. Fukushima and thereafter: Reassessment of risks of nuclear power. *Energy Policy* **2013**, *52*, 726–736. [CrossRef]
14. China's National Energy Administration (CNEA). Available online: http://zfxxgk.nea.gov.cn/auto82/201401/t20140124_1756.htm (accessed on 4 September 2014).
15. The State Council. Available online: http://www.gov.cn/ldhd/2012--10/24/content_2250357.htm (accessed on 4 September 2014).

16. World Nuclear Association. Nuclear Power in China, Updated March 2012. Available online: http://www.world-nuclear.org/ (accessed on 4 September 2014).

17. Lu, D. The Current Status of Chinese Nuclear Power Industry and Its Future. Available online: http://www.jsm.or.jp/ejam/Vol.2.No.1/GA/12/article.html (accessed on 15 October 2014).

18. World Nuclear Association. Nuclear Power in China. Available online: http://www.world-nuclear.org/info/Country-Profiles/Countries-A-F/China--Nuclear-Power/ (accessed on 16 August 2014).

19. CEIC China Database. Available online: http://www.ceicdata.com/countries/china (accessed on 16 August 2014).

20. World Nuclear Association. World Energy Needs and Nuclear Power. Available online: http://www.world-nuclear.org/info/Current-and-Future-Generation/World-Energy-Needs-and-Nuclear-Power/ (accessed on 16 August 2014).

21. Butler, D. Nuclear safety: Reactors, residents and risk. *Nature* **2011**, *472*, 400–401. [CrossRef] [PubMed]

22. China's National Energy Administration. 2014 Guidance for Energy. Available online: http://zfxxgk.nea.gov.cn/auto82/201401/t20140124_1756.htm (accessed on 16 August 2014).

23. Quan, S.W.; Zeng, Y.C.; Huang, B. Public perception and acceptance of nuclear power in Beijing, China. *Soc. Sci. Beijing* **2012**, *5*, 55–60. (In Chinese)

24. Schively, C. Understanding the NIMBY and LULU Phenomena: Reassessing Our Knowledge Base and Informing Future Research. *J. Plan. Lit.* **2007**, *21*, 255–266. [CrossRef]

25. Greenberg, M.R. NIMBY, CLAMP, and the Location of New Nuclear-Related Facilities: U.S. National and 11 Site-Specific Surveys. *Risk Anal.* **2009**, *29*, 1242–1254. [CrossRef] [PubMed]

26. Refineries and petrochemicals plants. Available online: http://www.bp.com/en/global/corporate/about-bp/company-information/group-organization/downstream/refineries-and-petrochemicals-plants.html (accessed on 16 August 2014).

27. Qu, G.H. PX Projects and Their Effect on Sustainability of Chinese Oil Refining Industry. *Sino Glob. Energy* **2013**, *7*, 1–7. (In Chinese)

28. Singapore integrated manufacturing site. Available online: http://www.exxonmobil.com/AP-English/Files/Combined_Site_Brochure_FINAL.pdf (accessed on 16 August 2014).

29. Steenhof, P.A.; Fulton, W. Scenario development in China's electricity sector. *Technol. Forecast. Soc. Chang.* **2007**, *74*, 779–797. [CrossRef]

30. Romanello, V.; Salvatores, M.; Schwenk-Ferrero, A.; Gabrielli, F.; Vezzoni, B.; Rineiski, A.; Fazio, C. Sustainable Nuclear Fuel Cycles and World Regional Issues. *Sustainability* **2012**, *4*, 1214–1238. [CrossRef]

31. Van der Zwaan, B.C.C. Nuclear energy: Tenfold expansion or phase-out? *Technol. Forecast. Soc. Chang.* **2002**, *69*, 287–307. [CrossRef]

32. Pearce, J.M. Limitations of Nuclear Power as a Sustainable Energy Source. *Sustainability* **2012**, *4*, 1173–1187. [CrossRef]

33. Lozano, R.L.; Hernández-Ceballos, M.A.; Adame, J.A.; Casas-Ruíz, M.; Sorribas, M.; Miguel, E.G.S.; Bolívar, J.P. Radioactive impact of Fukushima accident on the Iberian Peninsula: Evolution and plume previous pathway. *Environ. Int.* **2011**, *37*, 1259–1264. [CrossRef] [PubMed]

34. Wittneben, B.B.F. The impact of the Fukushima nuclear accident on European energy policy. *Environ. Sci. Policy* **2012**, *15*, 1–3. [CrossRef]

35. Kim, Y.; Kim, W.; Kim, M. An international comparative analysis of public acceptance of nuclear energy. *Energy Policy* **2014**, *66*, 475–483. [CrossRef]

36. Stoutenborough, J.W.; Sturgess, S.G.; Vedlitz, A. Knowledge, risk, and policy support: Public perceptions of nuclear power. *Energy Policy* **2013**, *62*, 176–184. [CrossRef]

37. Dalla Valle, A.; Furlan, C. Diffusion of nuclear energy in some developing countries. *Technol. Forecast. Soc. Chang.* **2014**, *81*, 143–153. [CrossRef]

38. Guidolin, M.; Guseo, R. A nuclear power renaissance? *Technol. Forecast. Soc. Chang.* **2012**, *79*, 1746–1760. [CrossRef]

39. Aoki, M.; Rothwell, G. A comparative institutional analysis of the Fukushima nuclear disaster: Lessons and policy implications. *Energy Policy* **2013**, *53*, 240–247.

40. Homma, T.; Akimoto, K. Analysis of Japan's energy and environment strategy after the Fukushima nuclear power plant accident. *Energy Policy* **2013**, *62*, 1216–1225. [CrossRef]

41. Heffron, R.J. Nuclear new build in the United States 1990–2010: A three state analysis. *Technol. Forecast. Soc. Chang.* **2013**, *80*, 876–892. [CrossRef]

42. Heffron, R.J. Nuclear energy policy in the United States 1990–2010: A federal or state responsibility? *Energy Policy* **2013**, *62*, 254–266. [CrossRef]

43. Roh, S.; Kim, W. How can Korea secure uranium enrichment and spent fuel reprocessing rights? *Energy Policy* **2014**, *68*, 195–198. [CrossRef]

44. Siegrist, M.; Visschers, V.H.M. Acceptance of nuclear power: The Fukushima effect. *Energy Policy* **2013**, *59*, 112–119. [CrossRef]

45. Bird, D.K.; Haynes, K.; van den Honert, R.; McAneney, J.; Poortinga, W. Nuclear power in Australia: A comparative analysis of public opinion regarding climate change and the Fukushima disaster. *Energy Policy* **2014**, *65*, 644–653. [CrossRef]

46. Park, E.; Ohm, J.Y. Factors influencing the public intention to use renewable energy technologies in South Korea: Effects of the Fukushima nuclear accident. *Energy Policy* **2014**, *65*, 198–211. [CrossRef]

47. Rosa, E.A.; Dunlap, R.E. The Pools–Poll trends: Nuclear power: Three decades of public opinion. *Public Opin. Q.* **1994**, *58*, 295–324. [CrossRef]

48. Van der Horst, D. NIMBY or not? Exploring the relevance of location and the politics of voiced opinions in renewable energy siting controversies. *Energy Policy* **2007**, *35*, 2705–2714. [CrossRef]

49. Zhang, L.; Tong, X. Analysis of public NIMBY attitude and its factors. *Soc. Sci. Res.* **2014**, *1*, 105–111. (In Chinese)

50. Pineda-Solano, A.L.; Carreto-Vazquez, V.H.; Mannan, M.S. The Fukushima Daiichi Accident and its Impact on Risk Perception and Risk Communication. *Chem. Eng. Trans.* **2013**, *31*, 517–522.

51. Ansolabehere, S.; Konisky, D.M. Public Attitudes toward Construction of New Power Plants. *Public Opin. Q.* **2009**, *73*, 566–577. [CrossRef]

52. Hüppe, M.; Weber, J. Effects of Distance, Age and Sex upon Attitudes toward Nuclear Power Plants: An empirical study: Untersuchung zu Einstellungen gegenüber Atomkraftwerken in Abhängigkeit von Wohndistanz, Alter und Geschlecht. *Zentralblatt für Hygiene und Umweltmedizin* **1999**, *202*, 331–344. [PubMed]

53. Davidson, L.M.; Baum, A.; Collins, D.L. Stress and Control-Related Problems at Three Mile Island1. *J. Appl. Soc. Psychol.* **1982**, *12*, 349–359. [CrossRef]

54. Baum, A.; Gatchel, R.J.; Schaeffer, M.A. Emotional, behavioral, and physiological effects of chronic stress at Three Mile Island. *J. Consult. Clin. Psychol.* **1983**, *51*, 565–572. [CrossRef] [PubMed]

55. Balzekiene, A.; Rinkevicius, L. Global issues, local solutions: Sociological analysis of public risk perceptions and attitudes to nuclear waste disposal. *Socialinial Mokslai* **2002**, *37*, 42–47.

56. Wolsink, M. Entanglement of Interests and Motives: Assumptions behind the NIMBY-theory on Facility Siting. *Urban Studies* **1994**, *31*, 851–866. [CrossRef]

57. Bell, D.; Gray, T.; Haggett, C. The 'Social Gap' in Wind Farm Siting Decisions: Explanations and Policy Responses. *Environ. Polit.* **2005**, *14*, 460–477. [CrossRef]

58. Mitchell, R.C.; Carson, R.T. Property Rights, Protest, and the Siting of Hazardous Waste Facilities. Siting of Hazardous Facilities. *Am. Econ. Rev.* **1986**, *76*, 285–290.

59. Marsh, D.; Mkwara, L.; Scarpa, R. Do Respondents' Perceptions of the *Status Quo* Matter in Non-Market Valuation with Choice Experiments? An Application to New Zealand Freshwater Streams. *Sustainability* **2011**, *3*, 1593–1615. [CrossRef]

60. Del Saz-Salazar, S.; Hernández-Sancho, F.; Sala-Garrido, R. The social benefits of restoring water quality in the context of the Water Framework Directive: A comparison of willingness to pay and willingness to accept. *Sci. Total Environ.* **2009**, *407*, 4574–4583. [CrossRef] [PubMed]

61. Carson, R.T. Constructed Markets. In *Measuring the Demand for Environmental Quality*; Braden, J.B., Kolstad, C.D., Eds.; Elsevier: Amsterdam, The Netherlands, 1991; pp. 121–160.

62. Gawande, K.; Jenkins-Smith, H. Nuclear Waste Transport and Residential Property Values: Estimating the Effects of Perceived Risks. *J. Environ. Econ. Manag.* **2001**, *42*, 207–233. [CrossRef]

63. Zweifel, P.; Schneider, Y.; Wyss, C. Spatial effects in willingness-to-pay: The case of nuclear risks. Available online: http://www.actuaries.org/ASTIN/Colloquia/Zurich/Zweifel_Schneider_Wyss.pdf (accessed on 28 September 2014).

64. Ferreira, S.; Gallagher, L. Protest responses and community attitudes toward accepting compensation to host waste disposal infrastructure. *Land Use Policy* **2010**, *27*, 638–652. [CrossRef]

65. Zhou, L.; Peng, X.; Guan, E.; Zhang, Y.; Huang, S. Public NIMBY attitude survey and WTA estimate of waste incineration facility. *Ecol. Environ.* **2012**, *12*, 174–177. (In Chinese)

66. Yamane, F.; Matsushita, K.; Ohgaki, H.; Asano, K. Study Plans Concerning Monetary Evaluation of Mitigation Measures for the Fukushima Daiichi Accident. *Energy Procedia* **2013**, *34*, 937–944. [CrossRef]

67. Choi, K.S.; Lee, K.J.; Lee, B.W. Determining the value of reductions in radiation risk using the contingent valuation method. *Ann. Nucl. Energy* **2001**, *28*, 1431–1445. [CrossRef]

68. Pelekasi, T.; Menegaki, M.; Damigos, D. Externalities, NIMBY syndrome and marble quarrying activity. *J. Environ. Plan. Manag.* **2012**, *55*, 1192–1205. [CrossRef]

69. Ouyang, X.; Lin, B. Impacts of increasing renewable energy subsidies and phasing out fossil fuel subsidies in China. *Renew. Sustain. Energy Rev.* **2014**, *37*, 933–942. [CrossRef]

70. Dziegielewska, D.; Mendelsohn, R. Does "No" mean "No"? A protest methodology. *Environ. Resour. Econ.* **2007**, *38*, 71–87. [CrossRef]

71. Haab, T. Nonparticipation or Misspecification? The Impacts of Nonparticipation on Dichotomous Choice Contingent Valuation. *Environ. Resour. Econ.* **1999**, *14*, 443–461. [CrossRef]

72. Ramajo-Hernández, J.; del Saz-Salazar, S. Estimating the non-market benefits of water quality improvement for a case study in Spain: A contingent valuation approach. *Environ. Sci. Policy* **2012**, *22*, 47–59. [CrossRef]

73. Heckman, J.J. Sample selection bias as a specification error. *Econometrica* **1979**, *47*, 153–161. [CrossRef]

74. Calia, P.; Strazzera, E. A sample selection model for protest votes in contingent valuation analyses. *Statistica* **2001**, *61*, 473–485.

75. Liao, S.Y.; Tseng, W.C.; Chen, C.C. Eliciting public preference for nuclear energy against the backdrop of global warming. *Energy Policy* **2010**, *38*, 7054–7069. [CrossRef]

76. Jun, E.; Joon Kim, W.; Hoon Jeong, Y.; Heung Chang, S. Measuring the social value of nuclear energy using contingent valuation methodology. *Energy Policy* **2010**, *38*, 1470–1476. [CrossRef]

77. Petition for rulemaking to improve emergency planning regulation. Available online: http://www.nirs.org/reactorwatch/emergency/petitionforrulemaking22012.pdf (accessed on 12 September 2014).

78. IAEA Safety Standards for protecting people and the environment. Available online: http://www-pub.iaea.org/MTCD/publications/PDF/Pub1534_web.pdf (accessed on 12 September 2014).

79. Zhao, B.; Qiu, L. Selection of Emergency Release Source Term and Partition of EPZ in the Chinese PWR NPP. *Radiat. Prot. Bull.* **2003**, *2*, 6–9. (In Chinese)

80. Hüppe, M.; Janke, W. The nuclear plant accident in chernobyl experienced by men and women of different ages: Empirical study in the years 1986–1991. *Anxiety Stress Coping* **1994**, *7*, 339–355. [CrossRef]

81. China National Energy Administration. Available online: http://www.nea.gov.cn/2012-10/24/c_131927804.htm (accessed on 12 September 2014).

82. Ansolabehere, S. *Public Attitudes toward America's Energy Options: Insights for Nuclear Energy*; CANES Publications: Cambridge, MA, USA, 2007.

83. Sun, C.; Zhu, X. Evaluating the public perceptions of nuclear power in China: Evidence from a contingent valuation survey. *Energy Policy* **2014**, *69*, 397–405. [CrossRef]

84. Arrow, K.; Solow, R.; Protney, P.R.; Leamer, E.E.; Radner, R.; Schuman, H. Report of the NOAA panel on contingent valuation. 9 May 1993, pp. 4601–4614. Available online: http://www.cbe.csueastbay.edu/~alima/courses/4306/articles/NOAA%20on%20contingent%20valuation%201993.pdf (accessed on 28 September 2014).

85. Carson, R.T. Contingent Valuation: A Practical Alternative when Prices Aren't Available. *J. Econ. Perspect.* **2012**, *26*, 27–42. [CrossRef]

86. Poe, G.L.; Vossler, C.A. Consequentiality and Contingent Values: An Emerging Paradigm. In *The International Handbook on Non-Market Environmental Valuation*; Bennett, J., Ed.; Edward Elgar Publishing: Cheltenham, UK, 2011; pp. 122–141.

sustainability

MDPI

Article

Determinants of Farmers' Willingness to Pay and Its Level for Ecological Compensation of Poyang Lake Wetland, China: A Household-Level Survey

Fanbin Kong, Kai Xiong and Ning Zhang *

Institute of Poyang Lake Eco-economics, Jiangxi University of Finance and Economics, Nanchang 330032, China; kongfanbin@aliyun.com (F.K.); xk06gg@163.com (K.X.)

* Author to whom correspondence should be addressed; zn928@naver.com or zhangn@jxufe.edu.cn; Tel.: +86-791-8381-0553; Fax: +86-791-8381-0892.

External Editor: Marc A. Rosen

Received: 29 July 2014; in revised form: 31 August 2014; Accepted: 23 September 2014; Published: 29 September 2014

Abstract: This study examines the determinants of farmers' willingness to pay (WTP) and their payment levels for ecological compensation of the Poyang Lake Wetland in China. We developed a farmer household survey and gathered 292 effective responses. The contingent valuation method (CVM) and Heckman's two-step model were employed for the empirical study. Results show that 46.58% of farmers are willing to pay ecological compensation, with an average price of $64.39/household per year. The influencing factors that significantly influence farmers' WTP include household income, residential location, emphasis on improvement of wetland resources, arable land area, and contracted water area. In addition, household income, residential location, arable land area, and contracted water area are significantly related to their payment levels. The results of this empirical study inform important policy implications and recommendations.

Keywords: household survey; ecological compensation; willingness to pay (WTP); Poyang Lake Wetland; China

---

1. Introduction

Known as the "kidneys of the earth," [1] wetlands play an extremely important role in alleviating pollution of water resources caused by human activities. Wetlands are not only important natural ecosystems but also a vital economic resource, playing an important role in water supply, water storage, and water construction projects [2]. China has a total wetland area of about 69.4 million ha, accounting for 10% of the world's wetlands [3]. The area of Poyang Lake Wetland is about 2698 km^2 [4]. It is the largest and the most important freshwater wetland in China [5,6]. Poyang Lake Wetland plays an irreplaceable ecological role in flood storage and biodiversity conservation, so much so that it is credited with the maintenance of regional, and even, national ecological security.

However, due to the long-term degradation and depletion of wetland resources, China's wetland areas have been decreasing, and their functions are gradually eroding [7]. Between 1954 and 1997, rampant construction activity significantly reduced the total area of Poyang Lake Wetland from 5160 km^2 to 3859 km^2, translating into a cumulative reduction of 1301 km^2 [8]. Since the late 1990s, a series of ecological restoration measures have been implemented in the Poyang Lake region to curb this trend of wetland degradation. However, the excessive use of the wetland's resources has led to the deterioration of habitats and declining biodiversity, which have not yet been fundamentally reversed. Some rare aquatic animals, such as dolphins and porpoises, are nearly extinct [9].

Given that the status of this wetland ecosystem continues to be exceedingly fragile, its restoration and protection have become key concerns for the national and local governments. A variety of lake wetland management mechanisms operate in China and globally. There are two main types of mechanisms: one is the mandatory regulation mechanism based on administrative means, while the other is the ecological compensation mechanism based on economic means. The ecological compensation mechanism is a new type of resource and environmental management method designed to balance economic development and ecological conservation [10]. These methods are widely used in natural resource compensation research in various venues including water [11], forests [12], and farms [13]. In market economies, the eco-compensation mechanism is also an important and effective management approach for ecological protection. For example, Chicago's corporate wetlands banks are part of its entrepreneurial wetland banking program [14], which aims to effectively resolve the contradictions and conflicts between wetland conservation and utilization. Similar success stories are not uncommon in the "new" economies [15]. In China, ecological compensation was initiated in the 1990s solely to address compensation for the ecological benefits of forests. Without corresponding laws, regulations, policies, and market mechanisms, this effort faced numerous challenges. Currently, the establishment of the Poyang Lake Wetland ecological compensation mechanism has been formally incorporated into the agendas of the central and local Chinese governments; however, the initiative continues to face difficulties in determining the compensating subjects. In terms of the entities managing wetland resources, difficulties in assigning responsibilities and ensuring effective implementation of ecological compensation mechanisms have deterred progress. Previous studies mainly focused on the general resident's WTP; however, few studies have analyzed the WTP of wetland farmers. This study aims to fill this gap by investigating farmers' WTP. The wetland farmers play a very important role in the wetland eco-compensation in Poyang lake wetland; they are both polluters and beneficiaries of the wetlands. The current study is the preliminary study on wetland eco-compensation, further study will identity the farmers' (willingness to accept) WTA. Finally, we will estimate the ecological compensation standard for farmers with the WTP and WTA. Based the empirical studies, we aim to present some important policy suggestions for making the ecological compensation standard for local wetland farmers.

Therefore, understanding farmers' willingness to pay (WTP) for ecological compensation of the Poyang Lake Wetland, their payment levels, and factors influencing such ecological compensation can theoretically contribute to policy innovations in this area. This study aims to provide pertinent reference values that will help policy makers decide the finer points of the Poyang Lake Wetland compensation mechanism, and ultimately, assist in the overall establishment of a lake wetland ecological compensation policy for China. Notably, no study in China has focused on farmers' WTP in such cases. Therefore, this study aims to fill this gap by investigating the factors influencing farmers' WTP for ecological compensation in this area using a household-level survey.

The rest of this paper is organized as follows. Section 2 presents a literature review. Section 3 explains the data and methodology. Section 4 presents the empirical results and related discussion. Section 5 concludes and provides important policy implications.

2. Literature Review

Wetland ecosystem services are essential to human life, and they are essentially public goods. However, there is not a relative market that expresses these values in China [16]. Estimating the non-use values of public attributes requires a non-market economic valuation method to avoid "*The Tragedy of the Commons*" [17]. Two categories of non-market valuation methods, developed in previous research, are the revealed preference and stated preference methods [18]. The revealed preference category includes the hedonic pricing method (HPM) and the travel cost method (TCM). These methods have been applied to actual market valuation characterized by exchanging economic currency and market goods/services [17]. The stated preference method involves the choice experiment and the contingent valuation method (CVM,) which is used to estimate the value of total ecosystem services [19].

CVM is regarded as one of the most promising methods for valuing public goods [20]. It came into use to estimate the benefits of outdoor recreation in the Maine backwoods of the United States [20].

CVM is widely used in many fields, such as measuring valuation for publicly financed health care services [21], assessing landfill mining projects [22], understanding public perceptions of nuclear power [23], conducting an economic valuation of forest ecosystem services [17], and so on. However, few studies on CVM have focused on Chinese wetlands. No studies on CVM have examined the Poyang lake wetlands, which is one of the most important wetlands in China. This study aims to fill this gap in the literature.

CVM research has made an invaluable contribution to the field by demonstrating that an explicit link between non-market goods and market price is unnecessary [17]. However, there is still a need for understanding of respondents' valuation of public goods [24]. Therefore, CVM is highly suitable for researching farmers' willingness to pay and the level of ecological compensation.

The theoretical basis of China's policy regarding payments for environmental services lies in the principle "Users should protect, destroyers should restore, beneficiaries should pay, and polluters should be charged fees" [25]. Presently, most of the relevant research literature assigns the responsibilities for wetland resource development and utilization to farmers, while the government, private companies, and other social subject are referred to as the beneficiaries of wetland protection. Therefore, policy makers designing ecological compensation systems typically position farmers only as compensators for ecological restoration and not as compensators for ecological restoration [15,26]. For example, some past studies have focused on farmers' willingness to accept ecological compensation in the Poyang Lake Wetland area [27,28] and the Shanxi Crested Ibis National Nature Reserve [29]. Other related research has followed a similar line of thought [15]. While past research has highlighted the "beneficiaries should pay" principle, it ignores the fact that farmers are both the beneficiaries and the destroyers of wetland resources. Ignoring the negative impact of farmers on wetland resource development and utilization activities is clearly not in the interests of wetland protection and conservation. Therefore, the current system design does not truly reflect the principle guiding ecological compensation, namely, "Users should protect, destroyers should restore." Currently, farmers are not responsible for wetland ecological compensation, which is a major deficiency of the previous studies. Thus, this study contributes by offering a novel research perspective: Not only are farmers the beneficiaries of wetland ecosystems, they are also its destroyers, and thus, ecological compensation for wetlands should be examined from aspect of farmers' WTP and the factors influencing the same.

Methodologically, previous studies mainly used the logit, tobit, and multiple linear regression models to analyze farmers' WTP for ecological compensation. For example, some studies investigated the factors impacting the ecological compensation paid by farmers in the Poyang Lake area [28,30], while others have examined these factors for paddy farmers in the Shanxi Crested Ibis National Nature Reserve [29] using above methods. However, the above models do not examine the factors that influence willingness to pay and the level of payment simultaneously. In particular, the models do not avoid the disturbance of "WTP = 0" samples when examining the factors that influence payment levels. Heckman's two-step model can effectively solve this problem and prevent sample selection bias [31]. Based on the above considerations, we use the contingent valuation method (CVM) to assess farmers' WTP for the ecological compensation of Poyang Lake Wetland and their payment levels. We utilize Heckman's two-step model to analyze the factors influencing the two above mentioned research indexes and their mechanisms. In doing so, we hope to assess the importance of the complementary values on farmers' WTP for ecological compensation of Poyang Lake Wetland and its application to China's overall lake wetland ecological compensation policy.

3. Data and Methods

3.1. Area and Data

Poyang Lake is a freshwater lake fed by water from five important rivers in southern China [32]. The State Council has approved and established the Poyang Lake Ecological Economic Zone, which is divided into the core-protected area, efficient and intensive development area, and lakeside controlled development area. This study examines the core protected and lakeside controlled development areas, including Nanchang County, Xinjian County, Jinxian County, Lushan District, Gongqing cheng City, Dean County, Yongxiu County, Xingzi County, Hukou County, Duchang County, Poyang County, Yugan County, and Dongxiang County.

The data used in this study are sourced from the 2013 and 2014 household surveys designed to assess farmers' WTP for ecological compensation of the Poyang Lake Wetland. Farmers in this area are mainly engaged in traditional primary industries such as cultivation and plantation. In order to facilitate subsequent comparative studies, we adopt the data from the "2012 Statistical Yearbook of Poyang Lake Ecological Economic Zone" and divide the 13 counties/areas into 3 types based on the ratio of the primary industry production value to the gross regional domestic product. The categories are demarcated as seen in Table 1, with large, medium, and small depicting ratios >20%, 10%–20%, and <10%, respectively.

Table 1. Classification of the study area.

Type	Region	Ratio	Area
I	Duchang, Yugan, Poyang	>20%	Large
II	Xinjian, Jinxian, Yongxiu, Xingzi, Hukou, Dongxiang	10%–20%	Medium
III	Nanchang, Lushan, Dean, Gongqingcheng	<10%	Small

In order to ensure an effective and unbiased study, we use sampling methods appropriate to the town, village, and household levels (Table 2).

Table 2. Sampling methods.

Stage	Sampling Unit	Number	Method
1	Town	26	Stratified sampling
2	Village	1	Probability proportionate to size sampling (PPS)
3	Household	12	Simple random sampling (SRS)

In the first stage, two towns are selected from each county type seen in Table 1 using the stratified sampling method. In the second stage, we select one village from each of the selected towns using the probability proportionate to size sampling (PPS) method. In the last step, we select households from these villages using the simple random sampling method, and then, we survey the households. In total, 292 of 312 questionnaires are found to be effective. The total population is wetland farmers in the Poyang lake area. Our pilot test employed simple random sampling, and found at least 225 respondents fitting the need. We then used the three-stage sampling method to conduct door-to door interviews for 312 respondents, of which 292 were found to provide reliable data. This number is more than the minimum required sample size, and thus the sample is statistically valid for deducing the total population.

3.2. Research Methods

The CVM and Heckman's two-step model are used to quantitatively analyze the obtained household survey data.

3.2.1. Contingent Valuation Method

CVM is a stated preference method [33] involving the hypothetical choices in an administered and well-designed sample survey, based on the direct elicitation of individual's preference [34]. It creates a hypothetical market by asking respondents whether they want to pay as well as the amount they are willing to pay for certain non-market goods [35]. As previously stated, CVM is widely used and has many advantages. Notably, it can measure both use and nonuse values [36,37]. Therefore, CVM can overcome the limitations of the travel cost method [37] and other traditional calculation methods, such as the proxy goods method and opportunity cost method [38]. However, some researchers doubt its ability to provide valid measures for economic valuation of public goods [36]. For example, stated WTP may be a poor indicator of actual WTP [39]. However, CVM's fundamental utility is supported by most critics, and more careful WTP estimates are encouraged because of this [40].

In this study, we accurately assessed WTP using the valuation method. We used an open-ended WTP questionnaire so that responders would not be restricted by defined values (as in binary choice or closed-ended questions) [41]. We minimized missing responses and explained questions more clearly using face-to-face interviews [20]. Responses to open-ended questionnaires are likely to minimize standard error and lower estimates of central tendency [42], preventing bias [41]. In addition, we finalized the WTP questionnaires and the pre-testing process with experts to guarantee validity and make the questionnaire more clear to respondents.

It is also very important to select a realistic payment vehicle (*i.e.*, how respondents pay the WTP amount) in CVM [43]. Taxes and donations are often used as payment vehicles associated with preservation values [44]. However, donations are more useful payment vehicles for contingent valuation because they provide a reasonable approach for estimating the economic value of small-scale public goods, while respondents may object to mandatory payment schemes (*i.e.*, entrance fees or taxes) [45]. Thus, we used donation as the payment vehicle in this study.

In addition, WTP values are calculated based on mathematical expectation (discrete variables), and the formula is expressed as below:

$$E = WTP = \sum_{i=1}^{n} \alpha_i Pr_i \tag{1}$$

where α_i stands for the amount farmer i is willing to pay, Pr_i represents the probability that farmer i will pay that amount, and n stands for the sample size of farmers whose WTP is positive.

3.2.2. Heckman's Two-Step Model

Heckman's two-step method is a statistical method that allows for accurate sample selection bias, for which Heckman [46] accepted the Economic Nobel Prize in 2000 [47]. We had two reasons for using Heckman's two-step model in the study. First, it allowed us to examine the two steps leading to farmers' decisions in a single model while distinguishing the influence of different factors between these two steps [31]. In other words, we were able to investigate the influence factors of willingness to pay along with payment level in a single model. We could then use the model to analyze the factors influencing farmers' payment levels simultaneously, and prevent the disturbance of farmers whose WTP was zero. Secondly, the model could explicitly resolve potential sample selection bias [31,48]. Since the population in our study was quite large with no boundaries, sampling could only define the scope that was selected by the researchers. It is, therefore, possible to insert irrelevant variables, or to choose not to include associated variables in the sample, which may cause sample selection bias [46]. Therefore, we used Heckman's two-step model to prevent these problems.

Variables: Eight indicators/variables are designed [29,30,49,50] to evaluate the changes in WTP and the payment levels of farmers in the study area (Table 3).

Table 3. Variables and description.

Variable	Unit	Description	Related Supporting Documents
Gender (X_1)	Male = 1, Female = 0	These variables evaluate the possible impacts on farmers' WTP and their payment levels, using individual and household-level information.	[29,30,49]
Number of family members (X_2)	Persons		[29,30,50]
Annual household income (X_3)	Yuan (¥)		[29,30,50]
Source of income (X_4)	Cultivation = 1, Otherwise = 0		[30]
Residential location (X_5)	Region I or II = 1, Region III = 0		[29]
Emphasis on improvement of wetland resources (X_6)	Yes = 1, No = 0	This variable evaluates the impacts of the farmers' concern and knowledge about environmental issues pertaining to wetlands on WTP and their payment levels.	[49,50]
Arable land area (X_7)	Acres	These variables examine whether the cultivation area and contracted water area impact farmers' WTP and their payment levels.	[29,30]
Contracted water area (X_8)	Acres		[29,30]

Model selection: This study uses Heckman's two-step model to estimate the factors influencing WTP and payment levels. First, we use the probit model to test the factors influencing WTP. Second, we use the multiple linear regression model to further investigate the factors influencing payment levels. Specifically, the models are expressed as follows:

$$Z = \partial_0 + \partial_1 X_1 + \partial_2 X_2 + \partial_3 X_3 \cdots + \partial_n X_n + \varphi \tag{2}$$

Equation (2) is the first-stage Heckman probit model. Z is the dependent variable, which represents the probability of wetland farmers' WTP. $\partial_0, \partial_1, \partial_2, \partial_3, \cdots, \partial_n$ are coefficients that will be estimated while examining the factors affecting farmers' WTP $X_1, X_2, X_3 \cdots, X_n$ are the explanatory variables, and φ is the residual term

$$Y = \beta_0 + \beta_1 X_1 + \beta_2 X_2 + \beta_3 X_3 \cdots + \beta_n X_n + \delta\lambda + \mu \tag{3}$$

Equation (3) is the multiple linear regression model used in the second stage of our analysis. Y is the dependent variable, which examines factors affecting the farmers' payment levels. In this paper, we add Mills ratio, λ, to overcome the sample selection bias [36]. $\beta_0, \beta_1, \beta_2, \beta_3, \cdots, \beta_n$ and δ are the coefficients to be estimated. $X_1, X_2, X_3 \cdots, X_n$ are the explanatory variables, and μ is the residual term.

4. Empirical Study

4.1. WTP and Payment Levels

As shown in Table 4, 46.58% of farmers have positive WTP, while 53.42% of farmers do not.

Table 4. Frequency of willingness to pay (WTP).

WTP	Number	Sample Size	Proportion
Yes	1	136	46.58%
No	0	156	53.42%

Sustainability **2014**, 6, 6714–6728

We use Equation (1) to estimate the payment levels in regions I, II, and III. The results appear as Equations (4)–(7) (see Figure 1).

$$E(WTP_I) = \sum_{i=1}^{n} \alpha_i Pr_i = 97.05 \tag{4}$$

$$E(WTP_{II}) = \sum_{i=1}^{n} \alpha_i Pr_i = 62.80 \tag{5}$$

$$E(WTP_{III}) = \sum_{i=1}^{n} \alpha_i Pr_i = 34.32 \tag{6}$$

$$E(WTP\ all) = \sum_{i=1}^{n} \alpha_i Pr_i = 64.39 \tag{7}$$

Figure 1. Distribution of farmers' payment levels in the Poyang Lake Wetland area.

The value measured as the Chinese currency (RMB Yuan) is converted into US $ value by the average exchange rate during 2012–2013 (RMB 6.252 yuan to one dollar) per household per year.

The results in Equations (4)–(7) and Figure 1 show that the payment levels of all farmers toward the ecological compensation of Poyang Lake Wetland area is $64.39/household per year. The highest payment levels, $97.05/household per year, occurs in region I. The second-highest level of household payment, $62.80/household per year, occurs in region II. The lowest level of household payment, $34.32/household per year, is seen for region III. The results also indicate that the higher the regional agricultural production, the higher the payment levels of the household willing to pay for ecological compensation.

4.2. Results of the Regressions

Heckman's two-step model is applied using Stata11.0. The farmers' WTP and their payment levels are used as the dependent variables, while household characteristics are used as the independent variables. The result is shown in Tables 5 and 6.

Table 5. First-stage probit analysis.

Variable	C	SE	Z	P > |Z|
Constant	−2.245 ***	0.575	−3.900	0.000
X_1	0.651	0.433	1.510	0.132
X_2	−0.056	0.080	−0.690	0.488
X_3	1.63×10^{-7}	2.00×10^{-6}	0.08	0.935
X_4	1.256 ***	0.274	4.580	0.000
X_5	−1.051 **	0.315	−3.330	0.001
X_6	2.415 ***	0.313	7.730	0.000
X_7	0.349 **	0.104	3.360	0.001
X_8	0.152 *	0.092	1.650	0.098

Note: ***, **, and * represent significance at 1%, 5%, and 10%, respectively.

Table 6. Second-stage multiple linear regression analysis.

Variable	C	SE	Z	P > |Z|
Constant	−60.250	89.297	−0.670	0.500
X_3	0.004 ***	0.001	4.330	0.000
X_5	271.517 ***	90.725	2.990	0.003
X_7	28.609 ***	4.049	7.060	0.000
X_8	30.946 ***	3.277	9.440	0.000
λ	155.600 **	77.718	2.000	0.045

Note: *** and ** represent significance at 1% and 5%, respectively.

It should be noted that eight explanatory variables are incorporated in the first stage, and four explanatory variables are introduced in the second stage. This is because Heckman's model should include at least one variable in the first stage that is different from the variables included in the second stage. That is, all explanatory variables must be contained in the first stage, while the second stage must contain fewer variables than the first stage [51]. Based on this principle, the second stage regress the variables with statistically significant values.

4.3. Factors Affecting WTP

The probit model indicated in Table 5 shows that source of income (X_4), residential location (X_5), emphasis on the improvement of wetland resources (X_6), arable land area (X_7), and contracted water area (X_8) are significantly related to WTP, while gender (X_1), family size (X_2), and household income (X_3) do not show statistical significance. X_4 is statistically significant with WTP, and the coefficient is positive, which means that farmers relying mainly on agricultural products for their incomes have stronger WTP. It may be that when a farmer's household income is sourced mainly from planting, breeding, and other traditional industries, environmental quality improvements are likely to be more beneficial to him, and therefore, such farmers are more willing to compensate the environment. X_5 is statistically significant with WTP, and the coefficient is negative, which means that farmers living in regions I and II have stronger WTP than those living in region III. This may be because the different levels of agricultural production in regions I, II, and III may affect farmers' WTP; farmers living in regions I and II will earn more from their ecological environment, and therefore, they have a stronger WTP. X_6 is statistically significant with WTP, and the coefficient is positive, indicating that farmers who pay close attention to wetland environmental improvements are more willing to compensate their environment. It may be that such farmers are dissatisfied with the current environmental quality of the wetland, which enhances their willingness to compensate the environment in order to improve it. X_7 is statistically significant with WTP, and the coefficient is positive; the more arable land the farmers have, the stronger their WTP. It may be that farmers with more arable land earn well from farming. Thus, if their environmental quality deteriorates, their incomes from farming would reduce. As a result, they are more willing to compensate the environment. X_8 is also statistically significant with WTP, and the coefficient is positive. Thus, the higher the contracted water area, the stronger the WTP. It may be that farmers with higher contracted water areas earn more revenue from fishing. Given the relation between fishing and the quality of the wetland environment, these farmers would be more willing to compensate the environment in order to protect it.

4.4. Factors Affecting Payment Levels

The multiple linear regression model shown in Table 5 indicates that household income (X_3), residential location (X_5), arable land area (X_7), and contracted water area (X_8) are significantly related to payment levels. X_3 is statistically significant with the payment levels, and the coefficient is positive; thus, the payment levels will increase as the incomes of the farmers with positive WTP increases. It maybe that the incomes of such farmers are closely linked with the wetland resources; therefore, their increasing incomes encourage them to pay more money to protect the wetland environment. That is, the higher the increase in farmers' incomes, the more their WTP. X_5 is also statistically significant with the payment levels and displays a positive coefficient. This means that the farmers living in regions I and II have higher WTP than those living in region III. This result may be attributed to their sources of income. The incomes of the farmers living in regions I and II depend more on agricultural (grain) production and fishing. Therefore, they are more willing to compensate the environments o as to potentially increase their incomes.

X_7 is also statistically significant with the payment levels and shows a positive coefficient. Thus, farmers having WTP and possessing more arable land will have higher payment levels; the more their arable land, the higher the portions of their incomes from planting, which in turn is closely connected to the environment. Therefore, farmers who have more arable land are willing to pay higher sums in order to protect the wetland environment. X_8 is statistically significant with the payment levels as well and has a positive coefficient. Therefore, farmers who are willing to pay have contracted a higher area of water and will have higher payment levels. It maybe that the higher the contracted water area, the higher the portions of their incomes from aquatic products. Therefore, the better the environmental quality is, the higher the farmer's potential income and his payment levels are. In addition, the coefficient of λ is not zero and is statistically significant, which indicates that the sample suffers from selection bias. Therefore, this result confirms our selection of Heckman's two-step model to examine the factors affecting farmers' WTP and their payment levels.

5. Conclusions and Implications

This study examined the determinants of farmers' WTP for ecological compensation of the Poyang Lake Wetland area in China and their payment levels, using farmer household-level survey data. The CVM and Heckman's two-step model were employed. The results show that 46.58% of farmers have positive WTP, with their average annual WTP being $64.39/household. The empirical results show that household income, residential location, emphasis on improvement of wetland resources, arable land area, and contracted water area have a significant correlation with the farmers' WTP, and household income, residential location, arable land area, and contracted water area have a significant correlation with the farmers' payment levels.

In order to effectively improve the farmers' WTP for the ecological compensation of Poyang Lake Wetland and their payment levels, it is necessary to promote the establishment and implementation of the Poyang Lake Wetland ecological compensation mechanism. The following policy implications would serve the purpose.

First, the government should raise the farmers' awareness about their obligations to wetland ecological protection and their liabilities for damage caused to the area. Experience has shown that it is difficult to levy compensation funds from the farmers, who traditionally view the long-term use wetland resources as being free. Thus, there are serious gaps between the concept's ideology and actual implementation. Although the law obligates citizens to protect natural resources and the environment and mandates legal liabilities for any breaches, farmers residing in the National Lake District consider the use of all wetland resources as their traditional right. The uninhibited and excessive use of wetland resources causes ecological losses, which could be lessened by improving farmers' awareness about these issues. Increased raising of awareness on the topic will help farmers recognize the illegality of such exploitative behavior and the negative impacts of wetland resource depletion and degradation, thus laying a solid ideological foundation for the successful establishment of an ecological compensation system for lake wetlands throughout the country. Secondly, establish rural cooperatives to produce wetland agricultural products such as fish, shrimp and vegetables for farmers. Encourage farmers to join cooperatives for joint development of wetland resources. In addition, the government should proactively support capital loans and technology that benefit more farmers in terms of wetland resources. Thus, the farmers will have the willingness to continually expand the sale of wetland products. Based on empirical results of this study, income and land area are positively linked to payment level. Therefore, when more farmers are willing to pay for wetland resources, it benefits development of these resources and increases the economic benefits of these wetland resources. Third, we recommend developing a special wetland protection fund for real money generated by farmers' willingness to pay, using the fund for the wetland ecological protection. We also recommend that state and local governments offer financial support to continually increase investment in wetland conservation. The local government should also communicate with transparency. Improving and protecting wetland environments promise to increase farmer's incomes and their quality of life, therefore benefiting China as a whole. Fourth, it is important to clarify the property rights of the Poyang Lake Wetland area. Field surveys show state-owned and collective-owned property rights for Poyang Lake Wetland resources, but the limits of the geographical boundaries are unclear. The operating property rights of the farmers have not been implemented. Blurred property boundaries not only increase the difficulties of wetland management but also hinder the establishment and implementation of wetland ecological compensation systems. Defining property rights to the wetland's resources can provide the fundamental institutional guarantees so necessary for ecological compensation mechanisms. Fifth, establishing an ecological compensation system database to serve rural households around lakes should be the government's priority. This exercise may be taken up as part of an annual census, wherein the relevant government departments would collate all the information related to ecological compensation, such as household income sources, arable land area, contracted water area, *etc.* Improved survey data would provide an important foundation for assessing farmers' WTP and help the development of specific standards in the field. Sixth, the government should develop differentiated ecological compensation standards. In accordance with the varying characteristics/heterogeneity of rural households, it may be prudent to develop different ecological compensation fund levies or disbursement criteria. Seventh, the in-depth study of the specific ecological compensation mode/operation system for the Poyang Lake Wetland shows that it is necessary for farmers to be able to pay for ecological compensations using payment patterns convenient to them. These patterns would differ by regional characteristics and may include payment methods such as compensation via labor, equipment, and/or money. Such choices would improve the farmers' ability to make payments toward ecological compensation.

This study has some limitations. The empirical analysis is based on data only for the 2012–2013 period. Therefore, future research should consider a longer period, by considering a broader sample. Another limitation is there is no reference set for farmer's WTP answer; thus, the answer might be biased. To overcome this limitation, future study may consider using the open-ended survey. Further study could investigate willingness to accept of farmers. By combining WTP and WTA, the ecological compensation standard can be estimated for wetland farmers.

Acknowledgments: This research was funded by the National Major Social Science Fund of China (12&ZD213), National Science Foundation of China (41261110, 41461118), China Postdoctoral Foundation (2014M551849) and Humanities and Social Science Fund of Jiangxi (JJ1420).

Author Contributions: Fanbin Kong designed research idea; Kai Xiong collected research and analyzed the data; Ning Zhang revised the manuscript. All authors read and approved the final manuscript.

Conflicts of Interest: The authors declare no conflict of interest.

References

1. Gopal, B.; Ghosh, D. Natural wetlands. In *Reference Module in Earth Systems and Environmental Sciences Encyclopedia of Ecology*; Academic Press: Waltham, MA, USA, 2008; pp. 2493–2504.
2. Bostian, M.B.; Herlihy, A.T. Valuing tradeoffs between agricultural production and wetland condition in the U.S. Mid-Atlantic region. *Ecol. Econ.* **2014**, *105*, 284–291.
3. Liu, H.Y. China's wetland resources characteristics, present situation and ecological security. *Resour. Sci.* **2005**, *29*, 54–60.
4. Huang, J.G.; Guo, Z.Y. Poyang Lake wetland conservation of biological diversity and its countermeasures. *Res. Soil Water Conserv.* **2007**, *23*, 305–306.
5. Wei, Y.H.; Zhang, J.Y.; Zhang, D.W.; Tu, T.H.; Luo, L.G. Metal concentrations in various fish organs of different fish species from Poyang Lake, China. *Ecotoxicol. Environ. Saf.* **2014**, *104*, 182–188. [PubMed]
6. Zhao, Z.H.; Zhang, L.; Cai, Y.J.; Chen, Y.W. Distribution of polycyclic aromatic hydrocarbon (PAH) residues in several tissues of edible fishes from the largest freshwater lake in China, Poyang Lake, and associated human health risk assessment. *Ecotoxicol. Environ. Saf.* **2014**, *104*, 323–331. [PubMed]
7. Zhang, Q.; Xiao, M.Z.; Li, J.F.; Singh, V.P.; Wang, Z.Z. Topography-based spatial patterns of precipitation extremes in thePoyang Lake basin, China: Changing properties and causes. *J. Hydrol.* **2014**, *512*, 229–239.
8. Qian, D.Q.; Liu, C.Y. Poyang lake wetland ecological protection and sustainable utilization research. *Acta Pedol. Sin.* **2002**, *23*, 318–326.
9. Liu, Y.; Peng, W. Social economic driving force analysis of the Poyang lake wetland ecosystem degradation. *Jiangxi Soc. Sci.* **2003**, *24*, 231–233.
10. Kong, F.B. Improving ecological compensation mechanism of China: Theory, practice and research prospects. *Issues Agric. Econ.* **2007**, *10*, 50–53.
11. Shen, N.; Pang, A.P.; Li, C.H.; Liu, K.K. Study on ecological compensation mechanism of Xin'an Spring Water Source Protection Zone in Shanxi province, China. *Procedia Environ. Sci.* **2010**, *2*, 1063–1073.
12. Li, F.; Li, W.H.; Zhen, L.; Huang, H.Q.; Wei, Y.J.; Naomi, I. Estimating eco-compensation requirements for forest ecosystem conservation: A case study in Hainan province, southern China. *Outlook Agric.* **2011**, *40*, 51–57.
13. Robert, H.; Oliver, B.; Ingrid, J.; Matthias, S.; Lukas, P. Motivations for implementation of ecological compensation areas on Swiss lowland farms. *J. Rural Stud.* **2014**, *34*, 26–36.
14. Robertson, M.; Hayden, N. Evaluation of a market in wetland credits: Entrepreneurial wetland banking in Chicago. *Conserv. Biol.* **2008**, *22*, 231–233.
15. Kong, F.B. *Poyang Lake Ecological Economic Zone Issue of Environmental Protection and Ecological Poverty*; China Environmental Science Press: Beijing, China, 2011.
16. Robert, C.; Ralph, A.; Rudolf, G.; Stephen, F.; Monica, G.; Bruce, H.; Karin, L.; Shahid, N.; Robert, V.O.; Jose, P.; *et al.* The value of the world's ecosystem services and natural capital. *Nature* **1997**, *387*, 253–260.
17. Tao, Z.; Yan, H.M.; Zhan, J.Y. Economic valuation of forest ecosystem services in Heshui watershed using contingent valuation method. *Procedia Environ. Sci.* **2012**, *13*, 2445–2450.
18. Monica, I.O.; Alex, S.M.; Barry, D.S. Economic valuation of environmental services sustained by water flows in Yaqui River Delta. *Ecol. Econ.* **2008**, *65*, 155–166.

19. Loomis, J.B.; Kent, P.; Strange, L.; Fausch, K.; Covich, A. Measuring the total economic value of restoring ecosystem services in an inpaired river basin: Results from a contingent valuation survey. *Ecol. Econ.* **2000**, *33*, 103–117.

20. Mitchell, R.C.; Carson, R.T. *Using Surveys to Value Public Goods: The Contingent Valuation Method*; Resources for the Future Press: Washington, DC, USA, 1989.

21. Tambor, M.; Pavlova, M.; Rechel, B.; Golinowska, S.; Sowada, C.; Groot, W. Willingness to pay for publicly financed health care services in Central and Eastern Europe: Evidence from six countries based on a contingent valuation method. *Soc. Sci. Med.* **2014**, *116*, 193–201. [PubMed]

22. Marella, C.; Raga, R. Use of the Contingent Valuation Method in the assessment of a landfill mining project. *Waste Manag.* **2014**, *34*, 1199–1205. [PubMed]

23. Sun, C.W.; Zhu, X.T. Evaluating the public perceptions of nuclear power in China: Evidence from a contingent valuation survey. *Energy Policy* **2014**, *69*, 397–405.

24. Venkatachalam, L. The contingent valuation method: A review. *Environ. Impact Assess. Rev.* **2004**, *24*, 89–124.

25. Wang, D.H. Issues to explore the establishment of ecological compensation mechanism. *Environ. Prot.* **2006**, *34*, 12–17.

26. Wang, Y.; Yan, J. Farmers' ecological compensation Willingness to accept analysis of the Nature Reserve—Take Shaanxi crested ibis nature reserve as example. *Chin. Rural Econ.* **2010**, *26*, 63–73.

27. He, J. Based on Poyang Lake Wetland Ecosystem Services and Ecological Compensation Community Research. Jiangxi Normal University, Nanchang, China, 2009.

28. Jiang, H.Y.; Wen, Y.L. Based on the WTA wetlands surrounding farmers willingness to compensation and influencing factors research. *Resour. Environ. Yangtze Basin* **2011**, *20*, 489–494.

29. Wang, C.H.; Cui, L.J.; Mao, X.F. Wetland ecological compensation area surrounding farmers willingness comparison. *Acta Ecol. Sin.* **2012**, *32*, 5345–5354.

30. Li, F.; Zhen, L.; Qing, H.Q. Willingness of farmers to compensate the impact of ecological factors in Poyang Lake region. *Resour. Sci.* **2010**, *34*, 824–830.

31. Kim, J.; Jang, S.C. Dividend behavior of lodging firms: Heckman's two-step approach. *Int. J. Hosp. Manag.* **2010**, *29*, 413–420.

32. Cui, L.J. Poyang lake wetland ecosystem service function value evaluation research. *Chin. J. Ecol.* **2004**, *23*, 47–51.

33. Hanemann, M.W. Discrete/continuous models of consumer demand. *Econometrica* **1984**, *52*, 541–562.

34. Arrow, K.J.; Solow, R.; Leamer, E.; Portney, P.; Radner, R.; Schuman, H. Report of the NOAA panel on contingent valuation. *Fed. Regist.* **1993**, *58*, 4601–4614.

35. Bengochea-Morancho, A.; Fuertes-Eugenio, A.M.; del Saz-Salazar, S. A comparison of empirical models used to infer the willingness to pay in contingent valuation. *Empir. Econ.* **2005**, *30*, 235–244.

36. Johnson, B.K.; Whitehead, J.C.; Mason, D.S.; Walker, G.J. Willingness to pay for downtown public goods generated by large, sports-anchored development projects: The CVM approach. *City Cult. Soc.* **2012**, *3*, 201–208.

37. Armbrecht, J. Use value of cultural experiences: A comparison of contingent valuation and travel cost. *Tour. Manag.* **2014**, *42*, 141–148.

38. Van den Berg, B.; Al, M.; Brouwer, W.; von Exel, J.; Koopmanschap, M. Economic valuation of informal care: The conjoint measurement method applied to informal caregiving. *Soc. Sci. Med.* **2005**, *61*, 1342–1355. [PubMed]

39. Carson, R.T.; Mitchell, R.C. The issue of scope in contingent valuation studies. *Am. J. Agric. Econ.* **1993**, *75*, 1263–1267.

40. Sattout, E.J.; Talhouk, S.N.; Caligari, P.D.S. Economic value of cedar relics in Lebanon: An application of contingent valuation method for conservation. *Ecol. Econ.* **2007**, *61*, 315–322.

41. O'Conor, R.M.; Johannesson, M.; Johansson, P. Stated preferences, real behavior and anchoring: Some empirical evidence. *Environ. Econ.* **1999**, *13*, 235–248.

42. Boyle, K.J.; Johnson, F.R.; McCollum, D.W.; Desvousges, W.H.; Dunford, R.W.; Hudson, S.P. Valuing public goods: Discrete *versus* continuous contingent-valuation responses. *Land Econ.* **1996**, *72*, 381–396.

43. Lee, C.K.; Han, S.Y. Estimating the use and preservation values of national parks' tourism resources using a contingent valuation method. *Tour. Manag.* **2002**, *23*, 531–540.

Sustainability **2014**, *6*, 6714–6728

44. Lee, C.K.; Mjelde, J.W. Valuation of ecotourism resources using a contingent valuation method: The case of the Korean DMZ. *Ecol. Econ.* **2007**, *63*, 511–520.

45. Champ, P.; Bishop, R.; Brown, T.; McCollum, D. Using donation mechanisms to value nonuse benefits from public goods. *J. Environ. Econ. Manag.* **1997**, *33*, 151–162.

46. Heckman, J. Sample selection bias as a specification error. *Econometrica* **1979**, *47*, 153–161.

47. Heckman Correction. Available online: http://en.wikipedia.org/wiki/Heckman_correction (accessed on 23 August 2014).

48. Bett, H.K.; Peters, K.J.; Nwankwo, U.M.; Bokelmann, W. Estimating consumer preferences and willingness to pay for the underutilised indigenous chicken products. *Food Policy* **2013**, *41*, 218–225.

49. Ge, Y.X.; Liang, L.J.; Wang, B.B. Residents the Yellow River basin ecological compensation intention and pay level analysis—Take Shandong province as an example. *Chin. Rural Econ.* **2009**, *25*, 77–85.

50. Cai, Z.J.; Zhang, W.W. Nanjing Yangtze River water quality improvement of the public's willingness to pay and the payment of the investigation. *Ecol Econ.* **2007**, *23*, 116–119.

51. Baum, C.F. *An Introduction to Modern Econometrics Using Stata*; Stata Press: College Station, TX, USA, 2006.

sustainability

MDPI

Article

Sustainable E-Governance: The Relationship among Trust, Digital Divide, and E-Government

Seunghwan Myeong [1,†,*], Yongmin Kwon [1,†] and Hyungjun Seo [2,†]

[1] Department of Public Administration, Inha University, Nam-gu, Incheon 402-751, Korea; kym@inha.edu
[2] Department of Global e-Governance, Inha University, Nam-gu, Incheon 402-751, Korea; 22132106@inha.edu
[*] Author to whom correspondence should be addressed; shmyeong@inha.ac.kr; Tel.: +82-032-860-7951.
[†] These authors contributed equally to this work.

Received: 4 June 2014; in revised form: 12 August 2014; Accepted: 25 August 2014; Published: 5 September 2014

Abstract: This study empirically examines the correlation between the quality of e-government and trust in government. It used survey data collected in 2013 from the metropolitan areas of Seoul. An index was developed to measure the quality of e-government services, and the Gov 3.0 values were reflected in the analysis, including openness, sharing, communication, and collaboration. The results show a partial correlation between the quality of e-government service and trust in government. In addition, the level of trust varied according to the different type of the digital divide groups. It suggests that as ICT (Information Communication Technology) has become more sophisticated, a willingness to share information among organizations and stakeholders may become a major factor to thoseactively seeking information and resources to make value-added products. It also suggests that more integrated data management including network securityand an open attitude toward information sharing will be more important beyond the level of technical issues.

Keywords: ICT; trust in government; digital divide

1. Introduction

The current smart society suggests the beginning of a post-information society. Although this information society can make people's lives more convenient and efficient, it may fail to sufficiently address technology-driven initiatives, in which government-driven ICT (Information Communication Technology) policies often ignore individuals' creative and cognitive processes in response to the government's actions. A smart society focuses on the process of mutual communication and the incorporation of each individual's thoughts into some social agreement. There are four major attributes of a smart society [1]. First, mobilitians deal with theirmobile environments freely, facilitating environments that are "always connected" through mobile devices. Second, personalized social networks facilitate communication between individuals anytime, anywhere as a result of many smartphone users and activated social networks. Third, ethics, trust, and fairness are some of the major values floated as new norms to dominate social activities because the public's rights can strengthen from large corporations to netizens, groups to individuals, and producers to consumers. Finally, a smart society can foster smart workplace environments where people can work without being limited by time or space through advanced ICT applications.

With the rise of this smart society, "smart e-government" has been proposed as a new model of government in a smart society. Smart e-government is a system in which cooperative governments strengthen the partnership between the public and private sectors; intelligent governments provide administrative services that better meet national requirements; transparent governments facilitate the public's communication, participation, and trust. People in a smart society are more active than those in an information society. As in the case of smartphones and social media, smart technologies facilitate people's participation in their environments. In the past, it was difficult to disseminate the voice of people, despite their ICT use. However, a smart society enables faster, real-time, and personalized communication. In particular, personalized services reflect one of the most representative characteristics of a smart society. Not only enterprises, but also governments, can focus more on the provision of personalized services.

In a smart society, based on a model of future government, e-government is connected to Gov 3.0 [1]. Gov 3.0 is a national administrative system that strengthens the role of individuals by redesigning administrative methods and processes based on highly intelligent ICT applications and social connections. In Gov 3.0, the government shares information and knowledge with firms, citizens, and global communities and provides common platforms that can produce democratic value added by exchanges between social members.

The government not only governs but also provides public goods. The government requires the public's participation in policymaking and providing public services. In addition, the government manages and provides data for transparency, trust, and value added. In some respects, the issue of the "Big Brother" is outdated. Monitoring and participation have become easier because of cross-checking mechanisms enabling people's use of smart technologies. In the initial stages of ICT adoption by the government, the emphasis was on accurate, efficient, and fast public administration. However, innovative ICT applications have changed the world, as illustrated by the "Jasmin Revolution" of 2011 in the Middle East. This event demonstrates that smart technologies can provide citizens with the power to change outdated customs and norms through the process of public discourse. The world's least corrupt countries show a high correlation between the quality of e-government and the level of trust in government. According to a 2007 Pew survey, in countries where people generally trust one another, there is greater confidence in the integrity of political leaders. Countries with a high level of e-government maturity tend to show a high level of trust (e.g., Sweden, Canada, and Britain). On the other hand, in low-trust countries, such as Nigeria and Lebanon, political corruption is widespread [2].

If there is some information asymmetry, then trust cannot be established. In the past, it was difficult to know what a government was really doing in every process of policy implementation. Even when a government provides well-designed e-government services, a high level of trust in government cannot be guaranteed. Unfortunately, many governments mistakenly believe that e-government services can promote trust in government. Therefore, many governments fail to transform their e-government into e-governance. This suggests a need to verify the factors driving the effect of e-government services on trust in government. Choi [3] stated that sustainability is a major subject of interest in the field of business and environmental management. Choi and Lee [4] emphasized the importance of long-term sustainability inKorea's regional innovation system and suggested that the governance approach can address sustainability. According to the literature, sustainability is an important factor in diverse fields. This suggests that a high level of trust in government can facilitate sustainable e-governance.

This study empirically examines the correlation between the quality of e-government and trust in government. The results have important policy implications for enhancing trust in government. Measurement instruments will be constructed to measure the quality of e-government services, and Gov 3.0 values are reflected in the analysis, including openness, sharing, communication, and collaboration. From this perspective, the digital divide issue may be one of the most serious factors to influence Gov3.0 policy and management. Although the advent of modern ICT has already relieved officials of the manytedious and routine managerial tasks, however, the question remains as to whatdegree the use of modern ICT can be more utilized which are greatly interactive with environments and related to human problems. In this research, the interests, conceptual relationships between the quality of e-government and trust will be discussed as well as examining the possible predictor of digital divide in e-government practices.

2. Literature Review

2.1. E-Government and Trust in Government

E-government plays an important role in fostering public trust and government transparency. Here the development of e-government services is necessary for transparency and trust. In this regard, it is conceivable that the Scandinavian model of governance, which "combines a high cost of government with high levels of trust and citizen participation," can deliver good public services.

Tolbert and Mossberger [5] suggested that "e-government can increase process-based trust by improving interactions with citizens and perceptions of responsiveness" and that "e-government has been proposed as a way to increase citizen trust in government and improve citizen evaluations of government". The least corrupt countries show a high correlation between the level of e-government and that of trust in government. They conducted empirical research about relationship between trust and e-government. They used the Pew Internet and American Life Project with 815 people who had previously reported that they used government Web sites. At the result, they found that the perception of government responsiveness at the local level led to greater trust in local government.

Moon [6] claimed that the public's trust in government has continued to weaken because of various administrative, political, sociocultural, economic, and media-related factors. Focusing on the administrative dimension, he explored selected administrative factors responsible for the decline in the public's trust, including the public's perception of administrative corruption (a lack of transparency), inefficiency (wastefulness), ineffectiveness, and policy alienation. He argued that IT offers a potentially useful tool for governments by helping them to restore the public's trust through improvements in transparency, cost efficiency, effectiveness, and policy participation. He illustrated this argument based on four selected cases (the OPEN system in Seoul, e-VA in Virginia, e-Filing for IRS tax returns, and online policy forums in Seoul and Pennsylvania).

Welch *et al.* [7] addressed the relationships between Internet use, citizen satisfaction with e-government, and trust in government. They first reviewed the literature on trust and explored how radical IT applications influence the production and maintenance of trust. They then developed some hypotheses about the relationships between citizens' experience with e-government, satisfaction with e-governmentand government websites, and trust in government. In addition, their model of e-government and website satisfaction incorporated citizens' perspectives on electronic transaction, transparency, and interactivity. Using data obtained from the Council on Excellence in Government, they developed and tested a two-stage, multiple-equation model that simultaneously predicted experience, satisfaction, and trust and found positive relationships of the use of government websites to e-government satisfaction and website satisfaction and a positive relationship between e-government satisfaction and trust in government. They concluded that e-government strategies (transaction, transparency, and interactivity) are important factors directly influencing e-government satisfaction and indirectly influencing trust. Individuals who use government websites are not only major consumers but also demanding citizens.

McNeal *et al.* [8] stated that, in addition to improving the efficiency and transparency of government services, e-government can increase the frequency of interactions between citizens and governments as well as improve perceptions of quality and trust in government. Previous studies of citizen-initiated contact with governments based on the Pew Internet and American Life Project survey data have found that e-government can motivate citizen-initiated contact with governments in some demographic groups and magnify existing gaps in others. Online citizen-initiated contact can improve the quality of interactions with governments, but evidence provides no support for the argument that e-government increases users' trust.

Hong [9] stated that recent years have witnessed the increasing use of online media such as websites, blogs, and social networking sites by governments for various public relations purposes. The study used a dataset of a national survey on Americans' use of the Internet, which was conducted by Princeton Survey Research Associates International and released by Pew Research

Center. The survey was completed in December 2009, selecting approximately 2200 adults based on the random-digit dialing (RDD) technique using both landline and mobile connections in order to ensure the representativeness of the sample. In this study, the respondents' experience with social media had a positive effect on their trust in government at the local and state levels. Those respondents who interacted with the government through social media were more likely to trust state and local governments than those who did not. However, the online use of transactional services (e.g., renewing a driver's license and registering an automobile) showed a difference in public trust in government only at the federal level. The researcher suggest that state and local governments should prioritize their interactions with citizens by emphasizing social media, updating high-quality information, and enhancing the accessibility of information on government websites.

To examine the role of trust in e-government, Horsburgh *et al.* [10] analyzes three types of trust drawing on 438 telephone surveys in Australia and 498 in New Zealand. The analysis of data from our study of Australians and New Zealanders found no relationship between trust in government institutions and in various e-government functions. Compared to other studies, they explained the disjuncture that they found may be a function of the fact that the respondents were from different countries to those where other studies were based.

Morgeson *et al.* [11] highlighted large gaps in the literature on the relationship between e-government and citizen trust. They addressed some of these gaps by using a cross-sectional sample of 787 end users of U.S. federal government services, data from the American Customer Satisfaction Index study, and structural equation modeling techniques and exploring the structure of the relationship between e-government and citizen trust. Although they find evidence that e-government adoption positively predicts citizen confidence in an agency, this relationship is relatively weak. Further, they find no evidence that e-government is positively related to trust in government. Instead, the findings suggest that e-government may help build or rebuild trust in local government not federal government.

Park and Cho [12] designed a preliminary causal link between use of social media in public relations and change in the public trust in organization. They concluded that by minimizing the distortion of message and strengthening connectedness between government and public, social media promises the possibility of restoring public trust in government by case study.

Parent *et al.* [13] tests the extent to which online initiatives have succeeded in increasing trust and external political efficacy in voters. An Internet-based survey of 182 Canadian voters shows that using the Internet to transact with the government had a significantly positive impact on trust and external political efficacy. They agree with that e-government usage increase trust in government, but the research shows that e-government intensifies existing levels of trust if these are positive, with no positive effect on those whose trust is either neutral or negative.

Butter *et al.* [14] analyzed how to use IT to deploy trust-based regulation in the government-to-business (G2B) relationship, with the Authorized Economic Operator (AEO) certification in the Netherlands between the Tax and Customs administrations and the businesses as a case study. The article discusses how to implement the AEO by utilizing the modern ICT, at lower transaction costs, in the meanwhile enhancing the trust and reputation between the government and businesses.

Omari and Omari [15] suggested the proposed e-Government trust model and showed that trust was a multidimensional issue. Each part was fully integrated with the others in a certain relationship that formulates trust. The main building blocks of trust are: IT security, process automation, policies and procedures, social and culture practices, and legislation. This model represents a suitable guideline for any government who wishes to build or rebuild trust with its customers. It is necessary to use modern technologies to complete the trust architecture.

Teo *et al.* [16] examined the role of trust in e-government success using the updated DeLone and McLean IS success model as the theoretical framework. The model was tested via a survey of 214 Singapore e-government Web site users. They found that online trust is partly affected by the offline trust in the government. Therefore, while Web site attributes, such as information quality, system quality, and service quality perceptions, are usually regarded as key success factors having effects on the final outcomes of e-government in terms of efficiency and effectiveness, these perceptions are in fact dependent on the trusting relationship between users and the government. They said that government agencies need to emphasize trust-building mechanisms in retaining users for their online public services.

Table 1 shows theories of E-government and trust in government. In previous studies, the relationship between e-Government and trust in government is divided into two opinions. However, in this study, we hypothesize that e-Government can lead greater trust in government. In Korea, many citizens are familiar with using ICT for public administration. According to UNPAN (United Nations Public Administration Network) in 2014, Korea was the highest ranked in index of e-Government. Horsburgh *et al.* [10] said that their research results depend on the countries because the results did not follow the other studies, which agree with positive relationship between e-Government and trust in government. Korea government utilized e-services for citizens in various ways. It is not only administrative work such as civil complaint and EDI but also tool for policy participation and value creation. It means that e-Government is not just technology for citizen in Korea but social platform, which can communicate with citizens and government. Through these trends in Korea, we expect that quality of e-Government can affect greater trust in government.

Table 1. Theories of e-government and trust in government.

Relationship between E-government and Trust in Government	Authors
Positive relationship	Tolbert and Mossberger [5], Welch *et al.* [7], Hong [9], Park &Cho [12], Butter *et al.* [14], Omari and Omari [15], Teo *et al.* [16]
No relationship or neutrality	McNeal *et al.* [8], Horsburgh *et al.* [10], Morgeson *et al.* [11], Parent *et al.* [13]

2.2. Digital Divide

The term "digital divide" comes from Gray Andrew Pole, a New York Times journalist in 1995. Since then, many researchers have defined this. Anderson and Bickson [17] highlighted the range of services available through the Internet and its equity implications when certain segments of the population are excluded from these services. Norris [18] defined the digital divide as a gap between the social haves and have-nots in their access to powerful new IT applications, particularly those embodied in the Internet. DiMaggio *et al.* [19] referred to the inequality in access to the Internet, the extent of use, knowledge of search strategies, the quality of technical connections and social support, the ability to evaluate information quality, and the diversity of use. Bélanger and Carter [20] distinguished between the information haves and have-nots, highlighting a gap between computer-literate individuals and those who are not. The digital divide is composed of two major barriers: access to and familiarity with technologies. Warren [21] stated that the digital divide can describe a situation in which a discrete sector of the population faces significant and possibly indefinite lags in its adoption of ICT through circumstances beyond its immediate control. Halford and Savage [22] stated that the notion of the digital divide implies a simple and singular boundary between digitally engaged and disengaged individuals, which glosses the possibility of a more complex process of stratification.

Doong and Ho [23] analyzed the secondary data from 2000 to 2008 for 136 countries to examine the gap of ICT country-by-country. They found that the factors for difference of ICT accessibility were not only demographic factor(gender, ages, education, income, and job) but also various factors, which range from micro level to macro level. Even residential area, urban form and countries cause difference of ICT accessibility.

Billon *et al.* [24] found the type of digital divide by difference of ICT adoption for 142 countries including developing countries and developed countries. According to the research, the type of digital divide is classified by countries, degree of economic development, demographic factor and institutional infrastructure. Especially, income is main description factor for technology adoption like Internet, personal computer and broadband.

One the other hand, some studies suggest that non-economical factors like rival, communication infra and human capital can affect adoption of ICT [25–28].

Bélanger and Carter [20] explored the effects of demographic variables identified in the digital divide literature on usage of e-Government services. Consistent with previous literature, income, education, age, and frequency of Internet use significantly impact use of e-government services. Typically, those more likely to use e-government services include younger citizens, citizens with higher levels of income, citizens with higher levels of education, and citizens who use the Internet for other tasks. This confirms that the digital divide has a major impact on e-Government usage.

Warren *et al.* [21] said that there is a danger that non-users of the Internet are disenfranchised by such developments, and these include some of the most disadvantaged and vulnerable sectors of rural populations. Thus, the paper explores the links between digital exclusion and social exclusion in a rural context, to identify the likely consequences of this "digital vicious cycle". They concluded that Internet offers the rural citizen significant benefits, helping to overcome the disadvantages of distance and social dispersion.

Halford and Savage [22] discussed conceptual tools, which might allow an elaborated sociological analysis of the relationship between information and communication technology on the one hand, and social inequalities on the other. They suggest that we need new perspectives and new tools which will enable us to go beyond established approaches to both technology and inequality and to find new ways of thinking, analyzing, and researching that get inside the complex and evolving nature of digital social inequalities.

Donnermeyer and Hollifield [29] examined the utilization of email and the Web, based on a sample of 471 residents from four rural communities in Nebraska and Wisconsin, in which the study found nearly identical levels and patterns of use across the communities. The findings are discussed in terms of the two variations on the digital divide. The first is a digital divide between rural people at the same place, based on their location within networks of co-workers and friends, which in turn influences awareness, knowledge, and eventual adoption of information technologies. The second divide is between rural communities that have growing economies and populations and those that are no growing, based on their locations relative to metropolitan areas and urban consumers.

Many digital divide researches are focusing on the factor of digital divide which cause gap of ICT accessibility. But some studies address trend of digital divide and criticize the bias of studies. Thus, they suggest that new concept is requested for deal with new digital divide.

Van Dijk [30] said that the main reason is that digital divide research suffers from a lack of theory. In the past 10 years, it has remained at a descriptive level, emphasizing the demographics of income, education, age, sex, and ethnicity. The deeper social, cultural, and psychological causes behind the inequality of access have not been addressed so far. In addition, he said that physical access the divide seems to be closing in the most developed countries whereas concerning digital skills, the use of applications for the divide persists or widens. Thus, it is needed to focus on utilization and outcome of ICT in a digital divide research.

Barzilai-Nahon [31] suggested an integrated analysis tool to measure digital divide, because previous studies could not address multidimensional digital divide. The researchers criticized that previous studies were limited to single-issues studies which focused on specific factor causing digital divide. These studies could not understand the whole aspect of multidimensional digital divide.

Park and Kwon [32] suggested multidimensional aspects of the digital divide by conceptualizing the magnitude of digital gaps in social, economic, cultural, and political relationships, going beyond its familiar definition. Because of digital disparity closely reflects social polarization, efforts to narrow digital inequality should be customized at four structural levels: individuals, communities, regions, and countries. According to these four levels, they examined various multidimensional approaches to the digital divide, including not only the accessibility and availability of information resources but also conscious and acceptable attitudes toward perceived gaps between the haves and have-nots.

3. Theoretical Model and Hypotheses

3.1. Theoretical Model

The theoretical model in Figure 1 was employed to describe the relationship between the quality of e-government services and trust in government. Previous studies have generally suggested that trust in government is a key driver of the use of e-government services. In the present study, measurement methods for Gov 3.0 were included for the quality of e-government services. In addition, different groups of the digital divide were included because of its key role in explaining the relationship betweenthe quality of e-government and trust in government, which may vary across these groups. If individuals favorably perceive the quality of e-government services, then they are likely to actively collect data and participate in cyberspace, which is related to the formation of trust in government. The theoretical model was used to examine the relationship between the perceived quality of e-government and trust in government, which was considered to potentially vary across various groups of the digital divide.

The model in Figure 2 was used to classify groups of the digital divide and examine how the level of trust would vary across the groups. As classified in Seo [33], the digital divide is categorized as "passive", "progressive", "alienation", and "desire" groups based on the ability and willingness to use ICT. As Park and Kwon [32] suggested, an individual's personal ability to use ICTs has now understood as a key variable, attracting academic interests on a possible correlation between an individual's intentions and behavior of ICT use. Even if individual users lack sufficient ability to use ICT, their willingness to use ICTs may influences traditional factors, which determined the pattern of the digital divide. Seo [33] examines individuals' ICTs understanding and willingness and finds that individuals with similar intentions tend to belong to similar information groups.

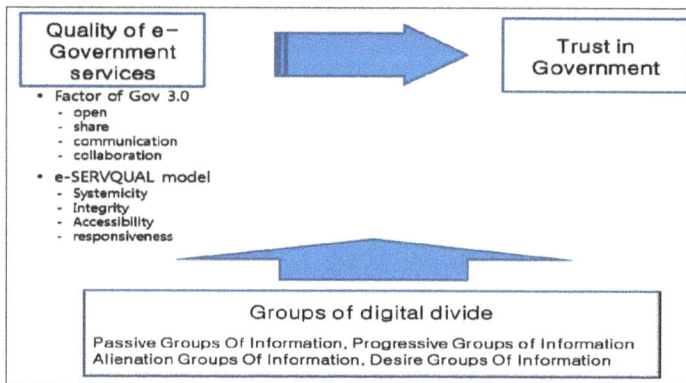

Figure 1. Research model.

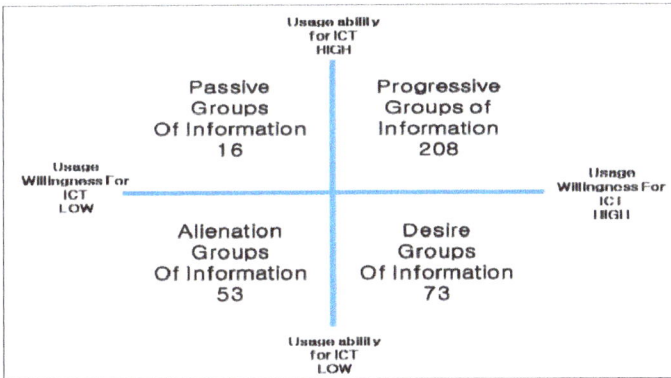

Figure 2. Digital divide groups.

3.2. Hypotheses

The effects of the perceived quality of e-government services on trust in government were examined to extend the literature to the perception of e-government services in the context of Gov 3.0, a newly emerging phenomenon. In addition, the correlation between the digital divide and trust in government was examined. To test the hypotheses, SPSS 18.0 was employed. The research methods included a multiple regression analysis and an ANOVA. Here two hypotheses were tested.

First, e-government may be an effective solution to the decline in trust in government [5]. This suggests that the perceived quality of e-government services may influence trust in government. Systemicity is measured by functional aspects from access and processing. Integrity is measured by perfection for service offer. Accessibility is measured by how many channels for information alienation groups. Responsiveness is measured by possibility for understanding and accepting user's needs. Open is measured by quality of information. Sharing is measured by problem for security, possibility for wide use service and possibility for cooperative service by sharing information. Communication is measured by effort for pay attention to public opinion. Collaboration is measured by effort for communicating with people and providing service based on people's needs. In this regard, the following hypotheses are proposed:

H1: The perceived quality of e-government services has a positive effect on trust in government.

H1-1: Systemicity has a positive effect on trust in government.

H1-2: Integrity has a positive effect on trust in government.

H1-3: Accessibility has a positive effect on trust in government.

H1-4: Responsiveness has a positive effect on trust in government.

H1-5: Openness has a positive effect on trust in government.

H1-6: Sharing has a positive effect on trust in government.

H1-7: Communication has a positive effect on trust in government.

H1-8: Collaboration has a positive effect on trust in government.

Second, we suggest that digital divide research is, not just a problem between information have and information have-not, but a problem for social-economic gap. In addition, as previous studies explained, digital divide includes not only accessibility but also information literacy, which is more comprehensive problem. Based on this premise, we should avoid dichotomous frame like ordinary people and information have-not. We should address the digital divide among information have groups. In Korea, many Korean researchers are dealing with the issue on a new digital divide, because digital divide is related to social integration. On the other hand, Seo [33] classified "leading", "indifference", "desire", and "alienation" groups by using understating for ICT and usage willingness for ICT. Unfortunately his study did not conduct an empirical research based upon his theoretical classification nor it reflect recent paradigm shift such as service creation by active individual. In this study, thus, the digital divide is categorized as "passive", "progressive", "alienation", and "desire" groups, based on the ability and willingness to use ICT. Willingness for ICT is measured by ICT usefulness(e.g., possibility for acquiring useful information, possibility for using information), ICT availability(e.g., convenience for ICT equipment), and ICT acceptance intention(e.g., possibility for using the newest ICT equipment). Ability for ICT is measured by PC/Internet use ability(e.g., possibility for purchasing goods by PC), Mobile/Smart equipment use ability(e.g., possibility for downloading and using application, possibility for augmented reality by using smart equipment), ability to reacting information dysfunction(e.g., possibility for checking and curing virus program, possibility for screening harmful contents). Based on this theoretical classification, we examine the difference of trust in government by four groups. We hypothesize that each groups have different perception on trust in government.

H2: The level of trust in government varies depending upon the different type of the digital divide group.

4. Data Collection and Measurement Methods

Table 2 shows demographic profile of respondents. Data were collected from a national survey conducted from 10 October to 31 October 2013. A pilot survey was conducted to assess the reliability and validity of the questionnaire, which was sent to a total of 350 randomly sampled individuals who reside in Seoul metropolitan city by e-mail. The metropolitan area of Seoul was assessed having top-quality information systems and programs in the Local Informatization Evaluation Reports [34]. The organizational size is reported by many studies as the critical factor influencing the process of decision making or implementing the electronic government projects in U.S. cities [6,35–39]. They maintain that higher degrees of horizontal and vertical differentiation in larger organizations often bring an increased need for control and coordination within an organization. Therefore, metropolitan city governments might need ICT that could provide faster methods of information. The impact of ICT policies and projects could be perceived more diversely by citizen.

Table 2. Demographic profile of respondents (*N* = 350).

Variables	Index	Frequency (no. of Individuals)	%
Sex	Male	173	49.4
	Female	177	50.6
Age	20s	67	19.1
	30s	75	21.4
	40s	78	22.3
	50s	66	18.9
	60s and over	64	18.3
Area of residence	Seoul	145	41.4
	Incheon	40	11.4
	Gyunggi Province	165	47.1
Education	Middle school	28	8.0
	High school	185	52.9
	College	131	37.4
	Graduate school	6	1.7

5. Measurement Data and Construct Validity

For the constructs "the quality of e-government services" and "trust in government," Myeong and Lee's [40] instruments were adopted and measured using a five-point Likert-type scale ranging from "strongly disagree" (1) to "strongly agree" (5). Table 3 shows the measurement methods for variables and the rotated pattern of factors. A principal component analysis was conducted using items for each variable.

In this study, we utilize the e-SERVQUAL model, which is used for assessing quality of e-service. Kim [41] used e-SERVQUAL model to evaluate quality of e-Government services. Parasuraman *et al.* [42] developed SERVQUAL, which consist of five dimensions such as reliability, responsiveness, assurance, empathy and tangibles to measure quality of service. Kim [41] suggests e-SERVQUAL including systemicity, integrity, accessibility, and responsiveness by exploiting SERVQUASL. Additionally, we added the factors of Gov 3.0 which are slogan by Gun Hae Park administration: openness, sharing, communication, and collaboration, because e-SERVUAL cannot sufficiently reflect trend of the smart society which is pervaded by mobile environment. This means that Gov 3.0 is different from previous e-Government services. Gov 3.0 emphasizes the role of private sector and government is not unilateral service provider but supporter for private sector in Gov 3.0. In addition, Gov 3.0 is interested in value creation by private sector. According to this paradigm shift, we apply factors of Gov 3.0 to the measurement on e-Government services. By utilizing the research model, we suggest a research model which assumes the relationship between quality of e-Government service and trust in government.

Table 3. Measurement instrument and rotated pattern of factors (Varimax Rotation).

Variable	Measurement Items	Factor Loading	Cron-bach's α	EigenValue	KMO (Kaiser-Meyer-Olkin)	Bartlett Sphericity
	-Provision for total search function	0.772				
	-Provision for sectoral search function	0.716				
	-Statement for relevant organization	0.733				
Systemicity	-Search function within results	0.751	0.902 ***	5.329	0.935	1553.470
	-Provision for button to return	0.765				
	-Search function for two more items	0.670				
	-Provision for button to move an write	0.702				
	-Function to view before and next info	0.704				
	-Function to print information provided	0.727				
	-Provision for viewer program	0.754				
	-Provision for real time complaints/publicity	0.702				
	-Function to apply online complaints	0.710				
	-Provision for ONE-STOP service	0.750				
Integrity	-Provision for ZERO-STOP service	0.701	0.885 ***	4.688	0.927	1236.126
	-Open for complaints process	0.703				
	-Immediate treatment until time limit	0.735				
	-Statement for complaints answer date	0.733				
	-Real time update for Q&A, FAQ	0.677				
	-Appointment of persons for service	0.780				
	-Provision for service via Internet/call center	0.711				
	-Provision for service via various method	0.719				
Accessibility	-Provision for add service to the disabled	0.685	0.832 ***	3.291	0.872	698.275
	-English version homepage for foreigners	0.822				
	-Exclusive homepage for youth	0.824				
	-Possession for digital divide guideline	0.667				

Table 3. Cont.

Variable	Measurement Items	Factor Loading		Cron-bach's α	Eigen Value	KMO (Kaiser-Meyer-Olkin)	Bartlett Sphericity
	-Provision for info on citizen participation	**0.617**					
	-System for online opinion	**0.685**					
	-Operation for bilateral policy forum	**0.697**					
Responsiveness	-Implementation for e-voting	**0.656**		**0.868 *****	4.607	0.910	1172.432
	-Implement for public survey/cyber poll	**0.656**					
	-Operation for bulletin board	**0.629**					
	-Function to check satisfaction for process	**0.727**					
	-Spontaneous announce for process/results	**0.689**					
	-Reflection for FAQ into processing	**0.703**					
	-Collect opinion for policy improvement	**0.721**					
	-Accuracy	0.257	**0.776**				
	-No error	0.135	**0.768**				
Openness	-Objectivity	0.225	**0.754**	**0.820 *****	Factor1: 2.696 Factor2: 2.010	0.863	794.420
	-Provision for APP	**0.745**	0.184				
	-Provision for up to date info on civil	**0.772**	0.114				
	-Usefulness for policy info	**0.631**	0.241				
	-Usefulness for info on website and APP	**0.642**	0.341				
	-Support for immediate admin process	**0.774**	0.167				
	-No error and crash	**0.656**					
	-Rapid handling	**0.691**					
Sharing	-Trust for technological function	**0.665**		**0.863 *****	4.127	0.887	1053.393
	-Possibility for tele-com service	**0.683**					
	-Support for mobile platform	**0.768**					
	-Convergence service for website and App	**0.709**					
	-Provision for new service via agency	**0.817**					
	-Provision for converge service via agency	**0.742**					

$p < 0.1$; * $p < 0.05$; ** $p < 0.01$; *** $p < 0.001$; (In Factor loading, values in bold mean more than a cutoff level 0.60).

Table 3. *Cont.*

Variable	Measurement Items	Factor Loading		Cron-bach's α	EigenValue	KMO (Kaiser-Meyer-Olkin)	Bartlett Sphericity
Communication	-Various communication channel	0.369	**0.635**				
	-Possibility for policy suggestion	0.196	**0.709**				
	-Possibility for immediate connection	0.194	**0.794**				
	-Use for necessary info anytime	0.274	**0.762**	0.879 ***	Factor1: 2.951 Factor2: 2.495	0.898	1195.408
	-Possibility for finding location	**0.722**	0.171				
	-Possibility for identifying civil complaint	**0.736**	0.228				
	-Timely provision for policy info	**0.611**	0.391				
	-Quick loading speed	**0.757**	0.248				
	-Availability for connection with Venders	**0.81**	0.288				
Collaboration	-Effort for reducing cost of admin process	**0.764**					
	-Effort for understanding people needs	**0.733**					
	-Effort for providing people service	**0.735**		0.879 ***	4.558	0.917	1266.736
	-Effort for interagency cooperation	**0.734**					
	-Effort for cooperation to various Venders	**0.747**					
	-Effort for interaction with people	**0.753**					
	-Effort for service provision by gender/age	**0.735**					
	-Effort for personalized service provision	**0.833**					
	-General trust	**0.785**					
	-Perceived professional competence	**0.763**					
Trust in Government	-Perceived content service	**0.753**		0.883 ***	4.131	0.905	1089.501
	-Perceived efficient service	**0.761**					
	-Perceived spontaneous effort	**0.724**					
	-Perceived of providing various information	**0.792**					
	-Perceived improvement for old procedure	**0.795**					

$p < 0.1$; * $p < 0.05$; ** $p < 0.01$; *** $p < 0.001$; (In Factor loading, values in bold mean more than a cutoff level 0.60).

The reliability of the items was assessed using Cronbach's alpha. As shown in Table 2, all items loaded on their proposed factors, satisfying the KMO threshold of 0.60 [43]. Cronbach's alpha for all items exceeded 0.60. Devellis [44] suggested that there is insufficient reliability if Cronbach's alpha for a scale is less than 0.60. All items for each variable loaded onto one factor except for openness and communication. First, systemicity was used as a factor to evaluate functional aspects from service access to processes in service provision. A total of 10 items were used, and according to a reliability analysis, Cronbach's α was 0.902.

Second, integrity was used as a factor to evaluate whether e-government service users would obtain sufficient content and complete services ($\alpha = 0.885$).

Third, accessibility was used as a factor to evaluate whether the diversity of channels for service provision and whether vulnerable social groups would facilitate easy access to those channels ($\alpha = 0.832$).

Fourth, responsiveness was used as a factor to evaluate whether the government would aggressively accept and reflect the user's interests and opinions ($\alpha = 0.868$).

Fifth, openness was used for the issue of Web 3.0, which emphasizes more individualized services based on information and service platforms provided by the government. A total of eightitems loaded onto two factors (factor 1 = accuracy, factor 2 = usefulness of information; $\alpha = 0.820$).

Sixth, sharing was used for the level of security and convergence, which were considered to play crucial roles in the provision of safer and reliable information services based on solid networks and systems. A total of eightitems loaded onto one factor ($\alpha = 0.863$).

Seventh, communication was used for interactions between the government, firms, and citizens. Communication refers to respecting other opinions and listening carefully to meet others'expectations. Therefore, to evaluate the level of communication, the extent to which the government pays careful attention to changing patterns and leading issues concerning public opinion was examined. A total of nineitems loaded onto two factors (factor 1=personalized accessibility, factor 2 = openness of communication; $\alpha = 0.879$).

Eighth, collaboration was used to address how the government, the private sector, and people create value-added information content and services based on mutual understanding and cooperative infrastructure/institutional settings. A total of eight items loaded onto one factor ($\alpha = 0.879$).

The dependent variable was the level of trust in government. Unlike general trust, trust in government is not a reciprocal but unilateral expectation because people do not trust the government if it fails to meet their performance expectations. As defined earlier, trust is the belief that the government would behave as expected in a socially responsible manner and thus that it would meet the trusting public's expectations [45–48]. In the present study, trust in government was evaluated through people's perceived expectations for the government's services and capability based on professional competence, content quality, efficient service, spontaneous efforts, information diversity, and procedural improvements. Here a total of sevenitems were used, and Cronbach's α was 0.883.

6. Analysis Results and Discussion

6.1. Results of a Multiple Regression Analysis

Table 4 shows the multiple regression results with the independent variable and the control variable. The coefficient of determination in the regression model was 56.1%, indicating the model to be significant (*F*-value = 31.276, $p < 0.001$).

Table 4. Results of a multiple regression analysis.

Items			Standardized Coefficients(B)	t value
Independentvariable	Openness	Systemicity	−0.068	−0.83
		Integrity	−0.122	−1.428
		Accessibility	0.093	1.15
		Responsiveness	0.052	0.594
		Accuracy	**0.399 *****	7.628
		Useful of information	0.072	1.015
		Sharing	**0.162 ***	2.261
	Communication	Openness of communication	−0.014	−0.193
		Personalized accessibility	−0.047	−0.797
	Collaboration		**0.385 *****	5.835
Items			B	t
Invariable			0.217	1.09
R^2			0.567	
adjusted R^2			0.548	
F value			31.276 ***	

* $p < 0.05$; ** $p < 0.01$; *** $p < 0.001$.

Accuracy (B = 0.399, $p < 0.001$), integration (B = 0.162, $p < 0.05$), and collaboration (B = 0.385, $p < 0.001$) were significant. The results provide partial support for H1, which predicted a positive effect of the perceived quality of e-government services on trust in government. As shown in Table 3, accuracy (openness), integration (sharing), and collaboration had significant positive effectson trust in government.

The empirical result shows that the level of trust is increased when the quality of e-Government services are more related with the Gov3.0 factors including Openness, Sharing, and Collaboration. Interestingly, accuracy is the most important factor in influencing the level of trust in government. It implies that people in the era of Gov3.0 ask more accurateinformation and data without error as well as objective. Collaboration among agencies is also critical for the Gov3.0 because of the environmental changes include less cost of administration process, understanding people's needs, interagency cooperation, interaction with citizen and venders, and a personalized service provision. As ICT has become more sophisticated, with a widely connected government system, willingness to share information among organizations and stakeholders may become a major factor to thoseactively seeking information and resources to make value-added products. It suggests that more integrated data management including network securityand an open attitude toward information sharing will be more important beyond the level of technical issues. For this reason, the MOSPA [49] enacted "The Act of Provision and Use of Public Data" in 2013. It suggests that policy remedies be provided for overcoming obstacles in information sharing under thegov3.0 environment. Issues of protection of privacy and official authorization for providing information on individuals have also become a major agenda before the adoption of a new system in the publicsector. For example, the MOSPA in 2011 has initiated the revision of theIndividual Information Protection Act of 2006 through public hearings, which was more focused on the protection of individuals used in the government portal sites and related systems [50].

6.2. ANOVA Results

Table 5 shows differences in the perception of trust in government between digital divide groups F-value = 3.275, $p < 0.05$). The desire information group showed the highest level of trust in government (3.28), followed by the progressive information group (3.25) and the alienation information group (3.01). The passive information group showed the lowest level of trust in government.

Table 5. Differences in the perception of trust in government among digital divide groups.

Groups	Number	Trust in Government	
		Mean	Standard deviation
Alienation information group	53	3.01	0.685
Passive information group	16	2.93	0.536
Desire information group	73	3.28	0.554
Progressive information group	208	3.25	0.662
F		3.275 *	

* $p < 0.05$; ** $p < 0.01$; *** $p < 0.001$.

These results imply that the digital divide may vary the degree of trust in government. For example, the alienation information group did not show the lowest level of trust in government. On the other hand, noteworthy is that the desire information group showed the highest level of trust in government. Although the desire information group can be considered a digital divide group, the results show clear differences in the perception on ICT between the desire and alienation information groups. The results suggest that the willingness to use ICT may be a possible predictor of trust in government. In a smart society, many people have opportunities to access smart and mobile devices because various services converge and inexpensive mobile technologies spread even to less developed countries. Therefore, to increase the level of trust, governments need to promote policies based on the willingness to use ICT instead of simply increasing the accessibility of hardware.

The results suggest that governments require policies that can increase the usability of ICT for alienation and passive information groups. In Gov 3.0, governments can play diverse roles such as platform providers, information collectors, intermediaries of governance systems, and market monitors. Such roles are crucial in unequal markets. Although participants themselves create value and establish environments to exchange services through various platforms, not all market participants are equal in terms of their ability and qualification. Therefore, to realize Gov 3.0, governments should provide accessible platform services with universal smart devices for groups who are not familiar with ICT use. If a government is always open and easy to access, then isolated information groups can employ public data and create value, thereby increasing the level of trust in government in the long term.

7. Conclusions

This study examined the effects of the quality of e-government services on trust in government by focusing on various groups of the digital divide in the era of a smart society and Gov 3.0. The results show a partial correlation between the quality of e-government service and trust in government. In addition, the level of trust varied according to the different type of the digital divide groups. It also suggests that governments need to provide policy remedies for overcoming obstacles in information sharing surrounding issues of privacy protection, network security, collaboration among governance structures, and official authorization processes or providing information on individuals.

This study has some limitations, which require more comprehensive and interpretive measurement methods. As measurement instruments, various indicators of user satisfaction, including accessibility, usefulness, and convenience, were adopted, based on the acceptance theory of the information system. Although the analysis included new Gov 3.0 factors, better indicators are required to measure the complex patterns of self-governance forming the new paradigm of Gov 3.0 and a new model of governance.

Acknowledgments: This work was supported by the National Research Foundation of Korea(NRF) grant funded by the Korean Government (NRF-2012-2012S1A3A2033666). This work was supported by the Inha University in South Korea. This paper used a data set conducted by a SSK(Social Science Korea) research team funded by NRF and partially adopted a theoretical framework in Yongmin Kwon's doctorate thesis "A Study on the Effects of Quality of e-Government Services on the Trust of Government in the Era of Government 3.0: Focusing on the Digital Divide Among Users in Metropolitan Area".

Author Contributions: Seunghwan Myeong (co-first author/correspondent author) designed a research framework and wrote the paper with editing; Yongmin Kwon (co-first author) performed a survey and analyzed the data; Hyungjun Seo updated a literature review and re-conducted a data analysis.

Conflicts of Interest: The authors declare no conflict of interest.

References

1. Myeong, S.H.; Hur, C.H. A study on change of e-Government and paradigm based on Gov3.0 through shift of smart society. In Proceedings of the Korean Association for Policy Studies Spring Conference, Jeonju, Korea, 13 April 2012; Korean Association for Policy Studies: Seoul, Korea, 2012; pp. 325–341.
2. Wike, R.; Holzwart, K. Where Trust is High, Crime and Corruption are Low—Since Communism's Fall, Social Trust Has Fallen in Eastern Europe. Available online: http://www.pewglobal.org/2008/04/15/where-trust-is-high-crime-and-corruption-are-low/ (accessed on 5 April 2014).
3. Choi, Y. Green management of logistics enterprises and its sustainable performance in Korea. *Afr. J. Bus. Manag.* **2012**, *6*, 1475–1482.
4. Choi, Y.; Lee, E.Y. Optimizing risk management for the sustainable performance of the regional innovation system in Korea through metamediation. *Hum. Ecol. Risk Assess.* **2009**, *15*, 270–280.
5. Tolbert, C.J.; Mossberger, K. The effects of e-government on trust and confidence in government. *Public Adm. Rev.* **2006**, *66*, 354–369.
6. Moon, M.J. Can IT help government to restore public trust? Declining public trust and potential prospects of IT in the public sector. In Proceedings of the 36th Annual Hawaii International Conference on System Sciences, Hawaii, HI, USA, 6–9 January 2003.
7. Welch, E.W.; Hinnant, C.C.; Moon, M.J. Linking citizen satisfaction with e-government and trust in government. *J. Public Adm. Res. Theory.* **2005**, *15*, 371–391. [CrossRef]
8. McNeal, R.; Hale, K.; Dotterweich, L. Citizen–government interaction and the Internet: Expectations and accomplishments in contact, quality, and trust. *J. Inf. Technol. Polit.* **2008**, *5*, 213–229.
9. Hong, H. Government websites and social media's influence on government-public relationships. *Public Relat. Rev.* **2013**, *39*, 346–356. [CrossRef]
10. Horsburgh, S.; Goldfinch, S.; Gauld, R. Is public trust in government associated with trust in e-government? *Soc. Sci. Comput. Rev.* **2011**, *29*, 232–241.
11. Morgeson, F.V.; vanAmburg, D.; Mithas, S. Misplaced trust? Exploring the structure of the e-government-citizen trust relationship. *J. Public Adm. Res. Theory.* **2011**, *21*, 257–283. [CrossRef]
12. Park, J.; Cho, K. Declining relational trust between government and publics, and potential prospects of social media in the government public relations. In Proceedings of the EGPA Conference 2009—"The Public Service: Service Delivery in the Information Age", St Julian, Malta, 1–4 September 2009.
13. Parent, M.; Vandebeek, C.A.; Gemino, A.C. Building citizen trust through e-government. *Gov. Inf. Q.* **2005**, *22*, 720–736. [CrossRef]
14. Den Butter, F.A.G.; Liu, J.W.; Tan, Y.-H. Using IT to engender trust in government-to-business relationships: the Authorized Economic Operator (AEO) as an example. *Gov. Inf. Q.* **2012**, *29*, 261–274.
15. Omari, H.A.; Omari, A.A. Building an e-Government e-trust infrastructure. *Am. J. Appl. Sci.* **2006**, *3*, 2122–2130. [CrossRef]
16. Teo, T.S.; Srivastava, S.C.; Jiang, L. Trust and electronic government success: An empirical study. *JMIS* **2003**, *25*, 99–131.
17. Anderson, R.H.; Bikson, T.K.; Law, S.A.; Mitchell, B.M. *Universal Access to E-Mail—Feasibility and Societal Implica-tions*; RAND: Santa Monica, CA, USA, 1995.

18. Norris, P. *Digital Divide: Civic Engagement, Information Poverty, and the Internet Worldwide*; Cambridge University Press: New York, NY, USA, 2001.

19. DiMaggio, P.; Hargittai, E.; Neuman, W.R.; Robinson, J.P. Social implications of the Internet. *Annu. Rev. Sociol.* **2001**, *27*, 307–336.

20. Bélanger, F.; Carter, L. The impact of the digital divide on e-government use. *Commun. ACM.* **2009**, *52*, 132–135.

21. Martyn, W. The digital vicious cycle: Links between social disadvantage and digital exclusion in rural areas. *Telecommun. Pol.* **2007**, *31*, 374–388.

22. Halford, S.; Savage, M. Reconceptualizing digital social inequality. *Inf. Commun. Soc.* **2010**, *13*, 937–955.

23. Doong, S.H.; Ho, S.-C. The impact of ICT development on the global digital divide. *Electron. Commer. Res. Appl.* **2012**, *1*, 518–533.

24. Billon, M.; Lera-Lopez, F.; Marco, R. Differences in digitalization levels: A multivariate analysis studying the global digital divide. *Rev. World Econ.* **2010**, *146*, 39–73.

25. Quibria, M.G.; Shamsun, A.N.; Tschanh, T.; Reyes-Macasaquit, M. Digital divide: Determinants and policies with special reference to Asia. *J. Asian Econ.* **2003**, *13*, 811–825.

26. Andonova, V. Mobile phones, the Internet and the institutional environment. *Telecommun. Pol.* **2006**, *30*, 29–45.

27. Guillén, M.F.; Suárez, S.L. Explaining the global digital divide: Economic, political and sociological drivers of cross-national Internet use. *Soc. Forc.* **2006**, *84*, 681–708.

28. Oyelaran-Oyeyinka, B.; Lal, K. Internet diffusion in sub-Saharan Africa: A cross-country analysis. *Telecommun. Pol.* **2005**, *29*, 507–527.

29. Donnermeyer, J.F.; Hollifield, C.A. Digital divide evidence in four rural towns. *IT Soc.* **2003**, *1*, 107–117.

30. Van Dijk, J.A. Digital divide research, achievements and shortcomings. *Poetics* **2006**, *34*, 221–235.

31. Barzilai-Nahon, K. Gaps and bits: Conceptualizing measurements for digital divide/s. *Inf. Soc.* **2006**, *22*, 269–278.

32. Park, J.Y.; Kwon, Y.M. New stratification perspective on the digital divide: A four-scale analysis model. *Int. J. eGov. Netw.* **2013**, *1*, 24–44.

33. Seo, J.W. Policy direction and strategies for the policy of digital divide in korea: Focusing on the local information centers. In Proceedings of the Korean Association for Public Administration Spring Conference, Cheonan, Korea, 19–20 April 2002; Korean Public Association for Administration: Seoul, Korea, 2002; Volume 2002, pp. 213–228.

34. Korean Association for Local Informatization. *Local Informatization Evaluation Report*; Korean Association for Local Informatization: Seoul, Korea, 2013.

35. Brudney, J.; Selden, S. The Adoption of innovation by smaller local governments: The case of computer technology. *Am. Rev. Public Adm.* **1995**, *25*, 71–86. [CrossRef]

36. Holden, S.H.; Norris, D.F.; Fletcher, P.D. Electronic government at the local level: Progress to date and future issues. *Public Perform. Manag. Rev.* **2003**, *26*, 1–20.

37. Norris, D.F.; Demeter, L.A. Computing in American city governments. In *The 1999 Municipal Yearbook*; International City/County Management Association: Washington, DC, USA, 1999; pp. 10–19.

38. Norris, D.F.; Kraemer, K.L. Mainframe and PC computing in American myths and realities. *Public Adm. Rev.* **1996**, *56*, 568–576. [CrossRef]

39. Norris, D.F.; Moon, M.V. Advancing e-government at the grassroots: Tortoise or hare? *Public Adm. Rev.* **2005**, *65*, 64–75.

40. Myeong, S.H.; Lee, B.J. A study on elderly people's behavior for information use: Focusing on the elderly people's perception on information technologies. *Korean J. Reg. Inf. Soc.* **2010**, *13*, 23–47.

41. Kim, D.S. A Study on the Quality of e-Government Services. Ph.D. Dissertation, University of Sunmoon, Asan, Korea, 2009.

42. Parasuraman, A.; Zeithaml, V.A.; Berry, L.L. SERVQUAL: A multiple-item scale for measuring customer perceptions of service quality. *J. Retail.* **1988**, *64*, 12–40.

43. Kaiser, H.F. An index of factorial simplicity. *Psychometrika* **1974**, *39*, 31–36. [CrossRef]

44. DeVellis, R.F. *Scale Development: Theory and Applications (Applied Social Research Methods)*; Sage Publications: Thousand Oaks, CA, USA, 2011.

45. Gefen, D. E-Commerce: The role of familiarity and trust. *Omega* **2000**, *28*, 725–737. [CrossRef]

46. Lewis, J.D.; Weigert, A. Trust as a social reality. *Soc. Forc.* **1985**, *63*, 967–985. [CrossRef]
47. Luhmann, N. *Trust and Power*; John Wiley and Sons: London, UK, 1979.
48. Mayer, R.C.; Davis, J.H.; Schoorman, F.D. An integration model of organizational trust. *Acad. Manag. Rev.* **1995**, *20*, 709–734.
49. Ministry of Security and Public Administration (MOSPA). *The Act of Provision and Use of Public Data*; MOSPA: Seoul, Korea, 2013.
50. Ministry of Security and Public Administration (MOSPA). *The Act of Personal Information Protection*; MOSPA: Seoul, Korea, 2011.

![sustainability logo] *sustainability*

MDPI

Article

Carbon Emissions in China: A Spatial Econometric Analysis at the Regional Level

Yu Liu [1], Hongwei Xiao [2,*], Precious Zikhali [3] and Yingkang Lv [4]

[1]   Institute of Policy and Management, Chinese Academy of Sciences, Beijing 100190, China; liuyu@casipm.ac.cn
[2]   Economic Forecasting Department, State Information Center, Beijing 100045, China
[3]   Postnet Suite 122, Private Bag X1, Die Wilgers 0041, Pretoria, South Africa; prehgabadela@gmail.com
[4]   College of Economics and Management, China Agricultural University, Beijing 100083, China; lvyingkang@cau.edu.cn
*   Author to whom correspondence should be addressed; xiaohw@cei.gov.cn; Tel.: +86-10-6855-7128.

Received: 23 July 2014; in revised form: 1 September 2014; Accepted: 2 September 2014; Published: 5 September 2014

Abstract: An extended Stochastic Impacts by Regression on Population, Affluence and Technology (STIRPAT) model, incorporating factors that drive carbon emissions, is built from the regional perspective. A spatial Durbin model is applied to investigate the factors, including population, urbanization level, economic development, energy intensity, industrial structure, energy consumption structure, energy price, and openness, that impact both the scale and intensity of carbon emissions. After performing the model, we find that the revealed negative and significant impact of spatial-lagged variables suggests that the carbon emissions among regions are highly correlated. Therefore, the empirical results suggest that the provinces are doing an exemplary job of lowering carbon emissions. The driving factors, with the exception of energy prices, significantly impact carbon emissions both directly and indirectly. We, thus, argue that spatial correlation, endogeneity and externality should be taken into account in formulating polices that seek to reduce carbon emissions in China. Carbon emissions will not be met by controlling economic development, but by energy consumption and low-carbon path.

Keywords: carbon emissions; spatial Durbin panel data model; spatial externality; Stochastic Impacts by Regression on Population, Affluence and Technology (STIRPAT)

---

1. Introduction

The challenge of climate change continues to put pressure on countries to shift to a low-carbon economy, which is loosely defined as an economy that produces minimal greenhouse gas (GHG) emissions. As a result, most developed or emerging countries have created their own strategies to save energy and reduce GHG emissions. As the world's biggest GHG emitter driven largely by energy use as the population and economy continue to expand, the importance of China's participation to reducing global emissions cannot be overemphasized. The growth in China's economy at an unprecedented average of 10.4 percent per year between 1990 and 2010 was accompanied by a tripling of the country's carbon dioxide emissions. By 2010, China's carbon emissions constituted 24 percent of global emissions. Projections indicate that China, together with India, will continue to lead not only future global economic growth, but, also, future growth in energy demand, making up 34 percent of projected total world energy consumption in 2040.

The importance of China reducing its global emissions has attracted the attention of many researchers as they attempt to identify factors that may determine the country's transition towards a low-carbon economy. This research has benefited from the development of spatial econometrics, which allows for analyses of China's trends and drivers of carbon emissions that permit variation both in the patterns and drivers across regions. Some impressive studies have applied spatial panel models to analyze China's regional or industrial environmental Kuznets curve [1–10]. However, most of these studies tend to focus on the impact of economic growth and foreign direct investment (FDI) on carbon emission, while the impacts of other factors, such as population size, urbanization, and energy price, are often ignored. Secondly, most of the researchers opt for either a fixed-effects model or a spatial lag and spatial error model, which usually give different empirical results and thus lead to some discrepancies. Although studies have used spatial econometric techniques to analyze carbon emissions, most of the models used generally face selection bias problems associated with the choice of a spatial lag model or spatial error model, fixed-effects or random-effects model, spatial heterogeneity model, and the construction of a spatial weight matrix.

This paper seeks to contribute to the literature that studies patterns and drivers of growth in China's carbon emissions using spatial econometric techniques that incorporate spatial effects, thereby making the estimates more effective. This can guide policy makers in designing carbon emissions policies and respond to climate change through a transition towards low-carbon economies.

2. Expanded Stochastic Impacts by Regression on Population, Affluence and Technology (STIRPAT) Carbon Emission Model

The Impacts of Population, Affluence, and Technology (IPAT) equation, originally proposed by Ehrlich *et al.* [11], is often used to study the impact of human activities on the environment. Its simplicity and ability to connect factors that impact environmental quality have resulted in its being widely used in studies of environmental problems (see, for example, Harrison [12], Raskin [13], York [14], Shi [15], Cole [16], Rosa [17], among others). IPAT is an accounting identity that is expressed as follows:

$$I = PAT \tag{1}$$

where *I* represents environmental impact, *P* is population size, *A* is affluence or wealth per capita (measured by GDP per capital), and *T* is technology level (measured by environmental impact per unit of GDP). The IPAT equation allows for the investigation of the role of a specific factor on environmental change while keeping other factors constant.

The equation has been criticized for not allowing room for diagnostic analysis. This has led to an evolution of the IPAT equation. One modification was proposed by Waggoner and Ausubel [18]: adding "consumption" *C* as a fourth variable on the right-hand side of Equation 1 to create the ImPACT model. *C* represents the intensity of energy use. The fact that the IPAT and ImPACT equations are mathematical identities under which the concerned factors impact the environment proportionally, thus limits the application of the models. Moreover, the relationship between the driving factors and carbon emissions is usually nonlinear and disproportionate, rendering the application of IPAT and ImPACT problematic.

In response to these limitations, Dietz and Rosa [19] proposed another variation—the Stochastic Impacts by Regression on Population, Affluence and Technology (STIRPAT) model. They present the IPAT equation in a stochastic manner under which carbon emissions are modeled stochastically via regressing it on population, wealth, and technology. The STIRPAT is expressed as follows:

$$I = aP^b A^c T^d e \tag{2}$$

where *a* represents model coefficient, *b*, *c* and *d* are the coefficients for population, wealth and technology, respectively, and *e* is the error term. Environmental pressure is represented by *I*, population size by *P*, wealth by *A*, and finally, technology by *T*. Since $a = b = c = d = 1$, STIRPAT is simplified to the

IPAT equation. The inclusion of the coefficients in STIRPAT ensures that the disproportional impacts of factors driving carbon emissions can be modeled. Taking a natural logarithm on both sides gives:

$$InI = Ina + b(InP) + c(InA) + d(InT) + Ine \tag{3}$$

Each coefficient in Equation 3 is interpreted as an elasticity between the independent variables and the dependent variable, *i.e.*, they show the percentage of change of the dependent variable due to a percentage changes of the dependent variable. STIRPAT allows both the estimation of the coefficients as well as decomposition of factors affecting environmental quality. Several studies have been conducted based on the model and its adjustment (see, for example, Dietz and Rosa [20], York *et al.* [21], among others). This paper extends STIRPAT by including variables such as urbanization, industry structure, energy consumption structure, energy price and openness. The extended STIRPAT model is expressed as in Equations (4) and (5).

$$\ln CS = \ln a + \beta_1(\ln P) + \beta_2(\ln UR) + \beta_3(\ln GDPPC) + \beta_4(\ln EI) + \beta_5(\ln IS) + \beta_6(\ln ECS) + \beta_7 ln(EP) + \beta_8 ln(OPEN) + Ine$$
$$= \alpha + \beta_1(lnP) + \beta_2(lnUR) + \beta_3(lnGDPPC) + \beta_4(lnEI) + \beta_5(lnIS) + \beta_6(lnECS) + \beta_7(lnEP) + \beta_8 ln(OPEN) + \varepsilon \tag{4}$$

$$\ln CI = \ln a + \beta_1(\ln P) + \beta_2(\ln UR) + \beta_3(\ln GDPPC) + \beta_4(\ln EI) + \beta_5(\ln IS) + \beta_6(\ln ECS) + \beta_7 ln(EP) + \beta_8 ln(OPEN) + \ln e$$
$$= \alpha + \beta_1(lnP) + \beta_2(lnUR) + \beta_3(lnGDPPC) + \beta_4(lnEI) + \beta_5(lnIS) + \beta_6(lnECS) + \beta_7(lnEP) + \beta_8 ln(OPEN) + \varepsilon \tag{5}$$

where CS denotes the level or scale of carbon emissions (measured in 10,000 tons of carbon emission), CI is carbon intensity (CO_2 emission per unit of GDP, measured by in 10,000 Yuan/ton), P represents population (population size, in 10,000), UR denotes the urbanization level (measured by the percentage of urban population in total population), $GDPPC$ denotes economic development (measured by GDP per capital), EI is energy intensity (measured by energy consumption per unit of GDP), IS represents industrial structure (measured by the secondary industry share of GDP), ECS represents energy consumption structure (measured by the percentage of coal in total energy consumption), EP is energy price (measured by producer's price index for manufactured products), and $OPEN$ is openness (measured by the gross investment the registered foreign-funded enterprises by region at the year-end).

3. Construction of Carbon Emission Spatial Econometric Model and Spatial Weight Matrix

The State Council has issued the 12th Five-Year Work Plan for Controlling Greenhouse Gas Emissions, setting a goal of reducing CO_2 emissions per unit of GDP by 17 percent in 2015 compared to 2010. Plans to reduce CO_2 emissions need to be included by the regions in their plans for economic and social development and the yearly plan, making carbon emissions an important indicator of development. In addition, in 2011, the National Development and Reform Commission issued *Notice Regarding the Development of Carbon Emissions Trading Pilot*, whose aim is to implement a pilot trading of carbon emissions rights in seven provinces, including Beijing, Tianjin, Shanghai, Chongqing, Guangdong, Hubei, and Shenzhen. These regions are required to draft a regulation and formulate the rules for the pilot carbon emissions trading and to set a regional GHG emissions reduction target. This makes the scale of carbon emissions an important monitoring indicator of regional carbon emissions. In line with this, this paper uses two variables—the scale and intensity of carbon emissions—as independent variables to obtain a comprehensive result.

Based on the extended STIRPAT, the papers build a spatial econometric model by taking into account the fact that carbon emissions are heterogeneous and spatially correlated across regions and industries. A spatial panel data econometric model, which integrates spatial econometrics (spatial effects) and panel data (time effects), makes spatial econometric analysis more efficient. The spatial panel data econometric model includes three basic models: the spatial lag panel data model, spatial error panel data model, and spatial Durbin panel data model. These models are further discussed below.

3.1. Spatial Lag Panel Data Model (SLPDM)

Where $lnCS_{it}$ and $lnCI_{it}$ denote scale and intensity of carbon emissions of the ith region at time t, respectively. $\Sigma w_{ij}lnCS_{it}$ and $\Sigma w_{ij}lnCI_{it}$ represent the spatial correlation between $lnCS_{it}$ and $lnCI_{it}$ of the region i and that of its adjacent regions. lnP_{it}, $lnUR_{it}$, $lnGDPPC_{it}$, $lnEI_{it}$, $lnIS_{it}$, $lnECS_{it}$, $lnEP_{it}$ and $lnOPEN_{it}$ are independent variables of region i at time t. δ is spatial auto-correlation index, w_{ij} is an element of the spatial weight matrix representing the spatial relations between region i and j. α is the constant term, β is are coefficients to be estimated, μ_i is the individual-fixed effect and λ_t is the time-fixed effect.

$$
\begin{aligned}
\ln CS_{it} &= \delta\sum_{j=1}^{N} w_{ij} \ln CS_{it} + \ln a + \beta_1(\ln P_{it}) + \beta_2(\ln UR_{it}) + \beta_3(\ln GDPPC_{it}) + \beta_4(\ln EI_{it}) \\
&\quad + \beta_5(\ln IS_{it}) + \beta_6(\ln ECS_{it}) + \beta_7(\ln EP_{it}) + \beta_8(\ln OPEN_{it}) + \mu_i + \lambda_t + \ln e_{it} \\
&= \delta\sum_{j=1}^{N} w_{ij} \ln CS_{it} + \alpha + \beta_1(\ln P_{it}) + \beta_2(\ln UR_{it}) + \beta_3(\ln GDPPC_{it}) + \beta_4(\ln EI_{it}) \\
&\quad + \beta_5(\ln IS_{it}) + \beta_6(\ln ECS_{it}) + \beta_7(\ln EP_{it}) + \beta_8(\ln OPEN_{it}) + \mu_i + \lambda_t + \varepsilon_{it}
\end{aligned}
\tag{6}
$$

$$
\begin{aligned}
\ln CI_{it} &= \delta\sum_{j=1}^{N} w_{ij} \ln CI_{it} + \ln a + \beta_1(\ln P_{it}) + \beta_2(\ln UR_{it}) + \beta_3(\ln GDPPC_{it}) + \beta_4(\ln EI_{it}) \\
&\quad + \beta_5(\ln IS_{it}) + \beta_6(\ln ECS_{it}) + \beta_7\ln(EP_{it}) + \beta_8(\ln OPEN_{it}) + \mu_i + \lambda_t + \ln e_{it} \\
&= \delta\sum_{j=1}^{N} w_{ij} \ln CI_{it} + \alpha + \beta_1(\ln P_{it}) + \beta_2(\ln UR_{it}) + \beta_3(\ln GDPPC_{it}) + \beta_4(\ln EI_{it}) \\
&\quad + \beta_5(\ln IS_{it}) + \beta_6(\ln ECS_{it}) + \beta_7(\ln EP_{it}) + \beta_8(\ln OPEN_{it}) + \mu_i + \lambda_t + \varepsilon_{it}
\end{aligned}
\tag{7}
$$

3.2. Spatial Error Panel Data Model (SEPDM)

The Spatial Error Panel Data model (SEPDM) is specified as follows:

$$
\begin{aligned}
\ln CS_{it} &= \ln a + \beta_1(\ln P_{it}) + \beta_2(\ln UR_{it}) + \beta_3(\ln GDPPC_{it}) + \beta_4(\ln EI_{it}) \\
&\quad + \beta_5(\ln IS_{it}) + \beta_6(\ln ECS_{it}) + \beta_7(\ln EP_{it}) + \beta_8\ln(OPEN_{it}) + \mu_i + \lambda_t + \ln e_{it} \\
&= \alpha + \beta_1(\ln P_{it}) + \beta_2(\ln UR_{it}) + \beta_3(\ln GDPPC_{it}) + \beta_4(\ln EI_{it}) + \beta_5(\ln IS_{it}) \\
&\quad + \beta_6(\ln ECS_{it}) + \beta_7(\ln EP_{it}) + \beta_8(\ln OPEN_{it}) + \mu_i + \lambda_t + \phi_{it} \\
\phi_{it} &= \rho\sum_{j=1}^{N} w_{ij}\phi_{it} + \varepsilon_{it}
\end{aligned}
\tag{8}
$$

$$
\begin{aligned}
\ln CI_{it} &= \ln a + \beta_1(\ln P_{it}) + \beta_2(\ln UR_{it}) + \beta_3(\ln GDPPC_{it}) + \beta_4(\ln EI_{it}) \\
&\quad + \beta_5(\ln IS_{it}) + \beta_6(\ln ECS_{it}) + \beta_7\ln(EP_{it}) + \beta_8(\ln OPEN_{it}) + \mu_i + \lambda_t + \ln e_{it} \\
&= \alpha + \beta_1(\ln P_{it}) + \beta_2(\ln UR_{it}) + \beta_3(\ln GDPPC_{it}) + \beta_4(\ln EI_{it}) + \beta_5(\ln IS_{it}) \\
&\quad + \beta_6(\ln ECS_{it}) + \beta_7(\ln EP_{it}) + \beta_8(\ln OPEN_{it}) + \mu_i + \lambda_t + \phi_{it} \\
\phi_{it} &= \rho\sum_{j=1}^{N} w_{ij}\phi_{it} + \varepsilon_{it}
\end{aligned}
\tag{9}
$$

where $InCS_{it}$, $InCI_{it}$, α, β, μ_i, λ_t, ε_{it}, InP_{it}, $InUR_{it}$, $InGDPPC_{it}$, $InEI_{it}$, $InIS_{it}$, $InECS_{it}$, $InEP_{it}$ and $InOPEN_{it}$ are defined same as in (6) and (7). ϕ_{it} denotes spatial error auto-correlation, ρ is spatial auto-correlation index.

3.3. Spatial Durbin Panel Data Model (SDPDM)

The Spatial Durbin Panel Data model (SDPDM) is specified as follows:

$$\ln CS_{it} = \delta \sum_{j=1}^{N} w_{ij} \ln CS_{it} + \ln a + \beta_1 (\ln P_{it}) + \beta_2 (\ln UR_{it}) + \beta_3 (\ln GDPPC_{it}) + \beta_4 (\ln EI_{it})$$

$$+ \beta_5 (\ln IS_{it}) + \beta_6 (\ln ECS_{it}) + \beta_7 (\ln EP_{it}) + \beta_8 (\ln OPEN_{it}) + \theta_1 \sum_{j=1}^{N} w_{ij} \ln P_{ijt} +$$

$$\theta_2 \sum_{j=1}^{N} w_{ij} \ln UR_{ijt} + \theta_3 \sum_{j=1}^{N} w_{ij} \ln GDPPC_{ijt} + \theta_4 \sum_{j=1}^{N} w_{ij} \ln EI_{ijt} + \theta_5 \sum_{j=1}^{N} w_{ij} \ln IS_{ijt} +$$

$$\theta_6 \sum_{j=1}^{N} w_{ij} \ln ECS_{ijt} + \theta_7 \sum_{j=1}^{N} w_{ij} \ln EP_{ijt} + \theta_8 \sum_{j=1}^{N} w_{ij} \ln OPEN_{ijt} + \mu_i + \lambda_t + \ln e_{it}$$

$$= \delta \sum_{j=1}^{N} w_{ij} \ln CS_{it} + \alpha + \beta_1 (\ln P_{it}) + \beta_2 (\ln UR_{it}) + \beta_3 (\ln GDPPC_{it}) + \beta_4 (\ln EI_{it})$$

$$+ \beta_5 (\ln IS_{it}) + \beta_6 (\ln ECS_{it}) + \beta_7 \ln(EP_{it}) + \beta_8 \ln(OPEN_{it}) + \theta_1 \sum_{j=1}^{N} w_{ij} \ln P_{ijt} +$$

$$\theta_2 \sum_{j=1}^{N} w_{ij} \ln UR_{ijt} + \theta_3 \sum_{j=1}^{N} w_{ij} \ln GDPPC_{ijt} + \theta_4 \sum_{j=1}^{N} w_{ij} \ln EI_{ijt} + \theta_5 \sum_{j=1}^{N} w_{ij} \ln IS_{ijt} +$$

$$\theta_6 \sum_{j=1}^{N} w_{ij} \ln ECS_{ijt} + \theta_7 \sum_{j=1}^{N} w_{ij} \ln EP_{ijt} + \theta_8 \sum_{j=1}^{N} w_{ij} \ln OPEN_{ijt} + \mu_i + \lambda_t + \varepsilon_{it}$$

$$(10)$$

$$\ln CI_{it} = \delta \sum_{j=1}^{N} w_{ij} \ln CI_{it} + \ln a + \beta_1 (\ln P_{it}) + \beta_2 (\ln UR_{it}) + \beta_3 (\ln GDPPC_{it}) + \beta_4 (\ln EI_{it})$$

$$+ \beta_5 (\ln IS_{it}) + \beta_6 (\ln ECS_{it}) + \beta_7 (\ln EP_{it}) + \beta_8 (\ln OPEN_{it}) + \theta_1 \sum_{j=1}^{N} w_{ij} \ln P_{ijt} +$$

$$\theta_2 \sum_{j=1}^{N} w_{ij} \ln UR_{ijt} + \theta_3 \sum_{j=1}^{N} w_{ij} \ln GDPPC_{ijt} + \theta_4 \sum_{j=1}^{N} w_{ij} \ln EI_{ijt} + \theta_5 \sum_{j=1}^{N} w_{ij} \ln IS_{ijt} +$$

$$\theta_6 \sum_{j=1}^{N} w_{ij} \ln ECS_{ijt} + \theta_7 \sum_{j=1}^{N} w_{ij} \ln EP_{ijt} + \theta_8 \sum_{j=1}^{N} w_{ij} \ln OPEN_{ijt} + \mu_i + \lambda_t + \ln e_{it}$$

$$= \delta \sum_{j=1}^{N} w_{ij} \ln CI_{it} + \alpha + \beta_1 (\ln P_{it}) + \beta_2 (\ln UR_{it}) + \beta_3 (\ln GDPPC_{it}) + \beta_4 (\ln EI_{it})$$

$$+ \beta_5 (\ln IS_{it}) + \beta_6 (\ln ECS_{it}) + \beta_7 \ln(EP_{it}) + \beta_8 \ln(OPEN_{it}) + \theta_1 \sum_{j=1}^{N} w_{ij} \ln P_{ijt} +$$

$$\theta_2 \sum_{j=1}^{N} w_{ij} \ln UR_{ijt} + \theta_3 \sum_{j=1}^{N} w_{ij} \ln GDPPC_{ijt} + \theta_4 \sum_{j=1}^{N} w_{ij} \ln EI_{ijt} + \theta_5 \sum_{j=1}^{N} w_{ij} \ln IS_{ijt} +$$

$$\theta_6 \sum_{j=1}^{N} w_{ij} \ln ECS_{ijt} + \theta_7 \sum_{j=1}^{N} w_{ij} \ln EP_{ijt} + \theta_8 \sum_{j=1}^{N} w_{ij} \ln OPEN_{ijt} + \mu_i + \lambda_t + \varepsilon_{it}$$

$$(11)$$

where $lnCS_{it}$, $lnCI_{it}$, lnP_{it}, $lnUR_{it}$, $lnGDPPC_{it}$, $lnEI_{it}$, $lnIS_{it}$, $lnECS_{it}$, $lnEP_{it}$, $lnOPEN_{it}$, α, μ_i, λ_t are defined the same as in (6) and (7). θ is a vector of coefficients to be estimated. We test the hypothesis $H_0 : \theta = 0$ and $H_0 : \theta + \delta\beta = 0$. The reject of the hypothesis indicates that SDPDM best fits the data.

The extended STIRPAT model examines not only the impacts of the aforementioned independent variables on scale and intensity of regions' carbon emissions, but it also determines the impacts of the independent variables of the adjacent regions on carbon emissions scale and extent. It also measures the impact of the carbon emissions scale and intensity of the adjacent regions on the region's carbon emissions scale and extent.

3.4. Spatial Weight Matrix

A spatial weight matrix needs to be constructed to reflect spatial correlation among regions. A proper spatial weight matrix is of substantial importance to get a sound spatial econometric result. The construction of the spatial weight matrix influences whether a spatial correlation exists, as well as spatial econometric model selection and the empirical results. To improve model credibility, we consider both geographical and non-geographical spatial correlation among the regions.

We opt for both geographical and economical spatial weighted matrix. The former is constructed by the inverse distance method.

$$W^{GS}_{ij} = \begin{cases} \dfrac{1}{d_{ij}^{\alpha}} & i \neq j \\ 0 & i = j \end{cases} \tag{12}$$

where d_{ij} is the distance between regional i and j, which is calculated from their longitudes and latitudes. The economic spatial weight matrix W^* is a product of W. and the economic weight matrix, E.

$$E_{ij} = \begin{cases} \dfrac{1}{\left| \bar{G}_i - \bar{G}_j \right|^{\alpha} + m} & i \neq j \\ 0 & i = j \end{cases}, \quad \bar{G}_i = \frac{1}{5} \sum_{t=2006}^{2010} G_{it} \tag{13}$$

where G_{it} denotes per capita GDP, representing the income level of region i at time t (Deflated by the price index in 2006). Thus, W^* incorporates economic development into the weight matrix. α is the adjustable parameters of economic weight, usually 1 or 2. When two different geo-spatial locate at the same level of economic development with the same period of time, the denominator is zero. To avoid the zero distance problem, when there are any two different locations in the same period geospatial economic variables are the same, m take 1. When any two different locations in the same period geospatial economic variables are not the same, m is taken to 0.

The calculation of regional carbon emissions takes into account the spatial–temporal dynamics of regional carbon emissions from electricity and thermo. The regional carbon emissions from electricity are elicited under the Origination Principle. The dynamic energy conversion coefficient of energy resources is used. The data is from the *China Energy Statistical Yearbook* 2011 [22].

4. Model Selection

Two Lagrange Multiplier tests (LM-Lag and LM-Error tests) are applied to choose which model, described in Section 3.1 to 3.3, best fits the data. In classical panel data models, there are four categories of fixed effects, namely individual-fixed effects, time-fixed effects, individual and time-fixed effects, and no fixed effects. We test the four kinds of fixed-effect models through the LM test. Tables 1 and 2 show the LM test statistics for Model 1 and Model 2, in which the dependent variable is Log(CS) and Log(CI), respectively.

Table 1. LM test for Model 1 (dependent variable: Log(CS)).

Variable	Pooled ML	Individual-Fixed Effects	Time-Fixed Effects	Individual and Time-Fixed Effects
Constant	−3.3551 *** (−5.8748)	——	——	——
Log(P)	0.9307 *** (21.2903)	0.7383 *** (3.9259)	0.9269 *** (21.0747)	1.2101 *** (4.5873)
Log(UR)	−0.2600 (−1.2142)	0.1818 (0.8779)	−0.1983 (−0.8826)	0.4890 ** (2.2189)
Log(GDPPC)	0.8992 *** (9.6115)	0.9090 *** (8.0765)	0.8583 *** (8.2249)	1.1905 *** (6.6064)
Log(EI)	1.1225 *** (15.1500)	1.1579 *** (4.6128)	1.1284 *** (15.1838)	1.1928 *** (4.2843)
Log(IS)	0.1321 (1.0852)	0.2492 ** (2.2930)	0.1208 (0.9918)	0.1563 (1.3847)
Log(ECS)	0.2847 *** (3.4521)	0.2583 *** (2.6862)	0.2901 *** (3.5199)	0.2952 *** (3.0436)
Log(EP)	−0.0611 (−0.2379)	−0.1480 ** (−2.2421)	0.3289 (0.6455)	0.0590 (0.4786)
Log(OPEN)	0.0804 ** (2.4207)	0.0556 ** (2.7728)	0.0895 *** (2.6282)	0.0554 *** (2.6780)
σ^2	0.0069	0.0004	0.0068	0.0003
R^2	0.9432	0.8341	0.9431	0.4882
Adjusted R^2	0.9400	0.8259	0.9403	0.4630
Durbin–Watson	2.0312	1.8704	2.0661	1.9776
Log-Likelihood	164.6880	382.5538	165.5679	390.1138
LM Spatial Lag	25.6397 (0.000)	6.9517 (0.008)	25.0131 (0.000)	8.5919 (0.003)
Robust LM Spatial Lag	31.6000 (0.000)	3.6978 (0.054)	31.2468 (0.000)	0.3639 (0.546)
LM Spatial Error	1.1145 (0.291)	3.4387 (0.064)	1.3975 (0.237)	9.5364 (0.002)
Robust LM Spatial Error	7.0748 (0.008)	0.1847 (0.667)	7.6311 (0.006)	1.3083 (0.253)

Joint Test of Significance LR	Fixed-Effects	Statistics	df	p-value
	Individual-Fixed Effects	449.0918	30	0.0000
	Time-Fixed Effects	15.1200	5	0.0099

Note: t or z-values are in parentheses, *p*-values in the parentheses under the coefficients of the LM tests, * represents significance at 10%, ** 5%, and *** 1%, respectively.

Table 2. LM test for Model 2 (dependent variable: Log(CI)).

Variable	Pooled ML	Individual-Fixed Effects	Time-Fixed Effects	Individual and Time-Fixed Effects
Constant	0.6449 (1.1291)	——	——	——
Log(P)	−0.0693 (−1.5858)	−0.2616 (−1.3914)	−0.0731* (−1.6609)	0.2101 (0.7963)
Log(UR)	−0.2600 (−1.2142)	0.1818 (0.8779)	−0.1983 (−0.8826)	0.4890 ** (2.2189)
Log(GDPPC)	−0.1008 (−1.0772)	−0.0910 (−0.8083)	−0.1417 (−1.3574)	0.1905 (1.0571)
Log(EI)	1.1225 *** (15.1500)	1.1579 *** (4.6128)	1.1284 *** (15.1838)	1.1928 *** (4.2843)
Log(IS)	0.1321 (1.0852)	0.2492 ** (2.2930)	0.1208 (0.9918)	0.1563 (1.3847)
Log(ECS)	0.2847 *** (3.4521)	0.2583 *** (2.6862)	0.2901 ***3.5199)	0.2952 *** (3.0436)
Log(EP)	−0.0611 (−0.2379)	−0.1480 ** (−2.2421)	0.3289 (0.6455)	0.0590 (0.4786)
Log(OPEN)	0.0804 ** (2.4208)	0.0556 *** (2.7728)	0.0895 *** (2.6282)	0.0554 *** (2.6780)
σ^2	0.0069	0.0004	0.0068	0.0003
R^2	0.8942	0.8013	0.8932	0.3492
Adjusted R^2	0.8882	0.7915	0.8879	0.3171
Durbin–Watson	2.0312	1.8704	2.0661	1.9776
Log-Likelihood	164.6880	382.5538	165.5679	390.1138
LM Spatial Lag	12.3664 (0.000)	4.8069 (0.028)	11.8219 (0.001)	10.6239 (0.001)
Robust LM Spatial Lag	12.6202 (0.000)	1.4754 (0.224)	11.2804 (0.001)	1.1991 (0.274)
LM Spatial Error	1.1145 (0.291)	3.4387 (0.064)	1.3975 (0.237)	9.5364 (0.002)
Robust LM Spatial Error	1.3684 (0.242)	0.1072 (0.743)	0.8561 (0.355)	0.1116 (0.738)

Joint Test of Significance (LR)	Fixed-Effects	Statistics	df	p-Value
	Individual-Fixed Effects	449.0918	30	0.0000
	Time-Fixed Effects	15.1200	5	0.0099

Note: t or z-values are in parentheses, *p*-values in parentheses under the coefficients of the LM tests, * represents significance at 10%, ** 5%, and *** 1%, respectively.

Tables 1 and 2 show that for both models, the LM tests with the four kinds of fixed effects (pooled-effects, individual-fixed effect, time-fixed effect, and individual and time-fixed effect) all support the spatial lag model at the five percent significance level. Similarly, the LM test with individual and time-fixed effect supports the spatial error model. Thus, the hypothesis that spatial correlations do not exist can be rejected. Furthermore, the LR tests reject the hypothesis that individual-fixed effect and time-fixed effect do not exist, indicating that the individual and time-fixed effects model outperforms its alternatives. We further determine which model (SLPDM, SEPDM, and SDPDM) is more appropriate by means of a Wald and LR test.

5. Spillover Effects of Regional Carbon Emissions

It is common to use point estimate from one or more spatial regression to test the existence of spillover effects. Lesage and Pace [23], however, argue that the point estimate of multiple spatial regression will bias its prediction of the spillover effect. They further break down spillover effects into direct and indirect effects.

The SDPDM model (13) can be rearranged as (14) and (15).

$$Y_{it} = \delta \sum_{j=1}^{N} w_{ij} Y_{it} + \alpha + \sum_{i=1}^{m} \beta_i X_{it} + \sum_{j=1}^{N} wi_j Xi_{jt} \theta + \mu_i + \lambda_t + \varepsilon_{it}$$

$$Y_{it} = \delta W Y_{it} + X_{it}\beta + W X_{it}\theta + \mu_i + \lambda_t + \varepsilon_{it} \tag{14}$$

$$Y_{it} = (I - \delta W)^{-1}(X_{it}\beta + W X_{it}\theta) + (I - \delta W)^{-1}\mu_i + (I - \delta W)^{-1}\lambda_t + (I - \delta W)^{-1}\varepsilon_{it} \tag{15}$$

where Y_{it} is the dependent variable of region i at time t, X_{it} is a vector of independent variables of region i at time t, α is the constant term, θ is similar to β, which is a $K \times 1$ vector of coefficients, μ_i is individual-fixed effect, λ_t is time-fixed effect. Taking partial derivatives of the kth independent variable X in both sides results in the following:

$$\left[\frac{\partial Y}{\partial x_{ik}} \cdots \frac{\partial Y}{\partial x_{Nk}} \right] = \begin{bmatrix} \dfrac{\partial y_1}{\partial x_{ik}} & \cdots & \dfrac{\partial y_1}{\partial x_{ik}} \\ \cdots & \cdots & \cdots \\ \dfrac{\partial y_N}{\partial x_{ik}} & \cdots & \dfrac{\partial y_N}{\partial x_{ik}} \end{bmatrix}$$

$$= (I - \delta W)^{-1} \begin{bmatrix} \beta_k & w_{12}\theta_k & \cdots & w_{1N}\theta_k \\ w_{21}\theta_k & \beta_k & \cdots & w_{2N}\theta_k \\ \cdots & \cdots & \cdots & \cdots \\ w_{N1}\theta_k & w_{N2}\theta_k & \cdots & \beta_k \end{bmatrix} \tag{16}$$

where w_{ij} is the (i, j) element of the matrix W. The direct effect is defined as the sum of the diagonal elements in the right matrix while the indirect effect is defined as the average of all the elements other than the diagonal elements (Lesage and Pace, 2009). Calculation of the direct and indirect effects by this method has a drawback because calculation $(I - \delta W)^{-1}$ is time consuming. To solve this, Lesage and Pace (2009) propose another method as follows:

$$(I - \delta W)^{-1} = I + \delta W + \delta^2 W^2 + \delta^3 W^3 + \ldots \tag{17}$$

The estimates of direct and indirect effects from (16) are denoted as Method 1 and Method 2 for (17). Tables 3 and 4 displays the direct and indirect effect estimates through Method 1 and Method 2, respectively, for Model 5 with Log(CS) being dependent variable. The results differ slightly across Method 1 and Method 2. All the variables have direct and indirect effects. P, GDPPC, EI, IS, impact the scale of carbon emission positively and significantly, while UR impacts significantly and negatively. Although the direct effects of ECS, EP, and OPEN are insignificant, their signs are in line with expectation.

Tables 5 and 6 display the direct and indirect effects estimates for Model 5 with Log(CI) being the dependent variable. The chosen from Method 1 and Method 2 do not differ from results. All the variables have direct and indirect effects. The direct effect of EI, IS, and ECS on the carbon intensity is positive, whereas it is negative for *P*, *UR*. Moreover, the direct effect of *GDPPC*, *EP*, and *OPEN* on the carbon intensity is insignificant, though their signs are as expected. From the perspective of indirect effects, all of the variables except for energy price have significant indirect effects. We can thus argue that spillover effects do exist. Spillover effects mean the independent variables affect the dependent variable via the spatial lagged variables. The differences of direct and indirect effects of all the control variables are substantial, indicating that failing to explicitly account for spatial correlation leads to estimation bias.

Table 3. Direct, indirect and total effect of the spatial Durbin model (Method 1, dependent variable: Log(*CS*)).

Variable	Direct Effect	Indirect Effect	Total Effect
Log(P)	0.8695 *** (17.5550)	0.2562 *** (3.5963)	1.1257 *** (16.9993)
Log(UR)	−0.6102 *** (−2.6245)	1.4454 *** (4.8198)	0.8352 *** (4.0497)
Log(GDPPC)	1.1107 *** (9.2912)	−0.6206 *** (−3.9366)	0.4901 *** (4.3048)
Log(EI)	1.3005 *** (10.6820)	−0.4729 *** (−2.6714)	0.8276 *** (6.1398)
Log(IS)	0.3498 *** (3.8936)	0.7305 *** (5.2446)	1.0804 *** (7.0120)
Log(ECS)	0.1102 (1.4101)	−0.2659 ** (−2.2764)	−0.1558 (−1.1617)
Log(EP)	−0.0464 (−0.3767)	0.0799 (0.3984)	0.0335 (0.1862)
Log(OPEN)	0.0004 (0.0206)	−0.0528 ** (−2.2098)	−0.0524 (−1.7280)

Note: t-values are in parentheses, * represents significance at 10%, ** 5%, and *** 1%, respectively.

Table 4. Direct, indirect and total effect of the spatial Durbin model (Method 2, dependent variable: Log(*CS*)).

Variable	Direct Effect	Indirect Effect	Total Effect
Log(P)	0.8680 *** (16.9634)	0.2573 *** (3.7798)	1.1253 *** (16.8913)
Log(UR)	−0.5950 ** (−2.5072)	1.4454 *** (4.7180)	0.8404 *** (4.0538)
Log(GDPPC)	1.1075 *** (9.0225)	−0.6203 *** (−3.6545)	0.4872 *** (4.2317)
Log(EI)	1.3057 *** (10.4525)	−0.4845 ** (−2.6801)	0.8212 *** (5.9779)
Log(IS)	0.3525 *** (3.8938)	0.7284 *** (5.3623)	1.0809 *** (6.9873)
Log(ECS)	0.1053 (1.3456)	−0.2625 ** (−2.2113)	−0.1572 (−1.1692)
Log(EP)	−0.0451 (−0.3586)	0.0834 (0.4056)	0.0383 (0.2008)
Log(OPEN)	0.0003 (0.0139)	−0.0536 ** (−2.3221)	−0.0534 * (−1.7624)

Note: t-values are in parentheses, * represents significance at 10%, ** 5%, and *** 1%, respectively.

Table 5. Direct, indirect and total effect of the spatial Durbin model (Method 1, dependent variable: Log(*CI*)).

Variable	Direct Effect	Indirect Effect	Total Effect
Log(P)	−0.1333 ** (−2.5375)	0.2570 *** (3.8721)	0.1237 * (1.9022)
Log(UR)	−0.6072 *** (−2.6125)	1.4402 *** (4.8072)	0.8331 *** (4.1424)
Log(GDPPC)	0.1172 (0.9877)	−0.6246 *** (−3.7793)	−0.5075 *** (−4.4427)
Log(EI)	1.3100 *** (10.9563)	−0.4772 *** (−2.7687)	0.8328 *** (6.1855)
Log(IS)	0.3433 *** (3.9225)	0.7147 *** (5.5172)	1.0580 *** (7.4353)
Log(ECS)	0.1115 ** (1.4542)	−0.2536 ** (−2.3062)	−0.1421 (−1.1075)
Log(EP)	−0.0452 (−0.3634)	0.0797 (0.4023)	0.0345 (0.1890)
Log(OPEN)	0.0010 (0.0524)	−0.0506 ** (−2.2070)	−0.0496 (−1.6861)

Note: t-values are in parentheses, * represents significance at 10%, ** 5%, and *** 1%, respectively.

6. The Spatial Durbin Panel Data Model (SDPDM) for Carbon Emission

We consider three Durbin models: (i) individual and time-fixed effects model (Model 3), (ii) both time and individual effects with bias correction borrowed from Lee and Yu [24] (Model 4), (iii) individual random effects and time-fixed effects (Model 5). The models with Log(*CS*) and Log (*CI*) as dependent variables are reported in Tables 3 and 4, respectively. Model 3 and Model 4 show that the coefficients for *P*, *UR*, *GDPPC*, *EI*, *IS*, *ECS*, *EP*, *OPEN*, and σ^2 changed slightly after bias correction, while the coefficients for the spatial lagged dependent and independent variables are sensitive to it. Thus, the bias correction is necessary for the spatial Durbin model with both individual and time-fixed effects. The SDPDM has two hypotheses: $H_0 : \theta = 0$ and $H_0 : \theta + \delta\beta = 0$. Rejection of both hypotheses indicates that SDPDM fits the data best. Both the Wald and LR tests reject the two hypotheses, thereby suggesting that both SLPDM and SEPDM are rejected. We thus opt for SDPDM. Meanwhile, the Houseman test points to (Model 5), of which the coefficients are in line with expectation, and the square correlation coefficient is greater than that of (Model 4).

Table 6. Direct, indirect and total effect of the spatial Durbin model (Method 2, dependent variable: Log(*CI*)).

Variable	Direct Effect	Indirect Effect	Total Effect
Log(P)	−0.1331 ** (−2.4595)	0.2598 *** (3.9424)	0.1267 ** (1.9568)
Log(UR)	−0.6056 ** (−2.5655)	1.4450 *** (4.6130)	0.8394 *** (4.0677)
Log(GDPPC)	0.1181 (0.9869)	−0.6269 *** (−3.8520)	−0.5089 *** (−4.5164)
Log(EI)	1.3078 *** (10.7349)	−0.4754 *** (−2.8265)	0.8324 *** (6.2488)
Log(IS)	0.3486 *** (3.8477)	0.7194 *** (5.4372)	1.0680 *** (6.8492)
Log(ECS)	0.1116 (1.4192)	−0.2601 ** (−2.2649)	−0.1485 (−1.1442)
Log(EP)	−0.0507 (−0.3953)	0.0924 (0.4544)	0.0418 (0.2324)
Log(OPEN)	0.0008 (0.0423)	−0.0525 ** (−2.2719)	−0.0517 * (−1.7145)

Note: t-values are in parentheses, * represents significance at 10%, ** 5%, and *** 1%, respectively.

We only report the results of Model 5, which are in column four in Tables 3 and 4, respectively, for the two dependent variables. The empirical results show that coefficients for most of the independent variables are significant and the signs are as expected. The coefficients for the spatial lagged variable are negative and significant in both models (line 1, column 4 in Tables 7 and 8), indicating that carbon emissions among regions are correlated. A region's carbon emission level is estimated to decrease by 0.2 percent if the scale and intensity of carbon emissions of its neighbors increase by one percent. Therefore, provinces which successfully pursuing a low carbon strategy plays an important role in building a low-carbon economy for the whole country, they will drive other provinces to increase their emissions reduction. An effective regional emission reduction strategy plus government's support will lead the regional emission reduction to a virtuous cycle, and make the carbon emissions reduce effectively. Below, we discuss the impacts of the independent variables on carbon emission.

Population. The significant and positive coefficient (line 3, column 4 in Table 7) for population size *P* suggests that population growth increases the scale of China's carbon emissions. The demand for energy increases dramatically with population growth, which in turn raises CO_2 emissions. In carbon intensity estimation, *P* impacts the carbon intensity negatively and significantly (line 3, column 4 in Table 8), indicating that population growth did not enlarge the carbon intensity. Saving energy and reducing emissions have become important aspects in adjusting the structure of China's economy and the path to development. Thus we have seen a declining trend in carbon intensity. For instance, in the 2009 United Nations Climate Change Conference, held in Copenhagen, Denmark, the Chinese government committed to reduce 40 to 50 percent of its CO_2 emissions by 2020 compared to 2005. Considering the fact that China is still undergoing urbanization and industrialization, as well as a surge of population and consumption per capita, a decrease of the carbon intensity has become the priority. China should follow the principle of *"shared but differentiated responsibility"* to develop its low-carbon economy in a sustainable way. The spatial lagged variable $W \times Log(P)$ impacts both the scale and intensity of carbon emissions significantly and positively, proving that there are carbon emissions spillover effects of population size. One should also note that the spillover effect of population is stronger at the scale of carbon emissions than carbon intensity. The possible reason is that spillover effects are generated by flow of population, such as interregional and rural–urban migration, and by a surge of CO_2 emissions from infrastructure development and household consumption.

Table 7. The spatial Durbin model with both individual and time-fixed effect (dependent variable: $Log(CS)$).

Variable	Spatial and Time-fixed Effect	Both Time and Individual Effects (Bias Corrected)	Spatial Random Effect and Time-Fixed Effect
$W \times Log(CS)$	−0.2290 *** (−2.7392)	−0.1978 ** (−2.2988)	−0.2020 ** (−2.4198)
$Log(P)$	1.1820 *** (3.9562)	1.1880 *** (3.4908)	0.8871 *** (17.6901)
$Log(UR)$	−0.2978 (−1.1976)	−0.3110 (−1.1002)	−0.4915 ** (−2.2262)
$Log(GDPPC)$	1.3010 *** (7.6561)	1.3101 *** (6.7802)	1.0642 *** (9.5461)
$Log(EI)$	0.8258 *** (3.4713)	0.8429 *** (3.1212)	1.2663 *** (11.2678)
$Log(IS)$	0.2827 *** (2.6770)	0.2755 ** (2.2968)	0.4039 *** (4.4186)
$Log(ECS)$	0.1940 ** (2.2499)	0.1964 ** (1.9999)	0.0900 (1.1606)
$Log(EP)$	−0.0565 (−0.5608)	−0.0548 (−0.4775)	−0.0348 (−0.2952)
$Log(OPEN)$	0.0108 (0.6195)	0.0113 (0.5677)	−0.0030 (−0.1595)
$W \times Log(P)$	0.6424 (1.4861)	0.6118 (1.2460)	0.4634 *** (4.2059)
$W \times Log(UR)$	1.8219 *** (5.1834)	1.8099 *** (4.5221)	1.4938 *** (4.8326)
$W \times Log(GDPPC)$	−0.0443 (−0.1559)	−0.0787 (−0.2454)	−0.4749 ** (−2.5301)
$W \times Log(EI)$	−1.2913*** (−3.1092)	−1.3385 *** (−2.8564)	−0.2720 (−1.3163)
$W \times Log(IS)$	0.7874 *** (4.4070)	0.7861 *** (3.8624)	0.8859 *** (6.0133)
$W \times Log(ECS)$	−0.2082 (−1.4987)	−0.2113 (−1.3356)	−0.2700 ** (−2.0940)
$W \times Log(EP)$	−0.0378 (−0.2028)	−0.0360 (−0.1695)	0.0828 (0.3832)
$W \times Log(OPEN)$	−0.0319 (−1.2736)	−0.0325 (−1.1394)	−0.0588 ** (−2.2985)
teta	——	——	0.1256 *** (5.5030)
σ^2	0.0002	0.0003	0.0003
R^2	0.9982	0.9982	0.9974
Square Correlation Coefficient	0.6573	0.6566	0.9615
Log-Likelihood	422.9826	422.9826	333.4740
Wald Test Spatial Lag	68.7413 (0.000)	52.9481 (0.000)	71.8871 (0.000)
LR Test Spatial Lag	56.5236 (0.000)	56.5236 (0.000)	NA
Wald Test Spatial Error	65.5395 (0.000)	51.4416 (0.000)	63.8144 (0.000)
LR Test Spatial Error	52.4984 (0.000)	52.4984 (0.000)	NA

Hausman test	Statistics	df	*p*-Value
	11.1632	17	0.8480

Note: *t* or *z*-values are in parentheses, *p*-values in parentheses under the coefficients of the LM and Wald tests. * represents significance at 10%, ** 5%, and *** 1%, respectively.

Table 8. Spatial Durbin model with both individual and time-fixed effect (dependent variable: Log(*CI*)).

Variable	Spatial and Time-Fixed Effect	Both Time and Individual Effects (Bias Corrected)	Spatial Random Effect and Time-Fixed Effect
W × Log(CI)	−0.2290 *** (−2.7499)	−0.1980 ** (−2.3095)	−0.2220 *** (−2.6778)
Log(P)	0.1820 (0.6092)	0.1879 (0.5522)	−0.1105 ** (−2.2183)
Log(UR)	−0.2978 (−1.1977)	−0.3109 (−1.0999)	−0.4819 ** (−2.1899)
Log(GDPPC)	0.3010 * (1.7715)	0.3100 * (1.6045)	0.0593 (0.5332)
Log(EI)	0.8258 *** (3.4718)	0.8428 *** (3.1211)	1.2646 *** (11.3236)
Log(IS)	0.2827 *** (2.6774)	0.2756 ** (2.2975)	0.4093 *** (4.4913)
Log(ECS)	0.1940 ** (2.2500)	0.1964 ** (1.9997)	0.0890 (1.1512)
Log(EP)	−0.0565 (−0.5608)	−0.0549 (−0.4777)	−0.0393 (−0.3332)
Log(OPEN)	0.0108 (0.6195)	0.0113 (0.5675)	−0.0035 (−0.1831)
W × Log(P)	0.4135 (0.9741)	0.4141 (0.8563)	0.2617 *** (3.6790)
W × Log(UR)	1.8219 *** (5.1836)	1.8100 *** (4.5226)	1.4948 *** (4.8508)
W × Log(GDPPC)	−0.2733 (−1.0161)	−0.2764 (−0.9023)	−0.6770 *** (−4.0574)
W × Log(EI)	−1.2913 *** (−3.1103)	−1.3382 *** (−2.8563)	−0.2474 (−1.2043)
W × Log(IS)	0.7874 *** (4.4070)	0.7862 *** (3.8625)	0.8877 *** (6.0435)
W × Log(ECS)	−0.2082 (−1.4987)	−0.2113 (−1.3354)	−0.2651 ** (−2.0601)
W × Log(EP)	−0.0378 (−0.2028)	−0.0361 (−0.1696)	0.0849 (0.3932)
W × Log(OPEN)	−0.0319 (−1.2736)	−0.0325 (−1.1393)	−0.0577 ** (−2.2615)
teta	——	——	0.1266 *** (5.5034)
σ^2	0.0002	0.0003	0.0003
R^2	0.9967	0.9967	0.9951
Square Correlation Coefficient	0.5642	0.5634	0.9282
Log-Likelihood	422.9334	422.9334	333.6113
Wald Test Spatial Lag	66.1930 (0.000)	51.3633 (0.000)	65.0033 (0.000)
LR Test Spatial Lag	54.5750 (0.000)	54.5750 (0.000)	NA
Wald Test Spatial Error	65.5435 (0.000)	51.4385 (0.000)	63.7257 (0.000)
LR Test Spatial Error	52.3998 (0.00)	52.3998 (0.000)	NA
Hausman Test	Statistics	df	P-Value
	0.9612	17	1.0000

Note: *t* or z-values are in parentheses, P-values in parentheses under the coefficients of the LM and Wald tests, * represents significance at 10%, ** 5%, and *** 1%, respectively.

Urbanization. Population impacts carbon emission via human production and consumption. The population factor affects carbon emissions not only through its size, but also via urbanization. Urbanization levels affect both the scale of carbon emissions and carbon intensity positively and significantly, indicating the acceleration of urbanization restrains the increase of carbon emissions scale and carbon intensity. In the past decade, China's urbanization rate has been one percent per year, reaching 50 percent in 2011 and 51.27 percent by the end of 2011. The variable W × Log(*UR*) positively and significantly affects both the level and intensity of carbon emissions. This suggests that spillover effects of urbanization on carbon emissions do exist and that the spillover effect of urbanization on the scale of carbon emission is similar to that on the carbon intensity. This is due to the competition for homogeneity among regions. The differentiated levels of urbanization of different regions accelerate the urbanization process for the lagging regions that aim to "catch up" with regions with higher urbanization level. This extensive urbanization model leads to negative consequences such as low land use efficiency, imperfect infrastructure and improper urban planning and so on. All these factors lead to growth in carbon emissions.

Per capita GDP. China is in an era of rapid industrialization and urbanization, which translates into CO_2 emissions growth from economic growth and energy consumption. The positive and significant impact of per capita GDP on the scale and intensity of carbon emissions indicates that China's unprecedented economic growth is the main driver of carbon emissions growth. Rising carbon emissions are to some extent unavoidable in maintaining a high growth rate. Thus, the carbon emissions reduction target is not likely to be met by controlling economic development, but by adjusting the structure of energy consumption and following the low-carbon path. We argue that economic growth and carbon emissions reduction can both be achieved. The negative and significant coefficient of the spatial lagged variable $W \times Log(GDPPC)$ shows that the economic growth in some regions can affect carbon emissions of other regions through spillover effects. The results also indicate that the spillover effect of economic development on the carbon intensity is greater than on the scale of carbon emission. This is explained by the fact that the provinces are competing to develop lower carbon economies in the 11th Five-Year period. The provinces have attempted to save energy and reduce emissions by adjusting the structure of economic growth and shifting towards low-carbon development paths. As a result, the effect of economic growth on carbon emissions has been alleviated.

Energy intensity. The decrease in energy intensity is mainly from technological innovation, affecting both the scale and intensity of carbon emissions. We found a significant and positive impact of energy intensity on the level and intensity of carbon emissions, indicating that China's technological innovation and the associated decrease in energy intensity contributes to the reduction of carbon emissions. Since adjusting industry and energy consumption structure is difficult, China needs to search for other ways—as with technological innovation—to improve energy efficiency and reduce carbon emissions. The low-carbon technologies, including clean energy alternative technologies, renewable energy technologies, and new energy technologies, which are currently in the stages of energy exploration, transformation and application, give substantial support to meeting the 2020 carbon emissions reduction target. However, no spatial spillover effect is found for energy intensity on carbon emissions, since the coefficient for $W \times Log(EI)$ is negative but insignificant. This is because the flow of carbon emissions technology from one region to another is hard to fulfill. The imitation of developing carbon emissions reduction technologies is to a large extent influenced by regional economic development and innovation capability. The large differences on research capabilities among regions block diffusion of those technologies.

Industry structure. Industrial structure refers to the percentage of the secondary industry which includes manufacturing and construction sectors. Those are energy-intensive industries. However, the secondary industry is still the main industry of China's economy, which is in the phase of urbanization and industrialization. Under such circumstances, the scale and intensity of carbon emissions are influenced by the current economic structure. This is supported by the results that *IS* effects scale and intensity of carbon emissions positively and significantly. This means the change in industry structure is not successful in reducing high energy consumption and emissions and increasing energy efficiency, because China is historically concentrated on heavy industries. To meet the emissions reduction target, China should adjust its economic structure and develop high-tech and modern service industries, which have far lower carbon emissions. On the other hand, the spillover effect by industry structure on carbon emissions levels is found to be positive but insignificant, suggesting that, in the short term, changes in industry structure are unlikely to reduce levels of carbon emissions. However, we confirm there is a spillover effect of industrial structure on the intensity of carbon emissions. The reason is that the carbon intensity target is allocated by the central government to the provinces that compete to meet the carbon emissions target. Different carbon intensity indicators in the energy production and consumption phases give the provinces incentives to adjust their industrial structures and strategies of energy production and consumption, which again leads to carbon emissions reduction.

Structure of energy consumption. In the long run, China ought to transform its traditional coal-intensive energy structure to an oil- and gas-intensive one. However, given current resource status and the high consumption rate of coal, the coal-intensive structure will remain for a long period of time. ECS is positive but insignificant in affecting both the levels and intensity of carbon emissions, indicating that change in energy consumption structure does not play a role. To strengthen the role of changes in the energy consumption structure, it is necessary to increase, in proportional terms, the use of non-fossil energies such as wind, hydro, nuclear, solar and biomass. The use of gas should also be increased through adjusting industrial policy and international trade policies. Moreover, $W \times Log(ECS)$ impacts the scale and intensity negatively and significantly, suggesting the presence of spillover effects of the structure of energy consumption. The spillover is due to the competition among the regions in optimizing energy consumption structure and developing non-fossil energies. It is necessary to build a mechanism under which the scale and intensity of energy consumption is controlled and provincial energy structures are correlated in an optimal way.

Energy price. In this paper, energy price refers to producer's price index for manufactured products. In theory, factor prices negatively correlate with factor demands. The coefficient for energy price is negative but insignificant in affecting both the level and intensity of carbon emissions, indicating that although the role of energy price in affecting carbon emission is not statistically significant, but important. To meet the increasing demand for energy, a market-oriented price mechanism needs to be formed to reflect resource scarcity. While the government decides the price for electricity transmission and distribution, the price for electricity producers and consumers is determined by the market-oriented price mechanism. We do not find evidence that the spillover effect of the energy price exists, because the release of regional energy price information is inefficient. When energy price in one region increases, producers in this region will purchase energy from its adjacent regions, thereby causing an increase of total carbon emission. Therefore, China is in need of a sounder price information system.

Openness. Under the trend of globalization, China's opening up policy has been pushing its economy forward; many achievements have been made as a result. In recent years, the need for a low-carbon economy has made it necessary to import advanced technologies from abroad, with a preference for sustainable ones. Thus, openness decreases carbon emissions. However, this hypothesis is rejected by the model results. We find *OPEN* effects carbon emissions to impact negatively but insignificantly. Nonetheless, China needs to import low-carbon technologies and welcome FDI in developing low-carbon technologies, since the spillover effect of FDI lowers scale and intensity of carbon emissions. The coefficient for $W \times Log(OPEN)$ is negative and significant, confirming the presence of a spillover effect. The spillover effect is from the competition among regions on absorbing FDI. Not only cities along the coast have increased the intensity of their policies to open their borders for trade and investment, but also the provinces from Central and Western China have accelerated the pace of opening up, supporting the transition towards a low-carbon economy.

7. Conclusions and Policy Recommendations

An extended Stochastic Impacts by Regression on Population, Affluence and Technology (STIRPAT) model for the regional level is created to investigate factors that drive the scale and intensity of carbon emissions in China. Based on provincial panel data from 2006 to 2010, a spatial Durbin model is applied to test the impacts of the driving factors on the scale and intensity of carbon emissions and to examine spatial correlation of carbon emissions and the spillover effects of the determinants. The main conclusions from the analysis are as follows:

First, most of the factors impact the level and intensity of carbon emissions significantly and with expected signs. The revealed negative and significant impact of spatial-lagged variables suggests that the carbon emissions among regions are highly correlated. As a result, the exemplary role of the provinces with low-carbon emission is of great importance in developing a nationwide low-carbon economy.

Second, the driving factors impact carbon emission both directly and indirectly. From the perspective of indirect effects, all of the variables except for energy price have significant indirect effects. We can, thus, argue that spillover effects do exist. The transitional panel data model will bias the estimation. The spillover effect refers to the independent variables that affect the dependent variable via the spatial-lagged variables. The differences of direct and indirect effects of the control variables are substantial, indicating that failure to account for spatial correlation leads to estimation bias.

The analyses show that spatial correlation, heterogeneity and externality need to be taken into account when formulating policies. Carbon emissions will not be met by controlling economic development, but energy consumption and low-carbon path. Considering the fact that carbon emissions among regions and industries are different, we propose the following strategies to reduce

Sustainability **2014**, *6*, 6005–6023

carbon emission while maintaining economic growth: Accelerating the process of urbanization, to fully realize its function of reducing carbon emissions, fostering technological innovation, optimizing industry structure, moderately increasing energy prices, and extending opening up policies for trade and foreign investment while choosing FDI with low-carbon technologies.

Acknowledgments: This research is supported by the National Natural Science Foundation of China "A Research on the Operating Mechanism and Economic Impact of the Pilot Regional Carbon Trading—Based on the Term-Co2 Model (No.71473242)", National Basic Research Program of China (No. 2012CB955700) and Chinese Academy of Science Strategic technology Special Project "Climate Change and Carbon budget Certification related issue (XDA.05140300)".

Author Contributions: Yu Liu performed research, analyzed the data and wrote the paper. Hongwei Xiao contributed to the conceptual framework of the methodology and interpreted the results. Precious Zikhali drafted and revised the manuscript. Yingkang Lv performed the calculations and analyzed the data.

Conflicts of Interest: The authors declare no conflict of interest.

References

1. Huang, Y.; Wang, L.; Li, G.; Jiang, D. An empirical analysis for the environmental Kuznets curve in China based on spatial penal models . *South China J. Econ.* **2009**, *10*, 59–68. (in Chinese).

2. Su, Z.; Hu, R.; Lin, S. Spatial econometric analysis of Kuznets' relationship between environmental quality and economic growth. *Geogr. Res.* **2009**, *2*, 303–310. (in Chinese).

3. Zhu, P.; Yuan, J.; Zen, W. Analysis of Chinese Industry Environmental Kuznets Curve—Empirical Study Based on Spatial Panel Model. *China Ind. Econ.* **2010**, *6*, 65–74. (in Chinese).

4. Wang, L.; Guan, J.; Zhang, J. Environmental Pollution and Economic Growth in China: A Dynamic Spatial Panel Data Model. *Geogr. Res.* **2010**, *6*, 818–825. (in Chinese).

5. Yao, Y.; Ni, Q. The impact of foreign direct investment on carbon intensity empirical study based on Chinese provincial dynamic panel data. *Econ. Geogr.* **2011**, *9*, 1432–1438. (in Chinese).

6. Yu, Y. Innovation Cluster, Government Support and the Technological Innovation Efficiency: Based on Spatial Econometrics of Panel Data with Provincial Data. *Econ. Rev.* **2011**, *2*, 93–101. (in Chinese).

7. Zheng, Z.; Huang, H. Spatial panel statistical analysis on local government behavior and environmental pollution. *Stat. Inf. Forum* **2011**, *10*, 52–57. (in Chinese).

8. Chen, D.; Zhang, J. An empirical study on the environmental Kuznets curve for China's carbon emission: Based on Spatial Panel model. *Stat. Inf. Forum* **2011**, *5*, 48–53. (in Chinese).

9. Xu, H.; Deng, Y. Does FDI lead to environment pollution in China? A spatial econometric analysis based on provincial panel data. *Manag. World* **2012**, *2*, 30–43. (in Chinese).

10. Wang, H.; Teng, Y. Economic Development and Environmental Pollution Space Panel Data Analysis. *Technol. Econ. Manag. Res.* **2013**, *2*, 85–89. (in Chinese).

11. Ehrlich, P.R.; Holdren, J.P. Impact of population growth. *Science* **1971**, *3977*, 1212–1217.

12. Harrison, P. *Inside the Third World: The Anatomy of Poverty*; Penguin Books: New York, NY, USA, 1981.

13. Raskin, P.D. Methods for estimating the population contribution to environmental change. *Ecol. Econ.* **1995**, *3*, 225–233.

14. York, R.; Rosa, E.A.; Dietz, T. Bridging environmental science with environmental policy: Plasticity of population, affluence, and technology. *Soc. Sci. Q.* **2002**, *1*, 18–34.

15. Shi, A. The impact of population pressure on global carbon dioxide emissions, 1975–1996: Evidence from pooled cross-country data. *Ecol. Econ.* **2003**, *1*, 29–42. [CrossRef]

16. Cole, M.A.; Neumayer, E. Examining the impact of demographic factors on air pollution. *Popul. Environ.* **2004**, *1*, 5–21. [CrossRef]

17. Rosa, E.A.; York, R.; Dietz, T. Tracking the anthropogenic drivers of ecological impacts. *AMBIO A. J. Hum. Environ.* **2004**, *8*, 509–512.

18. Waggoner, P.E.; Ausubel, J.H. A framework for sustainability science: A renovated IPAT identity. *Proc. Nat. Acad. Sci. USA* **2002**, *12*, 7860–7865. [CrossRef]

19. Dietz, T.; Rosa, E.A. Rethinking the environmental impacts of population, affluence and technology. *Hum. Ecol. Rev.* **1994**, *1*, 277–300.

20. Dietz, T.; Rosa, E.A. Effects of population and affluence on CO_2 emissions. *Proc. Nat. Acad. Sci. USA* **1997**, *1*, 175–179. [CrossRef]

21. York, R.; Rosa, E.A.; Dietz, T. STIRPAT, IPAT and ImPACT: Analytic tools for unpacking the driving forces of environmental impacts. *Ecol. Econ.* **2003**, *3*, 351–365. [CrossRef]

22. National Bureau of Statistics of People's Republic of China. *China Energy Statistical Yearbook 2011*; China Statistics Press: Beijing, China, 2012.

23. LeSage, J.P.; Pace, R.K. *An Introduction to Spatial Econometrics*; CRC Press: Boca Raton, FL, USA, 2009; pp. 19–44.

24. Lee, L.; Yu, J. Estimation of spatial autoregressive panel data models with fixed effects. *J. Econ.* **2010**, *2*, 165–185. [CrossRef]

sustainability

MDPI

Article

Sources of China's Economic Growth: An Empirical Analysis Based on the BML Index with Green Growth Accounting

Minzhe Du [1], Bing Wang [1,*] and Yanrui Wu [1,2]

[1] Economic Department, School of Economics, Jinan University, Guangzhou 510632, China;
    minzhe_du@126.com (M.D.); yanrui.wu@uwa.edu.au (Y.W.)
[2] Business School, University of Western Australia, Crawley WA 6009, Australia
*   Author to whom correspondence should be addressed; twangb@jnu.edu.cn; Tel.: +86-20-8522-0173;
    Fax: +86-20-8522-0173.

Received: 7 July 2014; in revised form: 18 August 2014; Accepted: 26 August 2014; Published: 5 September 2014

Abstract: This study develops a biennial Malmquist–Luenberger productivity index that is used to measure the sources of economic growth by utilizing data envelopment analysis and the directional distance function. Taking restrictions on resources and the environment into account based on the green growth accounting framework; we split economic growth into seven components: technical efficiency change, technological change, labor effect, capital effect, energy effect, output structure effect and environmental regulation effect. Further, we apply the Silverman test and Li-Fan-Ullah nonparametric test in combination with kernel distribution to test for the counterfactual contributions at the provincial level in China from 1998 to 2012. The empirical results show that: (1) technological progress and TFP make positive contributions to economic growth in China, while technical efficiency drags it down; (2) the effect of output structure and CO_2 emissions with environmental regulation restrain economic growth in some provinces; and (3) overall, physical capital accumulation is the most important driving force for economic take-off, irrespective of whether the government adopts environmental regulations.

Keywords: economic growth; biennial Malmquist–Luenberger index; data envelopment analysis; green growth accounting framework; counterfactual distribution

---

1. Introduction

Over the past 30 years, economic growth in China has attracted worldwide attention since the country embarked on reform and opened up. However, China has paid a heavy price in terms of resources and the environment for its significant economic growth. After the Asian economic crisis in 1997, some scholars even began to question whether China's overheating economic growth is sustainable. Krugman [1] argued that Asia, including China, succeeded because of its investment in resources instead of a promotion of efficiency. During the period of the "11th five-year plan", China's resource productivity was at $320–$350 per tonnes with the rapid growth of direct material input, and the output efficiency of its resources was below those of developed countries. Its CO_2 emissions were generated by primary energy doubled from 3.47 to 7.18 billion tonnes from 2000 to 2009, making China a major contributor of CO_2 emissions in the world. By the end of 2006, however, China had made some substantial progress in pollution reduction. The economic benefits arising from the implementation of its cleaner production program amounted to 4.4 billion CNY, and the direct economic benefits generated by energy saving amounted to 5.5 billion CNY. However, the costs of environmental pollution abatement are still increasing along with economic development. In 2011, the country's environmental pollution control investment was 602.62 billion CNY, accounting for 1.27% of

GDP. Consequently, the high intensity of resource consumption and environmental pollution shows that Chinese economic growth is still mainly based on the extensive growth feature of high input, high consumption, high emission and growth without development, and is not driven by the green growth approach of improving TFP.

Suffering from the dual challenge of economic growth and resource and environmental constraints, China must implement strict or appropriate environmental regulation, energy savings initiatives and other mechanisms to reduce the negative impact on its environment without reducing the rate of economic growth. Further, China urgently needs to transform the pattern of economic growth so as to realize a win-win solution for environmental protection and economic growth. To this end, it is necessary to understand what the sources of the country's economic growth are. However, the traditional accounting of sources of economic growth does not consider the factors of energy and the environment. In addition, this accounting method may lead to a misleading result.

Thus, the main purpose of this study is to discover China's sources of economic growth with the constraints of resources and the environment. The study uses the frontier technology boundary analysis and output-oriented directional distance function (DDF) to propose a decomposition of the sources of economic growth within the green growth accounting framework (GGAF), and then to measure the sources of China's economic growth between 1998 and 2012 based on the new biennial Malmquist–Luenberger productivity index.

The rest of this paper is organized as follows. The next section features a brief review of the relevant literature pertaining to the sources of economic growth. The theoretical methods, which contain the biennial Malmquist–Luenberger productivity index and the GGAF, are introduced in Section 3. Section 4 discusses the data and empirical results. In Section 5 describes the above tests that were conducted to further analyze the distribution dynamics of economic growth from 1998 to 2012. Finally, Section 6 presents the conclusions and policy implications derived from the study.

2. Literature Review

Economic growth is an important foundation for the economic and social development of a country or region. Thus, its sources, internal mechanisms, and implementation have become core issues that economists continue to explore. Much of the existing literature has described and analyzed the sources of China's economic growth. Some researchers [2–4] showed that China's economic growth mainly comes from factor accumulation, especially capital. Chow [5] first discovered that capital accumulation played a major role in explaining China's growth from 1952 to 1980 with the absence of technical progress. Kim and Lau [6] applied the aggregate meta-production function framework and found that growth mostly resulted from the growth of tangible inputs, that is, capital and labor, and not technical progress or TFP. Other researchers later found that TFP was the primary driving force behind China's growth [7–10]. Borensztein and Ostry [11] believed China's technological progress was slow even though TFP made a remarkable contribution in the post-reform period. Hu and Khan [12] further found that the sharp and sustained increase in TFP accounted for the unprecedented economic growth observed during the reform period while capital accumulation played an important role in China's economic growth from 1952 to 1994. Chow and Li [13] found that productivity growth accounted for almost 32% of growth, while capital accounted for 54% and labor 13%. However, Ding and Knight [14] concluded that structural change and productive efficiency, benefiting from the improved resource allocation, technology and competition, helped to explain the remarkably high growth rate.

An assessment of the above literature indicates that previous studies have two shortcomings. On one hand, most studies used the parametric method, but this method's accounting accuracy in terms of economic growth has been questioned [15,16] because it needs to set the production function and the error term. On the other hand, the studies focused on traditional factors, but not on energy consumption and CO_2 emissions with environmental regulation. Energy and the environment are endogenous variables and double rigid constraints on economic growth. The dual reversed transmission mechanism of the influence of energy conservation and environmental regulation on economic growth, can promote energy productivity and the transformation of the pattern of economic development. Energy consumption is a forceful driver for the growth of GDP [17–20]. Koop [21] noted that input changes of CO_2 emissions are a negligible factor in explaining growth. Chang [22] concluded that GDP growth is indissociable from increases in both energy consumption and CO_2 emissions. Wang *et al.* [23] found that reducing CO_2 emissions may handicap China's economic growth to some degree. Kareem *et al.* [24] found a causal relationship between CO_2 emissions and economic growth with the causality running from CO_2 emissions to economic growth. However, most of the researchers investigated the existence and direction of Granger causality between economic growth, energy, and CO_2 emissions, rather than growth accounting incorporating energy and environmental regulation.

If the composition of output and the methods of production are immutable, then the environment would be inextricably linked to the scale of global economic activity [25]. CO_2 emissions, a measure of environmental regulation variables, can be chosen as an input [26,27] or an output by using the DDF with the nonparametric method such as data envelopment analysis (DEA) [28–31]. This nonparametric method does not set the form of production functions and especially can be used for growth accounting with multiple inputs and outputs. Therefore, to contribute to the existing literature, this study first expands the biennial Malmquist productivity index proposed by Pastor *et al.* [32] and constructs a biennial Malmquist–Luenberger productivity index with the biennial environmental DEA technology, which can avoid infeasibilities and measures technological progress and regress. Second, this study adds energy and environmental factors into the decomposition and proposes a GGAF emphasizing energy saving and environmental protection. The change in economic growth can be decomposed into seven components: technical efficiency change, technological change, and the effects of labor, capital, energy, output structure, and CO_2 emissions with environmental regulation. Finally, this study utilizes the Silverman test to test for multimodality and the nonparametric Li-Fan-Ullah test to analyze the distribution dynamics of economic growth between actual and counterfactual distributions.

3. Method

3.1. Environmental Production Technology

In order to take resources and the environment into account, we decompose change in economic growth by using the environmental production technology that produces desirable outputs jointly with undesirable outputs. For each time period $t = 1,2,...,T$, the environmental production technology is described by the output set $S(t)$ that can be jointly produced from the input vector (L, K, E) as follows:

$$S(t) = \left\{ \left(L^t, K^t, E^t, Y^t, C^t \right) : \left(L^t, K^t, E^t \right) \text{ can produce } \left(Y^t, C^t \right) \right\}$$

(1)

where the variables L,K,E $\tilde{Y}^{12} = EFF \times Y^{98}$ R_+ denote an input vector for labor, capital and energy, respectively; Y $\tilde{Y}^{12} = EFF \times Y^{98}$ R_+ denotes the desirable or good output of gross regional product (GRP); and C $\tilde{Y}^{12} = EFF \times Y^{98}$ R_+ represents undesirable or bad output of CO_2 emissions.

The output set $S(t)$ is assumed to satisfy the standard properties of a technology, that is, $S(t)$ is compact for each input and is a closed set; and inputs and the desirable output are strong or freely disposable. In order to formulate $S(t)$ as an environmental technology, we need to impose two additional environmental axioms: the null-jointness or by-product axiom; and the weak disposability of joint outputs axiom. The first axiom indicates that if firms do not produce a good output, then it is not possible to produce bad output. The second axiom indicates that if all inputs (L, K, E) can produce outputs (Y, C), then it is feasible to reduce these outputs proportionally by θ where $(Y', C') = (\theta Y, \theta C)$ and $0 \leq \theta \leq 1$. This axiom reveals that it is costly to dispose of an undesirable output with the environmental regulated technology. In other words, we can construct the output set that satisfies the above properties and axioms as

$$S(t) = \left\{ (Y^t, C^t) : \sum_{i=1}^{I} z_i^t Y_i^t \geq Y, \sum_{i=1}^{I} z_i^t C_i^t = C, \sum_{i=1}^{I} z_i^t L_i^t \leq L, \sum_{i=1}^{I} z_i^t K_i^t \leq K, \sum_{i=1}^{I} z_i^t E_i^t \leq E, z_i^t \geq 0 \right\}$$

(2)

where $i = 1, 2, ..., I$ denotes observations of inputs and outputs; z_i is the weight assigned to each observation when constructing the production possibilities frontier; and $z_i > 0$ means that the production technology exhibits constant returns-to-scale (CRS). In addition, the output set at the time period $t + 1$ can be similarly defined as $S(t + 1)$.

Based on the technologies at time periods t and $t + 1$, Pastor et al. [32] introduced a new technology called the biennial technology. The biennial technology can be defined as the convex hull of the period t and $t + 1$ technologies. Taking the undesirable output into account, we can obtain the biennial environmental technology, which can be denoted as

$$S(B) = conv\{S(t), S(t + 1)\}$$

(3)

3.2. Biennial Malmquist–Luenberger Index

The traditional production function does not reflect the effect of changes in desirable and undesirable outputs in the production process. In accordance with the shortage function [33], Chambers et al. [34] constructed the DDF, which measures the distance to the observation from the production boundary. The output-oriented DDF, which is an alternative representation of the above technology, measures the distance from an observation to the production frontier. The directional output distance function provides a good method for modeling economic and environmental performances. This function at time period t with the biennial technology is defined as

$$\vec{D}_o^B (L^t, K^t, E^t, Y^t, C^t; g) = \sup \{ \beta : (Y^t, C^t) + \beta g \in S(B) \}$$

(4)

where $g = (g_y, -g_c)$ is a direction vector, and $\vec{D}_o^B (L^t, K^t, E^t, Y^t, C^t; g)$ measures the maximum proportional expansion of both desirable and undesirable outputs (Y^t, C^t), given the input vector (L^t, K^t, E^t) and the biennial technology in the direction g. Following [32], we introduce a TFP index called the biennial Malmquist–Luenberger index (hereafter, BML index). Taking the biennial production technology as a reference, the BML index between period t and $t + 1$ is given by

$$
\begin{aligned}
BML &= \frac{1 + \vec{D}_o^B (L^t, K^t, E^t, Y^t, C^t; g^t)}{1 + \vec{D}_o^B (L^{t+1}, K^{t+1}, E^{t+1}, Y^{t+1}, C^{t+1}; g^{t+1})} = \left[\frac{1 + \vec{D}_o^t (L^t, K^t, E^t, Y^t, C^t; g^t)}{1 + \vec{D}_o^{t+1} (L^{t+1}, K^{t+1}, E^{t+1}, Y^{t+1}, C^{t+1}; g^{t+1})} \right] \\
&\times \left[\frac{1 + \vec{D}_o^B (L^t, K^t, E^t, Y^t, C^t; g^t)}{1 + \vec{D}_o^t (L^t, K^t, E^t, Y^t, C^t; g^t)} \times \frac{1 + \vec{D}_o^{t+1} (L^{t+1}, K^{t+1}, E^{t+1}, Y^{t+1}, C^{t+1}; g^{t+1})}{1 + \vec{D}_o^B (L^{t+1}, K^{t+1}, E^{t+1}, Y^{t+1}, C^{t+1}; g^{t+1})} \right] \\
&= EFF \times TC
\end{aligned}
$$

(5)

Equation (5) shows that the BML index is decomposed into two components: technical efficiency change, or EFF and technological change, or TC. The first component, EFF, which indicates a catching-up effect, measures the change in the distance towards the best practice frontier from time period t to $t + 1$. The second component, TC, which measures technological progress or regress, captures the degree to which the production function shifts from period t to $t+1$ by taking the biennial technology as a reference. Because the biennial technology is defined as the convex hull of the period t and $t+1$ technologies, we do not need to take the arithmetic mean or geometric mean when defining the BML index.

3.3. Green Growth Accounting Framework

The traditional economic growth accounting method only accounts for and analyses the traditional production factors (such as labor and capital). In contrast, the modern economic growth accounting method not only considers the effect of traditional factors, but also focuses on energy and environmental factors that can affect economic growth. Under the restrictions of resource and environment, combined with the DDF and the BML index, we measure the sources of economic growth by utilizing the GGAF method.

Using biennial CRS technology, we can decompose the change in economic growth between time periods t and $t+1$ as per the following equation: where Y^t, Y^{t+1} represent the actual desirable output at times t and $t+1$ respectively; the functions F^t (L^t, K^t, E^t, Y^t, C^t, g) and F^{t+1} (L^{t+1}, K^{t+1}, E^{t+1}, Y^{t+1}, C^{t+1}, g) represent the maximum potential desirable output at times t and $t+1$ given input, desirable output and technology, respectively; and similarly, the functions F^B (L^t, K^t, E^t, Y^t, C^t, g) and F^B (L^{t+1}, K^{t+1}, E^{t+1}, Y^{t+1}, C^{t+1}, g) represent the maximum potential desirable output given the biennial technology at times t and $t+1$, respectively.

$$\frac{Y^{t+1}}{Y^t} = \frac{F^{t+1}(L^{t+1},K^{t+1},E^{t+1},Y^{t+1},C^{t+1};g^{t+1})\big/\left[1+\vec{D}_o^{t+1}(L^{t+1},K^{t+1},E^{t+1},Y^{t+1},C^{t+1};g^{t+1})\right]}{F^t(L^t,K^t,E^t,Y^t,C^t;g^t)\big/\left[1+\vec{D}_o^t(L^t,K^t,E^t,Y^t,C^t;g^t)\right]}$$

$$=\left[\frac{1+\vec{D}_o^t(L^t,K^t,E^t,Y^t,C^t;g^t)}{1+\vec{D}_o^{t+1}(L^{t+1},K^{t+1},E^{t+1},Y^{t+1},C^{t+1};g^{t+1})}\right]\times\left\{\frac{Y^{t+1}\cdot\left[1+\vec{D}_o^{t+1}(L^{t+1},K^{t+1},E^{t+1},Y^{t+1},C^{t+1};g^{t+1})\right]}{Y^t\cdot\left[1+\vec{D}_o^t(L^t,K^t,E^t,Y^t,C^t;g^t)\right]}\right\}$$

$$=\left[\frac{1+\vec{D}_o^t(L^t,K^t,E^t,Y^t,C^t;g^t)}{1+\vec{D}_o^{t+1}(L^{t+1},K^{t+1},E^{t+1},Y^{t+1},C^{t+1};g^{t+1})}\right]\times\frac{F^B(L^{t+1},K^{t+1},E^{t+1},Y^{t+1},C^{t+1};g^{t+1})}{1+\vec{D}_o^B(L^{t+1},K^{t+1},E^{t+1},Y^{t+1},C^{t+1};g^{t+1})}$$

$$\times\frac{1+\vec{D}_o^B(L^t,K^t,E^t,Y^t,C^t;g^t)}{F^B(L^t,K^t,E^t,Y^t,C^t;g^t)}\times\frac{1+\vec{D}_o^{t+1}(L^{t+1},K^{t+1},E^{t+1},Y^{t+1},C^{t+1};g^{t+1})}{1+\vec{D}_o^t(L^t,K^t,E^t,Y^t,C^t;g^t)}$$

$$=\left[\frac{F^B(L^{t+1},K^{t+1},E^{t+1},Y^{t+1},C^{t+1};g^{t+1})}{F^B(L^t,K^t,E^t,Y^t,C^t;g^t)}\right]\left[\frac{1+\vec{D}_o^t(L^t,K^t,E^t,Y^t,C^t;g^t)}{1+\vec{D}_o^{t+1}(L^{t+1},K^{t+1},E^{t+1},Y^{t+1},C^{t+1};g^{t+1})}\right]$$

$$\times\left[\frac{1+\vec{D}_o^B(L^t,K^t,E^t,Y^t,C^t;g^t)}{1+\vec{D}_o^t(L^t,K^t,E^t,Y^t,C^t;g^t)}\times\frac{1+\vec{D}_o^{t+1}(L^{t+1},K^{t+1},E^{t+1},Y^{t+1},C^{t+1};g^{t+1})}{1+\vec{D}_o^B(L^{t+1},K^{t+1},E^{t+1},Y^{t+1},C^{t+1};g^{t+1})}\right]$$

$$= PEGCH\times EFF\times TC$$

(6)

$$
\begin{aligned}
PEGCH &= \frac{F^B(L^{t+1}, K^{t+1}, E^{t+1}, Y^{t+1}, C^{t+1}; g^{t+1})}{F^B(L^t, K^{t+1}, E^{t+1}, Y^{t+1}, C^{t+1}; g^{t+1})} \times \frac{F^B(L^t, K^{t+1}, E^{t+1}, Y^{t+1}, C^{t+1}; g^{t+1})}{F^B(L^t, K^t, E^t, Y^t, C^t; g^t)} \\[4pt]
&= LE \times \frac{F^B(L^t, K^{t+1}, E^{t+1}, Y^{t+1}, C^{t+1}; g^{t+1})}{F^B(L^t, K^t, E^{t+1}, Y^{t+1}, C^{t+1}; g^{t+1})} \times \frac{F^B(L^t, K^t, E^{t+1}, Y^{t+1}, C^{t+1}; g^{t+1})}{F^B(L^t, K^t, E^t, Y^t, C^t; g^t)} \\[4pt]
&= LE \times KE \times \frac{F^B(L^t, K^t, E^t, Y^{t+1}, C^{t+1}; g^{t+1})}{F^B(L^t, K^t, E^t, Y^{t+1}, C^{t+1}; g^{t+1})} \times \frac{F^B(L^t, K^t, E^t, Y^{t+1}, C^{t+1}; g^{t+1})}{F^B(L^t, K^t, E^t, Y^t, C^t; g^t)} \\[4pt]
&= LE \times KE \times EE \times \frac{F^B(L^t, K^t, E^t, Y^{t+1}, C^t; g^{t+1})}{F^B(L^t, K^t, E^t, Y^{t+1}, C^t; g^{t+1})} \times \frac{F^B(L^t, K^t, E^t, Y^{t+1}, C^t; g^{t+1})}{F^B(L^t, K^t, E^t, Y^t, C^t; g^t)} \\[4pt]
&= LE \times KE \times EE \times CAE \times \left[\frac{F^B(L^t, K^t, E^t, Y^{t+1}, C^t; g^{t+1})}{F^B(L^t, K^t, E^t, Y^t, C^t; g^{t+1})} \times \frac{F^B(L^t, K^t, E^t, Y^t, C^t; g^{t+1})}{F^B(L^t, K^t, E^t, Y^t, C^t; g^t)} \right] \\[4pt]
&= LE \times KE \times EE \times CAE \times OSE
\end{aligned}
\tag{7}
$$

Equation (6) shows that economic growth change can be decomposed into three components: maximum potential economic growth change (*PEGCH*), which is measured by using the biennial technology as a reference; technical efficiency change (*EFF*); and technological change (*TC*). The first term, *PEGCH*, measures the maximum potential economic growth change depending on the changes in *L*, *K*, *E*, *Y* and *C* along the current period's production frontier. When we assume that the reference technology exhibits CRS, it follows that we can further separate *PEGCH* into five components by isolating the effects of changes in *L*, *K*, *E*, *Y* and *C* between the two time periods with the biennial technology.

Combining Equations (6) and (7), the complete seven-factor decomposition of economic growth with the GGAF method can be obtained by:

$$
Y^{t+1}/Y^t = EFF \times TC \times LE \times KE \times EE \times CAE \times OSE = TFP \times IME \times OME
\tag{8}
$$

The decomposition result from Equation (8) suggests that economic growth with environment regulation is affected by these seven factors. The last five components, measure the effects on economic growth of changes in labor (*LE*), capital (*KE*), energy (*EE*), CO_2 emissions (*CAE*) and output structure (*OSE*) with environmental regulation, respectively. The product of *LE*, *KE* and *EE* is the change in the input mix effect (*IME*). Similarly, the product of the last two effects is the change in the output mix effect (*OME*).

It is noted that the decomposition of change in economic growth in Equation (8) considers the restrictions of energy and environment. Traditional economic growth accounting does not take energy and the environment into account; its inputs only include labor and capital stock, and its output is GRP, not CO_2 emissions. Because one output, GRP, is considered, the effect of the change in output structure is equal to 1 and we can ignore it in the decomposition. Thus, according to the above-mentioned accounting idea, the decomposition of economic growth in the traditional model without environment regulation is given by:

$$
Y^{t+1}/Y^t = EFF \times TC \times LE \times KE = TFP \times IME
\tag{9}
$$

According to the application of a DEA-type linear programming approach, we can use this method to calculate the value of the seven components and then solve the following LP problem:

$$\vec{D}_0^B (L_i^t, K_i^t, E_i^t, Y_i^t, C_i^t; g^t) = Max\beta$$

$$s.t. \quad \sum_{i=1}^{I} z_i^t Y_i^t + \sum_{i=1}^{I} z_i^{t+1} Y_i^{t+1} \geq Y^t(1+\beta); \quad \sum_{i=1}^{I} z_i^t C_i^t + \sum_{i=1}^{I} z_i^{t+1} C_i^{t+1} = C^t(1-\beta);$$

$$\sum_{i=1}^{I} z_i^t L_i^t + \sum_{i=1}^{I} z_i^{t+1} L_i^{t+1} \leq L^t; \quad \sum_{i=1}^{I} z_i^t K_i^t + \sum_{i=1}^{I} z_i^{t+1} K_i^{t+1} \leq K^t;$$

$$\sum_{i=1}^{I} z_i^t E_i^t + \sum_{i=1}^{I} z_i^{t+1} E_i^{t+1} \leq E^t; \quad z_k^t, \ z_k^{t+1} \geq 0, \quad i = 1, \cdots, I.$$

$$(10)$$

4. Data and Empirical Results

4.1. Data

This study considers 30 provinces in China as research subjects. Data for 15 years between 1998 and 2012 are collected for the empirical analysis. The variables include the inputs (labor, capital stock and energy consumption), and outputs (GRP and CO_2 emissions) in each region. As we aim to study the effects of resources and the environment on economic growth, especially the effect of CO_2 emissions on economic growth, we select energy consumption as one of inputs and CO_2 emissions as one of outputs [35,36]. CO_2, an environmental factor, is an undesirable by-product accompanied by the production. In addition, CO_2 is mainly due to the use of energy (especially fossil energy), so we should take energy into account.

The data on labor input and GRP are obtained directly from the *China Statistical Yearbook* [37]. Labor input is measured by the number of employees. Data for total energy consumption are collected from the *China Energy Statistical Yearbook* [38]. Energy consumption consists of coal, washing coal, coke, oven gas, oil, gasoline, diesel, fuel, kerosene, liquefied petroleum, natural gas, refinery gas and others. The physical quantity of all energy is converted to a standard amount. There are no official data available for the capital stock of Chinese provinces. Following the perpetual inventory method, the capital stock for each province in year t is calculated as [39]:

$$K_t = I_t + (1-\delta)K_{t-1} = \sum_{k=0}^{t=1901}(1-\delta)^k I_{t-k} + (1-\delta)^{t-1900} K_{1900}$$

$$(11)$$

where K_{1900} is the initial value of the capital stock in 1900, I is the real value of gross fixed capital formation, and δ is the depreciation rate. To estimate the capital stock, we need to determine the initial capital stock and depreciation rate. We assume that the initial capital stock in 1900 is 0. This assumption is based on the fact that the capital stock from 1900 to 1952 was completely depreciated. Using investment data from 1952 to 2012 obtained in all provinces, we perform regressions between the logarithmic of the existing investment data and time series data. In addition, then we simulate the 1900 to 1951 sequence investment data for all provinces. Following a recent study by [40], we adopt different depreciation rates for each province.

The actual provincial CO_2 emissions cannot be obtained directly from the official data. CO_2 emissions mainly result from fossil energy consumption. The publication *Guidelines for National Greenhouse Gas Inventories* [41] provides a reference formula to estimate CO_2 emissions. Following this method, we can use provincial-level energy consumption to forecast CO_2 emissions in each province. The forecasting equation is given by:

$$CO_2 = \sum_{j=1}^{n} CO_{2,\,j} = \sum_{j=1}^{n} E_j \times NCV_j \times CEF_j \times COF_j \times (44/12)$$

(12)

where j represents the type of energy; E represents a variety of energy consumption; and NCV, CEF and COF represent the average low calorific values of energy, carbon emission coefficients and the carbon oxidation factor, respectively.

Table 1 shows the summary statistics of all variables. All nominal variables are deflated to real variables by using a price index for the year 2000. The mean value of desirable output GRP is 6620.05 (100 million CNY), whereas the undesirable output of CO_2 is 23,104.14 (10000 tonnes). In addition, those of labor, capital stock and energy consumption are 2304.33 (10000 persons), 18,642.29 (100 million CNY), 8797.01 (10000 tonnes), respectively. From these values, we can know that China is a big country in terms of energy consumption and CO_2 emissions. Clearly, the high growth in China shows obvious features of high investment, high energy consumption and high emissions. Therefore, the study of China's economic growth can no longer ignore the source of energy and environmental elements.

4.2. Empirical Results

According to our GGAF method, we can estimate economic growth and its sources at the provincial level. Table 2 shows each of the components of the decomposition of economic growth from 1998 to 2012 [42]. The first row of Columns 2 to 9 for each province reports the contributions to changes in economic growth from the effects of the changes in TFP, technical efficiency, technology, labor and capital stock without environment regulation. The second row for each province with environment regulation shows the contributions to changes in economic growth from the effects of changes in output structure, CO_2 emissions, and energy consumption, including five other components.

Table 1. Summary statistics of input and output variables, 1998–2012.

Variables	Mean	S.D.	Max	Min
Gross regional product (100 million CNY)	6,620.05	6,671.37	42,860.33	223.88
Carbon dioxide emissions (10000 tonnes)	23,104.14	18,408.14	106,667.02	892.85
Labor (10000 persons)	2,304.33	1,525.40	6,288.00	230.40
Capital stock (100 million CNY)	18,642.29	17,905.59	110,064.98	953.54
Energy consumption (10000 tonnes)	8,797.01	6,970.46	40,630.76	384.48

Table 2. Decomposition indexes of Economic growth between 1998 and 2012.

Provinces	TFP	EFF	TC	OSE	CAE	LE	KE	EE
Beijing	1.004	0.983	1.022			1.018	1.087	
	1.031	1.002	1.029	1.002	0.998	1.079	1.037	0.964
Tianjin	1.034	1.014	1.019			1.015	1.090	
	1.044	0.991	1.053	0.994	0.978	1.037	1.106	0.983
Hebei	0.982	0.986	0.995			1.005	1.126	
	0.997	0.991	1.006	1.000	0.939	1.005	1.180	1.000
Shanxi	0.972	0.977	0.995			1.004	1.143	
	0.891	0.760	1.172	0.938	0.916	1.007	1.452	0.997

Table 2. *Cont.*

Provinces	TFP	EFF	TC	OSE	CAE	LE	KE	EE
Inner Mongolia	0.995	0.990	1.004			1.006	1.155	
	0.979	0.751	1.303	0.899	0.879	1.022	1.485	0.986
Liaoning	1.029	0.997	1.032			1.009	1.076	
	1.006	0.864	1.164	0.953	0.975	1.059	1.177	0.959
Jilin	0.988	0.986	1.002			1.005	1.130	
	0.993	0.983	1.010	0.997	0.951	1.005	1.186	1.000
Heilongjiang	1.007	1.011	0.996			1.005	1.094	
	0.978	0.939	1.042	0.976	0.980	1.018	1.175	0.990
Shanghai	1.018	1.000	1.018			1.032	1.056	
	1.014	1.000	1.014	0.999	1.001	1.110	1.041	0.947
Jiangsu	1.036	1.005	1.031			1.008	1.076	
	1.023	1.000	1.022	1.000	0.961	1.016	1.089	1.034
Zhejiang	1.023	0.993	1.030			1.014	1.076	
	1.010	0.994	1.016	1.000	0.921	1.012	1.130	1.049
Anhui	0.980	1.000	0.980			1.000	1.139	
	1.006	0.999	1.007	1.000	0.938	1.000	1.182	1.000
Fujian	1.013	0.997	1.016			1.012	1.091	
	1.005	0.987	1.018	1.000	0.975	1.020	1.049	1.067
Jiangxi	0.969	0.989	0.980			1.000	1.152	
	1.005	0.999	1.006	1.000	0.871	1.000	1.210	1.054
Shandong	0.999	0.995	1.004			1.005	1.119	
	0.999	0.993	1.007	1.000	0.953	1.006	1.142	1.026
Henan	0.959	0.974	0.984			1	1.164	
	1.004	0.996	1.007	1.000	0.865	1.000	1.287	0.998
Hubei	0.980	0.996	0.984			1.004	1.135	
	1.006	1.001	1.005	1.000	0.833	1.004	1.316	1.008
Hunan	0.973	0.993	0.980			1.000	1.145	
	1.006	1.000	1.006	1.000	0.910	1.000	1.175	1.036
Guangdong	1.001	1.000	1.001			1.018	1.099	
	1.000	1.000	1.000	1.000	1.000	1.053	1.060	1.003
Guangxi	0.946	0.965	0.981			0.999	1.181	
	0.993	0.988	1.005	1.000	0.865	1.000	1.214	1.071
Hainan	1.032	1.003	1.029			1.015	1.059	
	0.997	0.989	1.008	1.000	0.858	1.002	1.182	1.095
Chongqing	0.974	0.994	0.980			1.000	1.154	
	1.009	1.004	1.005	1.000	0.837	1.000	1.254	1.061
Sichuan	0.981	1.001	0.980			1.000	1.141	
	1.010	1.005	1.005	1.000	0.893	1.000	1.180	1.051
Guizhou	0.981	1.002	0.980			1.000	1.133	
	1.004	1.002	1.002	1.000	0.743	1.000	1.490	1.000
Yunnan	0.971	0.991	0.980			1.000	1.137	
	1.000	0.995	1.004	1.000	0.741	1.000	1.433	1.040
Shaanxi	1.004	1.008	0.996			1.002	1.119	
	1.003	0.998	1.005	1.000	0.704	1.002	1.527	1.042
Gansu	0.974	0.994	0.980			1.000	1.140	
	1.006	1.000	1.006	1.000	0.896	1.000	1.231	1.000
Qinghai	1.029	1.000	1.030			1.010	1.075	
	1.008	0.998	1.009	1.000	0.649	1.006	1.618	1.051
Ningxia	1.018	0.995	1.023			1.010	1.085	
	0.996	0.993	1.003	1.000	0.651	1.010	1.704	1.000
Xinjiang	1.020	0.992	1.028			1.011	1.069	
	1.004	0.991	1.014	1.000	0.801	1.011	1.355	1.000
Weighted Mean	0.996	0.994	1.002			1.007	1.115	
	1.001	0.974	1.032	0.992	0.883	1.016	1.256	1.017

If the government does not implement green policies, such as environmental controls, firms would not need to pay for pollution emissions from their production process and thus would have little incentive to innovate and improve clean production technologies. Evidently, the differences in the means of changes in TFP, technical efficiency and technology are not substantially altered by environmental regulation. The effects of technical efficiency change on economic growth are less than 1 on average, implying a negative contribution of technical efficiency to economic growth. The biggest efficiency improvements taking measures of environmental governance appear in developed regions, such as Beijing, Chongqing, Guangdong and Jiangsu, as well as in backward areas, such as Guizhou and Sichuan. The mean score of technological change increases from 1.002 to 1.032 with the incorporation of environmental regulation. This indicates that environmental regulation is conducive to regional enterprises adopting new technologies and promotes technological progress. Among them, the provinces demonstrating rapid technological progress are Beijing, Tianjin, Fujian, Inner Mongolia, Liaoning, and Shanxi. We specifically need to point out that some provinces, including Beijing, Inner Mongolia, Liaoning, Shanxi, and Tianjin, emerge with technological progress greater than 1, considering energy and environmental factors. With environmental regulation, TFP did not appear to deteriorate in the case of the deterioration of technical efficiency. The great improvement in TFP (from 0.996 to 1.001 on average) is driven primarily by the rapid increase in technological progress. The TFP indices are generally higher in developed regions such as Beijing, Guangdong, Jiangsu, Shanghai, Tianjin, Liaoning, Heilongjiang and Zhejiang. This study demonstrates that technological progress and TFP make positive contributions to economic growth in China, while technical efficiency drags it down.

As shown in Columns 5 to 6 in Table 2, the accounting results of the changes in output structure and CO_2 emissions are less than 1 on average, considering environmental regulation. These results indicate that the exacerbation of output structure and CO_2 emissions effects have an adverse impact on economic growth and inhibit the growth of GRP in the long run. The output structure effect in most provinces is not less than 1 and promotes economic growth. Compared with Beijing, Chongqing, Gansu and other provinces, Tianjin, Heilongjiang, Inner Mongolia, Liaoning and Shanxi exhibit the smallest output structure effects, which are 0.994, 0.976, 0.899, 0.953 and 0.938, respectively. In terms of the CO_2 emissions effect, 28 provinces have scores far smaller than 1, while rich regions such as Shanghai and Guangdong exhibit values equal to one. In fact, if there is no cycle of production technology and other advanced conditions, the more CO_2 emissions, the more inputs such as raw materials are needed in the production process, which causes enterprises to produce less desirable outputs. Thus, the regulation of CO_2 emissions could restrain GDP growth to some extent.

The last three columns of Table 2 report the effects of the input mix. As is shown, the accumulation of physical capital plays a decisive role in economic growth. The effect of physical capital rose to 1.256 with environmental regulation from 1.115 without environmental regulation. LE exhibited no significant change. It is interesting to note that the KE of 26 provinces greatly improved after the consideration of environmental regulation, while that of Beijing, Fujian, Guangdong and Shanghai declined, albeit their LE greatly improved. With regard to the energy effect, EE on average made some contribution to economic growth. Over the 15-year period, the energy effect had a greater impact on economic growth in Jiangsu, Shandong, Hainan, Chongqing, Fujian, Guangxi, Hunan, Qinghai, Sichuan and Zhejiang. EE was equal to 1 in Anhui, Jilin, Gansu, Guizhou, Hebei, Ningxia and Xinjiang, but EE exerted a negative influence on economic growth in eight provinces, including Beijing, Heilongjiang, and Shanghai.

To demonstrate the relationship between the contributing factors and the initial level of GRP, Figure 1 plots the decomposition indexes against GRP in 1998, along with GLS regression lines [43–45]. Figure 1a shows that TFP change was positively correlated to GRP in 1998. Figure 1b shows a similar relationship between technical efficiency change and GRP. Both regression slope coefficients were statistically insignificant, demonstrating that neither TFP change nor technical efficiency change contributed significantly to economic convergence at the provincial level in China from 1998 to

2010. The statistically significant negative slope coefficient in Figure 1c suggests that the effect of technological change significantly contributed to convergence in economic growth. The positive sign of the statistically insignificant slope coefficients in Figure 1d–f indicate that the effects of changes in output structure, CO_2 emissions and labor did not significantly contribute to convergence, even though the contribution of CO_2 emissions had a wide dispersion. Figure 1g shows that the regression coefficient for change in physical capital accumulation was negative and statistically significant, indicating that the change contributed to convergence. Finally, as shown in Figure 1h, even if the contribution of the energy effect showed a wide dispersion and its coefficient was negative, the coefficient was statistically insignificant, suggesting that the energy effect also contributed little to convergence.

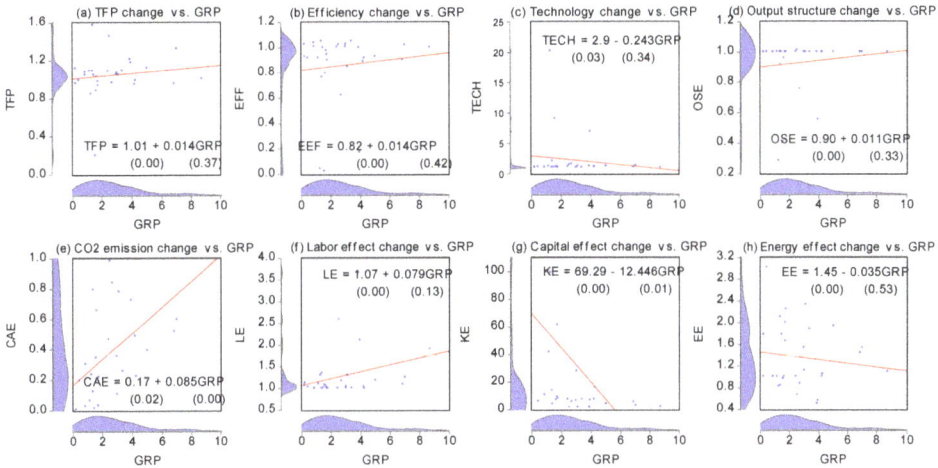

Figure 1. Decomposition components plotted against GRP in 1998.

5. Analysis of Distributions Dynamics of Economic Growth

Although we now understand the relationship between the contributing factors and the initial level of GRP, we should further analyze the distribution dynamics of economic growth from 1998 to 2012. Figure 2 describes the plots of the distributions of GRP across 30 provinces in 1998 and 2012. It is easy to determine that the distribution of GRP in 1998 is unimodal, but after 15 years, this distribution appears to bimodal with a higher mean in 2012.

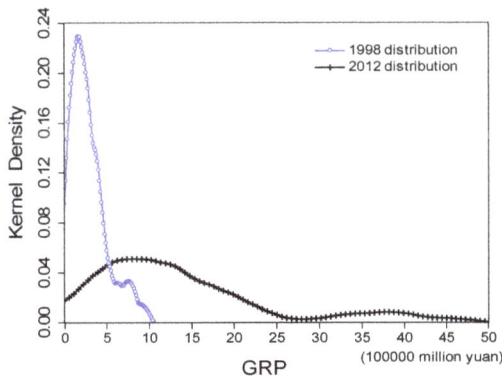

Figure 2. Actual distributions of GRP in 1998 and 2012.

Silverman [46] proposed a method (called the Silverman test) to test for the transformation theoretically [47,48]. With the application of this test for the multimodality of the actual distributions in 1998 and 2012, Table 3 reports the statistical significance levels for the tests of the null hypothesis that the kernel density has at most j modes against the alternative that it has more than j modes. As shown in Table 3, the *p*-value in the 1998 distribution is 0.262 with the null hypothesis that the kernel density has one mode, indicating that the 1998 distribution has a single mode. For the 2012 distribution, the null hypothesis that it has one mode is rejected (the *p*-value is 0.043) while the null hypothesis that it has two modes cannot be rejected (the *p*-value is 0.523). This shows that the 2012 distribution is indeed bimodal. Thus, it is true that the distributions of economic growth moved from being unimodal to bimodal over the 15-year period.

Table 3. Silverman test for multimodality of the actual distributions.

Distributions	*p*-values	
	H0: One Mode H1: More than One Mode	H0: Two Modes H1: More than Two Modes
Y98	0.262 (H0 not reject)	0.323 (H0 not reject)
Y12	0.043 (H0 reject)	0.523 (H0 not reject)

Note: Y^{98}, Y^{12} denote GRP across provinces in 1998 and 2012, respectively.

To further enhance this result of multimodality and understand the degree to which each of the seven components of the decomposition of economic growth change affect the distribution of economic growth from 1998 to 2012, we extend the analysis of the distribution dynamics by using the actual and counterfactual method with a nonparametric test, as developed by [49] and [50]. The method tests for the statistical significance of the differences between actual and counterfactual distributions that are two unknown distributions. Wang [51] also employed this test to study economics. The method indirectly tests for the statistical significance between the relative counterfactual distributions of the seven components of the decomposition of economic growth and the actual 2012 distribution. If we set the two unknown distributions as f and g, then the null hypothesis of this test is H_0: $f(x) = g(x)$ for all x, and the alternative is H_1: $f(x) \neq g(x)$ for some x. The decomposition of economic growth change with environment regulation in Equation (8) can be re-expressed as:

$$Y^{12} = (EFF \times TC \times LE \times KE \times EE \times CAE \times OSE) \times Y^{98} \tag{13}$$

Therefore, GRP across the provinces in 2012 can be constructed by successively multiplying GRP in 1998 by each of the seven components. According to this idea, we can segregate the effect on the counterfactual distribution dynamics of economic growth by the sequential introduction of each of these components. If we consider only the impact of change in technical efficiency, the counterfactual GRP distribution of the variable in 2012 can be given by

$$\tilde{Y}^{12} = EFF \times Y^{98} \tag{14}$$

If we multiply by the effect on technological change once more on the right side of Equation (14), the counterfactual GRP distribution of the variable in 2012 can be given by

$$\tilde{Y}^{12} = EFF \times TC \times Y^{98} \tag{15}$$

Analogously, we can obtain the remaining counterfactual GRP distributions of the variables generated by sequential introduction of components of the decomposition. Ultimately, these results test for the counterfactual distributions and the actual 2012 distribution as shown in Appendix A.

As Appendix A shows, the first t-test statistic value is 3.0925, which rejects the null hypothesis at the 1% significance level. This test result is consistent with Figure 2 and the result of the Silverman test in Table 3, suggesting that the counterfactual distribution is significantly different to the actual 1998 distribution. The next seven tests demonstrate the null hypothesis of identity of the counterfactual distributions by the sequential introduction of the seven contributing components of change in economic growth and the actual 2012 distribution. At the 1% significance level, Test 7 with physical capital accumulation alone easily accepts the null hypothesis and the other tests reject the null hypothesis that the counterfactual distributions are not identical to the actual 2012 distribution. These seven results indicate that physical capital accumulation is the key force for transforming the economic growth distribution and this factor alone made a big contribution to the shift to bimodality from 1998 to 2012. The other six factors played a minor role in explaining the comprehensive change in the distribution between 1998 and 2012. Tests 9 to 127 compare the actual distribution in 2012 with the counterfactual distribution with effects from the given two, three, four, five and six of the seven components.

The above analysis on economic growth distribution dynamics uses a formal test for the statistical significance of the differences between the counterfactual distributions and the actual distribution in 2012. Simultaneously, these results can be reinforced and illustrated by using figures of kernel distribution as shown in Figure 3 to Figure 4. Figure 3a, which is only combined with the effect of technical efficiency change, shows that the counterfactual distribution seems to be identical to the actual 1998 distribution, not the actual 2012 distribution. This indicates that technical efficiency made a small contribution to the promotion of convergence of the distribution. Even though the counterfactual distribution includes the effects from the changes in technology, output structure, CO_2 emissions and labor successively in Figure 3b–e, these results would not change dramatically. Until it takes physical capital accumulation into account, there is almost no significant difference between the counterfactual and the 2012 distributions (see Figure 3f). The results in Figure 3a–f are consistent with Test 2, 9, 30, 65, 100 and 121 in Appendix A.

Figure 4a compares the actual 1988 and 2012 distributions with the counterfactual 2012 distribution, combined only with technological change. It shows that the kurtosis of the counterfactual 2012 distribution reduces, but is still different to the actual 2012 distribution. When combined with output structure change in Figure 4b, the shape of these distributions does not change much. These results indicate that both the effect of technological change and the joint effect of technological change and output structure change played a minor role in economic growth over the 1998 to 2012 period. Considering the additional effect from the changes in CO_2 emissions and labor in Figure 4c,d, the counterfactual distribution moves much closer to the actual 1998 distribution. When physical capital accumulation is added to the counterfactual distribution in Figure 4e, its mode shifts to the left and it moves much closer to the actual 2012 distribution. This demonstrates that physical capital accumulation is the core contributor to change in economic growth. Figure 4f describes the counterfactual distribution with the joint effect of six components including the change in energy consumption. It illustrates that the counterfactual distribution moves further toward the actual 2012 distribution, though its shape changes only slightly and its tail extends. In addition, the six panels of Figure 4 can be reinforced by the nonparametric test corresponding to Tests 3, 15, 45, 85, 115 and 127 in Appendix A.

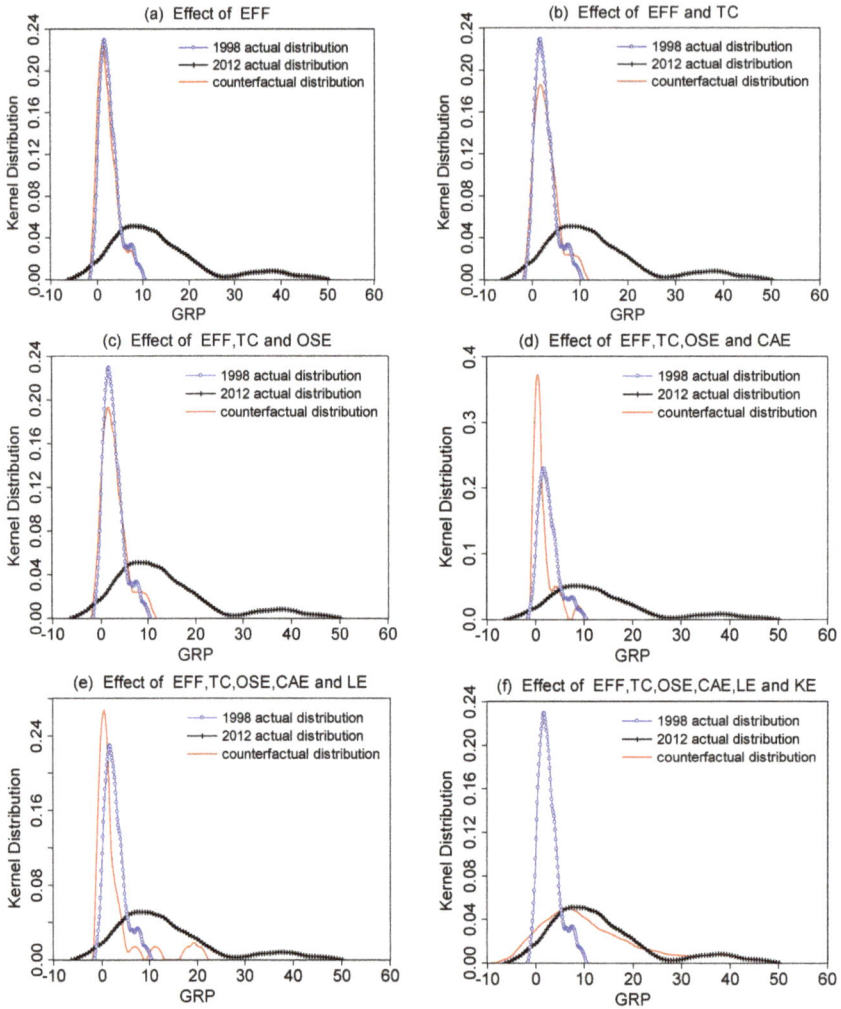

Figure 3. Counterfactual and actual distributions of economic growth with the effect of technical efficiency change (EFF).

According to the analysis, we can successively introduce the changes in output structure, CO_2 emissions, labor, physical capital accumulation and energy consumption in combination with each other. However, regardless of whether the combinations include two, three, four, five or six components of the decomposition, the shape of the counterfactual distribution does not change significantly. Only when physical capital accumulation is added to these combinations does the counterfactual distribution increasingly exhibit a bimodal shape and appear identical to the actual 2012 distribution. In summary, along with the process of economic growth, physical capital accumulation plays the most important role in changing the distribution from unimodal to bimodal during the period of 1998–2012.

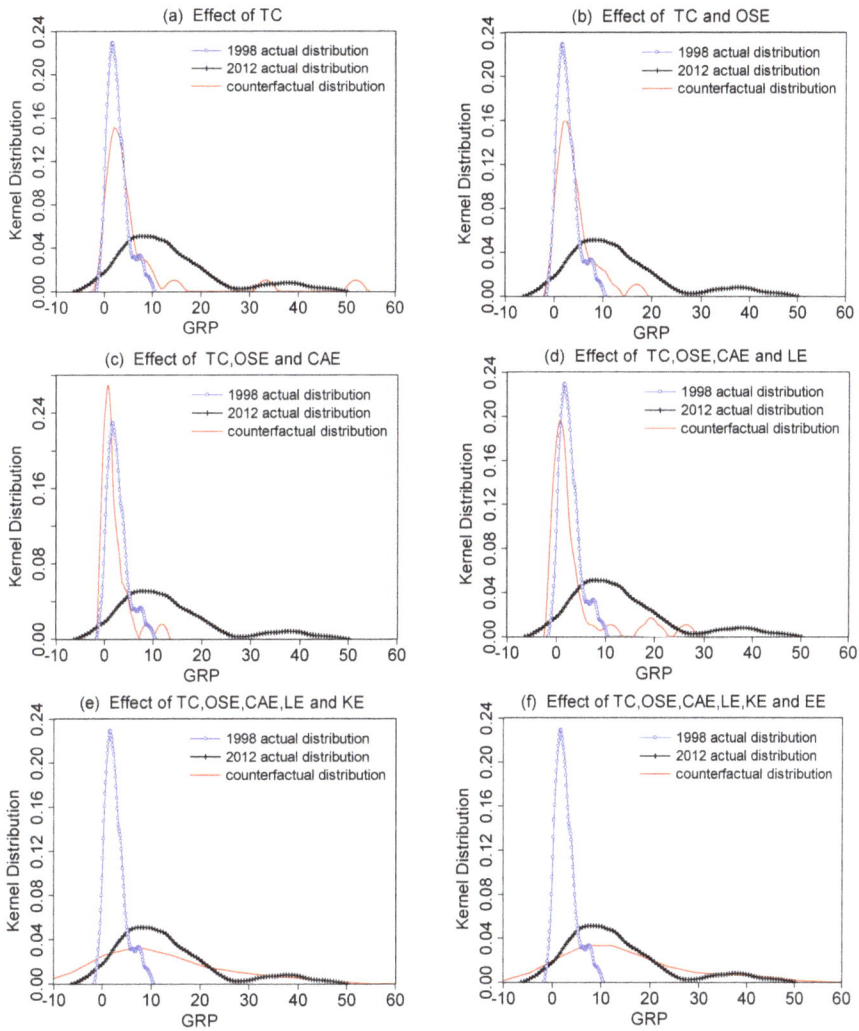

Figure 4. Counterfactual and actual distributions of economic growth with the effect of TC.

6. Conclusions

In this paper, we introduce a new biennial Malmquist–Luenberger productivity index by using the biennial environmental DEA technology and directional distance function. Based on the proposed BML index in consideration of resources and the environment, this article employs the green growth accounting framework to decompose economic growth change into seven components at the Chinese provincial level during the period from 1998 to 2012. These decompositions can measure the impact of the changes in technical efficiency, technology, output structure, CO_2 emissions, labor, physical capital accumulation and energy consumption on economic growth.

The results demonstrate that TFP promotes rapid economic growth, mainly because technology has made great progress, and even compensates for the negative effect brought about by the deterioration of efficiency, and technological progress contributes to convergence. However, the improvement of output structure is not apparent. The effect of CO_2 emissions with the emergence of a serious deterioration discouraged economic growth in some provinces between 1998 and 2012. Labor and energy are important sources of economic growth and their increase stimulates rapid economic growth. The energy effect contributed little to convergence. Undoubtedly, a high physical capital accumulation is the most important driving force for economic take-off, irrespective of whether the government implements environmental regulation or not, and it also makes a big contribution to convergence. In other words, economic growth is still mainly dependent on factor inputs, but not efficiency or TFP in China.

After that, we apply the Silverman test to confirm that the economic distribution changes from unimodal in 1998 to bimodal with a higher mean in 2012. In addition, the nonparametric test, in combination with some figures of kernel distribution, is performed to clarify the effect of each component of the decomposition on economic growth and makes the results more robust. Therefore, based on our research findings, the Chinese government needs to recognize that the high growth in factor inputs will not only result in a waste of resources, but also in environmental pollution. In order to achieve resource-saving, environmentally-friendly and sustainable macroeconomic growth, China should increase public investment in education and technology, accelerate industrial upgrading and then enhance the rate of technological progress and TFP. Only in this way can Chinese economic growth transform from an extensive program of increasing factor inputs to one with a green growth pattern driven by TFP.

The method of the green growth accounting framework can decompose economic growth change into seven components, and estimate the degree to which each of the seven components of the decomposition of economic growth change affect the distribution of economic growth from 1998 to 2012. However, there is sampling variability and thus statistical uncertainty about these estimates [30]. Parteka and Wolszczak-Derlacz [52] followed a bootstrap procedure to obtain bias-corrected estimates of Malmquist indices and their components and their confidence intervals [53]. Therefore, we can further adopt consistent bootstrap estimation procedures to obtain bias-corrected estimates of these indices and their confidence intervals, which test the significance of these indices' effects on economic growth.

Acknowledgments: The authors are grateful to the financial support provided by National Natural Science Foundation of China (71473105), the Fundamental Research Funds for the Central Universities (12JNYH002), New Century Excellent Talents in University (NCET-110856) and Guangdong Province Project of Key Research Institute of Humanities and Social Sciences at Universities—IRESD (2012JDXM_0009).

Author Contributions: Minzhe Du contributed to the acquisition of data, analysis and interpretation of the data and drafting the article; Bing Wang made substantial contributions to the concept and design of the article. Yanrui Wu provided the method of calculating capital stock and modified the draft. Both of the authors helped to revise the manuscript and approved its final publication.

Conflicts of Interest: The authors declare no conflict of interest.

Appendix A

Table A1. The counterfactual distribution hypothesis tests.

Null Hypothesis (H_0)	t-Test Statistics	Null Hypothesis (H_0)	t-Test Statistics
1. $f(Y^{12}) = g(Y^{98})$	3.0925	43. $f(Y^{12}) = g(Y^{98} \times EFF \times LE \times EE)$	1.6660 *
2. $f(Y^{12}) = g(Y^{98} \times EFF)$	3.1722	44. $f(Y^{12}) = g(Y^{98} \times EFF \times KE \times EE)$	7.2167
3. $f(Y^{12}) = g(Y^{98} \times TC)$	3.2513	45. $f(Y^{12}) = g(Y^{98} \times TC \times OSE \times CAE)$	3.9089
4. $f(Y^{12}) = g(Y^{98} \times OSE)$	3.1999	46. $f(Y^{12}) = g(Y^{98} \times TC \times OSE \times LE)$	0.6358 *
5. $f(Y^{12}) = g(Y^{98} \times CAE)$	4.5551	47. $f(Y^{12}) = g(Y^{98} \times TC \times OSE \times KE)$	8.3981
6. $f(Y^{12}) = g(Y^{98} \times LE)$	2.4344	48. $f(Y^{12}) = g(Y^{98} \times TC \times OSE \times EE)$	1.5624 *
7. $f(Y^{12}) = g(Y^{98} \times KE)$	-0.2006 *	49. $f(Y^{12}) = g(Y^{98} \times TC \times CAE \times LE)$	0.7044 *
8. $f(Y^{12}) = g(Y^{98} \times EE)$	2.6783	50. $f(Y^{12}) = g(Y^{98} \times TC \times CAE \times KE)$	9.9558
9. $f(Y^{12}) = g(Y_{98} \times EFF \times TC)$	2.7458	51. $f(Y^{12}) = g(Y^{98} \times TC \times CAE \times EE)$	2.7983
10. $f(Y^{12}) = g(Y^{98} \times EFF \times OSE)$	3.1313	52. $f(Y^{12}) = g(Y^{98} \times TC \times LE \times KE)$	0.5224 *
11. $f(Y^{12}) = g(Y^{98} \times EFF \times CAE)$	5.3561	53. $f(Y^{12}) = g(Y^{98} \times TC \times LE \times EE)$	0.0716 *
12. $f(Y^{12}) = g(Y^{98} \times EFF \times LE)$	2.8901	54. $f(Y^{12}) = g(Y^{98} \times TC \times KE \times EE)$	9.1998
13. $f(Y^{12}) = g(Y^{98} \times EFF \times KE)$	2.8901	55. $f(Y^{12}) = g(Y^{98} \times OSE \times CAE \times LE)$	4.1468
14. $f(Y^{12}) = g(Y^{98} \times EFF \times EE)$	2.2788	56. $f(Y^{12}) = g(Y^{98} \times OSE \times CAE \times KE)$	0.0276 *
15. $f(Y^{12}) = g(Y^{98} \times TC \times OSE)$	2.0906 *	57. $f(Y^{12}) = g(Y^{98} \times OSE \times CAE \times EE)$	5.1708
16. $f(Y^{12}) = g(Y^{98} \times TC \times CAE)$	2.9263	58. $f(Y^{12}) = g(Y^{98} \times OSE \times LE \times KE)$	7.7696
17. $f(Y^{12}) = g(Y^{98} \times TC \times LE)$	-0.0902 *	59. $f(Y^{12}) = g(Y^{98} \times OSE \times LE \times EE)$	1.8249 *
18. $f(Y^{12}) = g(Y^{98} \times TC \times KE)$	0.2784 *	60. $f(Y^{12}) = g(Y^{98} \times OSE \times KE \times EE)$	7.5675
19. $f(Y^{12}) = g(Y^{98} \times TC \times EE)$	0.9731 *	61. $f(Y^{12}) = g(Y^{98} \times CAE \times LE \times KE)$	9.1998
20. $f(Y^{12}) = g(Y^{98} \times OSE \times CAE)$	4.8776	62. $f(Y^{12}) = g(Y^{98} \times CAE \times LE \times EE)$	3.3905
21. $f(Y^{12}) = g(Y^{98} \times OSE \times LE)$	2.5605	63. $f(Y^{12}) = g(Y^{98} \times CAE \times KE \times EE)$	0.0212 *
22. $f(Y^{12}) = g(Y^{98} \times OSE \times KE)$	8.1129	64. $f(Y^{12}) = g(Y^{98} \times LE \times KE \times EE)$	8.7493
23. $f(Y^{12}) = g(Y^{98} \times OSE \times EE)$	2.4269	65. $f(Y^{12}) = g(Y^{98} \times EFF \times TC \times OSE \times CAE)$	4.5586
24. $f(Y^{12}) = g(Y^{98} \times CAE \times LE)$	3.7703	66. $f(Y^{12}) = g(Y^{98} \times EFF \times TC \times OSE \times LE)$	2.1208 *
25. $f(Y^{12}) = g(Y^{98} \times CAE \times KE)$	-0.0399 *	67. $f(Y^{12}) = g(Y^{98} \times EFF \times TC \times OSE \times KE)$	8.6480
26. $f(Y^{12}) = g(Y^{98} \times CAE \times EE)$	4.9706	68. $f(Y^{12}) = g(Y^{98} \times EFF \times TC \times OSE \times EE)$	2.3043 *
27. $f(Y^{12}) = g(Y^{98} \times LE \times KE)$	0.5651 *	69. $f(Y^{12}) = g(Y^{98} \times EFF \times TC \times CAE \times LE)$	3.2199
28. $f(Y^{12}) = g(Y^{98} \times LE \times EE)$	1.9149 *	70. $f(Y^{12}) = g(Y^{98} \times EFF \times TC \times CAE \times KE)$	-0.1126 *
29. $f(Y^{12}) = g(Y^{98} \times KE \times EE)$	8.7209	71. $f(Y^{12}) = g(Y^{98} \times EFF \times TC \times CAE \times EE)$	4.6026
30. $f(Y^{12}) = g(Y^{98} \times EFF \times TC \times OSE)$	2.9007	72. $f(Y^{12}) = g(Y^{98} \times EFF \times TC \times LE \times KE)$	1.6153 *
31. $f(Y^{12}) = g(Y^{98} \times EFF \times TC \times CAE)$	4.2116	73. $f(Y^{12}) = g(Y^{98} \times EFF \times TC \times LE \times EE)$	1.3714 *
32. $f(Y^{12}) = g(Y^{98} \times EFF \times TC \times LE)$	1.9787 *	74. $f(Y^{12}) = g(Y^{98} \times EFF \times TC \times KE \times EE)$	7.6552
33. $f(Y^{12}) = g(Y^{98} \times EFF \times TC \times KE)$	8.5744	75. $f(Y^{12}) = g(Y^{98} \times EFF \times OSE \times CAE \times LE)$	4.7471
34. $f(Y^{12}) = g(Y^{98} \times EFF \times TC \times EE)$	2.4802	76. $f(Y^{12}) = g(Y^{98} \times EFF \times OSE \times CAE \times KE)$	0.7412 *
35. $f(Y^{12}) = g(Y^{98} \times EFF \times OSE \times CAE)$	5.4615	77. $f(Y^{12}) = g(Y^{98} \times EFF \times OSE \times CAE \times EE)$	5.2877
36. $f(Y^{12}) = g(Y^{98} \times EFF \times OSE \times LE)$	2.8215	78. $f(Y^{12}) = g(Y^{98} \times EFF \times OSE \times LE \times KE)$	7.9339
37. $f(Y^{12}) = g(Y^{98} \times EFF \times OSE \times KE)$	8.3418	79. $f(Y^{12}) = g(Y^{98} \times EFF \times OSE \times LE \times EE)$	1.5858 *
38. $f(Y^{12}) = g(Y^{98} \times EFF \times OSE \times EE)$	2.2165 *	80. $f(Y^{12}) = g(Y^{98} \times EFF \times OSE \times KE \times EE)$	7.1302

Table A1. *Cont.*

Null Hypothesis (H_0)	t-Test Statistics	Null Hypothesis (H_0)	t-Test Statistics
39. $f(Y^{12}) = g(Y^{98}) \times EFF \times CAE \times LE)$	4.7027	81. $f(Y^{12}) = g(Y^{98}) \times EFF \times CAE \times LE \times KE)$	−0.0305 *
40. $f(Y^{12}) = g(Y^{98}) \times EFF \times CAE \times KE)$	0.7840 *	82. $f(Y^{12}) = g(Y^{98}) \times EFF \times CAE \times LE \times EE)$	3.9011
41. $f(Y^{12}) = g(Y^{98}) \times EFF \times CAE \times EE)$	5.2502	83. $f(Y^{12}) = g(Y^{98}) \times EFF \times CAE \times KE \times EE)$	0.0233 *
42. $f(Y^{12}) = g(Y^{98}) \times EFF \times LE \times KE)$	−0.0651 *	84. $f(Y^{12}) = g(Y^{98}) \times EFF \times LE \times KE \times EE)$	7.2847
85. $f(Y^{12}) = g(Y^{98}) \times TC \times OSE \times CAE \times LE)$	2.1985 *	107. $f(Y^{12}) = g(Y^{98}) \times EFF \times TC \times CAE \times LE \times EE)$	2.8757
86. $f(Y^{12}) = g(Y^{98}) \times TC \times OSE \times CAE \times KE)$	6.5094	108. $f(Y^{12}) = g(Y^{98}) \times EFF \times TC \times CAE \times KE \times EE)$	−0.0267 *
87. $f(Y^{12}) = g(Y^{98}) \times TC \times OSE \times CAE \times EE)$	3.9165	109. $f(Y^{12}) = g(Y^{98}) \times EFF \times TC \times LE \times KE \times EE)$	7.7859
88. $f(Y^{12}) = g(Y^{98}) \times TC \times OSE \times LE \times KE)$	8.1778	110. $f(Y^{12}) = g(Y^{98}) \times EFF \times OSE \times CAE \times LE \times KE)$	0.0060 *
89. $f(Y^{12}) = g(Y^{98}) \times TC \times OSE \times LE \times EE)$	0.8540 *	111. $f(Y^{12}) = g(Y^{98}) \times EFF \times OSE \times CAE \times LE \times EE)$	3.9147
90. $f(Y^{12}) = g(Y^{98}) \times TC \times OSE \times KE \times EE)$	8.5051	112. $f(Y^{12}) = g(Y^{98}) \times EFF \times OSE \times CAE \times KE \times EE)$	−0.0191 *
91. $f(Y^{12}) = g(Y^{98}) \times TC \times CAE \times LE \times KE)$	10.2244	113. $f(Y^{12}) = g(Y^{98}) \times EFF \times OSE \times LE \times KE \times EE)$	7.1642
92. $f(Y^{12}) = g(Y^{98}) \times TC \times CAE \times LE \times EE)$	1.0477 *	114. $f(Y^{12}) = g(Y^{98}) \times EFF \times CAE \times LE \times KE \times EE)$	−0.0649 *
93. $f(Y^{12}) = g(Y^{98}) \times TC \times CAE \times KE \times EE)$	9.8342	115. $f(Y^{12}) = g(Y^{98}) \times TC \times OSE \times CAE \times LE \times KE)$	2.1411
94. $f(Y^{12}) = g(Y^{98}) \times TC \times LE \times KE \times EE)$	8.9758	116. $f(Y^{12}) = g(Y^{98}) \times TC \times OSE \times CAE \times LE \times EE)$	2.2456 *
95. $f(Y^{12}) = g(Y^{98}) \times OSE \times CAE \times LE \times KE)$	−0.1248 *	117. $f(Y^{12}) = g(Y^{98}) \times TC \times OSE \times CAE \times KE \times EE)$	5.1559
96. $f(Y^{12}) = g(Y^{98}) \times OSE \times CAE \times LE \times EE)$	3.6693	118. $f(Y^{12}) = g(Y^{98}) \times TC \times OSE \times LE \times KE \times EE)$	8.8583
97. $f(Y^{12}) = g(Y^{98}) \times OSE \times CAE \times KE \times EE)$	−0.1008 *	119. $f(Y^{12}) = g(Y^{98}) \times TC \times CAE \times LE \times KE \times EE)$	9.9377
98. $f(Y^{12}) = g(Y^{98}) \times OSE \times LE \times KE \times EE)$	7.5982	120. $f(Y^{12}) = g(Y^{98}) \times OSE \times CAE \times LE \times KE \times EE)$	−0.0889 *
99. $f(Y^{12}) = g(Y^{98}) \times CAE \times LE \times KE \times EE)$	0.5346 *	121. $f(Y^{12}) = g(Y^{98}) \times EFF \times TC \times OSE \times CAE \times LE \times KE)$	−0.1959 *
100. $f(Y^{12}) = g(Y^{98}) \times EFF \times TC \times OSE \times CAE \times LE)$	3.5822	122. $f(Y^{12}) = g(Y^{98}) \times EFF \times TC \times OSE \times CAE \times LE \times EE)$	3.1966
101. $f(Y^{12}) = g(Y^{98}) \times EFF \times TC \times OSE \times CAE \times KE)$	0.3618 *	123. $f(Y^{12}) = g(Y^{98}) \times EFF \times TC \times OSE \times CAE \times KE \times EE)$	0.1709 *
102. $f(Y^{12}) = g(Y^{98}) \times EFF \times TC \times OSE \times CAE \times EE)$	4.8423	124. $f(Y^{12}) = g(Y^{98}) \times EFF \times TC \times OSE \times LE \times KE \times EE)$	7.1949
103. $f(Y^{12}) = g(Y^{98}) \times EFF \times TC \times OSE \times LE \times KE)$	7.6422	125. $f(Y^{12}) = g(Y^{98}) \times EFF \times TC \times CAE \times LE \times KE \times EE)$	0.1431 *
104. $f(Y^{12}) = g(Y^{98}) \times EFF \times TC \times OSE \times LE \times EE)$	1.4114 *	126. $f(Y^{12}) = g(Y^{98}) \times EFF \times OSE \times CAE \times LE \times KE \times EE)$	−0.0987 *
105. $f(Y^{12}) = g(Y^{98}) \times EFF \times TC \times OSE \times KE \times EE)$	7.2751	127. $f(Y^{12}) = g(Y^{98}) \times EFF \times TC \times OSE \times CAE \times LE \times KE \times EE)$	2.1060 *
106. $f(Y^{12}) = g(Y^{98}) \times EFF \times TC \times CAE \times LE \times KE)$	0.1907 *	128. $f(Y^{12}) = g(Y^{98}) \times EFF \times TC \times OSE \times CAE \times LE \times KE \times EE)$	0.00 *

Notes: * denotes $p < 0.01$.

References and Notes

1. Krugman, P. The myth of Asia's miracle. *Foreign Aff.* **1994**, *73*, 62–78.
2. Han, G.F.; Kalirajan, K.; Singh, N. Productivity and economic growth in East Asia: Innovation, efficiency and accumulation. *Jpn. World Econ.* **2002**, *14*, 401–424.
3. Wang, Y.; Yao, Y.D. Sources of China's economic growth 1952–1999: Incorporating human capital accumulation. *China Econ. Rev.* **2003**, *14*, 32–52.
4. Zhao, C.W.; Du, J. Capital formation and economic growth in western China. *Chin. Econ.* **2009**, *42*, 7–26. [CrossRef]
5. Chow, G.C. Capital formation and economic growth in China. *Q. J. Econ.* **1993**, *108*, 809–842. [CrossRef]
6. Kim, J.I.; Lau, L.J. The sources of economic growth of the East Asian newly industrialized countries. *J. Jpn. Int. Econ.* **1994**, *8*, 235–271. [CrossRef]
7. Young, A. Gold into base metals: Productivity growth in the People's Republic of China during the reform period. *J. Polit. Econ.* **2003**, *111*, 1220–1261. [CrossRef]
8. Arayama, Y.; Miyoshi, K. Regional diversity and sources of economic growth in China. *World Econ.* **2004**, *27*, 1583–1607. [CrossRef]
9. Islam, N.; Dai, E.; Sakamoto, H. Role of TFP in China's growth. *Asian Econ. J.* **2006**, *20*, 127–159.
10. Jefferson, G.H.; Hu, A.G.Z.; Su, J. The sources and sustainability of China's economic growth. *Brook. Pap. Econ. Act.* **2006**, *2*, 1–47. [CrossRef]
11. Borensztein, E.; Ostry, D.J. Accounting for China's growth performance. *Am. Econ. Rev.* **1996**, *86*, 224–228.
12. Hu, Z.F.; Khan, M.S. Why is China growing so fast? *Staff. Pap. Int. Monet. Fund* **1997**, *44*, 103–131. [CrossRef]
13. Chow, G.C.; Li, K.W. China's economic growth: 1952–2010. *Econ. Dev. Cult. Chang.* **2002**, *51*, 247–256. [CrossRef]
14. Ding, S.; Knight, J. Why has China grown so fast? The role of structural change. Available online: http://www.economics.ox.ac.uk/materials/working_papers/paper415.pdf (access on 1 September 2014).
15. Nadiri, M.I.; Prucha, R. Dynamic Factor Demand Models and Productivity Analysis. In *New Developments in Productivity Analysis*; Hulten, C.R., Dean, E.R., Harper, M., Eds.; University of Chicago Press: Chicago, IL, USA, 2001.
16. Gong, B.; Sickles, R. Finite sample evidence on the performance of stochastic frontiers and data envelopment analysis using panel data. *J. Econ.* **1992**, *51*, 259–284.
17. Shiu, A.; Lam, P.L. Electricity consumption and economic growth in China. *Energy Policy* **2004**, *32*, 47–54. [CrossRef]
18. Zhou, G.; Chau, K.W. Short and long-run effects between oil consumption and economic growth in China. *Energy Policy* **2006**, *34*, 3644–3655. [CrossRef]
19. Yuan, J.H.; Kang, J.G.; Zhao, C.H.; Hu, Z.G. Energy consumption and economic growth: Evidence from China at both aggregated and disaggregated levels. *Energy Econ.* **2008**, *30*, 3077–3094. [CrossRef]
20. Yalta, A.T.; Cakar, H. Energy consumption and economic growth in China: A reconciliation. *Energy Policy* **2012**, *41*, 666–675. [CrossRef]
21. Koop, G. Carbon dioxide emissions and economic growth: A structural approach. *J. Appl. Stat.* **1998**, *25*, 489–515. [CrossRef]
22. Chang, C.C. A multivariate causality test of carbon dioxide emissions, energy consumption and economic growth in China. *Appl. Energy* **2010**, *87*, 3533–3537. [CrossRef]
23. Wang, S.S.; Zhou, D.Q.; Zhou, P.; Wang, Q.W. CO_2 emissions, energy consumption and economic growth in China: A panel data analysis. *Energy Policy* **2011**, *39*, 4870–4875. [CrossRef]
24. Kareem, S.D.; Kari, F.; Alam, G.M.; Adewale, A.; Oke, O.K. Energy consumption, pollutant emissions and economic growth: China experience. *Int. J. Appl. Econ. Financ.* **2012**, *6*, 136–147. [CrossRef]
25. Grossman, G.M.; Krueger, A.B. Economic growth and the environment. *Q. J. Econ.* **1995**, *110*, 353–377. [CrossRef]
26. Hailu, A.; Veeman, T.S. Environmentally sensitive productivity analysis of the Canadian pulp and paper industry, 1959–1994: An input distance function approach. *J. Environ. Econ. Manag.* **2000**, *40*, 251–274. [CrossRef]

27. Coelli, T.; Lauwers, L.G.; Huylenbroeck, V. *Formulation of Technical, Economic and Environmental Efficiency Measures that are Consistent with the Materials Balance Condition*; CEPA Working Paper Series, No WP062005. The University of Queensland: Brisbane, Australia, 2005. Available online: http://www.uq.edu.au/economics/cepa/docs/WP/WP062005.pdf (access on 1 September 2014).

28. Chung, Y.H.; Färe, R.; Grosskopf, S. Productivity and undesirable outputs: A directional distance function approach. *J. Environ. Manag.* **1997**, *51*, 229–240. [CrossRef]

29. Fare, R.; Grosskopf, S.; Margaritis, D. APEC and the Asian economic crisis: Early signals from productivity trends. *Asian Econ. J.* **2001**, *15*, 325–342. [CrossRef]

30. Jeon, B.M.; Sickles, R.C. The role of environmental factors in growth accounting. *J. Appl. Econ.* **2004**, *19*, 567–591. [CrossRef]

31. Kumar, S. Environmentally sensitive productivity growth: A global analysis using Malmquist–Luenberger index. *Ecol. Econ.* **2006**, *56*, 280–293. [CrossRef]

32. Pastor, J.T.; Asmild, M.; Lovell, C.A. The biennial Malmquist productivity change index. *Soc. Econ. Plan. Sci.* **2011**, *45*, 10–15. [CrossRef]

33. Luenberger, D.G. New optimality principles for economic efficiency and equilibrium. *J. Optim. Theory Appl.* **1992**, *75*, 221–264. [CrossRef]

34. Chambers, R.G.; Chung, Y.; Färe, R. Benefit and distance functions. *J. Econ. Theory* **1996**, *70*, 407–419. [CrossRef]

35. Wei, C.; Ni, J.; Du, L. Regional allocation of carbon dioxide abatement in China. *China Econ. Rev.* **2012**, *23*, 552–565. [CrossRef]

36. Choi, Y.; Zhang, N.; Zhou, P. Efficiency and abatement costs of energy-related CO_2 emissions in China: A Slacks-based Efficiency Measure. *Appl. Energy* **2012**, *98*, 198–208. [CrossRef]

37. National Bureau of Statistics. *China Statistical Yearbook*; China Statistical Press: Beijing, China, 2011.

38. Department of Industry and Transport Statistics; National Bureau of Statistics (NBS); Energy Bureau; National Development and Reform Commission (NDRC) (Eds.) *China Energy Statistical Yearbook*; China Statistical Press: Beijing, China, 2011. (in Chinese)

39. Wu, Y. Openness, productivity and growth in the APEC economies. *Empir. Econ.* **2004**, *29*, 593–604. [CrossRef]

40. Wu, Y. China's contribution to productivity growth: New estimates. *China Econ. Q.* **2008**, *3*, 827–842.

41. Eggleston, H.S.; Buendia, L.; Miwa, K.; Ngara, T.; Tanabe, K. *IPCC Guidelines for National Greenhouse Gas Inventories in 2006*; IGES: Kanagawa, Japan, 2006.

42. These values are on weighted mean by GRP proportion of each province mean between 1998 and 2012.

43. Kumar, S.; Russell, R.R. Technological change, technological catch-up, and capital deepening: Relative contributions to growth and convergence. *Am. Econ. Rev.* **2002**, *92*, 527–548. [CrossRef]

44. Henderson, J.D.; Russell, R.R. Human capital and convergence: A production-frontier approach. *Int. Econ. Rev.* **2005**, *46*, 1167–1205. [CrossRef]

45. Kumar and Russell and Henderson and Russell use the same regression to describe labor productivity and its components growth rates. We also employ generalized least squares because the error term is likely to be heteroskedastic. These results are consistent with White test of OLS.

46. Silverman, B.W. Using kernel density estimates to investigate multimodality. *J. R. Stat. Soc.* **1981**, *43*, 97–99.

47. Bianchi, M. Testing for convergence: Evidence from non-Parametric multimodality tests. *J. Appl. Econ.* **1997**, *12*, 393–409. [CrossRef]

48. The proposed test was first applied to an OECD economic research by Bianchi, M.

49. Li, Q. Nonparametric testing of closeness between two unknown distribution functions. *Econ. Rev.* **1996**, *15*, 261–274. [CrossRef]

50. Fan, Y.; Ullah, A. On goodness-of-fit tests for weekly dependent processes using kernel method. *J. Nonparametric Stat.* **1999**, *11*, 337–360. [CrossRef]

51. Wang, C.H. Sources of energy productivity growth and its distribution dynamics in China. *Resour. Energy Econ.* **2011**, *33*, 279–292. [CrossRef]

Sustainability **2014**, *6*, 5983–6004

52. Parteka, A.; Wolszczak-Derlacz, J. Dynamics of productivity in higher education: Cross-european evidence based on bootstrapped Malmquist indices. *J. Product. Anal.* **2013**, *40*, 67–82. [CrossRef]

53. Simar, L.; Wilson, P. Estimating and bootstrapping Malmquist indices. *Eur. J. Oper. Res.* **1999**, *115*, 459–471. [CrossRef]

sustainability

MDPI

Article

Minimizing the Carbon Footprint for the Time-Dependent Heterogeneous-Fleet Vehicle Routing Problem with Alternative Paths

Wan-Yu Liu [1], Chun-Cheng Lin [2], Ching-Ren Chiu [3], You-Song Tsao [2] and Qunwei Wang [4,*]

[1] Department of Tourism Information, Aletheia University, New Taipei City 251, Taiwan; nellyliu@gmail.com
[2] Department of Industrial Engineering and Management, National Chiao Tung University, Hsinchu 300, Taiwan; cclin321@nctu.edu.tw (C.-C.L.); eric21358611@yahoo.com.tw (Y.-S.T.)
[3] Institute of Service Management, National Penghu University of Science and Technology, Penghu 880, Taiwan; d9508202@gmail.com
[4] School of Business, Soochow University, Suzhou 215006, China
* Author to whom correspondence should be addressed; wqw0305@126.com; Tel.:+86-512-6716-2489.

Received: 25 June 2014; in revised form: 13 July 2014; Accepted: 17 July 2014; Published: 23 July 2014

Abstract: To respond to the reduction of greenhouse gas emissions and global warming, this paper investigates the minimal-carbon-footprint time-dependent heterogeneous-fleet vehicle routing problem with alternative paths (MTHVRPP). This finds a route with the smallest carbon footprint, instead of the shortest route distance, which is the conventional approach, to serve a number of customers with a heterogeneous fleet of vehicles in cases where there may not be only one path between each pair of customers, and the vehicle speed differs at different times of the day. Inheriting from the NP-hardness of the vehicle routing problem, the MTHVRPP is also NP-hard. This paper further proposes a genetic algorithm (GA) to solve this problem. The solution represented by our GA determines the customer serving ordering of each vehicle type. Then, the capacity check is used to classify multiple routes of each vehicle type, and the path selection determines the detailed paths of each route. Additionally, this paper improves the energy consumption model used for calculating the carbon footprint amount more precisely. Compared with the results without alternative paths, our experimental results show that the alternative path in this experiment has a significant impact on the experimental results in terms of carbon footprint.

Keywords: carbon footprint; vehicle routing problem; heterogeneous fleet; alternative path; genetic algorithm

1. Introduction

Recently, the global warming has become more and more serious, and each country has paid more and more attention to the related issues of greenhouse gas effects. It cannot be denied that the greenhouse gases due to traffic transportation are harmful to the natural environment. If reckless greenhouse gas emissions continue, irreversible effects in the environment (e.g., global warming, desertification, and a rise in sea level) could result. Reducing the carbon footprint is a direct and effective method for reducing greenhouse gas emissions [1]. According to [2], carbon footprint can be defined as the CO_2 emission quantity produced (directly or indirectly) throughout the entire life cycle of a service or a product. Compared with the greenhouse gas emission term commonly used by the public, carbon footprint differs in that it includes all the CO_2 emission produced from the extraction and production of the product's raw materials, production and assembly of the product, and product use, disposal and recycling. Thus, a carbon footprint covers the entire life cycle of a product. Contemporary life is full of environmental pollution, and carbon footprint reduction is necessary to improve the environment for future generations.

According to the investigation by the Intergovernmental Panel on Climate Change (IPCC), transportation accounts for approximately 13% of total greenhouse gas emissions [1]. This means that millions of tons of CO_2 are being emitted into the environment, and the numbers are continuing to grow. Therefore, the design of logistics route planning to reduce vehicle exhaust is an effective method for reducing the carbon footprint. The focus of logistics operating system is how effectively to use vehicles. Reducing the number of vehicles through effective vehicle route planning to transport raw materials, semi-finished products, or finished products to their destinations can reduce vehicle exhaust and vehicle transportation costs. Thus, effective vehicle route planning is an important topic in delivery problems. Conventionally, logistics delivery centers determine vehicle routing manually. However, simple manual vehicle route planning methods cannot determine ideal route planning in a short time as a large number of customers and different vehicle fleets are involved. Effective vehicle route planning prior to vehicle assignment can result in the maximal resource utilization effectiveness and drastically reduce vehicle transportation costs. This naturally reduces vehicle exhaust and lowers carbon footprints.

The vehicle routing problem (VRP) is a research topic related to carbon footprint reduction [3]. VRP usually only considers a single depot, vehicle types, and a fixed number of customers. Each customer location has a variety of cargo quantity requirements, and the delivery center is responsible for assigning vehicle fleets with routes to satisfactorily deliver raw materials, finished products, and semi-finished products required by customers. Hence, route planning should achieve many objectives, e.g., the shortest route, the minimal cost, and the minimal required time under certain constraints. However, most practical situations are not as simple as previously described. The situations that affect computational complexity include different vehicle types and capabilities, and different road situations based on time and alternative path selection. How to formulate an effective route in these complex situations has been receiving a lot of attention. Compared with the conventional objectives that involve minimization of time or distance, the VRP with the objective of reducing the carbon footprint is a relatively novel subject. In previous related works on carbon-footprint VRP, Bektaş and Laporte [4] indicated that the factors related to vehicle fuel consumption and CO_2 emission, speed, load, distance, and time. Xiao *et al.* [5] developed an optimization model that adds a new factor, fuel consumption rate (FCR), and uses the simulated annealing method to resolve the model. Their results showed that the fuel consumption for 27 VRPs is reduced by an average of 5%. Although the previous works have addressed the basic VRP, real life VRPs often contain additional variables (e.g., road situations and vehicle types). Since it is unclear whether the basic VRP can be applied to the reality of multiple vehicle types and alternative path selection problems, and the factors in calculating carbon foot prints depend upon different vehicles, vehicle travel speeds, and road situations, most previous works on VRP often only considered a single characteristic, such as vehicle types [6], time-dependent [7], and multiple alternative path selection [8]. However, practical problems often include multiple variables, and applying the VRP that only consider one variable to practical problems may pose difficulties.

To move VRP closer to practical applications, this paper proposes the minimal-carbon-footprint time-dependent heterogeneous-fleet vehicle routing problem with alternative paths (MTHVRPP), which simultaneously considers different vehicle types and alternative path selections, to increase the applicability in practical situations. Since the FCR formula proposed in [5] is not suitable for multiple vehicle types and alternative path selection problems, this paper expands the FCR equation to consider the energy consumption in each time zone of a day, which enables the utilization tour complex MTHVRPP. Furthermore, this paper uses the minimal carbon footprint as the objective to reduce CO_2 emission. Compared with the conventional VRPs, the MTHVRPP can be broadly applied to practical situations, which is more in line with real life.

The MTHVRPP differs from conventional VRPs in that the MTHVRPP has different vehicle capacities and travel costs. In conventional VRPs, vehicles are of a fixed type and of a fixed capacity when satisfying the required customer demands; while in the MTHVRPP, the vehicle capacity depends on the vehicle type. Additionally, the conventional VRPs generally have fixed vehicle travel costs;

while in the MTHVRPP, the travel costs depend upon the vehicle type, road travel situation, and alternative path selection. Since the VRP is a proven NP-hard problem [9], and the MTHVRPP is an extension of VRP, the MTHVRPP is also an NP-hard problem. As the problem scale expands, the time for finding exact solutions increases with the increases in variables. Compared with the conventional VRPs, the MTHVRPP in this paper additionally considers vehicle types and alternative path selection, which increase the problem-solving complexity. Since typical exact algorithms (e.g., dynamic programming as well as branch and bound) cannot always guarantee finding an optimal solution, effective metaheuristic algorithms are more appropriate for solving large-scale NP-hard problems. In view of the importance of MTHVRPP in actual practice and the problem solving potential of metaheuristic algorithms, this paper uses the genetic algorithm (GA) as the basic framework to develop a problem-solving framework for MTHVRPP, which is expected to achieve an accurate optimal solution efficiently.

The MTHVRPP (which uses the minimal carbon footprint as the objective) concerned in this paper differs from the conventional VRPs (which typically use minimal transportation time and transportation distance as the objective). In addition, this paper proposes a GA to determine appropriate vehicle scheduling to satisfy some practical objectives, such as minimal carbon footprint, minimal total transportation time, and minimal total routing distance. The experimental design is expected to conform to practical problems. Detailed research contributions are given as follows:

- This paper proposes a GA for minimizing the carbon footprint for the time-dependent heterogeneous-fleet vehicle routing problem with alternative paths (MTHVRPP).
- In solution representation, time is divided into numerous time steps so that the average vehicle speed on different alternative paths and in different time zones can be expressed.
- Compared with previous VRPs, the factors that influence carbon footprints such as vehicle type, alternative path selection, vehicle load, and time zone speed are considered in this paper, in order to conform to real life situations.

2. Literature Review

The MTHVRPP in this paper is a type of VRP. This section reviews the previous VRP works related to MTHVRPP, and then the GA.

2.1. VRP

This subsection organizes the previous works on MTHVRPP, such as heterogeneous-fleet VRP (HVRP), time-dependent VRP (TDVRP), and the VRP with alternative paths, and explores their corresponding approaches.

2.2. Description of VRP

Prior to talking about VRP, we must first understand the traveling salesman problem (TSP). The TSP considers a single vehicle that visits multiple customers before returning to the depot, while the total routing time or distance of the vehicle is minimized. Furthermore, when the vehicle capacity limitation is concerned (*i.e.*, the total customer demand requirement of each route of the vehicle cannot exceed the vehicle capacity) this becomes a VRP. The difference between a VRP and a TSP is that a VRP can produce numerous routes to pass through all customer nodes under vehicle capacity limitations. The difference between TSP and VRP is illustrated in Figure 1, in which the TSP is a single-route node-service-combination problem with no vehicle capacity limitation and a VRP is a multiple-route node-service-combination problem with vehicle capacity limitation.

VRP [3] is defined as follows: (1) A vehicle starts from the depot and returns to the depot; (2) the vehicle must satisfy the required demand quantity of each customer; (3) each customer can only be serviced once by the vehicle; (4) the total customer demand quantity serviced by the vehicle cannot exceed the vehicle capacity limitation.

The mathematical model of VRP pursues an optimal vehicle route solution with the minimal total generalized cost that considers practical constraints, e.g., road network characteristics, customer requirements, facility resources, and delivery conditions. The generalized cost refers to the penalty of various negative effects during the vehicle delivery process. A commonly seen negative effect is the transportation cost, which can be divided into fixed cost and variable cost. Fixed costs include vehicle-use costs (e.g., purchase cost and depreciation) and the driver salary, while variable costs are related to delivery route scheduling (e.g., routing distance, time, fuel consumption, and loading/unloading time). Additionally, penalty costs could be generated if delays occur or customer requirements cannot be satisfied.

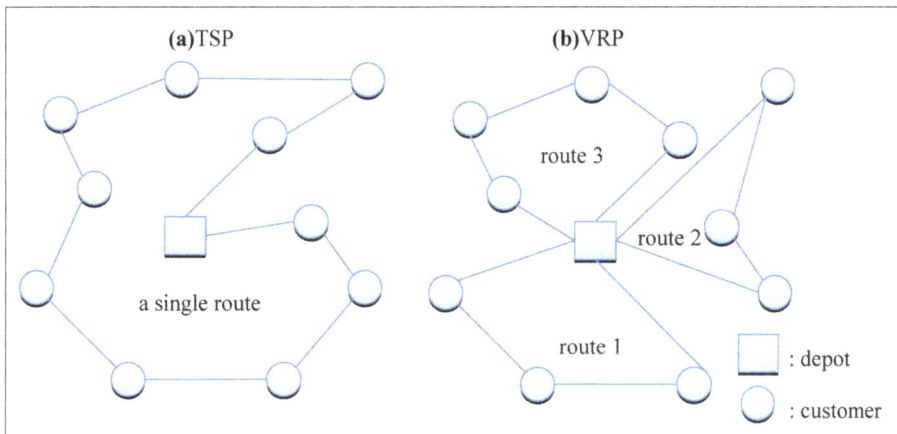

Figure 1. Illustration of the traveling salesman problem (TSP) and vehicle route problem (VRP) route patterns.

Application of VRP in actual practice can derive numerous problem types because of different conditions and changes in limitations, e.g., heterogeneous fleet VRP (HVRP), time-dependent VRP (TDVRP), and VRP with alternative paths. The HVRP differs from conventional VRPs in that it considers more than one vehicle type. Each vehicle type has different cost variables, and the parameters between vehicles are independent [6]. HVRP also does not have limitations on the number of vehicles used [10], and the main objective of HVRP is the maximal utilization of vehicles.

The TDVRP is primarily used in the situation with time window limitations, and its greatest difference from the conventional VRPs is the time change at different customer locations. Specifically, each customer node includes a time window, and the penalty costs could result if a customer node cannot be achieved within the time window [7]. The objective of TDVRP is to arrive at all customer nodes within the time window.

The VRP with alternative paths differs from conventional VRPs in that it has more than one transportation method between customer nodes. Conventional VRPs usually have only one vehicle transportation method. In additional to truck transport, the VRP with alternative paths can transport cargos by trains, airplanes, and other additional transportation methods, and may select more than one path between customer nodes. Regardless of additional transportation method or alternative path selection, the costs for each selection vary [8]. The objective of the VRP with alternative paths is to find one (or multiple) optimal route combinations to obtain an optimal solution. Note that the MTHVRPP proposed in this paper has the problem characteristics of HVRP, TDVRP, and VRP with alternative paths.

Sustainability **2014**, *6*, 4658–4684

2.3. Approaches for VRP

VRP is an NP-hard problem, and numerous previous works existed in the literature. The commonly seen approaches to the VRPs can be classified into mathematical programing and heuristic methods.

In the mathematical programming methods for VRPs, mathematical notations are used to construct high-complexity mathematical models, and then mathematical software is used to obtain the optimal solutions for moderate-size and low-limitation problems within a reasonable time. This method converts the VRP into an easily-solvable mathematical programming model with comparisons for the other optimization works, such as the Lagrangian relaxation method [11], assignment problem [12], set partition problem [13], and set covering problem [14]. However, VRP has numerous related factors in real life that cause difficulties in constructing a mathematical model or is ineffective for large-scale problems. Thus, many previous works have invested in other high-level solution-searching methods or computing technologies to improve this problem.

Since mathematical programming methods may encounter an excessive time consumption bottleneck when solving large-scale VRPs, many previous works have proposed various heuristic algorithms (e.g., generic algorithm, random search strategies, and speculative problem solving methods) to iteratively improve the objective value. This conforms to the practical requirement of efficiently obtaining a solution. The previous works related to heuristics can further be divided into conventional heuristics and metaheuristics.

Conventional heuristics use the greedy method and the local improvement concept to design an easily-implemented problem-solving method, which can generally be discussed in the following two stages: the *route construction* as well as the *route improvement*. *Route construction* is the initial developed heuristic method, which uses its own design rules to complete a possible solution by iteratively considering all the customer nodes to be routed. Clark and Wright [15] used a saving algorithm to calculate the amount of route cost reductions when combining two nodes (while not violating vehicle capacity), and then arranged priority node combinations according to the amount of location savings. Rosenkrantz *et al.* [16] proposed the insertion algorithm, which starts with a simple route, and then greedily finds the other node with the minimal cost to be inserted into the route until all customer nodes have been serviced. On the other hand, we consider the *route improvement* stage after the initial route is constructed. At this stage, the nodes and arcs of the initial route are exchanged and rearranged to improve the route solution. Popular route improvement methods include *arc exchange* and *node exchange*. The K-Opt arc exchange method proposed by [17] is one of the most commonly-used exchange method, which is based by [18–22].

Metaheuristics use iterative search to randomly jump in feasible solution space, so that the defect of converging on local minimum in conventional metaheuristical gorithms can be eliminated and the solution quality can be improved. Main metaheuristic methods include tabu search (TS), simulated annealing (SA), genetic algorithm (GA), ant colony optimization (ACO), and threshold accepting (TA). TS has a short-term memory effect to avoid repeated searches so that the optimal solution can be approached gradually. SA and TA operate under similar concepts of a certain probability of accepting inferior solutions and escaping local optimal solution constraints to continue searching. GA [23] simulates the genetic evolution process and uses crossover and mutation mechanisms to search for the optimal solution. ACO simulates the habit of ants leaving pheromones, and gives different alternative path selection probabilities for VRP to find superior routes. Many other works have also combined different algorithms to obtain a superior solution. For example, Osman [24] combined TS and SA concepts for the solution search during routing improvement. Van Breedam [25] used three types of routing improvement methods, and then added SA mechanisms for improvements. Tan *et al.* [26] combined TS, SA, and GA to solve the VRP with time window.

3. Our Genetic Algorithm Approach for MTHVRPP

No previous works have simultaneously considered the VRP with alternative path selection and multiple vehicle type limitations. Thus, alternative paths and multiple vehicle types in this paper are focused to explore VRP road network configuration. By using genetic algorithm (GA) design, we expect to find possible solutions and use these solutions to get close to the optimal solution. The previous works on VRP did not usually consider alternative path selection. Furthermore, the objective of this paper is carbon footprint minimization, and the factors that affect carbon footprints include road conditions, vehicle speed, vehicle load, and the weight of the empty vehicle. Therefore, this paper additionally considers the mechanisms for multiple alternative path selections and multiple vehicle types to conform to the factors that affect carbon footprint. Additionally, as for alternative path selection, different paths have different road conditions, and different vehicles have different capacities and empty vehicle weight. Thus, the focus of this paper is to obtain the optimal solution with the above multiple conditions.

3.1. Problem Description

Derived from the VRP, the MTHVRPP optimization model includes many concepts and limitations similar to typical VRP optimization models. However, since the vehicle and route limitations in MTHVRPP are different than those in VRP, the differences between MTHVRPP and VRP must be explored before constructing the MTHVRPP optimization model. Compared with VRP, the most prominent characteristics of MTHVRPP are as follows:

- The objective of the MTHVRPP is to minimize the total carbon footprint, not distance or time.
- The MTHVRPP has more than one vehicle type, and the capacity and basic costs of each vehicle are different.
- In the MTHVRPP, multiple paths exist between customer nodes; the distance of each path and the speed of different time zones of a day and different vehicles are also different.
- Because multiple vehicle types exist, the basic costs for each vehicle are different. The carbon emissions also change based on the load and travel speed during the routing trip.

In the conventional VRP model with a single vehicle type, only the road section variables are required to determine whether the vehicle travels on each road section, but the vehicle type traveling on the road is not considered. However, the MTHVRPP requires consideration of multiple vehicle types; therefore, conventional solution representation for VRP cannot easily express the solution characteristics in MTHVRPP.

In addition, note that the MTHVRPP and the conventional heterogeneous fleet vehicle routing problem (HVRP) are also different. Because the conventional solution representation only uses a single path between customers and does not consider alternative path selection problems, additional path selection mechanism in the solution representation compensates for the added alternative paths, which is an important topic in this paper.

3.1.1. Problem Assumptions

To simplify complexity and maintain reasonable cost assumptions, this paper has the problem limitations and makes the following assumptions:

(1) Route information:

- There is only a single depot, and its location is fixed.
- The distance between customers, the customer locations, the customer demand quantity, and the vehicle speed on routes between customer nodes in different time zones are known and fixed.

- Vehicles leave from the depot and return to the depot after servicing all the customers.
- The capacities for different vehicles are fixed and known.
- The total customer demand requirements on each route cannot exceed the vehicle capacity.
- More than one path between nodes can be selected.
- Each customer node must be visited, and is only visited once.
- Different vehicle types can be used for delivery according to the number of the required routes and the routing distance.

(2)   Costs and time:

- There is a positive proportional relationship between the vehicle routing distance and the vehicle carbon emission.
- There is a positive proportional relationship between the vehicle load and the vehicle carbon emission.
- The carbon emission from servicing customers is not considered.
- The vehicle types and vehicle number limitations are not considered.
- The routing time of each vehicle is limited.
- The vehicle fixed costs are not considered.
- The time window limitations are not considered.

3.1.2. Notations

- Node information: 1]

I	: $I = \{V_1, V_2, V_3 \dots V_S\}$, where v_i is a customer nodes for $i \in \{1, 2, \dots, S\}$.
v_0	: v_0 is the depot node.
I_0	: $I_0 = I \cup \{v_0\}$

- Vehicle information

U	: The number of vehicle types.
A_u	: The surface area of each vehicle type.
W_u	: The empty weight of each vehicle type.

- Constant

q_i	: The cargo demand requirement of node i.
Z_{ij}	: The number of selectable paths from node i to node j.
Q_u	: The maximum load capacity of vehicle type u.
V_{ijz}^m	: The speed in time zone m on path z between nodes i and j.
D_{ijz}	: The distance of path z between nodes i and j.
S	: The total number of customer nodes.
N	: The number of vehicle routes.
T_m	: The starting time point for time zone m.
L	: The vehicle routing time limitation.

- Label

i, j, k	: Node label.
z	: Route label.
m	: Time zone label.
u	: Vehicle type label.

- Variables:

s	: The number of customers' nodes that have already been serviced.
TA_i^n	: The cargo load of vehicle type u on route n after passing node i.
TL_i^n	: The time point when the vehicle reaches node i on route n.
T_{ijz}^{nm}	: The time point when the vehicle leaves node i on route n.
T_{ijz}^{nm}	: The time consumed by traveling on route n in time zone m on path z between i and j.
T_{ij}^n	: The total routing time between nodes i and j on route n.
D_{ijz}^{nm}	: The routing distance taken on route n in time zone m on path z between nodes i and j.
L_n	: The time traveling on route n.
g_{iju}^n	: The total carbon emission of vehicle u between node i and j on route n.
g_n	: The total carbon emission on route n.
TG	: The total carbon emission for the entire route.
TD	: The total routing distance.
TT	: The total routing time.

- Variables:

$$x_{i,u}^n = \begin{array}{l} 1, \text{if thevehicle type } u \text{ passes customer node } i \text{ on route } n; \\ 0, \text{otherwise.} \end{array}$$

$$r_{i,j,z,u}^n = \begin{cases} 1, \text{if the vehicle type } u \text{ passes path } z \text{ between nodes } i \text{ and } j \text{ on route } n; \\ 0, \text{otherwise.} \end{cases}$$

Bektaş and Laporte [9] indicated that the amount of carbon footprint is determined by the vehicle energy consumption between customer nodes, as calculated as follows:

$$P_{ij} \approx \alpha_{ij}(w + f_{ij})d_{ij} + \beta v_{ij}^2 d_{ij} \tag{1}$$

where P_{ij} is the energy (J) required by the vehicle from customer nodes i to j; w represents the weight of an empty vehicle (kg); f_{ij} represents the vehicle load (kg) between customer nodes i and j; d_{ij} represents the distance (m) between customer nodes i and j; v_{ij} represents the travel speed (m/s) of the vehicle between customer nodes i and j; α_{ij} is the specific route-related constant and β is the vehicle-related constant, respectively calculated as follows:

$$\alpha_{ij} = a + g\sin\theta_{ij} + gC_r\cos\theta_{ij} \tag{2}$$

$$\beta = 0.5C_d A\rho \tag{3}$$

where a represents the vehicle acceleration (m/s²); g represents the gravitational constant of 9.81 (m/s²); θ_{ij} represents the road inclination angle between customer nodes i and j; C_r represents the rolling resistance coefficient; C_d represents the road resistance coefficient; A represents the surface area of the vehicle (m²); ρ represent the air viscosity coefficient. However, the aforementioned equation is only appropriate for the ordinary VRP and is not completely suitable for the MTHVRPP proposed in this paper. Thus, we improve the previously described equation and enable the equation to be used in MTHVRPP with different vehicle speeds at different time zones, as shown below:

$$P_{iju}^{nm} = \alpha_{ij}(W_u + C_{iu}^n)D_{ijz}^{nm} + \beta(V_{ijz}^m)^2 D_{ijz}^{nm} \tag{4}$$

where P_{iju}^{nm} is the energy (J) required by the vehicle type u going from customer node i to node j in time zone m on route n; W_u is the empty weight of vehicle type u (kg);

$$TA_i^n$$

is the load (kg) of vehicle type u on route n after passing through node i;

$$V_{ijz}^m$$

is the vehicle speed (m/s) in time zone m on path z between nodes i and j;

$$D_{ijz}^{nm}$$

is the distance (m) traveled by the vehicle on route n in time zone m on path z between customer nodes i and j. Furthermore, because the surface area of each vehicle type is different, Equation (3) is modified to:

$$\beta = 0.5 \, C_d A_u \rho \tag{5}$$

3.1.3. Mathematical Model

- Objective equation:

The objective of our problem is to minimize the amount of the energy used based on the improved equation combined with variables $r_{i,j,z,u}^n$, which is given as follows:

$$\min \sum_{i \in I_0} \sum_{j \in I_0} \sum_{n=1}^{N} \sum_{m=0}^{M} \sum_{z=1}^{Z_{ij}} \sum_{u=1}^{U} r_{i,j,z,u}^n \{ \alpha_{ij}(W_u + C_{iu}^n)D_{ijz}^{nm} + \beta V_{ijz}^{m2} D_{ijz}^{nm} \} \cdot \frac{2.32}{8.8} / 3600000$$

Note that

$$r_{i,j,z,u}^n$$

is one or zero according to the condition whether vehicle type u has passed through path z between nodes i and j on route n. If the condition is true, then

$$r_{i,j,z,u}^n$$

= 1; otherwise,

$$r_{i,j,z,u}^n$$

= 0. Because the result unit obtained by the original objective equation is in $J \cdot m^2 / s^2$, our requirement is that this unit must be converted to a kilowatt-hour. One liter of gasoline can produce approximately 8.8 kilowatt-hours of energy [9] and approximately 2.32 kg of CO_2 [9]. Thus, this objective equation is multiplied with a coefficient of 2.32/8.8/360000.

- The constraints of vehicle flow rate conservation:

The following constraint ensures that each node is only passed once, where x_{iu}^n represents whether vehicle type u passes node i on route n. If so, then $x_{iu}^n = 1$; otherwise, $x_{iu}^n = 0$.

$$\sum_{n=1}^{N}\sum_{u=1}^{U} x_{iu}^n = 1 \ \forall i \in I.$$

(6)

The following constraint ensures that the number of vehicles entering and leaving the node is the same.

$$\sum_{n=1}^{N}\sum_{z=1}^{Z_{ij}}\sum_{u=1}^{U} r_{ijzu}^n = \sum_{n=1}^{N}\sum_{z=1}^{Z_{jk}}\sum_{u=1}^{U} r_{jkzu}^n \ , \forall j \in I \wedge \forall i, k \in I_0 \wedge i \neq j.$$

(7)

The following constraint ensures that the vehicle does not return.

$$\sum_{n=1}^{N}\sum_{z=1}^{Z_{ij}}\sum_{u=1}^{U} r_{ijzu}^n + \sum_{n=1}^{N}\sum_{z=1}^{Z_{ji}}\sum_{u=1}^{u} r_{jizu}^n = 1 , \forall i, j \in I \wedge i \neq j$$

(8)

The following constraint ensures that only one path is chosen between nodes.

$$\sum_{n=1}^{N}\sum_{z=1}^{Z_{ij}}\sum_{u=1}^{U} r_{ijzu}^n = 1 , \forall i, j \in I \wedge i \neq j.$$

(9)

The following constraint ensures that the number of vehicles leaving the depot is N.

$$\sum_{i \in I}\sum_{z=1}^{Z_{v_0 i}}\sum_{u=1}^{U} r_{v_0 izu}^n = 1 , \forall n = 1, 2, \dots, N.$$

(10)

The following constraint ensures that the number of vehicles returning to the depot is N.

$$\sum_{i \in I}\sum_{z=1}^{Z_{iv_0}}\sum_{u=1}^{U} r_{iv_0 zu}^n = 1 , \forall n = 1, 2, \dots, N.$$

(11)

- Vehicle load capacity constraint:

The following constraint ensures that the total cargo requirement on the route does not exceed the maximum vehicle load capacity, where q_i represents the demand quantity requirement of each node.

$$Q_u \geq \sum_{i \in I}\sum_{u=1}^{U} x_{iu}^n q_i , \forall n = 1, 2, \dots, N.$$

(12)

- Vehicle routing time constraint:

The following constraint ensures that the routing time of each vehicle is smaller than the maximum routing time limitation, where L_n represents the routing time of each route n and L is the maximum routing time.

$$L_n \leq L, \forall n = 1, 2, \ldots, N. \tag{13}$$

- Definition constraint:

The following constraint ensures that

$$x_{i,u}^n$$

only equals 0 or 1.

$$x_{i,u}^n \in \{0, 1\}, \forall i \in I, u \in U, n = 1, 2, \ldots, N. \tag{14}$$

The following constraint ensures that

$$r_{i,j,z,u}^n$$

only equals 0 or 1. If vehicle u passes through path z between nodes i and j on route n, then $r_{i,j,z,u}^n z$ equals 1; otherwise, equals 0.

$$r_{i,j,z,u}^n \in \{0, 1\}, \forall i, j \in I_0, z = 1, 2, \ldots, Z_{i,j}, u \in U, n = 1, 2, \ldots, N. \tag{15}$$

- Calculation of parameters:

The following equation calculates the routing time $T_{i,j,z}^{n,m}$ in each situation.

$$T_{i,j,z}^{n,m} = \begin{cases} \frac{D_{ijz}}{v_{ijz}^m}, if\ TL_{i,j}^n \in m \wedge TL_{i,j}^n + \frac{D_{ijz}}{v_{ijz}^m} \leq T_{m+1}, \forall i,j \in I \wedge i \neq j, z = 1, \ldots, Z_{ij}, m = 0, 1, \ldots \\ T_{m+1} - Td_{i,j}^n, if\ TL_{i,j}^n \in m \wedge TL_{i,j}^n + \frac{D_{ijz}}{v_{ijz}^m} > T_{m+1}, \forall i,j \in I \wedge i \neq j, z = 1, \ldots, Z_{ij}, m = 0, 1, \ldots \\ T_m + \frac{D_{ijz} - \sum_{m=0}^{m-1} D_{i,j,z}^{n,m}}{v_{i,j,z}^m}, if\ TL_{i,j}^n \notin m \wedge T_m + \frac{D_{i,j,z} - \sum_{m=0}^{m-1} D_{i,j,z}^{n,m}}{v_{i,j,z}^m} \leq T_{m+1}, \forall i,j \in I \wedge i \neq j, z = 1, \ldots, Z_{ij}, m = 0, 1, \ldots \\ T_{m+1} - T_m, if\ TL_{i,j}^n \notin m \wedge T_m + \frac{D_{i,j,z} - \sum_{m=0}^{m-1} D_{i,j,z}^{n,m}}{v_{i,j,z}^m} > T_{m+1}, \forall i,j \in I \wedge i \neq j, z = 1, \ldots, Z_{ij}, m = 0, 1, \ldots \end{cases} \tag{16}$$

The following equation calculates the time point $TA_{i,j}^n$ that the vehicle reaches customer node j on route n, where $TL_{k,i}^n$ represents the time that the vehicle left node i.

$$TA_{i,j}^n = TL_{k,i}^n + \sum_{n=1}^{N} \sum_{m=0}^{M} T_{i,j,z}^{n,m}, \forall i, j \in I \wedge i \neq j, z = 1, \ldots, Z_{i,j}. \tag{17}$$

The following equation calculates the total routing time $T_{i,j}^n$ from node i to j on route n.

$$T_{i,j}^n = TA_{i,j}^n - TL_{k,i}^n. \tag{18}$$

The following equation calculates the routing distance $D_{i,j,z}^{n,m}$ on route n in time zone m on path z between nodes i and j, where $Z_{i,j}$ is the path selected between i and j.

$$D_{i,j,z}^{n,m} = V_{i,j,z}^m T_{i,j,z}^{n,m} \ \forall i,j \in I \ \wedge i \neq j \ , z = 1, \dots, Z_{i,j}, m = 0, 1, \dots, M. \tag{19}$$

The following equation calculates the total time spend on route n.

$$L_n = \sum_{i \in I_0} \sum_{j \in I_0} T_{i,j}^n , \forall n = 1, 2 \dots, N. \tag{20}$$

Note that according to Constraint (13), L_n must be smaller than L.

3.1.4. Example Description

We describe a sample problem with five customer nodes and two vehicle types. The locations of the customers and their related distance are shown in Figure 2. We assume that the weights of vehicle types 1 and 2 without cargo loading are 3 tons and 5 tons, respectively. Customer nodes 1 to 6 separately require 2, 3, 1, 1, 2, and 5 tons, and the delivery of those cargos require three routes to be completed. The routing sequence of route1is 0-1-3-0, and requires vehicle type 1. The routing sequence for route2is 0-2-4-5-0, and requires vehicle type 1. Note that the gravitational constant is $g = 9.81 \ (m/s^2)$, the vehicle front surface area $A = 5 \ (m^2)$, the vehicle acceleration speed $a = 0 \ (m/s^2)$, the road inclination angle between customer nodes is $\theta_{ij} = 0$, the rolling resistance coefficient $C_r = 0.01$, the road resistance coefficient $C_d = 0.7$, and the air viscosity coefficient $\rho = 1.2041(kg/m^3)$. Detailed calculation for this route configuration is shown in Table 1.

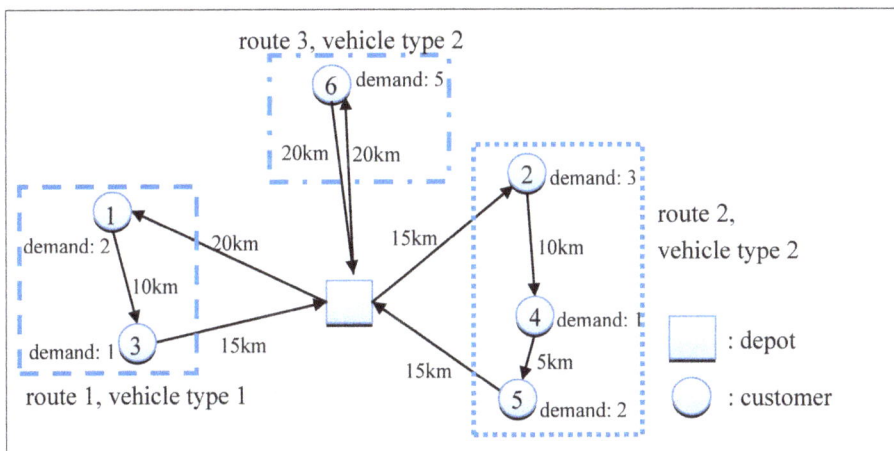

Figure 2. Description of node configuration example.

3.2. Genetic Algorithm Design

This subsection states the main components of our GA for MTHVRPP in detail.

3.2.1. Solution Representation

The solution representation of MTHVRPP is primarily used to determine the route of each vehicle of a different vehicle type (passing each customer node).

Consider the MTHVRPP with U vehicle types and S customer nodes. The length of the chromosome (solution) used in the GA is $(U - 1) + S$, where $U - 1$ zeros are used to change vehicle types; the other S numerals are a permutation of numbers 1, 2, ... , S, which are used to represent the ordering of the customer nodes serviced. Figure 3 is an example for chromosome expression with 2vehicle types and 6 customer nodes, where 0 separates two sequences of customer permutations that require services, *i.e.*, the first vehicle type delivers to customers 1 and then 3; the second vehicle type delivers to customers 2, 4, 5, and finally 6. Next, our method checks the vehicle capacity. When a vehicle type exceeds its maximum capacity when loading cargos in sequence, a separate route is required. In the example in Figure 3, loads from customers 1 and 2 do not exceed the maximum loading capacity of the first vehicle type. Therefore, the cargo can be transported in one route. However, vehicle type two exceeded its capacity after loading the cargos of customers 2, 4, and 5. Thus, an additional route must be made to load customers 6. In other words, Figure 3 included three routes. Furthermore, our method selects the paths with the least carbon footprint between customers as the final solution.

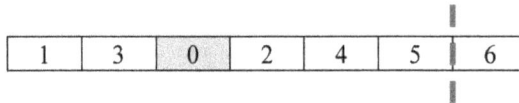

| 1 | 3 | 0 | 2 | 4 | 5 | 6 |

Figure 3. Description of node configuration example.

Table 1. The detailed spreadsheet for the problem in Figure 1.

Route	Vehicle type	Path	Distance	Weight	Time Zone 1 Speed	1 Routing distance	1 CO$_2$	2 Speed	2 Routing distance	2 CO$_2$	3 Speed	3 Routing distance	3 CO$_2$	4 Speed	4 Routing distance	4 CO$_2$	5 Speed	5 Routing distance	5 CO$_2$	6 Speed	6 Routing distance	6 CO$_2$	Total
r = 1	u = 1	0-1	20	3+3 = 6	40	6.67	0.41	50	8.33	0.60	60	5	0.42										1.45
		1-3	10	3+1 = 4							60	5	0.35	50	5	0.29							0.65
		3-0	15	3+0 = 3										50	3.33	0.17	40	6.67	0.27	50	5	0.25	0.7
n = 2	u = 2	0-2	15	5+6 = 10	50	8.33	0.84	50	6.67	0.67													1.52
		2-4	10	5+3 = 8				40	1.34	0.10	40	6.67	0.51	40	2.00	0.15							0.77
		4-5	5	5+2 = 7										60	5	0.46							0.46
		5-0	15	5+0 = 5										45	1.33	0.08	45	7.50	0.45	45	6.17	0.37	0.9
n = 3	u = 2	0-6	20	5+5 = 10	60	10.00	1.14	50	8.33	0.84	40	1.67	0.15										2.14
		6-0	20	5+0 = 5							40	5	0.27	50	8.33	0.54	60	6.67	0.52				1.35
Total																							9.95

3.2.2. Our Algorithm

Initially, we input all data constants, including customer locations, demand requirements, vehicle type, vehicle capacity, basic consumption, load consumption rate, the distance between nodes, and the vehicle speed on each path within each time zone. When all data has been set, GA is used to solve the problem. The GA process is shown in Figure 4. After the initial group is produced, the GA first starts with a population of chromosomes and evaluates this population. Next, selection, crossover, mutation, capacity check, alternative path selection, and evaluation are repeated until the termination conditions are met.

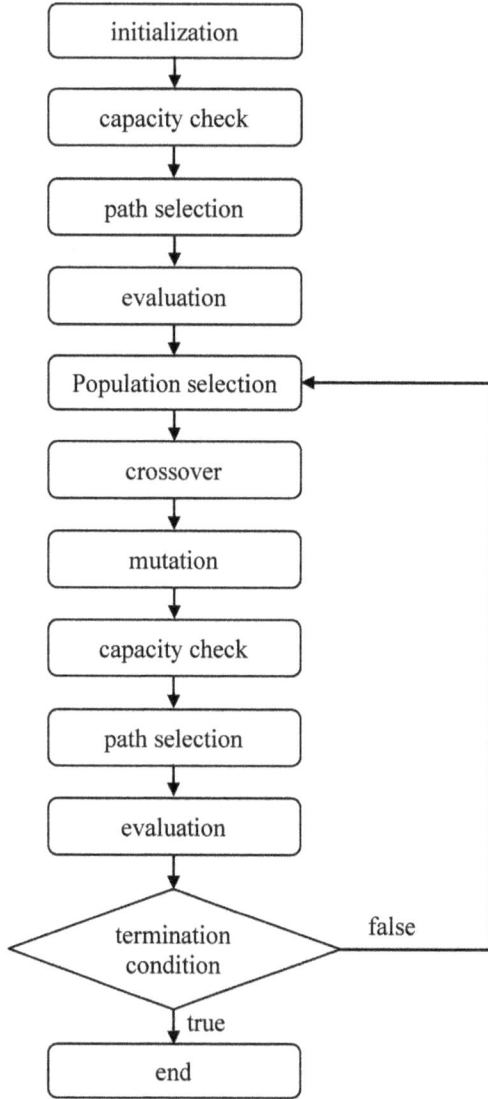

```
        ┌─────────────────────┐
        │   initialization    │
        └─────────┬───────────┘
                  ▼
        ┌─────────────────────┐
        │   capacity check    │
        └─────────┬───────────┘
                  ▼
        ┌─────────────────────┐
        │   path selection    │
        └─────────┬───────────┘
                  ▼
        ┌─────────────────────┐
        │     evaluation      │
        └─────────┬───────────┘
                  ▼
        ┌─────────────────────┐◄──────────┐
        │ Population selection │           │
        └─────────┬───────────┘           │
                  ▼                        │
        ┌─────────────────────┐           │
        │     crossover       │           │
        └─────────┬───────────┘           │
                  ▼                        │
        ┌─────────────────────┐           │
        │     mutation        │           │
        └─────────┬───────────┘           │
                  ▼                        │
        ┌─────────────────────┐           │
        │   capacity check    │           │
        └─────────┬───────────┘           │
                  ▼                        │
        ┌─────────────────────┐           │
        │   path selection    │           │
        └─────────┬───────────┘           │
                  ▼                        │
        ┌─────────────────────┐           │
        │     evaluation      │           │
        └─────────┬───────────┘           │
                  ▼                        │
           ◇─────────────◇     false       │
          ◇  termination   ◇───────────────┘
           ◇  condition   ◇
            ◇───┬───────◇
                ▼ true
        ┌─────────────────────┐
        │        end          │
        └─────────────────────┘
```

Figure 4. Our genetic algorithm process.

(1)   Initial population

We initialize a number of chromosomes to form a population. When each chromosome is a string of length $(U - 1) + S$, where U is the number of vehicle types and S is the number of customer nodes. Considering the initialization of each chromosome, each chromosome can be regarded as $(U - 1) + S$ blank spaces. Next, we randomly produce a permutation of $1, 2, \ldots, S$, and randomly put the S numbers to these $(U - 1) + S$ spaces. Then, the $U - 1$ remaining spaces are filled with 0.

(2)   Capacity check

Each chromosome include a permutation of numbers $1, 2, \ldots, S$ which is separated by $U - 1$ zeros. That is, a total number of U divisions exist, and the permutation in division i represents the customer service ordering provided by vehicle type i. Next, from left to right, the vehicle type permutation is considered to calculate the loading weight of the concerned vehicle type for the route. If the load of the currently concerned vehicle type exceeds the maximum loading capacity for the vehicle type, then a new route must be considered. Otherwise (*i.e.*, there is no new route generated), we enter the path selection stage and then the fitness evaluation stage. For example, the example in Figure 3 is divided into two divisions: $<1, 3>$ and $<2, 4, 5, 6>$. The second division must be divided into two routes because its requirement exceeds the vehicle capacity: $<2, 4, 5>$ and $<6>$. In other words, the first vehicle type only has one route: 0-1-3, while the second vehicle type has two routes: 0-2-4-5-0 and 0-6-0.

(3)   Alternative path selection

After completing a capacity check, each route of each vehicle type must be determined. In our problem, furthermore, multiple paths between any two customer nodes can be chosen. Thus, we calculate the carbon footprint of each route between any two customer nodes and then select the path with the lowest footprint as the final route for this chromosome.

(4)   Fitness evaluation

Fitness is primarily used to represent chromosome performance efficacy and as a basis for selecting decisions. The reciprocal of the total carbon emission is used as the fitness in this paper; that is, the smaller the total costs, the higher the fitness value. In case of chromosome i, the aforementioned capacity check and path selection can be used to decide the route and paths of each vehicle type, which can be used to calculate the total carbon emission $TG(i)$. The fitness $F(i)$ is calculated as follows:

$$F(i) = \frac{1}{TG(i)}$$

(21)

(5)   Population selection

The primary reason for reproduction is to retain high-performance chromosomes of the parent generation in the new off spring by using the acceleration of the population convergence speed. To match the survival of the fittest and the elimination of the weak when selecting individuals for reproduction, the probability of individuals with large fitness values being selected for reproducing offspring is higher. This paper uses the tournament selection method to make selections. First, two chromosomes are randomly chosen and compared for their fitness. The chromosome with a larger fitness value can proceed with the crossover. This process is repeated until sufficient parent-generation number has been obtained.

(6)   Crossover and mutation

The crossover strategy in this paper is the partially matched crossover (PMX), which is explained as follows. Two parent chromosomes are selected from the parent generation by the above tournament selection. Then, two cutoff points in the chromosome representation are randomly generated, and the partitions between the two cutoff points in the two parent chromosomes are exchanged to reproduce the offspring chromosomes. The genes without conflict from the parent chromosomes are reproduced to the offspring chromosomes. If a conflict exists, then seek other corresponding values for replacement. As for the mutation strategy, we adopt the ordering-oriented mutation, which is explained as follows. Two genes are randomly selected from the chromosomes and their positions are exchanged. A new population of chromosomes is created after crossover and mutation operations are complete.

(7)   Termination condition

Two types of termination conditions exist. The first type is to set the number of maximal generations. If the total generation number satisfies the upper bound, the entire evolutional process is stopped. The second type is the maximum unimproved generation number. If the best fitness value in the latest several generations have not improved (the values converge), the evolution process is stopped.

4. Experimental Design and Results

In this section, the previously mentioned GA approach is tested via a series of experiments. Different costs such as carbon footprint, time, or distance are analyzed and compared with the results of the problems without multiple alternative path selections. The design in this paper refers the model of fuel consumption rate (FCR) developed in [5]. However, because the problem pattern in [5] primarily explored the influence of FCR and the energy conversion effectiveness on energy consumption in different situations (*i.e.*, the experiment and problem pattern is different from that in this paper), it is not compared with our experimental results. Section 4.1 describes the experiment problem instances in this paper. Section 4.2 describes the experimental results of each problem i instance with different objectives and conducts the related parameter analysis on each problem instance. This includes whether routes can be selected, variation of experimental results with different objectives, and combined analysis and comparison of experimental results.

This paper usesC++ program language to implement the proposed algorithm, and all the experiments in this paper are evaluated on PCs with Intel® Core™ (Santa Clara, CA, USA) i7-3610QM CPU@ 2.30GHz 2.30 GHz and memory of 8 GB.

4.1. Description of Experimental Problems and Parameter Setting

Our experimental problems are designed based on those with different numbers of nodes and different vehicle fleet configurations used in [2]. Additional nodes and alternative path selection between nodes are added for different numbers of customer nodes and different vehicle types used for our experiments. An average speed table is established for each route in different time zones.

4.1.1. Parameter Settings

Three experimental problem instances have 20, 50, and 100 customer nodes, respectively, and each customer has a customer label. The x-and y- coordinates of each customer and the customer requirements are known. The number of vehicle types is three or five, and the capacity of each vehicle type is different. Let cS-U denote the name of the experimental problem instance with S customer nodes and U vehicle types. For example, c20-3 represents that the problem instance has 20 customer nodes and 3 vehicle types. Thus, there are six experimental problem instances, *i.e.*, c20-3, c20-5, c50-3, c50-5, c100-3, and c100-5.

The vehicle speed design considers that vehicles have a maximum routing time limitation of 10 h. We define the average vehicle speed to be modified every 10 min. Hence, 60 time zones are planned.

Each time zone has a basic speed, which then changes according to the selected vehicle type and the selected route. The basic vehicle speed V_{b_m} for each time zone m is as follows:

$$V_{b_m} = 70 - 5 \cdot \cos\left(\frac{4\pi \cdot m}{60}\right) \tag{22}$$

The above basic speed equation is shown in Figure 5.

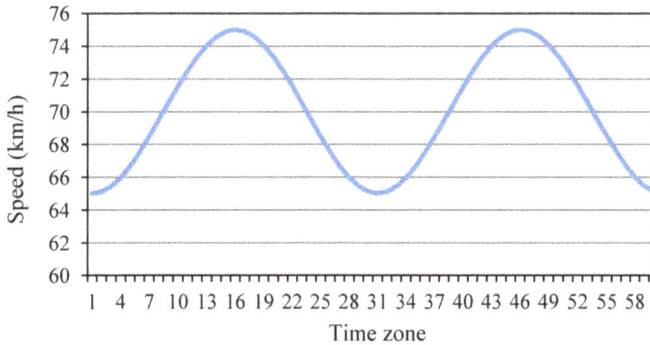

Figure 5. Illustration of basic vehicle speeds.

Considering that the routing distance affects the road selection, our experiment design categorizes the routes less than 30 km as the regular roads (e.g., highways, county highways and urban roads). Therefore, the vehicle speed is reduced by 20 (km/h), as calculated as follows:

$$V_{ij0}^m = V_{b_m} - 20 \text{ if } D_{ij0} < 30 \tag{23}$$

Since the alternative path selection is also a consideration factor in this paper, eight possible paths between any two customer nodes are selected in our experiments. Routes1, 2, and 3 allow the basic vehicle speed; routes 4, 5, and 6 allow the basic speed times 0.95; routes 7, 8, and 9 allow the basic speed times 1.05. The distance of each of routes 1, 4, and 7 is the original distance between customer nodes. The distance of each of routes 2, 5, and 8 is 0.95 times the original distance. The distance of each of routes 3, 6, and 9 is 1.05 times the original distance. Vehicle type is also a consideration factor in vehicle speed. Thus, the speed of vehicle types 1 and 2 in our experiment design is 1.025 times faster than vehicle types 3 and 4, and 1.05 times faster than vehicle type 5 (under the same road conditions).

Since the vehicle weight and the maximum load capacity also affect the carbon footprint, our experiment design considers five different vehicle weights and maximum load capacities, as shown in Table 2.

Table 2. Vehicle type classification.

Vehicle type	Type 1	Type 2	Type 3	Type 4	Type 5
Capacity (ton)	1	1.5	2	2.5	3
Empty vehicle weight (ton)	0.75	1	1.5	2	2.5

Since the parameters related to the objective function include route-related constant σ_{ij}, vehicle-related constant β, vehicle acceleration a, road inclination angle θ_{ij} between customer nodes, rolling resistance coefficient C_r, road resistance coefficient C_d, and air viscosity coefficient ρ, our experiments refer the experimental settings in [4] (as shown in Table 3).

Sustainability **2014**, *6*, 4658–4684

Table 3. Objective-related parameters.

Parameter	Value
Vehicle acceleration a	0
Road inclination angle θ_{ij}	0.01
Rolling resistance coefficient C_r	0.7
Road resistance coefficient C_d	0
Air viscosity coefficient ρ	1.2041

4.1.2. Parameter Setting for our GA

The parameter setting for our GA has a considerable influence on the algorithm. Usually, the more important parameters include the number of generations and the mutation probability. To determine what number of generations and mutation probability can obtain superior solutions; this paper divides these two factors into 10 levels, respectively. That is, the number of generations may be 5000, 10,000, … , and 50,000, and the mutation probabilities may be 0.01, 0.02, … , and 0.1. To find the most appropriate parameter setting for our GA, problem c20-3 is tested, and the objective of minimizing the total carbon footprint is considered. Ten experiments are conducted on each combination of the two factors, and the experimental results are shown in Figure 6, in which the experimental result with the best mean occurs when the number of generations is 50,000 and the mutation probability is 0.05. Thus, this setting is adopted to conduct our subsequent experiments.

4.2. Influence of Different Objectives on Carbon Footprint Emission

This section focuses on changes in number of customers and selectable vehicle types, and determines whether the carbon footprint performance vary when testing different objectives. The Minitab and SPSS system software is used to conduct single-factor ANOVA and independent sample *t*-test on results of each experimental problem instance with different objectives. In the experiments, we consider the location of each customer, different routing distances, and different speeds in different time zones to conform to practical situations.

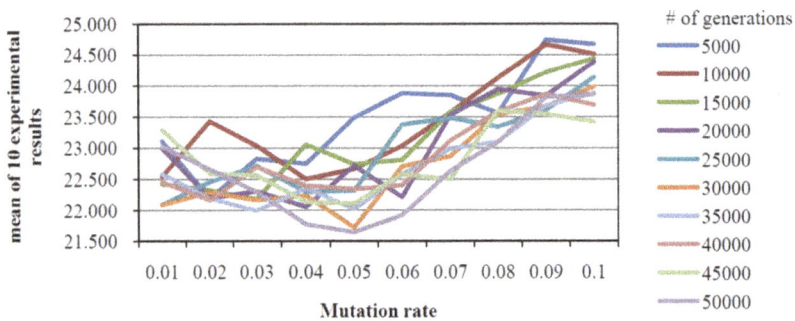

Figure 6. Experimental results with different combinations of numbers of generations and mutation rates.

4.2.1. Experimental Results

Consider the six aforementioned problem instances (c20-3, c20-5, c50-3, c50-5, c100-3, and c100-5) and design an experiment with three vehicle types transporting to 20, 50, and 100 customer nodes. Ten experiments are conducted with minimum carbon footprint, minimum time, and minimum distance as the objective. Carbon footprint (kg), routing time (minutes), and routing distance (km) results, means, and standard deviations from 10 experiments are obtained. However, because of the page limitation, only the results for problem c100-5are given in Table 4.

Table 4. Experimental results for problemc100-5 with different objectives.

Objective	Minimum Carbon Footprint			Minimum Routing Time			Minimum Routing Distance		
Number of Times	Carbon Footprint (kg)	Routing Time (minutes)	Routing Distance (km)	Carbon Footprint (kg)	Routing Time (minutes)	Routing Distance (km)	Carbon Footprint (kg)	Routing Time (minutes)	Routing Distance (km)
1	201.39	3522.89	3466.02	221.64	3118.71	3286.00	222.70	3045.60	3162.49
2	202.85	3496.71	3454.11	210.79	2984.85	3124.42	213.57	3121.18	3196.92
3	197.75	3440.53	3385.34	240.77	3095.69	3329.09	201.78	3217.58	3236.93
4	198.05	3415.39	3355.70	224.88	3019.47	3173.51	213.09	3215.16	3290.20
5	203.92	3552.83	3498.39	233.80	3093.27	3291.10	209.70	3249.87	3278.01
6	198.69	3421.67	3363.89	231.07	3015.33	3200.99	208.12	3147.69	3210.50
7	203.42	3494.83	3484.16	219.76	3123.51	3256.96	218.14	3156.72	3228.00
8	198.72	3480.55	3409.40	236.94	3089.65	3293.46	225.73	3141.88	3257.11
9	203.53	3358.02	3353.18	249.57	3142.63	3378.40	224.07	3125.42	3235.01
10	187.91	3194.74	3130.70	231.80	3136.67	3349.25	217.34	3092.43	3185.39
Average	199.62	3437.82	3390.09	230.10	3081.98	3268.32	215.42	3151.35	3228.06
Standard deviation	4.79	102.87	106.12	11.23	55.68	80.40	7.65	61.94	40.45

4.2.2. Comparison of Results Obtained with and without Alternative Path Selection Considerations

In this subsection, the SPSS statistical software is employed to compare the experimental results obtained using the models with and without alternative path selection considerations, respectively. The t-tests are conducted to determine whether the carbon footprints yielded from all problem instances are identical when alternative path selection is considered. Table 5 shows the results of the 10 carbon footprint experiments and the means and variances of the results when the minimal carbon footprint is used as the problem objective. The results show that, in all problem instances, the means of the experimental results obtained with alternative path selection considerations are superior to those obtained without such considerations. In addition, according to the ANOVA table of the carbon footprint results for all sample problems, the t-test results for all problems are less than 0.05, indicating a level of significance, *i.e.*, the alternative path selection has a significant influence on the carbon footprint results.

Table 5. Carbon footprint results for all problem instances (unit: kg).

Instance	c20-3		c50-3		c100-3		c20-5		c50-5		c100-5	
Route	Yes	No	Yes	No	Yes	No	Yes	No	Yes	No	Yes	No
1	22.53	22.93	82.51	89.51	195.82	202.29	21.30	23.80	83.00	88.07	201.39	212.50
2	20.53	23.27	80.11	90.28	193.65	206.02	20.00	23.53	84.56	91.24	202.85	210.07
3	21.90	24.18	84.32	87.23	196.88	207.01	20.70	23.81	84.23	87.15	197.75	210.66
4	21.63	24.85	82.77	85.62	197.28	207.64	20.48	22.40	79.64	89.66	198.05	212.05
5	22.66	23.62	83.07	88.28	197.74	207.53	20.86	24.51	82.23	89.99	203.92	210.04
6	20.48	25.29	83.56	85.97	196.42	208.03	19.95	22.36	80.30	88.96	198.69	209.65
7	22.01	24.04	82.32	90.34	196.82	207.68	21.81	22.87	83.85	91.33	203.42	203.56
8	22.83	25.73	82.84	89.35	199.21	210.20	20.87	23.20	86.17	88.93	198.72	208.24
9	21.26	24.10	79.85	88.11	192.69	204.05	21.82	21.96	83.44	90.15	203.53	210.41
10	21.56	24.20	79.28	87.71	197.23	201.44	21.70	22.77	81.13	91.70	187.91	211.31
Average	21.74	24.22	82.06	88.24	196.37	206.19	20.95	23.12	82.86	89.72	199.62	209.85
Standard deviation	0.82	0.87	1.71	1.66	1.92	2.76	0.70	0.79	2.04	1.48	4.79	2.52

4.2.3. Analysis of the Experimental Results Parameters for All Sample Problems

This subsection presents a single-factor ANOVA regarding the experimental results for problem c100-5. The ANOVA results are used to determine whether various objectives have significant effects on the carbon footprint results. The null hypothesis is that the three objectives have no effects on the carbon footprint results, and the alternative hypothesis is that the three objectives affect the carbon footprint results. The α for the level of significance is set at 0.05 before tests are conducted. When the ANOVA results reach the level of significance, a *t*-test is conducted between the experimental results obtained using minimal carbon footprint and minimal routing time as the objectives, respectively. The level of significance is set at 0.05. The *t*-test results are employed to investigate whether the carbon footprints obtained using minimal carbon footprint as the objective are significantly less than those obtained using other objectives.

An ANOVA analysis is conducted using the Minitab and SPSS software to calculate the carbon footprint results for problem c100-5 under various objectives. First, an equality of variance test is conducted to analyze the carbon footprint results under various objectives. The *p*-value of the test results is 0.65, greater than 0.05. Therefore, the null hypothesis, that is, "H_0: The variances of the carbon footprint results yielded under the three objectives are equal", is not rejected when the level of significance is set at $\alpha = 0.05$. Thus, considering the homogeneity of the samples, they can be used to conduct a single-factor ANOVA. The results show that the *p*-valueis0.000, which is smaller than 0.05. Hence, the null hypothesis, that is, "H_0: The carbon footprint results yielded under the three objectives are equal", is rejected when the level of significance is set at $\alpha = 0.05$. Subsequently, Scheffé's method is employed to conduct post hoc multiple comparisons. The results show the means of the carbon footprint results obtained under various objectives differ. Finally, a *t*-test is conducted between the carbon footprint results obtained using minimal carbon footprint as the objective and those obtained using minimal routing time or minimal routing distance as the objectives. The results show that the *p*-value is 0.000, which is smaller than $\alpha = 0.05$. Thus, we conclude that when the level of significance is set at $\alpha = 0.05$, the carbon footprint results obtained using minimal carbon footprint as the objective are significantly smaller than those obtained using minimal routing time or minimal routing distance as the objectives.

4.2.4. Analysis of the Decreases in the Carbon Footprint Results for All Sample Problems

The means of the carbon footprint results obtained under various objectives are used to explore the decreases in the carbon footprints and to determine whether vehicle types and the number of customers affect the observed decreases. Table 6 shows a comparison of the experimental results obtained for all problem instances using minimal carbon footprint as the objective. Compared with the carbon footprint results obtained using minimal routing time or minimal routing distance as the objective, the results obtained using minimal carbon footprint as the objective are superior in all problem instances although the results have less satisfactory performance in routing time and routing distance.

Figure 7 shows the decrease in carbon footprint as compared with the results obtained using minimal routing time or minimal routing distance as the objectives. The carbon footprint results obtained using minimal carbon footprint as the objective exhibit a satisfactory decrease as compared with the results obtained using minimal routing time as the objective. In contrast, the decrease in the carbon footprint results obtained using minimal carbon footprint as the objective are less satisfactory, as compared to those obtained using minimal routing distance as the objective. The *t*-test results obtained using Minitab and SPSS statistical software show that when the level of significance is set at $\alpha = 0.05$, the carbon footprint results obtained using minimal carbon footprint as the objective are superior to those obtained using minimal routing time or minimal routing distance as the objective. Furthermore, the number of customers is a factor that affects the decrease in the carbon footprint results. Figure 7 shows that when the number of customers is 20, the carbon footprint exhibits a more significant decrease compared with those when the number of customers is 50 or 100. Furthermore, the decrease in carbon footprint when the number of customers is 50 is more significant than when the number is 100. In other words, as the number of customers increase, the complexity of the problems rises and the decrease in carbon footprint declines. Although the decrease in carbon footprint obtained using a genetic algorithm declines as the number of customers increase, the experimental results confirm that carbon footprint is reduced effectively. Specifically, the *t*-test results obtained using Minitab and SPSS statistical software show that the carbon footprint decreases when the significance level of 0.05.

Table 6. Comparison of the results for all problems with objective of minimal carbon footprint.

Problem Instance	Performance	Using the Objective of Minimal Carbon Footprint	Comparison to the Results with Objective of Minimal Routing Time		Comparison to the Results with Objective of Minimal Routing Distance	
		Mean	Mean	Decrease (%)	Mean	Decrease (%)
c20-3	Carbon footprint (kg)	21.74	26.31	17.38	23.91	9.06
	Routing time (min)	564.09	484.47	16.43	513.84	−9.78
	Routing distance (km)	465.82	454.27	−2.54	445.96	−4.45
c50-3	Carbon footprint (kg)	82.06	96.11	14.62	85.79	4.34
	Routing time (min)	1580.70	1439.02	−9.85	1461.75	−8.14
	Routing distance (km)	1480.49	1476.98	−0.24	1426.82	−3.76
c100-3	Carbon footprint (kg)	196.37	219.13	10.39	203.09	3.31
	Routing time (min)	3441.72	3129.40	−9.98	3222.66	−6.80
	Routing distance (km)	3401.05	3288.08	−3.44	3254.69	−4.50
c20-5	Carbon footprint (kg)	20.95	27.07	22.60	23.68	11.52
	Routing time (min)	538.85	461.29	−16.81	482.37	−11.71
	Routing distance (km)	439.12	433.76	−1.23	418.20	−5.00
c50-5	Carbon footprint (kg)	82.86	100.85	17.84	88.95	6.85
	Routing time (min)	1575.54	1387.64	−13.54	1433.68	−9.89
	Routing distance (km)	1477.79	1441.01	−2.55	1398.84	−5.64
c100-5	Carbon footprint (kg)	199.62	230.10	13.25	215.42	7.33
	Routing time (min)	3437.82	3081.98	−11.55	3151.35	−9.09
	Routing distance (km)	3390.09	3268.32	−3.73	3228.06	−5.02

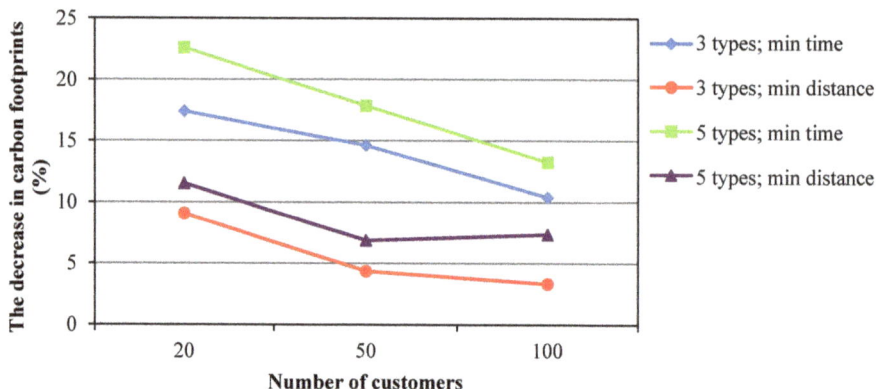

Figure 7. Comparison of the decreases in carbon footprints obtained using various vehicle types and objectives.

4.2.5. Analysis of the Computational Time Required for Executing our GA

This subsection presents an analysis regarding the computational time required for executing our GA for various objectives in differing problem instances. Figure 8 shows the means of the time required for executing our GA in the 10 experiments for each problem instance. As the number of customers increases, the computational time increases significantly. In addition, a significant difference is observed between the computational time required for solving problems that involve various objectives. The average time required for solving problems that involved minimal carbon footprint as the objective is the shortest, followed in order by the average time required for solving problems that involved minimal routing time and minimal routing distance, respectively, as the objective. From Figure 8, we see that the number of vehicle types has no significant effect on the average computational time.

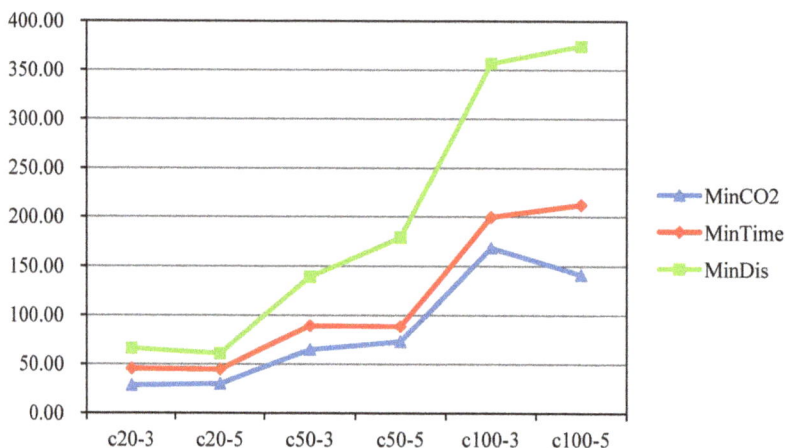

Figure 8. Comparison of the average time required for solving various problem instances.

5. Conclusions and Future Work

VRP is a vital problem in transportation and a crucial link in supply chain management. The problems that involve the basic VRP, and its variants have been investigated and solved in numerous

Sustainability **2014**, *6*, 4658–4684

previous works. However, the factors such as vehicle speed, vehicle type selection, vehicle load, and alternative path selection are often overlooked in VRP problems, although these factors often exist in real cases. This paper has developed a genetic algorithm (GA) for solving the MTHVRPP. Thus, the optimal vehicle routing is obtained to achieve the objectives of minimal carbon footprint, routing time, and routing distance. Experimental results confirm that the optimized vehicle routing obtained using the proposed GA yields superior results when the objective is to achieve minimal carbon footprint, although the routing results in relatively long routing time and routing distance. Therefore, determining a balance among various objectives is a critical topic of research.

In addition to the novel solution representation employed for the proposed GA, the concept of vehicle speed in different time zones is proposed, and the approximate optimal solutions are obtained by repeating the crossover and mutation operations in the GA. Based on the various locations of customers, the number of vehicle types, and the vehicle speed in different time zones, the alternative path selection is altered to obtain an approximate optimal solution and to achieve improvements. The results show that the experimental results obtained using minimal carbon footprint as the objective are superior to those obtained using minimal routing time or minimal routing distance as the objective. Furthermore, the decrease in the objective results declines as the number of customers increases. Nevertheless, this means reduced decreases instead of smaller reduced values. In conclusion, the proposed GA can be used to obtain satisfactory feasible solutions.

The main objective of this paper is to design a GA to obtain the vehicle routings that can result in the lowest carbon footprint. However, the objective weights and the relationships among various factors are not investigated. Extensions and improvements are necessary for practical applications. Hence, we offer the following recommendations for future studies. First, the road situations that truly reflect real situations should be explored. For example, real geographical situations can be employed as the samples for environment planning, and the actual change parameters can be integrated to the algorithm. Thus, the feasible solutions obtained can truly reflect the reality. Second, additional constraints can be introduced. For example, the common problems such as the time window problem, penalties, problems that involve multiple depots, and the truck and trailing routing problem can be integrated to enhance the applicability of the algorithm to reality. Third, the multi-objective problem that considers minimization of carbon footprints, routing time and routing distance is also of interest in the future work.

Acknowledgments: The first and second authors (Wan-Yu Liu and Chun-Cheng Lin) were supported in part by National Science Council, Taiwan (NSC102-2633-H156-001 and NSC 101-2628-E-009-025-MY3, respectively). The corresponding author (Qunwei Wang) was supported by the National Natural Science Foundation of China (no.71203151), the Postdoctoral Science Foundation of China (nos.2012M510139, 2013T60561), the Social Science Foundation of Jiangsu Province (no.12GLC008) and the Jiangsu Qing Lan Project.

Author Contributions: Wan-Yu Liu gave the framework of this research. Chun-Cheng Lin constructed the model. Ching-Ren Chiu and You-Song Tsao analyzed the results. Qunwei Wang gave some advices and checked the whole paper.

Conflicts of Interest: The authors declare no conflict of interest.

References

1. IPCC. *Climate Change 2007: Synthesis Report*; Intergovernmental Panel on Climate Change: Geneva, Switzerland, 2007; pp. 45–54.
2. Wiedmann, T.; Minx, J. A Definition of 'Carbon Footprint'. In *Ecological Economics Research Trends*; Pertsova, C.C., Ed.; Nova Science Publishers: Hauppauge, NY, USA, 2008; Chapter 1; pp. 1–11.
3. Dantzig, G.B.; Ramser, J.H. The truck dispatching problem. *Manag. Sci.* **1959**, *6*, 80–91. [CrossRef]
4. Bektaş, T.; Laporte, G. The pollution-routing problem. *Transp. Res. Part B Methodol.* **2011**, *45*, 1232–1250. [CrossRef]
5. Xiao, Y.; Zhao, Q.; Kaku, I.; Xu, Y. Development of a fuel consumption optimization model for the capacitated vehicle routing problem. *Comput. Oper. Res.* **2012**, *39*, 1419–1431. [CrossRef]

6. Golden, B.L.; Assad, A.; Levy, L; Gheysens, F.G. The fleet size and mix vehicle routing problem. *Comput. Oper. Res.* **1984**, *11*, 49–66. [CrossRef]

7. Ichoua, S.; Gendreau, M.; Potvin, J.Y. Vehicle dispatching with time-dependent travel times. *Eur. J. Oper. Res.* **2003**, *144*, 379–396. [CrossRef]

8. Garaix, T.; Artigues, C.; Feillet, D.; Josselin, D. Vehicle routing problems with alternative paths: An application to on-demand transportation. *Eur. J. Oper. Res.* **2010**, *204*, 62–75. [CrossRef]

9. Coe, E. *Average Carbon Dioxide Emissions Resulting from Gasoline and Diesel Fuel, Technical Report*; United States Environmental Protection Agency: Washington, DC, USA, 2005.

10. Taillard, E.D. A heuristic column generation method for the heterogeneous fleet. *RAIRO Oper. Res. Rech. Opér.* **1999**, *33*, 1–14. [CrossRef]

11. Lenstra, J.K.; Rinnooy Kan, A.H.G. Complexity of vehicle routing and scheduling problems. *Networks* **1981**, *11*, 221–227. [CrossRef]

12. Fisher, M.L.; Jaikumar, R. Ageneralized assignment heuristic for vehicle routing. *Networks* **1981**, *11*, 109–124. [CrossRef]

13. Bowerman, R.L.; Calamai, P.H.; Hall, G.B. Thespacefilling curve with optimal partitioning heuristic for the vehicle routing problem. *Eur. J. Oper. Res.* **1994**, *76*, 128–142. [CrossRef]

14. Cacchiani, V.; Hemmelmayr, V.C.; Tricoire, F. A set-covering based heuristic algorithm for the periodic vehicle routing problem. *Discret. Appl. Math.* **2014**, *163*, 53–64. [CrossRef]

15. Clarke, G.; Wright, J. Scheduling of vehicles from a central depot to a number of delivery points. *Oper. Res.* **1964**, *12*, 568–581. [CrossRef]

16. Rosenkrantz, D.; Sterns, R.; Lewis, P. An analysis of several heuristics for the traveling salesman problem. *SIAM J. Comput.* **1977**, *6*, 563–581. [CrossRef]

17. Lin, S. Computer solutions of the traveling salesman problem. *Bell Syst. Tech. J.* **1965**, *44*, 2245–2269. [CrossRef]

18. Baker, B.M.; Sheasby, J. Extensions to the generalized assignment heuristic for vehicle routing. *Eur. J. Oper. Res.* **1999**, *119*, 147–157. [CrossRef]

19. Kontoravdis, G.; Bard, J. *Improved Heuristics for the Vehicle Routing Problem with Time Windows*; Working Paper; Operations Research Group, Department of Mechanical Engineering, The University of Texas: Austin, TX, USA, 1992.

20. Potvin, J.; Rousseau, J. An exchange heuristic for routing problems with time windows. *J. Oper. Res. Soc.* **1995**, *46*, 1433–1446. [CrossRef]

21. Russel, R.A. Hybrid heuristics for the vehicle routing problem with time windows. *Transp. Sci.* **1995**, *29*, 156–166. [CrossRef]

22. Solomon, M.M. Algorithms for the vehicle routing and scheduling problems with time window constraints. *Oper. Res.* **1987**, *35*, 254–265. [CrossRef]

23. Holland, J.H. *Adaptation in Natural and Artificial System*; The University of Michigan Press: Ann Arbor, MI, 1975.

24. Osman, I.H. Metastrategy simulated annealing and tabu search algorithms for the vehicle routing problem. *Ann. Oper. Res.* **1993**, *41*, 421–451. [CrossRef]

25. Van Breedam, A. Comparing descent heuristics and metaheuristics for the vehicle routing problem. *Comput. Oper. Res.* **1995**, *28*, 289–315. [CrossRef]

26. Tan, K.C.; Lee, L.H.; Ou, K. Artificial intelligence heuristics in solving vehicle routing problems with time window constraints. *Eng. Appl. Artif. Intell.* **2001**, *14*, 825–837. [CrossRef]

sustainability

MDPI

Article

The Role of Intermediation in the Governance of Sustainable Chinese Web Marketing

Yongrok Choi * and Di Gao

Department of International Trade and Regional Studies, Inha University, 100 Inha-ro, Nam-gu, Incheon 402-751, Korea

* Author to whom correspondence should be addressed; yrchoi@inha.ac.kr;
  Tel.: +86-791-8381-0553; Fax: +86-791-8381-0892.

Received: 16 June 2014; in revised form: 21 June 2014; Accepted: 23 June 2014; Published: 30 June 2014

Abstract: This paper identifies the factors necessary for the sustainable performance of two Chinese web marketing companies. The companies are Alibaba and its twin, Taobao. This research is based on the structural equation model (SEM). The paper analyzes the core governance factors of Chinese trust (Guanxi) from outperforming web marketing mix strategies to determine if Guanxi can be applied to other web community marketing strategies. The empirical tests, in general, show the web marketing mix is important to create values in China. Three other web marketing strategies—communication, content, and commerce incorporate Guanxi with full mediation effects. Some implications concerning trust enhancement by the Chinese government and web companies are suggested.

Keywords: web marketing mix (4Cs); Chinese trust (Guanxi); mediation effect; structural equation model (SEM); governance

1. Introduction

China represents one of the most rapidly changing countries in the world. China has been a fast follower with respect to economic development, particularly in the fields of information and communication technology (ICT) and e-business. Recently, the economy has re-oriented its traditional export brick industry paradigm towards the evolving IT industry. This dynamic has brought innovation to the Chinese IT and e-business industry fields improving the economy. The Chinese web companies have made efforts to connect Chinese worldwide "Huaqiao" with their ethnic and cultural background. Huaqiao is defined as the Chinese population abroad who have an ethnically-based tendency to prefer Chinese interpersonal relationships that are based on Chinese trust (Guanxi). Huaqiao was originally based on individual Guanxi relationships. However, the rapidly evolving internet and related e-business has enabled many Chinese Huaqiaos worldwide to connect quickly, and their loyalty has ensured the success of ICT and e-business organizations.

Since the Chinese market is huge, diverse and rapidly evolving, with a unique cultural background, global e-business companies such as eBay and Amazon.com should change their strategies to adapt or localize Chinese Guanxi for successful operation in the global Chinese market. Figure 1 shows that the number of Internet users in China rapidly increased to 45.8 % in the year 2013. Moreover, internet shopping mall users represent 48.9 % (or 0.3 billion) of all internet users [1]. If overseas users and buyers are included, the statistics are even greater.

Sustainability **2014**, *6*, 4102–4118

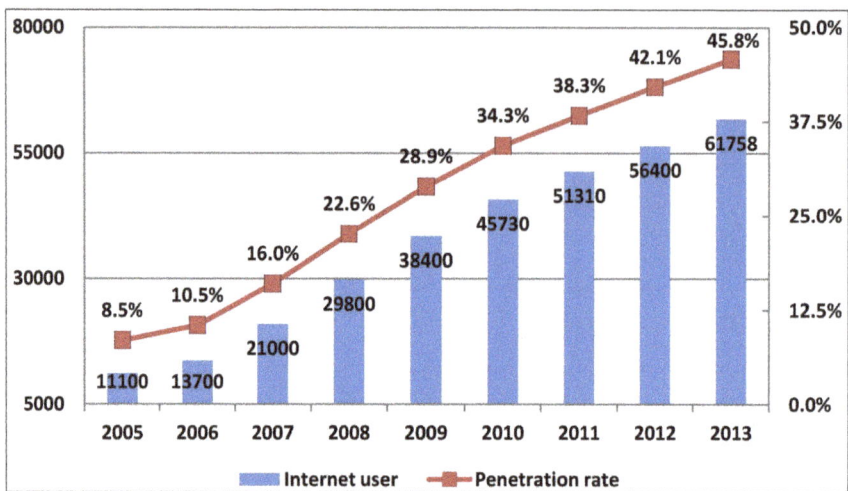

Source: Chinese Internet Network Information Center (CNNIC)

Figure 1. Internet users and the penetration rate for China (Unit: 10 million, %).

Alibaba Group is the most representatively successful web business in China. It is a private e-business group with business-to-business online web portals, online retail and payment services, a shopping search engine, and proprietary data-based cloud computing services. In 2012, the business portals of Alibaba and its twin web business of Taobao together achieved 1.1 trillion yuan ($170 billion) in sales, surpassing the global competitors, eBay and Amazon.com, combined [2]. The company began to connect Chinese manufacturers with overseas buyers, transforming off-line Huaqiaos worldwide into online customers. The consumer-to-consumer (C2C) portal Taobao, which is similar to eBay, features nearly a billion products and is one of the 20 most visited web sites globally. The Alibaba Group's sites account for over 60 % of the parcels delivered in China [2]. The C2C portal Taobao has gained popularity and claims 96.4 % of the C2C market as a result of viral marketing that is based on Chinese trust (Guanxi).

China is one of the largest countries in the world and, therefore, commerce can be beset with bottlenecks such as poor delivery systems, ineffective information security, weak infrastructure, and limited access to the Internet environment. The Chinese government imposes severe regulations on the internet and its users [3,4]. Nonetheless, the successful performance of Chinese web marketing companies may be a consequence of significant governance factors in web marketing strategy. This paper identifies the notable governance factors from a web marketing perspective. The remainder of this paper is organized as follows. Section 2 describes the conceptual characteristics of web marketing strategies and presents related hypotheses for web marketing strategies. Section 3 employs the methodology of the structural equation model (SEM) to empirically test the sustainable performance of Chinese web marketing companies. Section 4 concludes with some implications.

2. The Web Marketing Mix and Its Model

2.1. Conceptual Characteristics of the Web Marketing Mix

The rapid diffusion of e-business has revolutionized our daily lives. Although the traditional approaches of economics or business management remain popular, the "smart" use of the internet has changed the business and economic environment. The paradigm of traditional business management was to maximize profits, and it incorporated diverse marketing activities, particularly the strategic mix of the four marketing tools—product, price, place, and promotion. However, market leadership has transferred to the companies who integrate the consumer into the production process and cater to the "prosumer", who means the active consumers to participate in the production process. For these companies, the traditional push marketing model using the 4Ps is losing relevance. The leading products provide satisfaction, but the leading services provide an emotional relationship, which is the essence of pull marketing. Based on this pull marketing approach, the sustainable governance of marketing emphasizes relational management.

Web marketing is defined as relationship marketing that creates long-term network management value via collaboration and customization [5]. Web marketing is based on the creation of value from relationships among network members. There is a fundamental difference between web marketing and traditional marketing. Web marketers must reward customers for their loyalty with similar strategies as traditional marketers. Long-term success requires persistent loyalty as a core factor of web marketing. Customer loyalty enlarges future sales volume and exponentially increases sales through viral marketing. Relationship management is central to the creation of value for the network manager. Web marketing should emphasize relationship building, relationship management, and value creation from relationships. To identify the factors involved, the procedural structure of web marketing and its components with respect to the four Cs must be defined. Communications, contents, commerce, and community form the core of relational management. Because the Chinese commercial transaction is based on Chinese trust (Guanxi), this relational management factor is key with respect to governance for Chinese web marketers and their ability to outperform the Chinese and global markets.

Based on the procedural approach of web marketing, the first strategy that web marketers employ with respect to the new user is customer familiarization with the web site. Thus, communication is the starting point of the relationship. Once the new user feels comfortable with accessing and using the site, interest in frequent visits can be built, which is the basic strategy behind site contents. Frequent visits represent the core objective of web marketing, which is to create value based on commerce strategies. Users should sense a community that reflects the maxim "once a friend, forever a friend." The four strategies represent a step-by-step approach to create a relationship, maintain it, and utilize it for the creation of value. These strategies are interconnected and form a web marketing strategy matrix—the web marketing mix 4Cs.

2.2. Literature Review

The paradigm of the web marketing mix is to create value based on sustainable relationship management. The most significant characteristic of the sustainable relationship is loyalty. Substantial studies address customer loyalty, and the majority of previous literature emphasizes the intermediation of satisfaction for sustainable loyalty. This section addresses the basic theories and model with respect to the web marketing mix.

The paradigm of sustainable relationship building using the web marketing mix defines customer loyalty as faithfulness or devotion to a product, service, and/or the company. Loyalty could represent a consumer preference for a particular product (or brand) and a commitment to repeatedly purchase that brand despite other choices [6]. The majority of the literature differentiates between the perceived desire to buy that represents potential loyalty, and repeat purchase that represents behavioral loyalty [7–9]. The former emphasizes psychological factors such as organizational commitment, repurchase desire, and willingness to recommend the item to others, while the latter focuses on measurable levels of revealed preferences such as the repurchase ratio, the frequency of transactions, and the number of repurchases [9].

Customer loyalty is the outcome of effective company marketing activities, and it is also the case for web marketing companies in areas such as B2B, B2C or C2C. For example, to encourage customer loyalty, China's Tenmao of Alibaba and Taobao provided a quality guarantee that allowed the customer to return a product for any reason within seven days, and the repurchase value was returned as cash to spend on that same site at any time. This type of web marketing mix strategy provides customer loyalty through relationship management.

2.3. Direct Model Web Marketing Mix Hypotheses

Communication with respect to web marketing is defined as the activity of conveying information through the exchange of ideas, feelings, and attitudes by means of the internet. As the first step-wise approach to relationship management, communication is the initial catalyst in the web marketer and customer relationship. Effective communication should generate and sustain relationships.

To effectively communicate with new visitors, web marketers should eliminate the practical and psychological barriers that visitors might experience. For example, the Aribaba group developed a communication strategy with Ariwangwang, which is a one-to-one cyber troubleshooting platform to overcome practical barriers. Using this communication channel, new entrants can access necessary product information and related services. To address psychological barriers to effective access, web marketers should provide customized e-mails to web managers alerting them of reliability assurances and award records received from the public for exemplary service. To ensure practical and easy access to a web site, workable menus, real-time service updates, and a user-friendly web environment are necessary. Selnes [10] argued that loyalty is a consequence of a psychological barriers to transfer to other another option, or practical barriers such as high transfer costs. Therefore, the following communication hypothesis is proposed.

- H1: Communication strategies positively impact concerning web user loyalty.

  Internet users visit sites that provide real-time information such as exchange rates, weather, and news, and/or an interesting attraction such as a free game. All of these elements represent contents strategy. With respect to web marketing, content represents information and experiences that provide value for internet users in specific contexts [11]. The contents, therefore, can influence visit frequency. Frequent visits build familiarity with web sites that offer useful information and/or fun experiences. The customer becomes accustomed to the web sites, which maintains the relationship. Therefore, the following hypothesis with respect to content is proposed.

- H2: Contents strategies positively impact web user loyalty.

  The third stage of the web marketing mix is based on commerce strategy. Frequent visits themselves only provide an illusion of sales. Therefore, the basic core strategies of web marketing are connected with the creation of commercial value. However, commercial value should be differentiated from the traditional direct sales profits because web marketing may use one-source multi-use with its own web sites and may create revenues from diverse source of values. The web manager may tolerate a lower price than the cost of production because there may be complementary compensation from advertising commissions and/or membership fees. In some cases, the loss of profit may be compensated by rent from other web site residents and/or a consulting premium for offline activities. Therefore, diverse revenue sources with the same product or services are feasible in addition to traditional profits. Ahn lab, a leading Korean anti-vaccine company, obtains profits from membership fees, whereas another anti-vaccine company with free membership, Alyak, obtains value from advertising commission during on-line vaccine checking and updating. China's Tenmao uses diverse commerce strategies, such as new movie advertising commissions and rent for other small website retailers on the Tenmao web sites. Such diverse commerce strategies are based on customer loyalty, which in itself represents a diverse source of commerce [12]. Therefore, the following hypothesis with respect to commerce is proposed.

- H3: Commerce strategies positively impact web user loyalty.

  Web marketing follows the maxim "once a customer, forever a customer." Therefore, the post-purchase services provided to buyers are significant. For example, Tenmao of Alibaba created the Tenmao forum on which frequent visitors share ideas. This platform has become a social network where a loyal community engages in word-of-mouth marketing. An empirical test on the performance of the Taiwanese educational system concluded that managerial commitment and systems oriented toward the community are integral to organizational loyalty [13]. Based on these arguments, the following hypothesis concerning communication is proposed.

- H4: Community strategies positively impact web user loyalty.

All of the web marketing hypotheses are based on loyalty because value creation from relational loyalty is the goal of web marketing, not profit maximization. The successful performance of Chinese web marketing companies can be represented by the direct model in Figure 2.

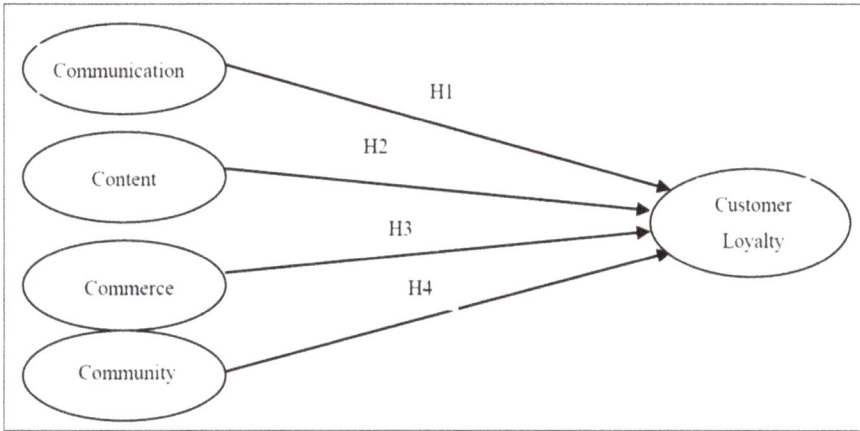

Figure 2. Direct model: The web marketing mix and hypotheses.

2.4. Indirect Model with Intermediation

Despite the significance of customer loyalty, particularly Chinese trust (Guanxi), some of the literature concludes that loyalty is not necessarily a central factor in the web marketing mix. The lack of consensus concerning loyalty may originate from a culture of pragmatism among the Chinese people because of continuous wars and severe poverty that have plagued the nation's history. The word "Shengyi" in China refers to the business characteristics of a person, not the life purpose of an individual [14]. Salesmanship is a born-in-characteristic in China; thus, loyalty may not be the direct result of web marketing. A website may possess no customer loyalty, but the traffic on the site from information seekers may result in a commercial transaction. This dynamic represents a missing link between loyalty and web marketing performance.

The majority of literature concerning trust and loyalty emphasize the governance factor of customer satisfaction, even with respect to the web marketing mix [15–18]. Customer satisfaction should affect customer loyalty, but not vice versa [18]. Kotler [16] defined satisfaction as an individual's sense of pleasure or disappointment resulting from a comparison of a product's perceived performance (or outcome) and expectations. According to Hansemark and Albinsson [17], satisfaction is an overall customer attitude towards a service provider, or an emotional reaction to the difference between the customer's anticipated fulfillment of some need, goal or desire and actual fulfillment. However, Oliver [18] summarizes the transaction-specific nature of satisfaction and differentiates it from attitude. The author states that the satisfaction is consumption-specific, whereas the attitude (or loyalty) comes from an enduring affective orientation for a product or service. From the consumer's perspective, satisfaction is a desirable end-state of consumption or patronization; it is a reinforcing pleasurable experience [19]. Satisfaction is provided by the product or service itself and may or may not result in loyalty. Chang [20] argued that loyalty may stem from repeat purchases, and satisfaction itself may not depend on loyalty.

All of these arguments imply a missing link between the web marketing mix and the goal of gaining customer loyalty. Therefore, an analysis of the intermediary variable of satisfaction can reveal the governance concerning the sustainable performance of the web marketing mix with respect to loyalty. To identify the missing link between loyalty and satisfaction concerning web marketing strategies, the hypotheses with respect to the intermediary variable of satisfaction represent the indirect model in Figure 3. The hypotheses consist of the following.

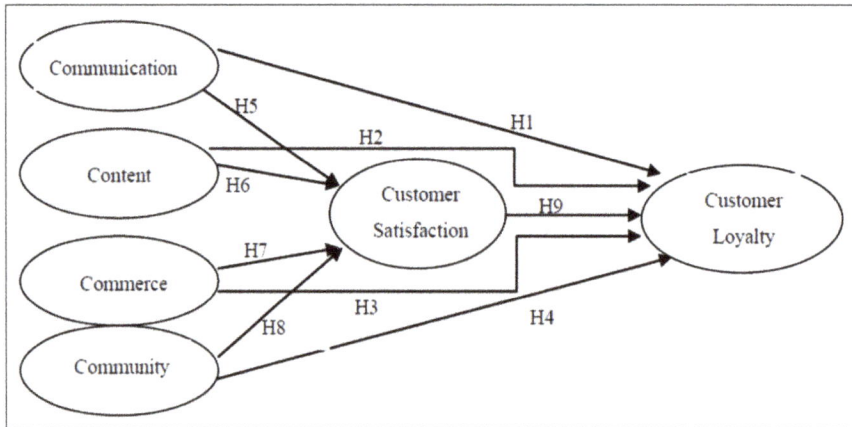

Figure 3. Indirect model with intermediation.

- H5: Communication strategies positively impact the consumer's satisfaction.
- H6: Content strategies positively impact consumer satisfaction.
- H7: Commerce strategies positively impact consumer satisfaction.
- H8: Community strategies positively impact consumer satisfaction.
- H9: Consumer satisfaction positively impacts consumer loyalty.

3. Empirical Tests and Implications

3.1. Data and Methodology

The data for the empirical tests were collected using a survey questionnaire. An initial pilot study was conducted. Fifty consumers with extensive online shopping experience were invited to complete the questionnaires. Based on the Cronbach alpha coefficients ($a > 6$), some items were modified. Additionally, Chinese web marketing experts were invited to complete the questionnaire as a pilot test. The questionnaire was then modified based on the expert feedback.

The questionnaire survey was administered during the period 16 January to 22 February 2014. A total of 350 questionnaires were sent randomly to Chinese online shoppers by e-mail or messenger. The shoppers were retrieved from business yellow pages for various sectors and provinces nationwide, only when they had an experience with Alibaba and/or Tabao web markets. A total of 153 unique and usable organizational responses were received (the response rate was 43.7%). Table 1 presents the demographic characteristics of the respondents. They represent most of internet users in China with high portions on 20s and 30s (90.4 %), and with university background (64.1%).

Table 1. Demographic characteristics.

Characteristic	Frequency	Percent (%)
Gender		
Male	66	43.1
Female	87	56.9
Education Level		
High school	36	23.5
University	98	64.1
Graduate school	19	12.4
Age		
20–29	64	41.8
30–39	59	38.6
40–49	30	19.6
Income (per month, Chinese Yuan)		
500–1000	17	11.1
1000–2000	53	34.6
2000–3000	65	42.5
3000 or over	18	11.8

We compared the early and late respondents to overcome the problem of non-response bias, as recommended by Armstrong and Overton [21]. The 175 questionnaires were divided into two groups based upon the time of completion. An independent *t*-test was employed to examine any differences between the early and late completion groups. The results indicated no significant differences in various items between these two groups, suggesting that our sample is free from non-response bias.

To measure all the observed variables in this study, we adopted existing well-established multiple-item, seven-point Likert scales. These scales ranged from 1 ("strongly disagree") to 7 ("strongly agree"). We chose seven-point Likert scales because some Chinese people do not want the extreme answers and thus it is difficult to handle with five-point Likert scales for some questions. The detailed measurement items are presented in Table A1. The communication strategies in the web marketing mix were analyzed using five categorical questions concerning the level of easy and effective access to the websites to evaluate the psychological and practical barriers to web site access. The contents strategies were analyzed using four questions designed to illicit insightful information concerning the overall design of website menus and the privacy or security level of the web content. The commerce strategies were analyzed using four questions concerning the quality of the product, price, promotion, and services. The final phase of web marketing strategies was analyzed using five community-related questions concerning the frequency of website participation. All of the questions were based on Taobao, the most representative e-shopping mall in China, and all the respondents possessed experience on this particular web site. Based on the two stepwise approaches, a reliability test was conducted followed by the structural empirical tests.

3.2. Reliability Test

Our proposed model must be statistically reliable and valid. Reliability is used to describe the overall consistency of a measure. The proposed method should reflect similar results when tested again under the same conditions. For the reliability test, we used the widely known Cronbach's alpha coefficient, the corrected item total correlation coefficient, and the construct reliability coefficient. These represent the most commonly used criteria for measuring reliability. Table 2 shows that each measure is above the suggested threshold at 0.7, 0.5, and 0.8 and thus, these values are considered adequate to confirm a satisfactory level of reliability in this study.

Table 2. Reliability test of the latent variables.

Latent variables	No. of items	Cronbach's αlpha (>0.7)	Corrected item-total correlation (>0.5)	Construct reliability (>0.8)
Communication	5	0.828	0.595–0.656	0.829
Content	4	0.796	0.551–0.636	0.796
Commerce	4	0.850	0.619–0.741	0.852
Community	5	0.910	0.736–0.818	0.910
Customer satisfaction	4	0.858	0.683–0.731	0.859
Customer loyalty	5	0.867	0.627–0.741	0.867

3.3. Validity Test

The validity of an assessment is the extent to which the target is accurately measured (the true information). The validity analysis includes both content validity and construct validity components. The content validity analysis tests the representativeness of the items in the questionnaire. We found no reports of any misunderstanding during the pilot test. The interviewees stated that the items were easily understood, which indicates content validity [22].

The confirmatory factor analysis (CFA) is an effective tool used to test construct validity. According to Campbell and Fiske [23], construct validity research typically tests the extent to which data provides (a) convergent validity—this is the extent to which different assessment methods show similar measurements of the same trait (*i.e.*, construct; ideally, these values should be moderately high), and (b) discriminant validity. Discriminant validity is the extent to which independent assessment methods show divergent measurements of different traits (ideally, these values should demonstrate minimal convergence).

As summarized by Choi and Yu [24], convergent validity occurs when (a) all factor loadings are significantly over the 0.5 cut-off point and, (b) the average variance extracted (AVE) from items by their respective constructs is greater than 0.5. Table 3 shows the results of the convergent validity measured using CFA. We recognize that the measurement scale shows a strong convergent validity because all of the factor loadings are significant and over 0.5, and the AVE of all the items is larger than 0.5.

Table 3. Convergent validity test on the measurement model.

Variable	SFL [a]	C.R [b]	AVE [c]
Communication strategies			0.615
Com1-Easy access in general	0.657	7.870	
Com2-Easy access by Aliwangwang	0.577	7.402	
Com3-Reply speed	0.685	7.764	
Com4-Effective access to information	0.555	7.381	
Com5-Credibility on access	0.600	-	
Content strategies			0.638
Con1-Design attractiveness	0.646	6.669	
Con2-Relevant content	0.662	6.653	
Con3-Accurate content	0.625	6.311	
Con4-Privacy concerning content	0.617	-	
Commerce strategies			0.706
Cmc1-Price competitiveness	0.724	7.882	
Cmc2-Advertisement usefulness	0.751	8.428	
Cmc3-Events and activities	0.739	8.540	
Cmc4-Coupon and promotion	0.600	-	
Community strategies			0.765
Cot1-Friendliness	0.687	10.507	
Cot2-Percieved acceptance	0.697	10.765	
Cot3-Knowledge of the community	0.822	12.357	
Cot4-Participation level of the community	0.808	12.006	
Cot5-Pro-active level of the community	0.755	-	
Customer satisfaction (CS)			0.710
Sat1-Perceived satisfaction with purchase	0.657	-	
Sat2-Satisfaction with web service	0.679	7.585	
Sat3-Satisfaction with price	0.743	7.957	
Sat4-Perceived evaluation of shopping experience	0.760	8.265	
Customer loyalty			0.659
Loy1-Visit frequency	0.728	-	
Loy2-Memory of the attraction	0.644	8.571	
Loy3-Recommendation level	0.721	9.309	
Loy4-Loyalty to the brand even with a higher price	0.652	7.936	
Loy5-Intention to purchase volume	0.564	7.404	
Goodness-of-fit and recommended cut-off point			
$\chi^2 = 289.8$ (direct model; DM), 405.551 (indirect model; IM); χ^2/df (<5) = 1.32 (DM), 1.31 (IM); CFI (>0.9) = 0.959 (DM), 0.954 (IM); RMSEA (<0.1) = 0.046 (DM), 0,045 (IM)			

[a] SFL represents an estimate of the standardized factor loading; [b] CR represents critical ratio; [c] AVE represents average variance extracted.

For the model fit of CFA, we also used a number of goodness-of-fit indices recommended in previous studies such as a normed chi-square (χ^2/df), goodness-of-fit (GFI), comparative fit index (CFI), root mean square residual (RMR), and root mean square error of approximation (RMSEA) [25]. We find in our measurement model that all of the various overall goodness-of-fit measures are superior to the recommended criteria. Thus, the construct validity of the measurement model is acceptable.

With respect to discriminant validity, the square root of the AVE for the constructs should be larger than any respective inter-construct correlations. Table 4 shows that the square roots of the AVE of all the variables are higher than their inter-correlations, which supports the discriminant validity.

Table 4. Discriminant validity test of the measurement model.

Construct items	Communication	Contents	Commerce	Community	CS	Loyalty
Communication	0.765 [a]					
Contents	0.466	0.706 [a]				
Commerce	0.448	0.417	0.638 [a]			
Community	0.427	0.299	0.544	0.615 [a]		
CS	0.591	0.478	0.545	0.534	0.710 [a]	
Loyalty	0.545	0.466	0.528	0.500	0.659	0.752 [a]

[a] The square root of the AVE as a criteria of the cutting point for correlation. CS: Customer Satisfaction.

3.4. Hypotheses Test

Following the confirmation of the reliability and validity of the questionnaire, we also conducted the goodness of fit test for overall model fit. Table 3 shows that all the statistics for the direct model (DM) and the indirect model with intermediary (IM) are statistically significant as a whole, compared with the critical values of χ^2/df (<5), CFI (>0.9), RMSEA (<0.10).

Based on these tests, we now test the proposed hypotheses. By using the SEM, we find that the ML estimation method fits our data most appropriately; therefore, ML estimation is used for the hypotheses testing. The empirical findings are presented in Figure 4. Our results show that all the web marketing strategies have a positive impact on customer loyalty. Therefore, H1 to H4 are supported (p < 0.005). Among the web marketing mix strategies, communication is the most influential concerning customer loyalty, whereas the content contribution is the least influential.

To test the mediating effect of organizational commitment and citizenship behavior, the relationships among the variables should satisfy all of the following conditions as suggested by the references [24,26]: (1) the independent variable should significantly influence the dependent variable; (2) the independent variable should influence the mediator significantly; (3) the mediator must influence the dependent variable significantly, and (4) the impact of the independent variable on the dependent variable must diminish after controlling for the effects of the mediator. If any of these conditions are not satisfied, there is no mediation. If all of these conditions are satisfied and the influence of the independent variable becomes non-significant in the presence of the mediator, the effects of the independent variable are said to be completely or fully mediated by the mediator. If all the conditions are satisfied, while the influence of the independent variable remains significant in the presence of the mediator, the effects of the independent variable are said to be partially mediated [26–28].

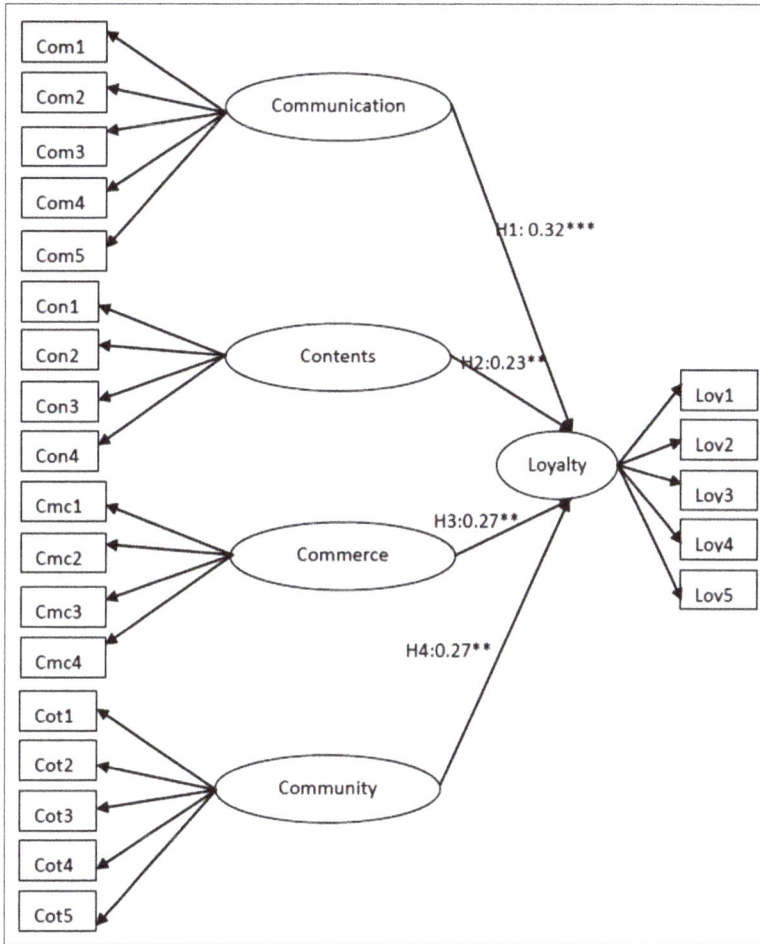

Figure 4. The results of the direct model.

Compared with the direct model in Figure 4, the results of the mediation model in Figure 5 show that the mediatory hypotheses H5, H6, H7, and H8 support condition (1); hypotheses H1, H2, H3, and H4 support condition (2), and H9 supports condition (3). With respect to the mediator condition (4) concerning consumer satisfaction, communication, contents, and commerce have no effect on consumer satisfaction, whereas the effect of community has a lower but marginally significant effect ($p > 0.01$). Therefore, we conclude that the relationship between communication, content, and commerce strategies are fully mediated by customer satisfaction, whereas the community strategy of the web marketing mix is partially mediated by customer satisfaction concerning loyalty.

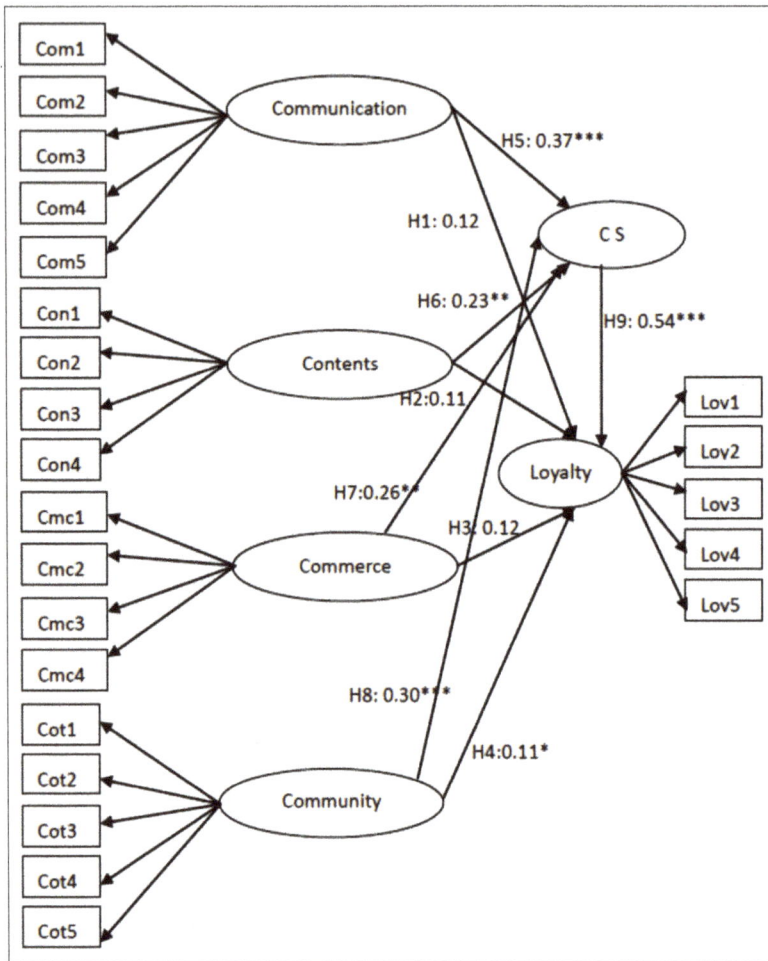

Figure 5. The results of the indirect model.

The results indicate that web marketing strategies concerning communication, content, and commerce influence customer loyalty fully and positively through customer satisfaction with online shopping. Customer satisfaction could be an important governance factor in the relationship between the web marketing mix and its sustainable performance.

If the community strategy attempts to create relationships in the final stage of the web marketing mix, the strategy also partially affects customer satisfaction. This implies that the final completion of the web marketing mix using community strategy may create customer satisfaction with governance for sustainable performance and loyalty together, while the community strategy does not exclude the role of intermediary in the creation of Chinese loyalty (Guanxi).

4. Conclusions

The sustainable governance of the web marketing mix is increasingly significant for the rapidly changing Chinese business environment. There is an urgent need to identify factors that contribute to web marketing performance. The leading global e-business companies, such as eBay, Amazon.com,

Sustainability **2014**, *6*, 4102–4118

Facebook, and Google could not outperform Chinese industry leaders such as Alibaba and its twin, Taobao, *etc*. This paper proposed web marketing mix strategies concerning the 4Cs for outstanding sustainable performance in Chinese online shopping. The study empirically tested the procedural approach to determine the governance factors contributing to customer satisfaction and Chinese loyalty (Guanxi) using the SEM. We find that the majority of web marketing mix strategies are fully mediated with customer satisfaction concerning loyalty, whereas community is partially mediated.

This paper did not examine Chinese loyalty (Guanxi) in detail. However, Chinese loyalty (Guanxi) differs from general trust or reliability because it considers relational-based responsibility as the benefactor of Chinese loyalty (Guanxi). Because of this highly responsible collaboration, creating, maintaining, and utilizing Chinese loyalty is complex. This relationship should be based on the win-win rule toward future monetary remuneration. Financial compensation provides Guanxi with governance, which is defined as the workable mechanism for sustainable performance of the collaboration network [5]. This research emphasizes the role of satisfaction concerning loyalty as the governance factor for the sustainable performance of web marketing. The majority of global e-businesses emphasize convenience and practical merits as governing factors, which results in the loss of potential customers. Therefore, entry to the Chinese web market should be based on relational management with respect to the 4Cs web marketing mix.

Acknowledgments: This work was supported by the National Research Foundation of Korea Grant funded by the Korean Government (NRF-2014S1A5B1011422).

Author Contributions: This research was designed, and written by the first as well as the corresponding author, and performed and analyzed the data by the coauthor.

Appendix A

Table A1. The measurement items for latent variables.

Questions	Strongly disagree → Strongly agree
The questions concerning communication	
1. No difficulty obtaining shopping information-(Com1)	1 2 3 4 5 6 7
2. No difficulty connecting with Aliwangwang customer service-(Com2)	1 2 3 4 5 6 7
3. It is easy to get a response concerning inquiries-(Com3)	1 2 3 4 5 6 7
4. Most of the Tmall(Taobao) information is useful-(Com4)	1 2 3 4 5 6 7
5. The product becomes more credible after communication-(Com5)	1 2 3 4 5 6 7
The questions concerning content	
1. Web design of Tmall is insightful-(Con1)	1 2 3 4 5 6 7
2. I feel comfortable e-shopping on Tmall-(Con2)	1 2 3 4 5 6 7
3. I feel the information in Tmall is accurate-(Con3)	1 2 3 4 5 6 7
4. Tmall is secure concerning private information-(Con4)	1 2 3 4 5 6 7

Table A1. *Cont.*

Questions	Strongly disagree → Strongly agree
The questions concerning commerce	
1. The price of the same product in Tmall is cheaper than the off-line shopping mall-(Cmc1)	1 2 3 4 5 6 7
2. There are many brand advertisements in Tmall-(Cmc2)	1 2 3 4 5 6 7
3. I support bonus points in Tmall-(Cmc3)	1 2 3 4 5 6 7
4. I appreciate e-purchase coupons in Tmall-(Cmc4)	1 2 3 4 5 6 7
The questions concerning community	
1. I feel like a family member of the Tmall community-(Cot1)	1 2 3 4 5 6 7
2. I am happy to receive communication from Tmall-(Cot2)	1 2 3 4 5 6 7
3. If asked questions by others, I answer them happily-(Cot3)	1 2 3 4 5 6 7
4. I participate in events in the Tmall community-(Cot4)	1 2 3 4 5 6 7
5. If I raise issues, I will certainly get a response-(Cot5)	1 2 3 4 5 6 7
The questions concerning customer satisfaction	
1. I feel happy whenever I purchase in Tmall-(Sat1)	1 2 3 4 5 6 7
2. I'm satisfied with the service of Tmall-(Sat2)	1 2 3 4 5 6 7
3. I'm satisfied with the price of products in Tmall-(Sat3)	1 2 3 4 5 6 7
4. The shopping experience with Tmall was one of the best-(Sat4)	1 2 3 4 5 6 7
The questions concerning customer loyalty	
1. I visit the Tmall homepage regularly-(Loy1)	1 2 3 4 5 6 7
2. When I buy products, Tmall is my first choice-(Loy2)	1 2 3 4 5 6 7
3. I will recommend Tmall to other people-(Loy3)	1 2 3 4 5 6 7
4. Even if the price of product in Tmall is higher than others, I will still choose Tmall-(Loy4)	1 2 3 4 5 6 7
5. I think I want to buy most items from Tmall-(Loy5)	1 2 3 4 5 6 7

References

1. Chinese Internet Network Information Center (CNNIC). Annual Statistics of Internet in China. Available online: http://www.199it.com/archives/187771.html and http://news.xinhuanet.com/tech/2014-01/16/c_126015636.htm (accessed on 28 May 2014).
2. The Economist. E-commerce in China: The Alibaba phenomenon. Available online: http://www.economist.com/news/leaders/21573981-chinas-e-commerce-giant-could-generate-enormous-wealthprovided-countrys-rulers-leave-it (accessed on 23 June 2014).
3. Wang, P.; Wang, H. The Implications and Suggestions of C2C web Marketing in China. Available online: http://www.cnki.com.cn/Article/CJFDTotal-AHNY200620154.htm (accessed on 20 May 2006). (In Chinese)
4. Bum, Y. The Bottlenecks of C2C web Marketing in China. Available online: http://wenku.baidu.com/link?url=lmX_8yMt7Xrt-1Ni7eCQFD9rgrEz1OGW0xy0vrC-ez8ZXptYi4Kx_MIy69mEzFfQRQJtjs9yzGjzOC-guDhpXPSjTqMeV0oVnCpSoFUmsiS (accessed on 20 February 2009). (In Chinese)
5. Choi, Y. *Global e-Business Management: Theory and Practice*; Bomyoung-books Publishing Co.: Seoul, Korea, 2014; p. 54.
6. Dick, A.S.; Basu, K. Customer Loyalty: Toward an Integrated Conceptual Framework. *J. Academy Market. Sci.* **1994**, *22*, 99–113. [CrossRef]

Sustainability **2014**, *6*, 4102–4118

7.   Bennettt, R.; Charnine, E.J.; Hartel, J.R. Experience as a moderator of involvement and satisfaction on brand loyalty in a business-to-business setting. *J. Ind. Market. Manag.* **2005**, *34*, 97–107. [CrossRef]
8.   Rauyruen, P. Relationship quality as a predictor of B2B customer loyalty. *J. Bus. Res.* **2007**, *60*, 21–31. [CrossRef]
9.   Chang, H.H.; Chen, S.W. The Impact of Customer Interface of Quality, Satisfaction and Switching Costs on E-loyalty: Internet Experience as a Moderator. *J. Comput. Hum. Behav.* **2008**, *24*, 2927–2944. [CrossRef]
10. Selnes, F. An Examination of the Effect of Product Performance on Brand Reputation, Satisfaction and Loyalty. *Eur. J. Market.* **1993**, *27*, 19–35. [CrossRef]
11. Odden, L. What is Content? Learn from 40+ Definitions. Available online: http://en.wikipedia.org/wiki/Content_(media)#cite_note-1 (accessed on 20 February 2014).
12. Amblee, N.; Bui, T. Harnessing the Influence of Social Proof in Online Shopping: The Effect of Electronic Word of Mouth on Sales of Digital Microproducts. *Int. J. Electron. Commerce* **2011**, *16*, 91–114. [CrossRef]
13. Lin, H.-F. Empirically testing innovation characteristics and organizational learning capabilities in e-business implementation success. *Internet Res.* **2008**, *18*, 60–78. [CrossRef]
14. Daylian (Korean Newspaper). China socialists, Korea Capitalists? Available online: http://dailian.co.kr/news/view/253506 (accessed on 23 June 2014). (In Korean)
15. Loiacono, E.T.; Watson, R.T.; Goodhue, D.L. WEBQUAL: A measure of website quality. *J. Market. Theor. Appl.* **2002**, *13*, 432–438.
16. Kotler, P.; Armstrong, G. *Principles of Marketing*, 11th ed.; Pearson/Prentice Hall: Upper Saddle River, NJ, USA, 2005.
17. Hansemark, O.C.; Albinson, M. Customer Satisfaction and Retention: The Experiences of Individual with Employees. *Manag. Serv. Q.* **2004**, *14*, 40–57. [CrossRef]
18. Oliver, R.L. Measurement and Evaluation of Satisfaction Process in Retail Settings. *J. Retail.* **1981**, *57*, 25–48.
19. Oliver, R.L. *Satisfaction: A Behavioural Perspective on the Consumer*, 2nd ed.; M.E. Sharpe Inc.: New York, NY, USA, 2007; p. 4.
20. Chang, H.H.; Chen, S.W. The Impact of Customer Interface of Quality, Satisfaction and Switching Costs on E-loyalty: Internet Experience as a Moderator. *J. Comput. Hum. Behav.* **2008**, *24*, 2927–2944. [CrossRef]
21. Armstrong, S.J.; Overton, T.S. Estimating non-response bias in a mail survey. *J. Mark.* **1977**, *14*, 396–402. [CrossRef]
22. Zeng, X.S.; Meng, X.H.; Yin, H.T.; Tam, C.Y.; Sun, L. Impact of cleaner production on business performance. *J. Clean. Prod.* **2010**, *18*, 975–983. [CrossRef]
23. Campbell, D.T.; Fiske, D.W. Convergent and discriminant validation by the multitrait-multimethod matrix. *Psychol. Bull.* **1959**, *56*, 81–105. [CrossRef]
24. Choi, Y.; Yu, Y. The Influence of Perceived Corporate Sustainability Practices on Employees and Organizational Performance. *Sustainability* **2014**, *6*, 348–365. [CrossRef]
25. Bagozzi, R.P.; Yi, Y. On the evaluation of structural equation models. *Acad. Mark. Sci.* **1988**, *16*, 74–93. [CrossRef]
26. Baron, R.M.; Kenny, D.A. The moderator-mediator variable distinction in social psychological research: Conceptual, strategic, and statistical considerations. *J. Personal. Soc. Psychol.* **1986**, *51*, 1173–1182. [CrossRef]
27. Tepper, B.J.; Shafer, S.; Meredith, J.R.; Marsh, R. A clarification on conceptual and methodological issues related to the job characteristics model: A reply. *J. Oper. Manag.* **1996**, *14*, 369–372. [CrossRef]
28. Chen, S.C.; Yen, D.; Hwang, M. Factors influencing the continuance intention to the usage of web 2.0: An empirical study. *Comput. Hum. Behav.* **2012**, *28*, 933–941. [CrossRef]

MDPI

St. Alban-Anlage 66

4052 Basel

Switzerland

Tel. +41 61 683 77 34

Fax +41 61 302 89 18

www.mdpi.com

Sustainability Editorial Office

E-mail: sustainability@mdpi.com

www.mdpi.com/journal/sustainability

www.ingramcontent.com/pod-product-compliance
Lightning Source LLC
Chambersburg PA
CBHW051849210326
41597CB00033B/5830